$\mathcal{A}$ VISITOR'S GUIDE
to Colonial *&* Revolutionary

Mid Atlantic America

A VISITOR'S GUIDE
to Colonial *&* Revolutionary

Mid Atlantic America

INTERESTING SITES TO VISIT
Lodging ✸ Dining ✸ Things to Do

Includes
New York, Pennsylvania, New Jersey, Delaware *&* Maryland

Patricia & Robert Foulke

The Countryman Press
Woodstock, Vermont

ISBN 978-0-88150-689-1

Book design by Joseph Kantorski
Composition by Eugenie S. Delaney
Cover photograph courtesy of Shutterstock
Maps by Paul Woodward, © The Countryman Press
Interior photographs by the authors

"Indian Pumpkin Griddle Cakes" recipe on p. 202 reproduced from
Old Bedford Village Hearth Cooking by Vi Laws, courtesy of Old Bedford
Village, Bedford, PA, www.oldbedfordvillage.com. "Reynolds Tavern Shepherd's
Pie" recipe on p. 302 provided courtesy of Reynolds Tavern, Annapolis, MD,
www.reynoldstavern.org. "Macaroons" recipe on p. 311 provided courtesy of
Mount Clare Museum House, Baltimore, MD, www.mountclare.org.

Published by The Countryman Press, PO Box 748, Woodstock, VT 05091

Distributed by W. W. Norton & Company, Inc.,
500 Fifth Avenue, New York, NY 10110

Printed in the United States of America

Book Club Edition

Contents

Introduction

This book is the second of three related guides. *A Visitor's Guide to Colonial & Revolutionary New England* was published in 2006, and a third volume, *A Visitor's Guide to the Colonial & Revolutionary South*, is planned for 2008. Each can be enjoyed and used by travelers independently, but there are many links between them, just as there came to be links between the disparate American colonies.

People who travel walk through human history, whether they are conscious of it or not. In this book we hope to enhance the pleasure of your travel along the eastern seaboard of the United States by developing and refining a sense of place. Heightened awareness of what happened where we walk now and whose footsteps preceded ours satisfies not only curiosity but also a natural longing to be connected with our surroundings.

Those who profess to live only in the present—a persistent myth in American popular culture—forget how disturbed they are when revisiting childhood sites that have changed almost beyond recognition. Constructing the past, and often idealizing it in the process, creates an orientation in time that is inseparable from the sense of place that defines who we are, both individually and collectively. Just as we rewrite our own internal autobiographies year by year, each generation recasts the past in its own molds.

Colonial and Revolutionary history is a kaleidoscope of movement and change, but it is clearly tied to many places that still remain. Rediscovering those places and expanding their meaning is the aim of this book and its companion volumes. They are not designed for committed antiquarians or for those who reduce the past to a prologue of the present. They are designed for travelers with a persistent curiosity, those who like to build contexts around what they see.

This book explores colonial and Revolutionary sites, forts, government buildings, churches, inns, houses, historic districts, museums, and living-history museums, as well as reenactments and festivals throughout the five Mid-Atlantic states. The time span begins in the early 1600s and extends into the early 1800s.

Our series on colonial and Revolutionary America combines the features of travel guides and historical narratives to re-create the conditions and ambience of colonial life for travelers and armchair travelers alike. As avid travelers of both sorts ourselves, we hope to bring you a vivid sense of place, time, and character, whether you go on the road or stay at home.

Some of the stories are about historical figures or events you may already know of, and others may tickle your fancy. You may enjoy reliving trips already taken, or you may be considering a new venture and want specific information on potential activities and sites within various regions.

A time line at the beginning of each chapter sets the stage for your personal orientation. An introduction describes the founding and development of each colony. Then the focus shifts to places that can still be seen by visitors who want to walk into their heritage to understand it better. Throughout the remainder of each chapter the focus remains on specific places, linking each town and building or site with the events that occurred there. In some cases we may mention the dates of early settlement in a village even if there is little or nothing left to see except the topography. In other cases the process of expanding and modernizing buildings has left a remnant of a colonial home or inn intact after two hundred years of addition and change. Those with observant eyes may be able to reconstruct what a place might have looked like in the colonial era and get some sense of how its inhabitants lived.

Our emphasis is both on memorializing important political and military events and understanding the context in which they occurred, so the book includes material on the social and cultural history of everyday life—architecture, clothing, food, transportation, occupations, religious practices, customs, folklore, and the like. Some early groups of colonists left Europe and endured the hardships of living in the wilderness of the New World to attain religious freedom and maintain their own cultures. Sometimes those cultures were challenged by later immigrants, as the Quaker founders of Pennsylvania were by Scotch-Irish Presbyterians, or as the Catholic founders of Maryland were by Puritans, who eventually managed to deprive them of the vote. In other cases the colonists were primarily interested in the profit of the company that financed their start in the New World, as evidenced in the early history of New York.

Thus the idea of a quintessential colonial America is itself more a convenience for historians than a reality. In fact there were many disparate settlements that gradually and often reluctantly banded together for limited common purposes. Since the Mid-Atlantic colonies were quite diverse in topography and economic activity, with peoples drawn from different ethnic, regional, and religious traditions in Europe, the story has to be retold for each within the larger framework of American expansion. The process of their amalgamation lasted through the Revolution and beyond, eliciting much controversy and sometimes bumptious behavior. Regionalism, by no means dead today, persisted throughout the colonial and Revolutionary eras and blocked many attempts at cooperation among the colonies.

Also, many early European attempts to establish colonies in America were dismal failures, often because the entrepreneurs and adventurers who came were bent on exploiting the new land. Those with money to invest in shares were not used to hard work and often ill equipped for the rigors of living in the wilderness. Some of these marginal ventures in the Mid-Atlantic region, especially those based on profits from the fur trade, were evanescent, while others, like New Netherland and New Sweden, suffered instability through the interference of European powers. Among the settlements that survived and prospered, some were abandoned later as economic or political conditions changed. Permanence, order, and stability were envisioned in royal land grants but seldom achieved in the proprietary charters most frequently given to Mid-Atlantic colonies.

One of the destabilizing forces was the constant flow in and out of colonies. People uprooted from their European homelands to escape religious persecution, political suppression, or the devastation of wars continued to migrate within and between the colonies, searching for better land or other opportunities. Many moved on simply to find a new place with topography reminiscent of their native regions, whether flat land, rolling hills, mountains, or river valleys.

The cultural diversity that we prize today also fragmented American experience. Succeeding waves of immigrants—English Puritans, French Huguenots, Welsh Quakers, German Mennonites, Moravians, and Lutherans, Scotch-Irish Presbyterians—clung together in enclaves united by religious principles, ethnic origins, language, and folk traditions. They maintained their identity through forms of worship and customs from home—precious objects from the past, Christmas or festival decorations, and clothing worn on special occasions.

Colonial America, then, is no single fabric but a patchwork quilt of many pieces, each with its own distinctive character and design. As you explore its many wonderful places, keep an eye out for change, instability, transience, variety, and anomaly, and be prepared for surprises. During our research for this book, most of the generalizations we had harbored from American history courses were shattered, to be replaced by sharper images and a keener sense of the many stories that are never fully or conclusively told. When you discard preconceptions and look closely at the places you visit, you too will begin rewriting colonial history in your own mind.

Trip Planning

We have grouped places you may want to visit geographically rather than chronologically, since you will be traveling in literal space and imaginative time. Each colony has its unique character, and we have tried to reflect that in the order of presentation.

Sometimes we choose to begin with the earliest settlement, branching out in various directions to follow people as they moved to new locations; in other cases we are more strictly geographical, moving from the sea inland or along the coast, according to patterns of migration.

In no case do we survey the whole state that developed from the original colony, for several reasons. Among them, the most important is the limited transportation available to settlers. Water was the primary means of movement, especially along great navigable rivers like the Hudson, Delaware, and Potomac or immense bays like the Chesapeake. Settlement clung to these waterways throughout most of the 17th century and slowly moved to other inland areas with the development of roads during the 18th century. Even so, only small portions of the Mid-Atlantic colonies had been settled before 1760.

Although the colonial settlements of particular interest are listed within their current states and grouped geographically, we cannot pretend to establish travel patterns that will match each reader's interests and timetable. Some may want to spend a week along the Hudson or in greater Philadelphia, while others will shoot through a string of cities from New York to Baltimore in the same time. Therefore we do not suggest stock itineraries that "cover" the colonial high points in any region, though any reader so inclined could construct one from this book. Most people will want to browse through a region without a rigid schedule, pausing to enjoy the unexpected glimpses of daily life two or three centuries ago.

The Internet can provide you with valuable information if you can separate out the advertorials luring people to specific sites or places. Some Web sites of regional and town tourist authorities are very helpful, and links may provide more detail. Yet guidebooks like this one are the most efficient starting place for objective and informed descriptions of the places you may want to visit, with follow-up on the Web to check seasons and opening hours of sites, special exhibits and events, and other current information. Because many historic sites are staffed by volunteers, their hours and seasons are subject to frequent change. It is always wise to call or check the Web site while planning your trip.

For the latest updates contact the state tourist offices or local convention and visitors bureaus, which offer detailed maps of towns and regions, guides to historic sites, locations for outdoor recreation, and lists of accommodations and restaurants. Such offices also have calendars of festivals and special events you may want to work into your travel plans. We list some of the traditional festivals, but their dates change, and some are not held every year, so it is always wise to check before making your plans. For your convenience, we list addresses, telephone numbers, and Web sites (when available) of state, regional, and town tourist offices.

Accommodations and Restaurants

In a country where plentiful wood was the primary building material, restricting suggestions for lodging and food to authentic colonial inns, B&Bs, and restaurants makes little sense, because most of these establishments have been torn down, burned down, or simply rotted away—you would be out in the cold and hungry in many regions of historic interest.

But you can find wonderful accommodations from former eras for an overnight stay if you are not too fussy about the date the structure was first built. This policy makes sense for another reason: Many inns and houses grew with the trade or the family as addition by addition formed an elongated T at the back of the original structure. Those who restore such buildings have to decide which era will set the pattern. Architectural purists may reject the additions that kept the house alive and full of people, but social historians understand such processes of growth and adaptation. Discriminating travelers usually find colonial, Federal, or Victorian lodgings preferable to larger but less interesting modern hotel and motel rooms, so we list the former, but seldom the latter, unless there is a special reason to do so.

Restaurants present another problem not so easily resolved. Only a handful of inns have survived from the colonial era, and most of them serve a mélange of contemporary cuisines, with a few colonial specialties. Others listed are located in authentic historic buildings or have succeeded in recreating the ambience of former eras. Although we have at some time enjoyed a meal in the restaurants we list, in no case can we guarantee the current quality of the food. Menus change by the season and the year, and good chefs are notoriously peripatetic.

We do not pretend to be comprehensive in our suggestions for a pleasant place to spend the night or eat a good meal. We like the establishments we list but know there are many others of equal quality that we have not yet discovered. For your convenience, we list the phone numbers and Web sites of recommended inns, bed & breakfasts, and restaurants so you can make reservations and get current information.

Acknowledgments

In the research for this volume, which involved many months of reading, as well as travel to colonial and Revolutionary sites, we found ourselves mentally rewriting and reenergizing the sometimes stale and dull history handed out to us in high school and even college history courses. For the first time we realized how vibrant and dangerous those eras were, and began to fully appreciate the bravery and persistence of our colonial and Revolutionary precursors. We turned to many acclaimed historians to reawaken that dormant understanding, and especially appreciate the help of Skidmore colleague Tom Lewis, whose research and writing on the Hudson Valley (*The Hudson: A History*, Yale University Press, 2005) provided both information and insight. Never before had we fully understood the crucial significance of the Hudson-Champlain corridor in the development and defense of America—even though we live within it—and his book helped to tell that story.

We also extend our gratitude to many persons who helped us plan our travels through colonial Mid-Atlantic states, provided maps, arranged appointments, and sometimes reviewed our text. They include directors of local and regional visitors bureaus and chambers of commerce, media specialists in state tourist authorities, public-relations representatives and guides at historical sites, friends, and a host of others who went out of their way to give us information and lead us to important places in their communities.

We also thank Kermit Hummel, editorial director of the Countryman Press, for his interest in this series of heritage tourism volumes on the colonial and Revolutionary eras—New England, the Mid-Atlantic states, and the South. Managing editor Jennifer Thompson has demonstrated both understanding of the complexity of the subjects and patience as the texts developed. And we especially thank Glenn E. Novak and his wife, Sarah, for their meticulous attention to detail, knowledge of history, and substantive contributions to the text. Never before in more than a quarter century of working with editors have we had such a pleasant and productive experience.

New York

Historical Introduction
to the
New York Colony

In an era when waterways provided the most expeditious and convenient way of moving people and goods through the roadless wilderness of the American continent, early settlements congealed along coastlines and riverbanks. From the outset the lifeblood of the New Amsterdam colony was the Hudson River, navigable from the lower harbor 150 miles upstream to Fort Orange (Albany). There the Dutch West India Company established a trading post for the beaver and otter pelts so valued in Europe, and a port settlement to tranship them grew on Manhattan Island at the mouth of the river. This waterway became the defining axis of the New York colony throughout the 17th century, and its extension through Lake George and Lake Champlain made it the primary highway of invasion in the second half of the 18th century between the British and French empires in North America and their Indian allies. During the French and Indian War and the Revolution, and briefly again during the War of 1812, holding a series of Adirondack forts became the key for sustaining or blocking invasions from north or south and thus for control of the continent.

Hudson and Champlain

As if by some hidden design of convergence, the year 1609 brought Henry Hudson and Samuel de Champlain to explore opposite ends of these water routes linking the mid-Atlantic with the St. Lawrence River. Hudson had heard from his friend Captain John Smith, lately of Virginia, that there was "a sea leading into the western ocean, by the north of the southern English colony." When the Dutch East India Company hired Hudson to find a speedy route to China, visions of

George Washington stands in front of the Federal Hall National Memorial on Wall Street.

> ✳ Henry Hudson set sail on a polar expedition in 1611, again seeking the tantalizing Northwest Passage through the bay named after him. After a long winter locked in ice, discontented crew members mutinied. They forced Hudson and his son, as well as seven others, into a small boat before sailing for England. The bay must have claimed the lives of those left behind; no remains were ever recovered.

instant wealth through trade in spices, pearls, and silk were enticing. Moreover, the Dutch East India Company guaranteed him 800 guilders with 200 more for his wife in case he did not come back. Not daunted by earlier failures (in 1607 and 1608, under an English flag) to reach China through a northeast passage, he set out again in 1609 with a mixed crew of eighteen English and Dutch sailors on the *Half Moon*. When ice fields and a threatened mutiny stopped his eastward track, he ignored his instructions and shifted his attention to finding a Northwest Passage.

He sailed to Newfoundland and caught "one hundred and eighteen great cods," met Indians in Penobscot Bay, headed south for Delaware Bay, and finally decided to cruise up into the river that now bears his name. By September 2, 1609, Hudson reached the lower bay off Sandy Hook, then sailed up "the great river of the mountain," as he called it, for seventeen days, almost all the way up to Albany. The *Half Moon* anchored when it came to a section of river that was only seven feet deep. Hudson then surmised that he was not going to reach the western ocean, but he sent men in a small boat upstream as far as they could go in half a day; the mate confirmed his suspicions.

On the voyage up and down the river, Hudson and his crew had encounters with many bands of Indians from various tribes along the shores, some of the encounters warlike and leading to bloodshed, others amicable. As Hudson's dreams of spices and pearls faded, they were replaced by the skins and furs that the local Indians were willing to trade for trinkets. Although he later wrote the Dutch East India Company about the value of the furs, the directors were disappointed that he had not found a magical route to China. However, other Dutch businessmen were intrigued by fur trading and proceeded to make money in that way.

NEW YORK *Time Line*

1609	**1609**	**1613**	**1624**	**1626**
Henry Hudson explores river named for him, as far as site of Albany	Samuel de Champlain explores lake named for him	Adriaen Block arrives at Hell's Gate in Manhattan	Dutch settle in New York Bay and at Fort Orange (Albany) on the Hudson River	Peter Minuit arrives and purchases Manhattan from Indian sachems

Like Hudson and many other European explorers, Frenchman Samuel de Champlain sought the illusory Northwest Passage to the riches of the Orient. After accompanying a fur-trading voyage up the St. Lawrence in 1603, he founded fur-trading posts at Port Royal in Acadia (Nova Scotia) and Quebec. In 1609, accompanied by a war party of Algonquians, Hurons, and Montagnais, he explored southward up the Richelieu River, to a large lake stretching even further to the south. Their canoes reached a Mohawk camp along the west shore at a promontory (either Crown Point or Ticonderoga) at night, and a battle followed the next morning. Champlain had a weapon new to the Mohawks—the arquebus—and it ultimately won the battle as the Mohawks scattered into the woods. The war road that would last through more than two centuries for Europeans was established that day.

Champlain named the lake for himself and wrote about the wild game in the forests and the fish in the lake. He claimed to have spotted "the Champlain Monster," and we haven't heard the last of that yet. According to his description, it was a five-foot fish, "as big as my thigh, and had a head as large as my fists, with a snout two feet and a half long, and a double row of very sharp, dangerous teeth. Its body has a good deal the shape of the pike."

From Exploration to First Settlement

Adriaen Block, a Dutch trader and explorer, sailed through the narrow strait east of Manhattan in 1613 and named it "Hellegat" (Hell passage) because strong, funneling tidal currents made it difficult to navigate. He sailed around Long Island, naming it for its shape. Block continued up the Hudson to Castle Island just south of Albany, where he built Fort Nassau. He returned home with a boatload of furs and a new map. His company, the United New Netherland Company, received the right to make four more trading trips over a three-year period.

The Dutch West India Company obtained a charter in 1621, and by 1624 its first group of settlers arrived in New Netherland. Most of them were French-speaking Huguenots, called Walloons, who had been persecuted in Belgium and France

1629
Establishment of patroonships to encourage settlement along the Hudson

1640
New England colonists begin to resettle on Long Island

1664
English rule established in New Netherland

1673
Dutch regain control of New York for fifteen months

A *Quadricentennial* CELEBRATION

The year 2009 will mark the 400th anniversary of the exploratory voyages of Henry Hudson and Samuel de Champlain on the waterways named after them. The Hudson-Fulton-Champlain Quadricentennial Commission will also mark the 200th anniversary of Robert Fulton's maiden steamship journey up the Hudson in 1807—three "critical advances in the settlement, expansion and development of North America." A similar commemoration took place in 1909, and all three milestones will be celebrated together again in 2009. Eight signature events will take place from July 4 to October 4, 2009, from New York City to the Quebec border. The Web site is up and running: www.exploreny400.com. Phone: 888.HFC.2009. E-mail: info@exploreny400.com.

for being Protestants. Cornelis Jacobsz Mey, the captain of the *Nieu Nederlandt,* landed eight men on Governor's Island off Manhattan in 1624. They called it Nut Island because of the wild chestnut and walnut trees growing there. Another group sailed to Fort Nassau (which had been flooded and abandoned in 1614) and replaced it with Fort Orange on higher ground. The third group settled south of the site of Philadelphia, where they built another Fort Nassau, while the fourth group settled near present-day Hartford.

Three months later forty-five Walloons arrived with cattle, sheep, horses, hogs, and farm equipment. The Manhattan Island colony reached 200 persons. New Amsterdam, as it was called, was planned by West India Company engineers down to the last street, school, and the Dutch Reformed Church. When Peter Minuit arrived as director-general of the colony in 1626, one of his first acts was a formal purchase of the land from Indian sachems. Manhattan Island was sold for sixty guilders, or about $24, in exchange for trading goods that the Indians liked. New Netherland slowly began to be settled by individuals.

Those who were persecuted in English colonies found the New Netherland

NEW YORK *Time Line*

1690	**1690**	**1691**	**1703**	**1754**
Leisler's Rebellion	King William's War, burning of Schenectady	New York becomes a royal colony under William and Mary	Queen Anne's War	French and Indian War begins; colonies meet in Albany to discuss defense

colony a safe place to settle in the 1630s and 1640s. Reverend John Throckmorton came with thirty-five families to settle in the Throg's Neck area of East Bronx. The Reverend Francis Doughty settled Newtown between Queens and Brooklyn. Lady Deborah Moody came to Gravesend Bay in Brooklyn. Anne Hutchinson came to Pelham Neck (she would be killed in an Indian attack in 1643).

Patroonships along the Hudson

Unlike the New England colonies held together by strong religious convictions and theocratic forms of government, New Netherland began as a commercial venture with a heterogeneous population. The nineteen directors of the Dutch West India Company began to worry about the slow growth of profits. Some argued that they should eliminate the high costs of colonization and fall back to a simple fur trading operation, while others saw the long-term benefits of settlement growth throughout the Hudson Valley. By 1629 they were offering parcels extending sixteen miles on one side of the Hudson River or eight miles on both sides to people who agreed to bring fifty colonists to settle over a period of four years. These individuals were called patroons, and they were required to give their tenants homes, cattle, and tools. The tenants had to pay rent to the patroons and conform to other requirements. The uptake was slow, so to attract more middle-class settlers, in 1640 the company also offered 200 acres to anyone bringing five immigrants.

This semifeudal system encouraged the development of huge landholdings along the Hudson and established a pattern that endured far beyond Dutch control of the colony. Kiliaen Van Rensselaer, one of the nineteen directors who promoted colonization, took advantage of the offer and became one of the largest absentee landlords at the head of navigation. His family's holdings at Rensselaerwick, stretching on both sides of the river from present-day Troy southward through Albany and halfway downstream to what is now the city of Hudson, added up to 750,000 acres. Robert Livingston, a secretary to Nicholaes Van Rensselaer, the resident patroon in Albany, married his widow and began accumulating another vast estate in the mid-Hudson region, eventually encompassing more than a million acres.

1755	**1757**	**1758**	**1759**	**1763**
Battle of Lake George	Montcalm destroys Forts Oswego and George	Montcalm defeats Abercrombie at Fort Carillon (Ticonderoga)	French abandon forts at Ticonderoga and Crown Point; British capture Fort Niagara	Treaty of Paris formally ends French and Indian War

Erratic Government

The search for profit at the core of New Netherland—perhaps an omen of New York City's future—did not provide stable government through its first decades. Corruption and fraud in officials, lack of essential goods from the home country, chaotic conditions in streets and buildings, and a transient, polyglot population impeded orderly development in the colony.

When Peter Stuyvesant arrived in New Amsterdam in 1645, he would have looked out at a dilapidated fort, crude wooden houses, and unfenced animals in the streets and heard the shouts of drunken residents and Indians. As director-general for the company, he had a difficult task to restore order, and the previously uncontrolled settlers complained when he established ordinance after ordinance to clean up the settlement on Manhattan. The son of a strict Calvinist minister in the Dutch Reformed Church, he had no qualms about imposing his principles and authority first in New Amsterdam and eventually upriver in a largely independent Rensselaerwick as well. Through seventeen years of his administration he established enough order to attract more colonists to the Hudson and with difficulty managed to quell a number of Indian uprisings as these original residents were displaced.

Ultimately, events in Europe would bring his efforts to an end when the Dutch lost control of New Netherland after forty years. Stuyvesant had to turn the colony over to the British in 1664. King Charles II had given a royal patent for lands that included New Netherland to his brother James, Duke of York, who dispatched four warships full of soldiers under the command of Colonel Richard Nicolls to back up the claim. When Nicolls arrived off New Amsterdam, Stuyvesant had neither the troops nor the powder and supplies to withstand a siege and was persuaded to negotiate a surrender. Nicolls renamed New Amsterdam New York. In November of 1673, during an Anglo-Dutch war, Dutch warships briefly took back control of the city for a few months, until the Treaty of Westminster gave it back to the British in February 1674. The long process of assimilation to British rule continued with some discontent among the Dutch settlers but few eruptions.

One of those occurred in 1689 when news of the "Glorious Revolution" that

NEW YORK *Time Line*

1765	**1775**	**1776**	**1777**
Stamp Act Congress meets in New York City	Ethan Allen and Benedict Arnold capture Fort Ticonderoga	Battle of Long Island; Fort Washington surrenders; Washington retreats through New Jersey; Arnold's hastily assembled fleet defeated by British on Lake Champlain but succeeds in delaying invasion	Burgoyne defeated at Saratoga

During the late decades of the 17th century the line between legal and illegal trade and enterprise was often crossed. For example, privateering was legal and very profitable for New Yorkers. The King of England granted privateers commissions, and the captain and crew eagerly divided up the spoils of capture. Some privateers became pirates when they seized a ship belonging to a neutral country. The trick was to off-load the cargo from the seized ship into an unarmed New York ship. Faked papers completed the job. Captain William Kidd, who lived on Sloat Lane (later called Beaver Street) in New York City, was well known for his privateering success. At one point his crew mutinied and he then became a pirate—or so he said. He surrendered in Boston, was sent to London for trial, and was executed in 1701.

brought William and Mary to the English throne reached New York. A royal fiat annexing New York to the Dominion of New England brought total collapse of the government. Six captains on duty at Fort James refused to take orders from Lieutenant Governor Francis Nicholson. The senior officer, Jacob Leisler, was appointed commander of the province by a convention of New York county. Leisler's Rebellion was short-lived. Although Leisler demonstrated some administrative ability, he assumed more authority than had been granted from vague wording in a royal letter and aroused opposition from wealthy Anglo-Dutch families, especially in Albany. By 1691 a new governor arrived in New York from England. Governor Henry Sloughter took control of the fort and arrested the Leisler group; Leisler was tried, convicted of treason, hanged, and beheaded.

Other wars had peripheral effects on parts of New York. During King William's War (1689–97) upstate New York was the focus of the French desire to control the fur trade. Governor Frontenac of New France sent a party of 200 French and Indians to attack Schenectady in 1690. When they reached the stockade on the night of February 9, they found only two sentries at the gate—and both of them were snowmen! Pouring through the open gate, the raiders massacred fifty-two people, took twenty-seven prisoners, and burned all but five of eighty homes. This brutal attack raised fears in Albany that proved groundless, and by the time Queen

1778	**1779**	**1783**	**1789**
France signs treaty with Americans and enters war against Britain	General Sullivan leads punitive expedition against Iroquois in western New York	Treaty of Paris recognizes American independence; British evacuate New York; Washington resigns his commission	Washington inaugurated as first president of the United States in New York City, then the federal capital

Anne's War broke out (1703–13) the Iroquois provided a buffer between French Canada and Albany. Tired of French incursions into their territory, the Iroquois had signed peace treaties with both Canada and New York in 1701.

French and Indian War

Also called the Seven Years War, this worldwide struggle between France and Britain began on the North American frontier and lasted from 1754 to 1763. The waterways in the state—the Hudson-Champlain corridor, the Mohawk Valley, and the St. Lawrence—were at the center of the conflict in North America. British regular troops and colonial militias were pitted against French regulars and Canadians, with Native American tribes participating on both sides. In June of 1754 representatives of seven colonies held a conference in Albany to make preparations for defense and try to enlist Indian help. The Iroquois negotiated with William Johnson, who had been appointed superintendent of Indian affairs, and he presented them with thirty wagons of trade goods to win their support.

The story of New York campaigns in the French and Indian War is largely told in the building, defending, attacking, destroying, and rebuilding of forts west and north of Albany. The important forts were located at key points to control troop movements on the waterways—Oswego, Niagara, Crown Point (Fort St. Frédéric), Ticonderoga (Fort Carillon), Lake George, Fort Edward.

In 1755 the British built Fort Oswego to control the water route from Lake Ontario to the Mohawk River but lost it to the Marquis de Montcalm the next year.

The campaigns along the Lake Champlain–Lake George corridor started in small encounters and grew into large battles to control access to the heart of New York. The first, in 1755, occurred at the head of Lake George where no fort yet stood. Baron de Dieskau, heading south to attack Fort Lyman (Fort Edward), met forces under Sir William Johnson and was defeated after several encounters on a single day. After the battle Johnson started building Fort William Henry on a bluff overlooking Lake George, and it repelled a French attack the following winter. But when the Marquis de Montcalm laid a massive siege against Fort William Henry

> With remarkable prescience, Benjamin Franklin, one of the Pennsylvania delegates to the Albany Congress, proposed a union of the colonies to handle matters of common defense and westward expansion, leaving all other affairs to the individual colonies. It would include a congress of selected representatives, based on each colony's population and wealth, and a president general appointed by the king. The Albany Plan passed and was forwarded to the colonial assemblies, which refused to consider it seriously, and to Parliament, where it was laid aside. In a letter to Governor Shirley of Massachusetts, Franklin commented, "Everyone cries, a union is necessary, but when they come to the manner and form of the union, their weak noodles are perfectly distracted."

in 1757 with batteries of artillery and nearly 8,000 soldiers and Indians, Colonel George Munro was forced to surrender under fair terms that were violated in the unintended massacre that followed.

The next year brought the most massive campaign yet seen in North America, led by British general James Abercrombie. He assembled 15,000 men, both regulars and colonials, and an armada of more than 1,000 bateaux and whaleboats to transport them thirty-two miles down the lake for an attack on Fort Carillon (Ticonderoga). Through brilliant strategy on the part of outnumbered Montcalm, this attack was repulsed and Abercrombie retired in defeat.

After the victories of 1758 the French initiatives faltered and they began to fall back toward Canada. When Jeffrey Amherst led a new attack on Fort Carillon (Ticonderoga) in 1759, the French abandoned the fort, and Crown Point as well. The tide had turned against them, and in the same year Sir William Johnson reoccupied Oswego and used it as a staging site for the campaigns against Forts Frontenac and Niagara. The fall of Fort Niagara gave the British control of the western waterways. Capping off a year of glorious victories, British General James Wolfe defeated Montcalm on the Plains of Abraham above Quebec. With the surrender of Montreal a year later, the military phase of the war was over and the negotiations for the Treaty of Paris began. In this aftermath, France gave up Canada to Britain, and the stage was set for the next conflict to control North America.

Revolutionary Rumblings

New York's reputation as a haven for Tory sympathizers during the Revolution was not undeserved—especially in New York City, Long Island, Westchester County, and the Mohawk Valley—but it's only half the truth. For some time before the Revolution, the colonists chafed under English rule, and New Yorkers were among the most aggrieved. The British army had been headquartered in New York, the center of action during the French and Indian War. By 1763 Parliament was trying to get the colonies to help pay for the cost of the war. Prime Minister Lord George Grenville started with an import tax, then a stamp tax, and soon followed with a host of other measures designed to wring money from the colonists.

In 1765 New York's merchants decided to boycott British goods. The Stamp Act Congress met in the city in October of 1765, with delegates from nine colonies, and proclaimed the right to self-determination in matters of taxation. The Sons of Liberty emerged as leaders of the resistance, and their members had no compunction about the use of force to bring the king's ministers into line. In 1774 two thousand Yorkers jumped on board the *London*, a ship loaded with tea, burst open the tea cases, and threw them into the river. Committees of correspondence were established to oppose the Tea Act, and delegates were sent to the congress in Philadelphia that agreed to prohibit importation of tea from Britain. But New York's loyalties remained divided, partly because city merchants had strong ties (and debts) to London, partly because of the strong presence of British troops and officials in the city.

New York Campaigns

About a third of the Revolutionary War battles took place in New York, including many crushing defeats and one crucial victory for the Americans. The most important actions occurred in two sectors, in and around New York City and along the Champlain-Hudson waterway in 1776 and 1777. The major disaster came first with the occupation of New York City, which was lost to British forces under Lord Howe in a series of battles during the late summer and fall of 1776. During this campaign Washington's army suffered defeat in Brooklyn at the Battle of Long Island, when his 10,000 troops were overwhelmed by 20,000 redcoats and Hessians, and in upper Manhattan in the defense of Fort Washington, where nearly 3,000 defenders were taken prisoner. By choosing to commit his whole army to defend New York City at the outset of the war, Washington risked losing it altogether but escaped twice. After the battle in Brooklyn he succeeded in ferrying 9,000 men across the East River to Manhattan during the night, and after the surrender of Fort Washington and the abandonment of Fort Lee he retreated across New Jersey with a remnant of his former strength, estimated at no more than 3,000 men.

Upstate, the water route—stretching from the St. Lawrence through the Richelieu River, Lake Champlain, and Lake George to the Hudson River—became the main warpath for invading British forces from the north. As the French had used it during the French and Indian War, the British now sought to cut the colonies in half, sealing New England off from the Mid-Atlantic colonies on this axis. The action in this sector was on a minor scale compared to the large forces involved in New York City, but delaying tactics here thwarted a major invasion from the north.

Ethan Allen and Benedict Arnold had already seized lightly defended Fort Ticonderoga in 1775, and after a failed American attempt to invade Canada later that year, the British mounted a southward response. During the summer of 1776 they built a fleet of thirty ships and gunboats at St. Johns (St.-Jean-sur-Richelieu) to wrest control of Lake Champlain, while Arnold was building a fleet of fifteen vessels at Skenesborough (Whitehall, New York) to oppose their advance. In October Arnold's little navy met the British fleet under the command of Sir Guy Carleton at Valcour Island, where much of the American fleet was destroyed by superior British firepower. After the battle Arnold's surviving ships managed to glide past the British blockade on a foggy night. Although Arnold lost most of his remaining vessels in the chase that followed, he had delayed Carleton's invasion down the lake long enough. When the British troops faced a heavily manned Fort Ticonderoga at the end of October, with snow already falling, they returned to Canada for the winter.

A more comprehensive British strategy emerged for the renewed campaign in 1777. In a three-pronged attack General John Burgoyne was to move south along the Champlain-Hudson waterway while Colonel Barry St. Leger moved east from Oswego along the Mohawk and General Howe moved north along the Hudson, all converging at Albany. Like many promising military plans, it went awry through lack of coordination and unforeseen obstacles. St. Leger's advance was stopped by a bloody battle at Oriskany and an unsuccessful siege of Fort Stanwix at Rome. General Howe sailed south to Philadelphia to encounter Washington, leaving the northward progress to Sir Henry Clinton, who never got beyond Kingston. Meanwhile Burgoyne captured Fort Ticonderoga, but his advance bogged down on the military road south of Skenesborough, partly destroyed by American forces, and by severe losses at battles in Hubbardton and Bennington.

By the time Burgoyne reached Saratoga, his forces numbered not much more than 5,000 men and he faced nearly 20,000 Americans under the command of General Horatio Gates. After two unsuccessful attacks at Saratoga, badly outnumbered and with no prospect of reinforcements from St. Leger or Clinton, Burgoyne finally surrendered. The ultimate significance of this victory—by far the

---

The split loyalties of New Yorkers were symbolized by the city's official welcome to two prominent figures on the same day, June 25, 1775. One was George Washington, on his way to Massachusetts to assume command of Patriot militias besieging the British army in Boston in the aftermath of the outbreak of hostilities at Lexington and Concord. The other was Royal Governor William Tryon, returning to New York after a year's absence in England.

A number of New York organizations provide maps and information about Revolutionary War sites and campaigns in the state. They include Heritage New York, www.heritageny.gov; the New York Independence Trail, www.independencetrail.org; Hudson River Valley National Heritage Area, www.hudsonrivervalley.com; and Mohawk Valley Heritage Corridor, www.mohawkvalleyheritage.com

most important of 1777—was not only stopping a potent strategy for dividing the colonies, but in helping to enlist the aid of France for the American cause. After Saratoga, the major actions of the Revolution moved south to New Jersey, Pennsylvania, and Virginia.

The Treaty of Paris confirmed American independence in September of 1783, but the British did not evacuate New York City until November.

Regions *to* Explore

NEW YORK CITY
LONG ISLAND
HUDSON RIVER VALLEY
CAPITAL DISTRICT/SARATOGA/GLENS FALLS
THE ADIRONDACKS
CENTRAL LEATHERSTOCKING REGION
FINGER LAKES
WESTERN NEW YORK/GREATER NIAGARA

NEW YORK CITY

Historical New York City is like an archipelago with many islands to explore. Did you know that the borough of the Bronx is located on the mainland and that the other four boroughs—Manhattan, Brooklyn, Queens, and Staten Island—are on islands? Brooklyn and Queens are on Long Island. Brooklyn dates back to 1658, when it was called Breukelen, from a Dutch town near Amsterdam. Queens was named for Queen Catherine Braganza, the wife of England's Charles II. Staten Island is home to Richmondtown Restoration; it was a thriving town during the Revolution.

That brings us to Manhattan, the most famous part of New York City and yet only twelve miles long. The Algonquian Indians named it "island of the hills." It is known as a world capital of tourism, as well as international finance, fashion, and higher education. Millions of visitors arrive every year, and there is more than

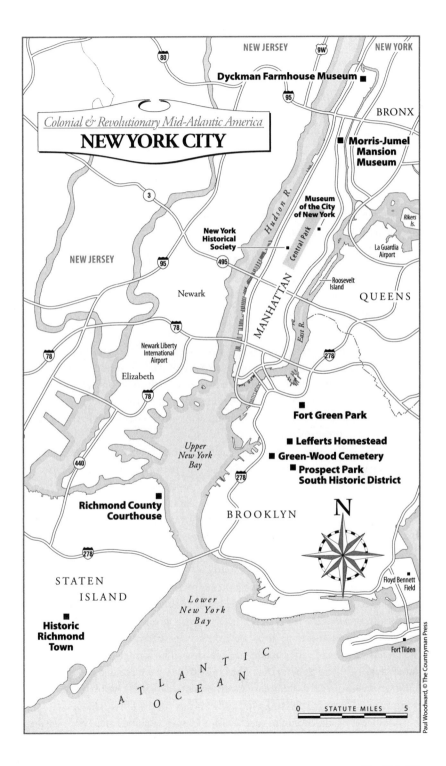

Colonial & Revolutionary Mid-Atlantic America
NEW YORK CITY

NEW JERSEY 9W NEW YORK

80

Dyckman Farmhouse Museum ■

95

BRONX

■ **Morris-Jumel Mansion Museum**

3

Museum of the City of New York

Rikers Is.

New York Historical Society

La Guardia Airport

95

495

Roosevelt Island

QUEENS

NEW JERSEY

Newark

78

78

Newark Liberty International Airport

Elizabeth

78

278

■ **Fort Green Park**

■ **Lefferts Homestead**
■ **Green-Wood Cemetery**
■ **Prospect Park South Historic District**

Upper New York Bay

440

278

Richmond County Courthouse

BROOKLYN

N

STATEN ISLAND

Lower New York Bay

Floyd Bennett Field

■ **Historic Richmond Town**

A T L A N T I C
O C E A N

Fort Tilden

0   STATUTE MILES   5

enough to interest everyone. Every time we visit we pick out an area that is new to us, but we'll never be able to finish our list.

Mentally recreating the colonial life of New York City is a bit like starting to assemble a jigsaw puzzle that has been in the attic too long, with many key pieces lost by generations of careless children. All the sites of major events are still there—from the first Walloon settlement at the Battery in 1625 to the route of Washington's parade down Bowery Lane when the British finally evacuated the city in 1783—but most have been transformed beyond recognition. New York, more than most large cities of the world, has used the wrecking ball freely to make room for the new on an island much too small for its ambitions. Finding where the pieces that remain mostly unchanged fit into the cityscape is not an easy task. The best place to start is in museums, including historic house museums, where you can see the pattern that no longer exists as a whole.

UPPER MANHATTAN

HISTORICAL SITES *and* MUSEUMS

The **Dyckman Farmhouse** (212-304-9422; www.dyckmanfarmhouse.org), 4881 Broadway at 204th St., is the northernmost stop on our colonial/revolutionary tour of Manhattan. Open Wed.–Sun. This modest 1784 farmhouse seems incongruous on a street bustling with people, with cars and trucks double parked, flinging open doors without looking to see if a vehicle might be zooming by. Look up the stone steps leading to the Dyckman House, past a black wrought-iron fence and mounds of roses, tulips, and daffodils. Walk up the steps and in through the Dutch door of the farmhouse.

The house has been recently opened after restoration. Some furniture belonging to the Dyckman family is back in place. The parlor on the right has a soft teal color on the mantel and window frames. A Chippendale-style drop-front desk has a serpentine front and dates to 1760–90. A display case includes clay pipes, the rim of a fish net, oyster shells, and a hook for locating lost fish traps and anchors. To the left, the dining room, probably used for sleep, work, and entertaining, has blue tiles around the fireplace. Downstairs are the kitchen and the relic room housing artifacts.

Jan Dyckman was the founding father who arrived in New Amsterdam in the 1660s. In 1689 he and Rebecca Nagel married after their spouses died. During the British occupation in 1776–83 the Dyckman family fled; they returned after the war ended to find their home destroyed. A new house was built. Today the house has a half-acre park outside the back door. The formal garden is shaded by large trees, including a cherry tree. The Hessian Hut was reconstructed from foundation stones from a Revolutionary encampment on former Dyckman land. There were once 60 huts on this land, with eight soldiers bunked in each one.

Our second historic home is just a few miles south, dating from 1765. Wealthy Loyalist families often built country estates outside the city. Roger Morris and his wife, Mary Philipse, built the **Morris-Jumel Mansion** (212-923-8008; www.mor risjumel.org), 65 Jumel Terrace. Open Wed.–Sun. Morris fought under Edward Braddock during the French and Indian War; he was also a friend of George Washington. But as the Revolution approached, the Morris family fled to England as staunch Loyalists.

Imagine George Washington standing on the wide porch overlooking New York harbor, Staten Island to the south, and the Hudson and Harlem Rivers to the west and east. His troops, after a stinging defeat on Long Island, had recently won the Battle of Harlem Heights. Washington lived in the house in the fall of 1776 as he tried to defend Manhattan. He chose a room at the end of a corridor because he liked peace and quiet. His personal servant, William Lee, slept in the hall outside the door on a pallet. Other bedrooms include Eliza Jumel's bedroom from 1826–30, and niece Mary Bowen's room, who was raised as a daughter. Aaron Burr's room, dating from 1833—after, at age 77, he had married Eliza—is there. But one year later she began divorce proceedings, and Burr died on the day the divorce was granted in 1836.

Afterward, the house became a tavern; then Stephen and Betsy Jumel purchased it. The house still contains its original fireplace in the old basement kitchen. Some of the furniture dates from the Morris period, before the Revolution, and some from the Jumel period.

If you want to whet your appetite for early colonial life, visit the **Museum of the City of New York** (212-534-1672; www.mcny.org), 1220 Fifth Ave. at 103rd St., which is the place to trace the history of the city from its days as a Dutch trad-

The Dyckman Farmhouse.

The Morris-Jumel Mansion.

ing post. Open Tue.–Sun. Exhibits include a model of Henry Hudson's *Half Moon,* dioramas showing the age of Dutch exploration in the 17th century and Dutch life in New Amsterdam, a model of a Dutch fort, and a scale model of New Amsterdam in 1660. The English and Revolutionary War Gallery explores the history of New York after the British arrived in 1664. Two Gilbert Stuart portraits of George Washington hang here. The Toy Gallery on the third floor features dollhouses and furniture dating from 1769.

MIDTOWN MANHATTAN

Another place to become immersed in the history of the area is the **New-York Historical Society** (212-873-3400; www.nyhistory.org) 170 Central Park West and 77th St. Open Tue.–Sun. The American silver collection has pieces from the 17th and 18th centuries. Period rooms feature those centuries as well. Don't miss the collection of 18th-century toys. The third floor houses American crafts, including weathervanes, pottery, and household utensils.

LOWER MANHATTAN

The site of the original Dutch settlement of Nieuw Amsterdam, now Lower Manhattan, flourished for many years, but the buildings have mostly disappeared. However, the **Fraunces Tavern Museum** (212-425-1778; www.frauncestavern.org), 54 Pearl St., stands in a reconstructed 1719 building. Open daily. Stephen De

Lancey built it as his home, then sold the building to Samuel Fraunces, who opened it as the Queen's Head Tavern in 1763.

Fraunces became chief steward for George Washington, and his tavern was the site of Washington's farewell to his officers in 1783. Forty-four officers attended the banquet in the Long Room, set for a dinner as it would have been that night. After the dinner Washington walked to Whitehall, took a boat to New Jersey, and proceeded from there to Annapolis, Maryland, where he resigned his commission at a ceremony in the State House.

The museum houses a permanent collection that includes Chinese export porcelain, silver, documents, prints, paintings, maps, clocks, weapons, and sculpture. Special exhibitions are held, as well as a full roster of educational programs on topics such as science and witchcraft in colonial times, Native American fare, 18th-century etiquette, New York City folklore, and medicinal plants in colonial America. You can also have lunch or dinner downstairs in **Fraunces Tavern Restaurant** (212-968-1776), a favorite spot for those working on Wall Street.

Next you'll hear about a pirate who wasn't all bad. The first **Trinity Church** (212-602-0800; www.trinitywallstreet.org), 74 Trinity Place, was built in 1697, and taxes collected from all citizens paid for it. William (Captain) Kidd contributed heavily to the building fund.

The Great Fire of 1776 demolished the church, and it has risen twice since. The fire was suspected of having been set by Washington's agents or rebel sympathizers, to discommode the occupying British. The graveyard contains many old stones; the oldest is that of Richard Church from 1681.

St. Paul's Chapel (212-602-0874; www.trinitywallstreet.org), Broadway at Fulton St., dates from 1776; it's considered to be the oldest public building in continuous use in Manhattan. Open daily. After George Washington's inauguration a service took place here. The tomb of Brigadier General Richard Montgomery, who was killed in the Battle of Quebec in December 1775, is on the east porch. Inside, the pulpit, communion rail, organ exterior, and the Waterford crystal chandeliers are all pre-Revolution. After Trinity Church burned in the fire of 1776, St. Paul's became the favorite Anglican church in New York. In fact, British officers worshipped here instead of turning it into a stable or a hospital, as was the fate of other churches. (After September 11, 2001, St. Paul's Chapel served as a place of rest and refuge for recovery workers. Inside, displays about the disaster and its aftermath are very poignant. The roots of the sycamore tree that fell on that day are preserved and on display in the south churchyard.)

> Most people would never guess that the most notorious donor to the building fund of Trinity Church on Wall Street was none other than William Kidd, better known as Captain Kidd. He was well respected until he turned to pirating. The borderline between privateering and piracy was thin indeed, and Kidd had won renown for his success as a privateer.

The pulpit at St. Paul's Chapel.

Although the **Statue of Liberty** (212-363-3200; www.nps.gov/stoi) is certainly of a later period, the Statue of Liberty Museum on Liberty Island offers immigration displays dating from 1600. The island itself belonged to Isack Bedloo, a merchant and "select burgher" of New Amsterdam. Bedlow's Island (an anglicized Bedloo) remained in the family until 1732, when it was sold for five shillings. Bedlow's Island was first a quarantine station, then a summer home (1746), and in 1756 was used as a smallpox quarantine station when the disease was raging through Philadelphia. When the English were in power, Tory sympathizers found safety here.

Much of the maritime activity centered on the East River, which was in the lee of Manhattan and therefore less subject to westerly winds, flooding, and ice floes of the Hudson River. The **South Street Seaport Museum** (212-748-8600; www.southstreetseaportmuseum.org), Fulton and Water Sts., has been restored as a port, reflecting life here from early days into the 19th century. Open Apr.–Oct., Tue.–Sun.; Fri.–Mon. the rest of the year. Although most of the historical buildings date from the 19th century, the flavor of colonial days is still here. Peter Schermerhorn consolidated his waterfront lots on Fulton Street in 1793, and the Schermerhorn Row landfill began to reclaim land from the sea. In 1811 he built a row of countinghouses.

WALKING TOUR *of the* COLONIAL TRIANGLE

Patriot Tours (718-717-0963; www.patriottoursnyc.com) offers a great way to experience colonial history in Lower Manhattan. You will hear stories of real people and political intrigue. Learn about spy rings during the Revolution. Who was the greatest spymaster of all? Where did the Sons of Liberty fight over a liberty pole? Who was Alexander McDougall?

We started our tour with Karen Quinones at City Hall, the site of the liberty pole known as "the Common" or "the Fields." Rabble-rousers were active there, eager to harass local Tories. Stamp Act protesters came in 1765. In 1766 residents angrily attacked British soldiers who had cut down the liberty pole—resulting in what is claimed to be the first blood shed in the colonial struggle against Great Britain. Alexander McDougall was the leader of the Sons of Liberty; he was jailed but continued to receive visitors in jail from 3 to 6 in the afternoon. On July 9, 1776, the Declaration of Independence was read on the Common by George Washington.

Moving on down Broadway, named the Broad Way, stop in St. Paul's Chapel (see description above). The chapel escaped the fire of 1776 when a bucket brigade vigorously poured water on the roof. Continue to the John Street Methodist Church (212-269-0014), which was on "Golden Hill." In 1770 a fight between British soldiers and colonists was called "the Battle of Golden Hill." The soldiers had been putting up broadsides complaining about their treatment, and the colonists objected. This action has also been called "the first blood of the Revolution." Who knows?

The Fly Market along the docks was where artisans and farmers sailed down

> ✿ The lead statue of King George III was toppled from its base on Bowling Green, dismembered, and pieces of it ended up in the woodshed behind Oliver Wolcott's house in Litchfield, Connecticut. The women and girls in town melted them down and made the lead into bullets to be used against the British. (See our Visitor's Guide to Colonial & Revolutionary New England, page 162.)

to sell their vegetables, fruits, and wares. Colonists tended to gather there to play backgammon. Ships came during spring and fall, and people shopped for the newest goods. Eventually, they boycotted British goods, and homespun became the fashion.

Wall Street was built by the Dutch to keep the colony contained. Peter Stuyvesant made the wall of wood, and colonists tended to set it on fire during riots.

Bowling Green, now a small public park, was rented by residents for the annual fee of one peppercorn. General Washington's headquarters stood here. Governor Cadwallader Colden's carriage was burned by Stamp Act rabble-rousers on the lawn. After the Declaration of Independence was read, colonists came here and pulled down the gilded equestrian statue of King George III.

Federal Hall National Memorial (212-825-6888; www.nps.gov/feha), 26 Wall St. Open Mon.– Fri. After a two-year renovation it reopened in October 2006. The museum is operated by the National Park Service. The Continental Congress met in 1787, and when the Constitution was ratified in 1788, New York remained the capital. The collection contains artifacts from George Washington's inauguration on April 30, 1789, including the Bible used on that day. The capital moved to Philadelphia in 1790.

In 1735 John Peter Zenger was jailed, tried, and acquitted of libel for exposing government corruption in his newspaper, a case that helped establish a precedent for freedom of the press. The press could print the truth—as long as it did not reflect poorly on the assembly!

Number 1 Broadway, the Archibald Kennedy mansion, was where George Washington for a time had his headquarters. After a Loyalist plot to kill Washington was uncovered, he moved his headquarters to City Hall. Thomas Hickey was the only soldier convicted in the plot, and he was hanged on June 28, 1776.

Spying was rampant during that time, and the chief spymaster was none other than George Washington himself. He had his sources active and used the information they provided. Perhaps 500 men and women were agents on both sides. Some of them even wrote with invisible ink!

The Battery is at the southern tip of Manhattan, and in 1624 a Dutch fort stood there. Castle Clinton commemorates the 1811 West Battery Fort. Today a damaged sculpture, "Sphere," represents world peace. It was taken from the World Trade Plaza after the September 11 attack.

Our tour ended at Fraunces Tavern, described above. It is the perfect place for lunch after walking for a couple of hours.

LODGING

ALGONQUIN HOTEL
59 W. 44th St., New York, NY 10036
888-304-2047, 212-840-6800;
www.algonquinhotel.com
The Algonquin Round Table, with its literary devotees, met here during the 1920s. Matilda the cat lives a life of leisure on a lobby sofa. 174 guest rooms.

THE EDISON HOTEL
228 W. 47th St., New York, NY 10036
800-637-7070, 212-840-5000:
www.edisonhotelnyc.com
The Hotel Edison opened in 1931, when Thomas Edison turned on its lights by remote control. The art deco hotel is in the heart of the Broadway theater district and steps away from Times Square. 45 guest rooms.

THE ESSEX HOUSE
160 Central Park South, New York, NY 10019
888-645-5697, 212-247-0300;
www.jumeirahessexhouse.com
This art deco hotel is right on Central Park, with unsurpassed views of the park year-round. 605 guest rooms.

THE FRANKLIN HOTEL
164 E. 87th St., New York, NY 10128
800-607-4009, 212-369-1000;
www.franklinhotel.com
This European-style hotel on the Upper East Side offers an old-world ambiance. Chandeliers and original mosaic art enhance the property. 49 guest rooms.

HOTEL ROGER WILLIAMS
131 Madison Ave., New York, NY 10016
888-448-7788, 212-448-7000;
www.hotelrogerwilliams.com
The hotel dates from 1929, and is a sister hotel of the Franklin Hotel. 190 guest rooms.

INTERCONTINENTAL THE BARCLAY
111 E. 48th St., New York, NY 10017
800-782-8021, 212-755-5900;
new-york-barclay.intercontinental.com
The hotel dates from 1926 under the aegis of the Vanderbilt family. 686 guest rooms.

LE PARKER MERIDIEN
118 W. 57th St., New York, NY 10019
800-543-4300, 212-245-5000;
www.parkermeridien.com
The hotel is just south of Central Park and close to Fifth Avenue. A rooftop pool overlooks the park. 731 guest rooms.

SALISBURY HOTEL
123 W. 57th St., New York, NY 10019
888-NYC-5757, 212-246-1300;
www.nycsalisbury.com
Near Central Park and the theater district, the Salisbury offers large guest rooms, some with several closets. 80 guest rooms.

HOTEL WALES
1295 Madison Ave., New York, NY 10128
866-WALESHOTEL, 212-876-6000;
www.waleshotel.com
Just over a century old, this hotel sits on top of Carnegie Hill and has hosted flappers, tycoons, war heroes, and writers. 87 guest rooms.

THE WARWICK NEW YORK HOTEL
65 W. 54th St., New York, NY 10019
800-2033232, 212-247-2700; www.warwickhotelny.com
The hotel was built by William Randolph Hearst in 1927. Actress and Hearst favorite Marion Davies had a suite on the 27th floor. 426 guest rooms.

WASHINGTON SQUARE HOTEL
103 Waverly Place, New York, NY 10011
800-222-0418, 212-777-9515;
www.washingtonsquarehotel.com
This art deco hotel is across from Washington Square Park. It has been a haven for writers, artists, and visitors to Greenwich Village for more than a hundred years. 160 guest rooms.

RESTAURANTS

CITY HALL RESTAURANT
131 Duane St., New York, NY 10013
212-227-7777; www.cityhallnewyork
.com
Black and white photos of old New York
are featured. The menu is classic American.

FRAUNCES TAVERN
54 Pearl St., New York, NY 10013
212-968-1776; www.frauncestavern
.com
The restaurant is in the 1719 building that
also houses the Fraunces Tavern Museum.

HEIDELBERG
1648 Second Ave., New York, NY 10028
212-628-2332; www.heidelberg
restaurant.com
Decorated with a grape arbor, beer steins,
and needlepoint on the walls. A variety of
German dishes.

L'ÉCOLE, FRENCH CULINARY INSTITUTE
462 Broadway, New York, NY 10013
212-219-3300; www.frenchculinary
.com/lecole.htm
Students prepare a prix fixe lunch as well
as dinner.

LINDY'S
825 Seventh Ave., New York, NY 10019
212-767-8343; lindysnyc.com
New York–style cheesecake is featured as
well as deli sandwiches.

ONE IF BY LAND, TWO IF BY SEA
17 Barrow St., New York, NY 10014
212-255-8649; www.oneifbyland.com
This 18th-century carriage house was once
owned by Aaron Burr.

Fraunces Tavern, the scene of Washington's farewell to his officers.

RAINBOW GRILL
30 Rockefeller Plaza, New York, NY
10012
212-632-5100; www.rainbowroom.com
In 1934 it opened as a supper club. The
views are panoramic.

SARDI'S
234 West 44th St., New York, NY 10035
212-221-8440; www.sardis.com
Signed caricatures of famous people. Prix
fixe pre-theater dinner menu.

TAVERN ON THE GREEN
Central Park at West 67th St.,
New York, NY 10023
212-873-3200; www.tavernon
thegreen.com

Murals, flowers, lights, and lanterns. A
variety of dishes on the menu.

EVENTS

February: George Washington's birthday,
Morris-Jumel House; 212-923-8008
September: Battle of Harlem Heights,
Morris-Jumel House; 212-923-8008

INFORMATION

**NYC & COMPANY (CONVENTION
AND VISITORS BUREAU)**
810 Seventh Ave., New York, NY 10019
212-484-1200; www.nycvisit.com

BROOKLYN

Just across the East River from Manhattan lies Brooklyn, meaning "broken land"
for its rolling hills, rock outcroppings, and varied topography. The Continental
Army and the British had their first battle here: the Battle of Brooklyn (also called
the Battle of Long Island) in 1776. In late June of that year a British fleet had
appeared in New York harbor, and in July the British had established their headquarters on Staten Island. On August 21 the city was drenched by a terrific storm.
Lightning flashed and set houses on fire.

The next day, in bright sunlight, the British prepared to attack. Lord Howe
eventually landed 20,000 troops on Brooklyn, but Washington at first was not
aware of the large number. The American force was reinforced to about 10,000.
After a daring British flanking attack,
the Continental Army suffered a devastating defeat in a pitched battle, with
heavy casualties. Washington's battered
army withdrew to defensive positions
on Brooklyn Heights and appeared
trapped.

On August 28 the temperature
dropped ten degrees and a cold rain
soaked the troops, the beginning of a
classic nor'easter. Washington rode his
horse around in the rain to comfort his
men. Faced as he was with almost cer-

Major Abner Benedict
wrote, "It was surcharged
with electricity, for the lightning
was constantly searching it from
limit to limit. . . . Then followed a
crash louder than a thousand
cannon. . . . In a few minutes the
entire heavens became black as
ink. . . . The thunder did not follow in successive peals, but in
one continuous crash."

tain defeat and the loss of his army—and in all probability the war as well—the weather was a lucky break for him. The nor'easter both provided cover for a precarious evacuation and prevented the British fleet from entering the East River to stop it. On the evening of August 29 Washington began a secret strategy by sending the troops to the Brooklyn ferry landing, where they thought they were to be relieved by replacements. No one was told that they were in fact going to be evacuated to the city. When the wind shifted to the southwest, the boats set out in the dark with no lights on board. As dawn drew near with many troops still at the ferry, a providential fog set in to obscure the operation. The boats made trip after trip across this narrow stretch of water. Washington stayed beside the ferry landing until the last of his troops were embarked, reaching Manhattan at about seven. That morning the British were astounded to find their prey had vanished.

HISTORICAL SITES *and* MUSEUMS

Green-Wood Cemetery (718-768-7300; www.green-wood.com), 500 25th St. Open daily. A statue of Minerva on top of the hill commemorates the Battle of Brooklyn. You can see the Statue of Liberty from the hill.

Fort Greene Park, Myrtle and DeKalb Ave., contains the Prison Ship Martyrs Monument. It is dedicated to the Continental soldiers who died on British prison ships in Wallabout Bay. Stanford White designed the monument. About 11,000 Americans died on the "hulks."

Lefferts Homestead (718-789-2822; www.prospectpark.org), 95 Prospect Park West (the main address for the park). Open Apr.– Nov., Fri.– Sun. The house dates from 1783 but was burned by Pennsylvania riflemen sent to harass the British. The Lefferts family was among the earliest European settlers in Brooklyn. They grew wheat, flax, hemp, and corn for trade. For their own kitchens they grew peas, potatoes, and other vegetables. Animals were kept for labor, dairy, meat, and wool.

STATEN ISLAND

The staging place for the British as they invaded Long Island, Staten Island was also where Benjamin Franklin, John Adams, and Edward Rutledge tried to negotiate peace with Lord Admiral Richard Howe on September 11, 1776. But they would not accede to his demand to place the colonies under Britain. Today the

The Lefferts Homestead in Brooklyn.

island is quieter than the rest of the city and still retains rolling hills and wood-land.

HISTORICAL SITES *and* MUSEUMS

Historic Richmond Town (718-351-1611; www.historicrichmondtown.org), 441 Clarke Ave. Open Wed.–Sun. This Williamsburg-like village is on 25 acres and contains about 40 buildings dating from the 17th to the 19th centuries. Some of them came from other parts of the island, and others were part of the original settlement.

Buildings from the colonial and Revolutionary periods include the 1670 Britton Cottage, which is the oldest building in town. It may have served as Staten Island's first government building. Britton family members occupied it from 1695 to 1714 and later from 1860 to 1915, when botanist Nathaniel Britton lived there. The 1695 Voorlezer's House was a church, school, and residence for the minister and teacher. The 1700 Treasure House was where British officers are said to have stashed gold coins in the walls. The 1720 Christopher House was a clandestine meeting place for local patriots; Joseph Christopher was a member of the Richmond County Committee of Safety. The 1740 Guyon-Lake-Tysen House has both Dutch and Flemish influence, and the original paneling is intact. The 1750 Boehm House was named for an educator, Henry Boehm, who lived there until 1862. We enjoyed watching inquisitive schoolchildren touring some of the houses.

EVENTS

At this writing a possible reenactment at Historic Richmond Town is under discussion. Please call 718-351-1611 x281 for more information.

INFORMATION

NYC & COMPANY
810 Seventh Ave., New York, NY 10019
212-484-1200; www.nycvisit.com

BROOKLYN TOURISM AND VISITORS CENTER
Brooklyn Borough Hall
209 Joralemon St., Brooklyn, NY 11201
718-802-3846; www.visitbrooklyn.org

STATEN ISLAND USA
10 Richmond Terrace, Staten Island, NY 10301
718-816-2000;
www.statenislandusa.com

LONG ISLAND

At 125 miles long and no more than 23 miles wide, Long Island has a shoreline that won't quit. Built of glacial moraines, its southern shore fronting the Atlantic Ocean has a long series of barrier beaches with shallow, sheltered bays behind them. At its eastern end the moraine splits into two peninsulas protecting a cleft of deeper bays with fine harbors. The northern shore along Long Island Sound provides easy access to the mainland, and its western end has some of the finest harbors on the East Coast.

It is not surprising that Long Island attracted settlers from New England looking for easier land to till than their own rock-strewn soil and eager to escape the constrictions of Puritan theocracy. The island provided flatter land for farming and bases for fishing and whaling. Unlike the Hudson Valley, it became an enclave for more English than Dutch settlers in the 17th century and by the Revolutionary War was noted for its Loyalist sympathies. George Washington established some of his spy networks on the island, and after the war he traveled along the north shore to thank his agents for their contribution to American independence.

Although now densely populated at its west end by the sprawl from New York City, the island still preserves significant remnants of its past, both along the north shore and at the forks. In spite of the influx of fashionable megamansions, the Hamptons hold on to their heritage, as do the old ports. Much of the farmland has been maintained, the wineries on both the North and South Forks prosper, and there are still great wild barrier beaches to enjoy.

North Shore

OYSTER BAY

Granted a patent from New Amsterdam in 1641, colonists from Connecticut were the first to settle here, but the town also attracted Dutch settlers in succeeding years. Like many north shore communities, it had both a protected harbor and arable farmland.

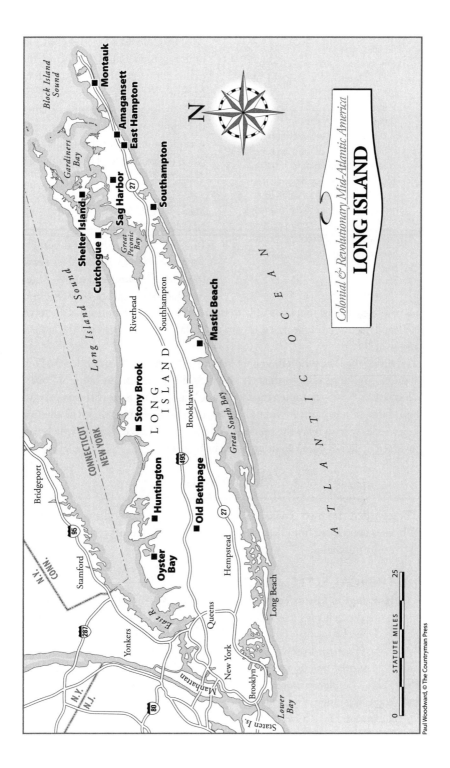

Colonial & Revolutionary Mid-Atlantic America
LONG ISLAND

Block Island Sound

Montauk ■

Amagansett ■
East Hampton ■

Gardiners Bay

Southampton ■

Shelter Island ■

Sag Harbor ■

Cutchogue ■

Great Peconic Bay

Southampton

Riverhead

Mastic Beach ■

Long Island Sound

CONNECTICUT
NEW YORK

Stony Brook ■

L O N G   I S L A N D

Brookhaven

Great South Bay

A T L A N T I C   O C E A N

Bridgeport

Huntington ■

Old Bethpage ■

Hempstead

Oyster Bay ■

Stamford

N.Y.
CONN.

Queens

Long Beach

East R.

287

Yonkers

New York

N.Y.
N.J.

Brooklyn

Manhattan

Lower Bay

Staten Is.

95

80

495

27

27

STATUTE MILES
0   25

Paul Woodward, © The Countryman Press

George Washington, who suffered a crucial lack of intelligence about British movements before the disastrous Battle of Long Island, organized networks of spies throughout the Revolutionary War and spent much of his own funds to finance them. In hatching the effective Culper Spy Ring, he gave instructions "not to divulge the names of those involved to anyone . . . Two years ago I sent a captain into New York without adequate preparation and he was caught and hanged."

Theodore Roosevelt designed and built Sagamore Hill (1885) here as his principal residence. Oyster Bay became a haven for wealthy New York City families who built mansions along this "gold coast" shore for their summer pleasure. F. Scott Fitzgerald captured the ambience of this era in *The Great Gatsby*.

HISTORICAL SITES *and* MUSEUMS

In 1738 Samuel Townsend bought **Raynham Hall** (516-922-6808; www.raynhamhallmuseum.org), W. Main St. Open daily except Mon. He and his wife, Sarah, lived in the house with their eight children. Samuel was the town clerk and the justice of the peace; he also controlled a fleet of trading ships, a store, and a small farm.

During the Revolution Raynham Hall served as the headquarters for the Loyalist Queen's Rangers. Unfortunately for the British, it was also the home of Robert Townsend, who had become a spy for George Washington. Robert Townsend gave his information to Samuel Woodhull, who then hung clothing on his clothesline in a special way to relay the message. Spies also used invisible ink, which was invented by James Jay, a physician living in England.

HUNTINGTON

The town dates from 1653 when Richard Holbrook, Robert Williams, and Daniel Whitehead purchased from Raseokan, sachem of the Matinecock tribe, land known as "the first purchase."

HISTORICAL SITES *and* MUSEUMS

The **Huntington Historical Society Museum** (631-427-7045; www.huntingtonhistoricalsociety.org), 209 Main St. Open Tue.–Sun. The society has four sites: the Dr. Daniel Kissam House (ca. 1795); the David Conklin Farmhouse (ca. 1750); the Huntington Sewing and Trade School (ca. 1905); and the Soldiers and Sailors Memorial Building (ca. 1892). The Conklin Farmhouse was occupied by the Conklin family for more than 150 years. Don't miss the table and chair used by George Washington in 1790.

The **Joseph Lloyd Manor House** (631-692-4664), Lloyd Lane. Open Memorial Day–Columbus Day, Sat.–Sun. The house dates from 1766 and is furnished to the 1793 inventory of John Lloyd II.

STONY BROOK

This is a hamlet in the town of Brookhaven. New Englanders arrived in 1665 to settle here. Shipping and shipbuilding were the industries. Ward Melville was a local businessman who owned most of the "Three Villages," including Stony Brook, Setauket, and Old Field. Don't miss seeing the wooden eagle on top of the post office who flaps his wings on the hour.

HISTORICAL SITES and MUSEUMS
Stony Brook Grist Mill (631-751-2244; www.wardmelvilleheritage.org), 111 Main St. Open Apr.–Dec., Fri.–Sun. The miller grinds grain and interprets the operations of this mill dating from 1751.

South Shore

OLD BETHPAGE

HISTORICAL SITES and MUSEUMS
Old Bethpage Village (516-572-8400 or 8401; www.oldbethpage.org), Round Swamp Rd. Open Mar.–Dec., Wed.–Sun. This living-history farm has 55 buildings, some dating from the 1700s. Today it is a reconstructed pre–Civil War village on 209 acres. The Powell farmstead is the original building in the Old Bethpage site. It contains the original farmhouse and an English-style barn. Don't miss the pigs, chickens, geese, sheep, and oxen that still call it home. The Schenk farmhouse dates from the early 1700s and has been restored to the style of 1765. The house has a large stone fireplace on one end. Both houses are furnished, and interpreters in period dress are there to speak with you.

MASTIC BEACH

Mastic Beach is a hamlet in the town of Brookhaven.

HISTORICAL SITES and MUSEUMS
The **William Floyd Estate** (631-399-2030; www.nps.gov), 245 Park Dr. Open from Memorial Day weekend to the last full weekend in October, Fri.–Sun. This is the ancestral home of William Floyd, a Revolutionary War general and Long Island's signer of the Declaration of Independence. The 25-room mansion was built in stages from 1724 to 1930.

North Fork
Farms and vineyards provide lush green landscape to explore. We remember visiting friends there almost forty years ago with our young children who enjoyed strolling around the village green in Cutchogue as well as running on the beach.

On another trip we visited many of the twenty-three wineries for a book and article.

CUTCHOGUE

Before Europeans came to the area it was home to an Indian tribe called the Corchaugs. In 1640 Reverend John Young sailed from New Haven with thirteen Puritan families and settled the town of Southold. Eastern Long Island was part of the New Haven Colony then. In 1661 the town fathers laid out lots, and Cutchogue was opened for settlement in 1667.

HISTORICAL SITES *and* MUSEUMS

The oldest English house still standing in New York State is **Old House** (631-734-7122; www.cutchogue/suffolkhistory.org), on the village green. Open the last week in June through Labor Day weekend, Sat.–Mon. John Budd built his home in 1649 after sailing with John Youngs from New Haven in 1640. Exposed sections inside the 1649 house let visitors see the English Tudor construction. The furniture was all handmade by the early settlers who lived in the area. **Wickham Farmhouse** on the village green dates from 1704. Antique quilts are featured in the house. Both houses contain colonial furnishings.

SHELTER ISLAND

Shelter Island lies between the North and South Forks of Long Island. Early settlers arrived from England seeking religious freedom. Wealthy sugar merchants from Barbados came to use the white oak for barrels. Nathaniel Sylvester arrived to settle with his sixteen-year-old bride, Grissel, in 1652. By 1673 Nathaniel owned the entire island.

HISTORICAL SITES *and* MUSEUMS

The **Havens House Museum** (631-749-0399), South Ferry Rd., was the home of James Havens, a member of the provincial congress, who lived here from 1743. The pleasant white house, located on a curve in the road, stayed in the family until 1925. The site of the first meetinghouse, dating from 1743, is on North Ferry Road next to the Presbyterian church.

A little farther north on North Ferry Road you will come to a little road leading to the **Quaker Cemetery**. A memorial sign at that point states that Nathaniel Sylvester and other Quakers came here to escape persecution. You can drive into the woods to the cemetery, which has a large stone table in the center and a number of grave markers surrounded by a fence. It was a poignant moment for us as we stood remembering our Quaker heritage; Edward Foulke and Eleanor Foulke left Wales in 1698 to find more economic opportunity in America.

INFORMATION

SHELTER ISLAND CHAMBER OF COMMERCE
631-749-0399; www.shelter-island.net

South Fork

SOUTHAMPTON

Colonists from Massachusetts settled here in 1640. By the mid-19th century visitors began to come for vacation. They stayed with fishermen and farmers.

HISTORICAL SITES *and* MUSEUMS

The **Thomas Halsey House** (631-283-3527; www.southamptonhistorical museum.com), S. Main St. Open Fri.–Sun. Dating from 1648, it is said to be one of the oldest English frame houses in the state. Phebe, the wife of Thomas, was murdered here by Connecticut Indians. Furnishings date from the 17th and 18th centuries. Don't miss the colonial herb garden.

SAG HARBOR

Sag Harbor's first inhabitants, the Indians, settled on a site that is now the center of town. They called it "Wegwagonock," or "Foot of the Hill." Later, as the place became a port, there was opportunity to take advantage of commodities going in or out, and by 1707 the British Crown was concerned enough about rum-running to appoint an officer to monitor this illegal activity.

Sag Harbor became a major whaling center during the 18th and early 19th centuries. The call "Ship in the Bay!" almost rings in your ears as you imagine the old days of whaling in town.

HISTORICAL SITES *and* MUSEUMS

The **Sag Harbor Whaling Museum** (631-725-0770), 200 Main St., is the place to go to ponder the maritime past and learn more about whaling and the people who spent their lives in that profession. Open mid-May–mid-Oct., daily. Inside, you'll see rooms chock-full of items brought back by whalers, made by them during long voyages, or enjoyed by their families. Both Sag Harbor and Nantucket inhabitants tried beach whaling taught to them by Native Americans before they ventured with their equipment onto ships. You'll see a collection of harpoons, ships' logs, and lots of scrimshaw.

The **Custom House** (631-725-0250), Garden St. Open Memorial Day weekend, daily July–Aug., then weekends until Columbus Day. It was the home of Henry Packer Dering, who was a U.S. customs master, in addition to raising nine children in his home. The office contains a history of Sag Harbor as one of two ports of entry—the other was New York. The kitchen must have been warm, with a huge fireplace and an oven for baking bread.

INFORMATION

SAG HARBOR CHAMBER OF COMMERCE
459 Main St., SagHarbor, NY 11963
631-725-0011; www.sagharborchamber.com

EAST HAMPTON

Estates line the shore, and they are lovely to look at. However, don't count on finding a place to park so that you can use a beach. Stickers are required in the parking lots; but you can cycle or walk to the beaches. East Hampton is an attractive village with a number of historic buildings on its shady streets.

HISTORICAL SITES *and* MUSEUMS

East Hampton Historical Society (631-324-6850; www.easthamptonhistory.org), 101 Main St. The society operates a number of historic houses: Clinton Academy; the Town House; the Osborn-Jackson House; and Mulford Farm. Open July–Labor Day.

The **Osborn-Jackson House,** at 101 Main St., dates from 1735. The house contains 18th- and 19th-century furnishings. Some rooms are used for galleries for temporary exhibits, and quilting and weaving are featured during the summer.

Clinton Academy, 151 Main St., was the first chartered academy in New York State; it dates from 1784. Boys came here from New York City to study for college. The house now contains East Hampton exhibits.

Across the green stands **Mulford Farm** (631-324-6869), dating from 1680. Here's a house with enough colonial particulars to form a glossary of colonial information. A costumed interpreter will take you around the house, supplying stories about the people who lived here and the items now displayed. Look for the patch of eel grass protruding from a hole in the wall up near the ceiling; although it was handy for insulation, inhabitants found that little creatures from the woods would hunker down in it during the winter and then find it difficult to get out.

Displays include one on the maritime triangular trade, which ran from Africa, where slaves were picked up, to the West Indies, whence a cargo of molasses was shipped to the Northeast to make rum. You can also see a chart of cattle earmarks villagers used to distinguish their

In 1648 settlers purchased East Hampton for "20 coats, 24 hatchets, 24 hoes, 24 looking glasses and 100 muxes [an early tool used for making wampum]" from the Shinnecock Indians.

own animals, a collection of wine bottles, silver, a Delft platter in blue and white, and a pewter platter.

Look for the "ghosts" of missing parts of hinges where the outline still reveals its original shape. Did you know that "spiles" are curly wood shavings used to light the fire?

The bedroom downstairs was used by the oldest and the youngest members of the family. The rope bed has straw on top and then a feather mattress. There's a twister to crank up the ropes on the bed—hence the phrase "sleep tight."

> ✳ Look for the "fleam," which was used to bleed people who became sick. They had to hold on to a pole tightly so the veins stood out for bleeding. Blood ran down the fabric wrapped around the pole, and the end result looked like a barber pole.

People used to congregate in the kitchen with its roaring fire to sew, weave on the loom, make candles in the mold, and cook in three-legged pots. A "temse" is a container covered with goatskin pierced with nails to be used as a sifter for hand-ground grain. There's a unique waffle iron, and also a toaster.

Home Sweet Home Museum (631-324-0713), 14 James Lane. Open

Costumed interpreters are there to answer questions at Mulford Farm in East Hampton.

May–Sep., Mon.–Sun.; Oct.–Nov., Fri.–Sun. This 1680 saltbox contains English ceramics and early American furniture and textiles. An herb garden and the 1804 Pantigo Windmill are on the grounds.

EVENTS

November: Holiday house tour; 631-324-6850

AMAGANSETT

The first European settlement here was in 1690, in what became a fishing village at the base of Montauk Point. By the 18th century whaling was in full swing.

HISTORICAL SITES *and* MUSEUMS

Amagansett Historical Society (631-267-3020), Watermill Lane. Miss Amelia's Cottage dates from 1725. The museum is furnished with period furniture and a rare clock.

MONTAUK

Fishing is very popular just off the banks of Montauk, at what is known as "cod ledge." Hither Hills State Park and Montauk County Park provide recreational facilities.

HISTORICAL SITES *and* MUSEUMS

Second House Museum (631-668-5340), Montauk Hwy., was built in Montauk by 1746 and rebuilt in 1797. The "First House," dating from 1744, burned in 1909. The 18th-century kitchen is a highlight.

George Washington ordered a lighthouse to be built on Montauk Point in 1795. Very wisely, he insisted that it be set almost 300 feet back from the shoreline to allow for erosion. In November 1797 Jacob Hand lit the 13 whale-oil lamps for the first time; he was up all night making sure they were all burning. By 1987 the era of manned lighthouses was over, as three Coast Guard seamen left their posts to the automated aerobeacon.

LODGING

THE AMERICAN HOTEL
Main St., Sag Harbor, NY 11963
631-725-3535;
www.theamericanhotel.com
Dating from 1846, the hotel is in the center of town for convenient exploring. 8 guest rooms.

THE BAKER HOUSE 1650
181 Main St., East Hampton, NY 11937
631-324-4081;
www.bakerhouse1650.com
Surrounded by gardens, these luxury accom-

modations began as a sea captain's house built in 1648. Inside there are wood-burning fireplaces and William Morris wallpaper. There is also a spa. 5 guest rooms.

BASSETT HOUSE
128 Montauk Hwy., East Hampton, NY 11937
631-324-6127; www.bassetthouseinn.com
Built in 1830, this charming house is decorated with a red-leather barber's chair, three stuffed bears, a stoplight, and a wooden sea chest. 12 guest rooms.

DERING HARBOR INN
13 Winthrop Rd., Shelter Island, NY 11965
631-749-0900; www.deringharborinn.net
This inn is located on the waterfront; closed during the winter. 21 guest rooms.

GANSETT GREEN MANOR
273 Main St., Amagansett, NY 11930
631-267-3133; www.gansettgreenmanor.com
The inn is surrounded by gardens and fountains. Some rooms have kitchens and electric fireplaces.13 guest rooms.

GURNEY'S INN
290 Old Montauk Hwy., Montauk, NY 11954
631-668-2345; www.gurneysinn.com
At the tip of Long Island,this inn dates from 1926. 109 guest rooms.

HUNTTING INN
94 Main St., East Hampton, NY 11937
631-324-0410; www.thepalm.com
Though in the center of town, this colonial inn is surrounded by pleasant country gardens. 20 guest rooms and The Palm restaurant.

MILL HOUSE INN
31 N. Main St., East Hampton, NY 11937
631-324-9766: www.millhouseinn.com
This historic inn is in the center of townand

overlooks Old Hook Windmill. 10 guest rooms.

RAM'S HEAD INN
108 Ram Island Dr., Shelter Island Heights, NY 11965
631-749-0811; www.shelterislandinns.com
This 1929 inn is on Coecles Harbor and provides sailboats, a paddleboat, and a kayak. Guests can also arrive in their own boats.17 guest rooms

1708 HOUSE
126 Main St., Southampton, NY 11968
631-287-1708; www.1708house.com
The house dates from the 18th century to the 21st (and part of the cellar dates to 1648). There are also three cottages on the property. 15 guest rooms.

THREE VILLAGE INN
150 Main St., Stony Brook, NY 11790
631-751-0555;
www.threevillageinn.com
This 1751 inn offers rooms in the main building plus cottages, all in colonial style. 26 guest rooms.

RESTAURANTS

B SMITHS
Long Wharf Promenade, Sag Harbor, NY 11963
631-725-5858; www.bsmith.com/restaurant
Mediterranean and southern cuisine on the waterfront.

GOSMAN'S DOCK RESTAURANT
500 W. Lake Dr., Montauk, NY 11954
631-668-5330; www.gosmans.com
Long Island produce and seafood.

THE PALM AT THE HUNTTING INN
94 Main St., East Hampton, NY 11937
631-324-0411; www.thepalm.com
Steak and seafood are featured.

LOBSTER ROLL
1980 Montauk Hwy., Amagansett, NY
11930
631-267-3740; lobsterroll.com
Seafood is a specialty.

SEA GRILLE AT GURNEY'S INN
290 Old Montauk Hwy., Montauk, NY
11954
631-668-2660; www.gurneysinn.com
Oceanfront seafood and other regional
specialties.

THREE VILLAGE INN
150 Main St., Stony Brook, NY 11790
631-751-0555; www.threevillageinn
.com
Traditional New England cuisine.

INFORMATION

**LONG ISLAND CONVENTION
& VISITORS BUREAU**
330 Motor Pkwy., Hauppauge, NY
11788
877-FUN-ON-LI, 631-951-3900;
www.discoverlongisland.com

HUDSON RIVER VALLEY

Giovanni da Verrazano discovered the Hudson River when he sailed along the coast under the flag of France in 1524. He wrote to Francis I, "We have found a pleasant place below steep little hills." Not until eighty-five years later, when Henry Hudson sailed almost all the way to Albany, did Europeans begin to explore the "great river of the mountain" well known and used by Native Americans. Although Hudson was disappointed that it turned out not to be the Northwest Passage to the riches of the Orient, his voyage began the story of the most important river in America for two centuries.

Hudson returned with enthusiastic reports of the broad, fertile valley surrounding this navigable waterway. Dutch fur traders and pioneering settlers led the way for other immigrants to follow as the valley became the central core of New Netherland and later New York. The great estates of patroons and smaller grants gradually filled the land, displacing the Indian tribes that had lived and hunted along the river. Hudson River sloops plied the broad reaches of the river, carrying goods and people between Manhattan and Albany. In the second half of the 18th century control of the Hudson and its extended water route northward to Canada became the key to the continent, the focal point of strategy in both the French and Indian War and the Revolution. During the Revolution about one-third of the battles took place somewhere along this corridor.

The invention of the steamboat extended the role of the river in the 19th century as the primary mode of transportation, even as railroads supplanted steamboats and their tracks lined the shores, contributing to the prosperity of some river towns. Others towns decayed, and industrialization brought pollution to the river, but in the last decades of the 20th century environmental movements succeeded in restoring much of the quality of the river's water and the beauty of its shore-

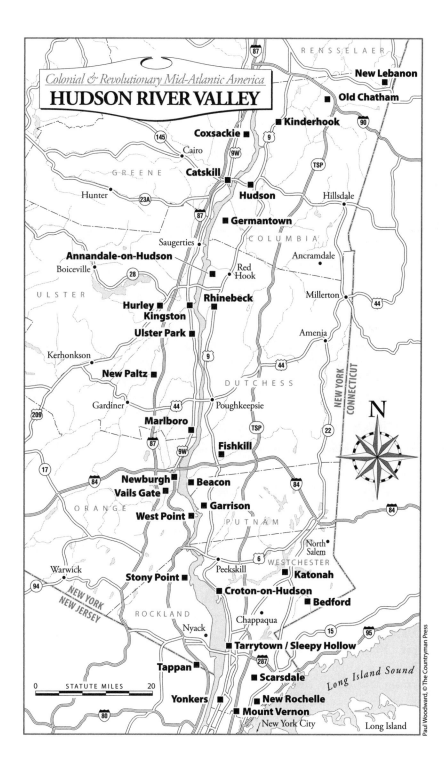

Colonial & Revolutionary Mid-Atlantic America

HUDSON RIVER VALLEY

RENSSELAER

New Lebanon ■

Old Chatham ■

Kinderhook ■

Coxsackie ■

Cairo •

Catskill ■

GREENE

Hunter • 23A

Hudson ■

Hillsdale •

Germantown ■

COLUMBIA

Saugerties •

Ancramdale •

Annandale-on-Hudson ■

Boiceville •

Red Hook •

ULSTER

Millerton •

Hurley ■

Rhinebeck ■

Kingston

Ulster Park ■

Kerhonkson •

Amenia •

New Paltz ■

DUTCHESS

Gardiner •

Poughkeepsie •

Marlboro ■

Fishkill ■

Newburgh ■

Beacon ■

Vails Gate ■

ORANGE

Garrison ■

West Point ■

PUTNAM

Warwick •

North Salem •

Peekskill •

WESTCHESTER

Stony Point ■

Katonah ■

Croton-on-Hudson ■

Bedford ■

ROCKLAND

Chappaqua •

Nyack •

NEW YORK NEW JERSEY

Tarrytown / Sleepy Hollow ■

Tappan ■

Scarsdale ■

Long Island Sound

Yonkers ■

New Rochelle ■

Mount Vernon ■

New York City

Long Island

NEW YORK CONNECTICUT

N

0 STATUTE MILES 20

Paul Woodward, © The Countryman Press

Hudson River sloops evolved from their prototypes in Holland as the prime vessels of the river. They were typically sixty-five to seventy-five feet in length, with a full forward section for cargo capacity and a raised quarterdeck for passengers, and a mast set well forward and rigged with a large mainsail, small jib, and topsail. Some were remarkably seaworthy, like the fifty-nine-foot *Experiment,* which made an unusual trading voyage to Canton in 1785–87; but most stuck to the river trade. They flourished well into the 19th century and multiplied rapidly after the opening of the Erie Canal in 1825. With good winds they could make faster passages than early steamboats. In 1966 Pete Seeger and others created a foundation to build the 106-foot *Clearwater* as an authentic but larger replica and floating classroom. Launched in 1969, she sails to educate both children and adults on the need to restore and preserve the environment of the Hudson.

lines. Today the visitor interested in the colonial and Revolutionary heritage of the valley will find many important and well-preserved sites along both shores and farther inland.

Since the great estates of the patroons had such a dominating influence on the settlement of the valley, and their imprint still survives in the organization of counties up and down the Hudson, this portion of the guidebook will use the counties as an organizing principle.

REGIONAL INFORMATION

800-762-8687, 845-291-2136; www.travelhudsonvalley.com

HUDSON VALLEY TOURISM
800-232-4782; www.travelhudsonvalley.com

Lower Hudson

The Lower Hudson includes the counties of Westchester, Rockland, Orange, and Putnam.

WESTCHESTER COUNTY

During the 1620s and 1630s settlers arrived from the Dutch West India Company. By the 1640s the English began arriving, some of them moving west from New England towns for religious freedom. Manors were established by royal grant; the largest was that of Frederick Philipse on the Hudson River. Westchester County was established by an act of the New York Assembly in 1683. By 1775 the county was the richest in the New York colony.

During the Revolution the county saw more devastating action than any other. The battles of Pelham and White Plains were fought in 1776. Then, because the

American headquarters was located at Continental Village just north of Peekskill and the British headquarters was in New York City, Westchester was the "neutral ground" in between. Soldiers and paramilitary groups from both sides were destructive as they raided and pillaged farms and homes.

Today Westchester County is a thriving, cosmopolitan suburb of New York City. It is known as a sophisticated shopping destination with upscale stores.

MOUNT VERNON

Mount Vernon sits at a high elevation; the Throgs Neck Bridge to Queens can be seen on a clear day. Although the city was not incorporated until 1892, the historic stone St. Paul's Church dates from the 18th century.

HISTORICAL SITES *and* MUSEUMS

St. Paul's Church National Historic Site (914-667-4116; www.nps.gov/sapa), 897 S. Columbus Ave. Open Mon.–Fri. This 18th-century church was used as a hospital during the Revolution. The burial ground is one of the oldest in the country. A museum is housed in the former carriage house.

During the 18th century a celebrated libel trial for John Peter Zenger was held in Mount Vernon. Its lessons were helpful in 1791 for the development of the Bill of Rights. The London foundry that cast the Liberty Bell also cast a second bell, called the Freedom Bell, and you can find it here.

NEW ROCHELLE

Thomas Pell bought the Pelham Manor tract in 1654 from the Siwanoy Indians. By 1689 Huguenots began to settle in the area. They were French Protestants who left France after the revocation by Louis XIV of the Edict of Nantes, which had protected them from religious persecution.

In 1775 General George Washington came through town on his way to assume command of the army besieging Boston. The British army arrived in the summer of 1776 but left by October 25. In 1784 land was given to Thomas Paine by New York State for his service in the struggle for independence.

New Rochelle has long been attracting artists and writers as well as commuters who work in New York City.

John Pell officially deeded New Rochelle to Jacob Leisler with the following requirement: "As an Acknowledgment to the Lord of the said Manor one Fatt Calfe on every fouer and twentieth day of Jun yearly and every Year Forever (if demanded)."

HISTORICAL SITES *and* MUSEUMS

Thomas Paine Cottage (914-633-1776; www.thomaspainecottage.org), 20 Sicard Ave. The cottage is open Tue., Thu., Sat., and Sun. Located on land given to Paine by New York State in 1784, the cottage contains some of his possessions, including a Franklin stove given to Paine by Ben Franklin himself. Rooms are furnished with 18th- and 19th-century pieces. There is a wax model of Paine from Madame Tussaud's museum.

Thomas Paine arrived in Philadelphia from England in 1774 and found himself in the middle of revolutionary ferment. His *Common Sense,* the anonymous and enormously influential pamphlet published in January 1776, argued fervently for independence from Britain. Paine wrote the stirring pamphlets called *Crisis* ("These are times that try men's souls") and, after the Revolution, *Rights of Man* (1791–92) in support of the French Revolution. An open letter attacking George Washington in 1796 later tarnished his reputation in America.

EVENTS

April: Encampment, Thomas Paine Cottage; 914-633-1776
September: Colonial fair and encampment, Thomas Paine Cottage; 914-633-1776

YONKERS

Manhattes Indians lived on the site of present-day Yonkers. In 1646 the Dutch West India Company granted land to Adriaen Cornelissen van der Donck. De Jonkheer, his title, became the name of the land.

Today Yonkers is a major industrial center as well as the home of Yonkers Raceway, a harness racing track.

HISTORICAL SITES *and* MUSEUMS

Philipse Manor Hall (914-965-4027; www.philipsemanorfriends.org), 255 Westchester Ave., Pound Ridge. Open Apr.–Oct., Wed.–Sun. This imposing Georgian mansion dates from 1680 to 1744. Frederick Philipse III, a wealthy Loyalist with a trading and shipping business in New York City, lived here. The original

In *Common Sense* Paine identifies the American cause with universal human rights: "The cause of America is in a great measure the cause of all mankind. Many circumstances hath, and will arise, which are not local, but universal, and through which the principles of all Lovers of Mankind are affected, and in the Event of which, their Affections are interested. The laying a Country desolate with Fire and Sword, declaring War against the natural rights of all Mankind, and extirpating the Defenders thereof from the Face of the Earth, is the Concern of every Man to whom Nature hath given the Power of feeling."

1750s papier-mâché ceiling is still here. Today the building houses a museum of history, art, and architecture. Portraits from the Cochran Collection of American Portraiture are on display.

INFORMATION

YONKERS CHAMBER OF COMMERCE
20 S. Broadway, Yonkers, NY 10701
914-963-0332; www.yonkerschamber.com

SCARSDALE

Scarsdale offers an upscale residential community with beautiful estates. The Greenburgh Nature Center is popular, with trails and a natural history museum. (914-723-3470; www.townlink.com/community_web/gnc).

HISTORICAL SITES *and* MUSEUMS

Cudner-Hyatt House (914-723-1744; www.scarsdalehistory.org), 937 Post Rd. Open year-round Mon.–Fri., weekends by appointment. This farmhouse dates from 1734 and is listed on the National Register of Historic Places. Its two stories are filled with mid-19th century furnishings, textiles, and tools.

TARRYTOWN/SLEEPY HOLLOW

Sleepy Hollow country contains three areas: Irvington, Sleepy Hollow, and Tarrytown. Sleepy Hollow was North Tarrytown until 1996. There are also interesting historic sites to visit from later eras: Kykuit (the Rockefeller estate), Lyndhurst, and Union Church of Pocantico Hills, which has marvelous stained-glass windows by Henri Matisse and Marc Chagall.

HISTORICAL SITES *and* MUSEUMS

Come to meet the man who made the "knickerbockers" come alive. *The Sketch Book* presented some of the characters that Washington Irving is remembered for: Ichabod Crane, the Headless Horseman, and Rip Van Winkle.

Irving described his house as "a little old-fashioned stone mansion all made up of gable ends and as full of angles and corners as an old cocked hat." The Van Tassel family built the stone house of 16 rooms in Tarrytown in 1656; Irving bought it in 1835 and called it **Sunnyside** (914-591-8763; www.hudsonvalley.org), W. Sunnyside Lane. Open in summer, daily except Tue.; winter Nov.–Dec., Sat.–Sun. Every time we go by on the train we search for the house and always manage to catch a glimpse.

Irving was known for poking fun at the Dutch who lived along the Hudson River, whom he called "knickerbockers." His *A History of New York* was published when he was 26 under the name Diedrich Knickerbocker.

Washington Irving planted the wisteria vine still growing at Sunnyside.

Irving was born in 1783 in New York City and was named after General George Washington, whom his Scottish immigrant parents greatly admired. He remembered being patted on the head by General Washington when he was a child.

As you approach the house, look at the southerly view of the Hudson; once there was a beach and also a boat dock there. When the railroad came through in 1849, the pleasures of the river were somewhat diminished.

Irving planted the wisteria vine beside the front door, and the iron benches on the porch were housewarming gifts. Irving loved planning innovations for his house and invented a number of refinements that other homes did not have for many years. For example, he created a water system for his house that was unknown to anyone else around.

He wrote *The Life of George Washington* in this house and completed it just before his death. His desk and books are still in the study as he left them. The house is completely furnished, with his favorite chair poised by a window for the view, and the dining room table set for dinner. Interpreters in costume, including Irving himself, are there to supply stories about the beloved author.

The **Old Dutch Church of Sleepy Hollow** (914-631-1123), US 9. The church was built by Frederick Philipse in 1685. Washington Irving is buried in Sleepy Hollow Cemetery, which is adjacent to the church's Burying Ground. Revolutionary War soldiers are buried in both cemeteries. Cemetery tours are given on Sun. at 2 from Memorial Day weekend to the end of October.

According to the story, Ichabod Crane rode off on his horse, Gunpowder, to visit Katrina Van Tassel and ask her to marry him. He was turned down, and, as he made his way home, "It was the very witching time of night that Ichabod, heavy-hearted, and crestfallen, pursued his travel homewards, along the sides of the lofty hills which rise above Tarry town. . . . In the dark shadow of the grove, on the margin of the brook, he beheld something huge, misshapen, and mounted on a black horse of powerful frame. . . . Ichabod was horror-struck, on perceiving that he was headless! . . . If I can but reach that bridge, thought Ichabod, I am safe."

He was, however, thrown from his horse by the "head" tossed at him by the headless horseman. In the morning Ichabod Crane was gone, his horse Gunpowder was there, and a pumpkin was lying in the road.

Philipsburg Manor (914-631-3992; www.hudsonvalley.org), US 9. Open daily except Tue. The house now re-creates the period from 1720 to 1750. Built as a fort in 1682 for Frederick Philipse, it was not a major residence for the family, who lived in Yonkers, but was used as business headquarters.

After you leave the visitor center you will cross a bridge over the river into that earlier era. Ducks and geese float and dive in the pond, and a mill wheel turns with a splashing sound. The interior is quite spartan, with bare floors and no curtains.

The dining room at Sunnyside.

Washington Irving is buried in Sleepy Hollow Cemetery, along with many Revolutionary War soldiers.

In the parlor stands a Dutch cupboard with painted scenes on it. You can visit the gristmill for a demonstration. **Historic Hudson**, which operates Sunnyside, Philipsburg Manor, and Van Cortlandt Manor, offers a variety of programs throughout the year.

CROTON-ON-HUDSON

Tellers Point, in Croton Point Park, is where Revolutionary War patriots attacked the HMS *Vulture* as British major John André was secretly meeting with Benedict Arnold to discuss how Arnold would hand over West Point. Because the sloop was forced to leave without him, André had to return overland and was waylaid in the no-man's-land between American and British lines by a group of AWOL American militiamen. Searching André for valuables, they discovered the plans of fortifications at West Point in his boot and concluded that he was a British spy.

Today Croton-on-Hudson is a popular destination, with its Croton Point Park offering swimming, boating, fishing, camping, and hiking (914-864-7053; www.westchestergov.com/parks).

HISTORICAL SITES *and* MUSEUMS
Van Cortlandt Manor (914-271-8981; www.hudsonvalley.org), S. Riverside Ave. Open summer daily except Tue.; winter Nov.–Dec. weekends. Closed Jan.–Mar.

In 1697 Stephanus Van Cortlandt's land was chartered by patent of King William III as the Lordship and Manor of Cortlandt. It included 86,000 acres at the junction of the Croton and Hudson Rivers. In 1749 Pierre Van Cortlandt, a grandson of Stephanus, lived in the house. He added a gristmill, store, church, school, and the Ferry House, an inn at the ferry crossing. Travelers came on the Albany Post Road and crossed the river on a family-owned ferry; local inhabitants frequented the inn's taproom to get news from peddlers and other travelers.

BEDFORD

Bedford Village has a New England flavor, with its green lined with white clapboard houses. The green dates from 1681. Actually, the town for a time was claimed as part of Connecticut. The historic buildings are managed by the Bedford Historical Society. In 1779 the British burned much of the town.

HISTORICAL SITES *and* MUSEUMS
Bedford Court House (914-234-9751; www.bedfordhistoricalsociety.org), NY 22 at the village green. Open May–Oct., Thu.–Sat. It was the northern county seat from 1787 to 1870. On the first floor the courtroom has been restored. A museum of local history is on the second floor. Historical Hall, next to the Old Burying Ground, was originally built in 1806 as a Methodist church. Twenty yoke of oxen moved it to its present site in 1837.

KATONAH

In the 1890s Katonah had to move to its present location as the New York City reservoir system expanded. This meant that it could be designed with care, as a planned community. The main residential streets are handsome, with green down the middle. The architecture is Victorian and painted in a riot of color.

HISTORICAL SITES *and* MUSEUMS

John Jay Homestead (914-232-5651; www.johnjayhomestead.org), 400 NY 22. Open Tue.–Sun. John Jay was the first chief justice of the United States. Rooms are furnished in Federal style. Don't miss the formal gardens and the herb garden.

LODGING IN WESTCHESTER COUNTY

ALEXANDER HAMILTON HOUSE
49 Van Wyck St.
Croton-on-Hudson, NY 10520
914-271-6737; www.alexanderham
iltonhouse.com
This B&B is on a hill overlooking the Hudson. It dates from 1889and has 8 guest rooms.

CASTLE ON THE HUDSON
400 Benedict Ave.
Tarrytown, NY 10591
800-616-4487 or 914-631-1980;
www.castleonthehudson.com
This turn-of-the-century castle features large marble fireplaces and carved wooden paneling. 31 guest rooms.

CRABTREE'S KITTLE HOUSE
11 Kittle Rd.
Chappaqua, NY 10514
914-666-8044; www.kittlehouse.com
The house dates from 1790; the inn has hosted Henry Fonda and other film stars. 12 guest rooms.

TARRYTOWN HOUSE
49 E. Sunnyside Lane
Tarrytown, NY 10591
800-553-8118 or 914-591-8200;
www.tarrytownhouseestate.com
Two historic mansions, King House and Biddle House, are part of the estate. 212 guest rooms.

RESTAURANTS IN WESTCHESTER COUNTY

BLUE HILL AT STONE BARNS
630 Bedford Rd.
Pocantico Hills, NY 10591 (near Tarrytown)
914-366-9600; www.bluehillstone
barns.com
A converted 1920s dairy barn on a self-sustaining farm; the "Farm Feast" features produce from the fields gathered that very day.

CRABTREE'S KITTLE HOUSE
11 Kittle Rd.
Chappaqua, NY 10514
914-666-8044; www.kittlehouse.com
Specialties include yellowfin tuna and Hudson Valley foie gras.

EQUUS RESTAURANT, CASTLE ON THE HUDSON
400 Benedict Ave.
Tarrytown, NY 10591
Continental-American cuisine is served in three dining rooms including one overlooking the Hudson River.

EVENTS

April, June, November, December:
Open-hearth cooking workshops at Van Cortlandt Manor, Croton-on-Hudson; 914-631-8200 x618; www.hudsonvalley.org
April: Sheep to Shawl, sheepherding with collies, sheep shearing, wool dyeing, and

weaving demonstrations, Philipsburg Manor, Sleepy Hollow; 914-631-8200; www.hudsonvalley.org

April: Crafts & Tasks, try historic skills and crafts like blacksmithing, weaving, and candle making, Van Cortlandt Manor, Croton-on-Hudson; 914-271-8981; www.hudsonvalley.org

May: Pinkster, colonial African American celebration of spring, Philipsburg Manor, Sleepy Hollow; 914-631-8200; www .hudsonvalley
Animals & Acrobats, celebration of the early American circus, Van Cortlandt Manor, Croton-on-Hudson; 914-271-8981; www.hudsonvalley.org

July: Independence Day 1806, Van Cortlandt Manor, Croton-on-Hudson; 914-271-8981; www.hudsonvalley.org

July: Independence Day, Washington Irving's Sunnyside, Tarrytown; 914-591-8763; www.hudsonvalley.org

July, September: Colonial birthday party, Philipse Manor Hall, Yonkers; 914-965-4027; www.philipsemanorfriends.org

October: Battle of Pell's Point encampment, St. Paul's Church National Historic Site, Mount Vernon; 914-667-4116, www.nps.gov/sapa

December: St. Nicholas Day celebration, Philipse Manor Hall, Yonkers; 914-965-4027; www.philipsemanorfriends.org
Twelfth Night, Van Cortlandt Manor, Croton-on-Hudson; 914-631-8200 x618; www.hudsonvalley.org

INFORMATION

WESTCHESTER COUNTY OFFICE OF TOURISM
222 Mamaroneck Ave., White Plains, NY 10605
800-833-9282, 914-995-8500;
www.westchestertourism.com

ROCKLAND COUNTY

Rockland County is less than fifteen miles from New York City, and yet it has a pastoral charm that makes getting away from the city appealing. With 35,670 acres of parkland, lakes, and mountains, visitors find more than enough to do. There are villages along the river, museums, and historic sites to visit.

Dutch settlers arrived in the area in the early 1600s. Along with some Huguenot and English settlers, they made a life for themselves by farming, hunting, fishing, and trapping. They built sawmills and gristmills on the creeks. Some of the historic homes have been in the same families since the 1600s. The first county courthouse in the area was built in Tappan in 1691. Tories torched it in the pre-Revolutionary years. The county seat moved to New City.

TAPPAN

Tappan is remembered as the place where Benedict Arnold and Major John André arranged Arnold's planned betrayal. The plot was uncovered, and André was hanged on André Hill.

HISTORICAL SITES *and* MUSEUMS

DeWint House (845-359-1359; www.dewinthouse.com), 20 Livingston Ave. Open daily. George Washington and his staff lived here in 1780 during the trial of Major John André. Washington closed the shutters of his room when André was hanged. He stayed again in the house in 1783 to meet with Sir Guy Carleton and discuss the British evacuation of New York. The house is also a shrine to the fraternal organization of the Masons; Washington was a Mason.

The house was made of Holland brick and sandstone in 1700. Seventeen Dutch patentees shared the land for farming. A carriage house museum contains pieces from the 1700s. If you visit in the spring, you will be treated to thousands of tulips in bloom.

Tappan Reformed Church (845-359-1694), 32 Old Tappan Rd. This church was organized by Dutch settlers in 1694; the present building dates from 1835. The Manse was built in 1726 and has been reconstructed.

STONY POINT

King's Ferry in Stony Point was the link between New England and the southern colonies. George Washington's army used it many times.

HISTORICAL SITES *and* MUSEUMS
Stony Point Battlefield State Historic Site (845-786-2521; www.nysparks.com), Park Rd. Off US 9W. Open Apr. 15–Oct. 31, Wed.–Sun. The American light infantry, commanded by Brigadier General Anthony Wayne, made a midnight assault against a British garrison here in July 1779. Wayne ordered his soldiers to attack with bayonets so that an accidental shot would not alert the enemy. Wayne suffered a head wound but continued to direct his soldiers. He earned a gold medal for this exploit and the nickname "Mad Anthony." The museum offers exhibits and a slide show. Docents in period dress demonstrate muskets, artillery, cooking, and camp life.

LODGING IN ROCKLAND COUNTY

BEAR MOUNTAIN INN
Palisades Pkwy. US 9W, 7 Lakes Dr.,
Bear Mountain, NY 10911
845-786-2731; www.bearmountaininn
.com
A 1915 example of rustic design, this lodge is right in the park on a lake. 48 guest rooms.

RESTAURANTS IN ROCKLAND COUNTY

OLD '76 HOUSE
110 Main St.
Tappan, NY 10983
845-359-5476

Built in 1668, this house once served as Washington's headquarters and Major John André's prison. The cuisine is American-Continental.

LANTERNA TUSCAN BISTRO
3 S. Broadway
Nyack, NY 10960
845-353-8361; www.lanternausa.com
Lanterns sit on the tables in this 1863 restaurant featuring the cuisine of northern Italy.

EVENTS

May: Loyal American weekend, a reenactment at Stony Point Battlefield; 845-786-2521; www.nysparks.com
June: Flag Day commemoration, retire-

ment of flags at Stony Point Battlefield; 845-786-2521; www.nysparks.com
July: Concert by the campfire at the Stony Point Battlefield, and storming of Stony Point military encampment; 845-786-2521; www.nysparks.com
October: Living History–Twin Forts Day at Bear Mountain State Park; 845-786-2701; www.nysparks.com

INFORMATION

ROCKLAND COUNTY OFFICE OF TOURISM
18 New Hempstead Rd., New City, NY 10956
800-295-5723; www.rockland.org

ORANGE COUNTY

Those of us eager to spend quality time on or near water will find Orange County appealing, with the Hudson River to the east and the Delaware River at the far western corner. The county was named for William, Prince of Orange, who was loved by the settlers.

Storm King Mountain, a prominent feature jutting into the Hudson, was originally named Klinkesberg, the Dutch for "brick mountain," by Henry Hudson. Dutch ship captains then called it Boterberg, for butter hill, because it looked like a mound of butter. Finally, a writer, Nathaniel Parker Willis, gave it the name Storm King, for the violent thunderstorms that took place there.

WEST POINT

HISTORICAL SITES and MUSEUMS
United States Military Academy at West Point (845-938-2638; www.usma.edu), US 9W. The academy and grounds are not open to the public except by a one-hour bus tour. Call 845-446-4724 for bus tour information. The visitor center is open daily.

The **West Point Museum** (845-938-3590; www.usma.edu/museum) is in Olmsted Hall at Pershing Center. Exhibits include military uniforms, flags, weapons, and military art. Open daily.

West Point was occupied from 1778 on because George Washington understood the location was a military site of great importance in controlling navigation on the Hudson. In 1778 a "great chain" was forged and placed across the river from West Point to Constitution Island to keep British ships from proceeding upstream.

Washington's headquarters was at West Point in 1779. Benedict Arnold was given command of the post in 1780; he was conspiring with Major John André, an aide to British general Sir Henry Clinton, to hand the defenses over to the British for 20,000

Although there are eight counties in the country with the name Orange, New York had the first. The others are in California, Florida, Indiana, North Carolina, Texas, Virginia, and Vermont.

pounds sterling, but the plan backfired when Americans captured André near Tarrytown. Incriminating papers, which André had hidden in his boot, were sent to General Washington. Arnold then fled to the British ship *Vulture* and later served in the British army. André was tried and hanged as a spy.

VAILS GATE

HISTORICAL SITES *and* MUSEUMS

New Windsor Cantonment (845-561-1765; www.nysparks.com), 374 Temple Hill Rd. Open mid-Apr.–Oct., Wed.–Sun. Seven hundred log cabins once filled the site of the last encampment of soldiers during the Revolution. One of the original cabins remains, and some buildings were reconstructed. Docents in period dress demonstrate weapons, trades, medicinal techniques, and camp life. The visitor center has a collection of 18th-century artillery. Military reenactments take place on the grounds.

    Knox Headquarters (845-561-5498; www.nysparks.com), Forge Hill Rd. Open Memorial Day–Labor Day, Wed.–Sun. Perhaps best known for his feat of hauling cannon overland in midwinter from Fort Ticonderoga to Washington's army outside Boston, General Henry Knox was a friend of Washington's and one of his key aides and officers, and he used this house several times as a headquarters. The 1734 house started life as a hunting lodge for John Ellison. The house is furnished with period pieces. Ruins of the 1741 mill are on the grounds.

MARLBORO

HISTORICAL SITES *and* MUSEUMS

Gomez Mill House (845-236-3126), Mill House Rd. Open May–Oct., Wed.–Sun. This home is the oldest surviving Jewish homestead in North America. It dates from 1714, when it began life as a sawmill and trading post. The Gomez family served those who were traveling north. Dard Hunter owned the paper mill, and it is still in operation with a gift shop.

NEWBURGH

Today the city of Newburgh has a 455-acre historic district to explore. The tour of 18th- and 19th-century homes is self-guided.

    Cruises to Bannerman Island are available from Hudson River Adventures (845-220-2120; www.prideofthehudson.com).

HISTORICAL SITES *and* MUSEUMS

From April 1782 to August 1783, **Washington's Headquarters** was in the Jonathan Hasbrouck house at 84 Liberty St. (845-562-1195; www.nysparks.com). Open mid-Apr.–Oct., Wed.–Sun. The army remained encamped at New Windsor and

George Washington originated the Order of the Purple Heart in 1782 in his headquarters in Newburgh. On May 3, 1783, he awarded the first "Badge of Military Merit" for acts of bravery. In 1932 it became the Purple Heart and was available to veterans of past wars; in 1942 it was restricted to those "wounded in action against any enemy." The Purple Heart is now presented to Americans wounded or killed in combat in service to the country.

In November 2006 the National Purple Heart Hall of Honor opened at the New Windsor Cantonment State Historic Site. Visitors walk along a corridor from the entry that features a timeline of the history of the Purple Heart. The Roll of Honor includes a computer database, which is regularly updated; you can search by a recipient's name and location of battle. A film, *Freedom Isn't Free,* is shown in the video theater.

grew restive while the long negotiations prior to the Treaty of Paris were in progress. Lack of pay and any prospect of pensions from Congress led to one of the most bizarre episodes of the Revolutionary era, generally called the Newburgh Conspiracy.

In March of 1783 petitions were circulating among officers at Newburgh that suggested a possible coup against Congress if no action on pensions was forthcoming. Although there are no records to verify conversations, some of Washington's key generals—Henry Knox and Horatio Gates—were apparently involved. When Washington learned that the officers had scheduled a meeting, he canceled it and called his own on March 16. In a carefully prepared, eloquent statement, he quashed the incipient revolt: "And let me conjure you, in the name of our Common Country, as you value your own sacred honor, as you respect the rights of humanity, and as you regard the Military and National Character of America, to express Your utmost horror and detestation of the Man who wishes, under any specious pretences, to overturn the liberties of our Country, and who wickedly attempts to open the flood Gates of Civil discord, and deluge our rising Empire in Blood."

LODGING IN ORANGE COUNTY

ANTHONY DOBBIN'S STAGECOACH INN
268 Main St.
Goshen, NY 10924
845-294-5526; www.dobbinsinn.com
The 1740s Georgian manor is furnished with family heirlooms. The owners are descended from Wild Bill Hickok and William Penn. 7 guest rooms.

CALDWELL HOUSE
25 Orrs Mills Rd.
Salisbury Mills, NY 12577
800-210-5565 or 845-496-2954;
www.caldwellhouse.com
This 1803 colonial home is furnished with antiques. 4 guest rooms.

CROMWELL MANOR
174 Angola Rd.
Cornwall, NY 12518
845-534-7136; www.cromwellmanor
.com

The estate includes an 1820 mansion and a 1764 cottage on seven acres; gardens abound. 12 guest rooms.

MEAD TOOKER HOUSE
136 Clinton St.
Montgomery, NY 12549
845-457-5770; www.meadtooker.com
This 200-year-old colonial is on the National Register of Historic Houses. 8 guest rooms.

THAYER HOTEL
674 Thayer Rd.
West Point, NY 10996
800-247-5047 or 845-446-4731;
www.thethayerhotel.com
This 1926 hotel overlooks the Hudson River and is on the grounds of West Point. The granite Gothic-style building has a Historic Hotels of American designation.151 guest rooms.

RESTAURANTS IN ORANGE COUNTY

IL CENA'COLO
228 S. Plank Rd.
Newburgh, NY 12550
845-564-4494
The building resembles a Tuscan villa, and northern Italian cuisine is served.

THAYER HOTEL
674 Thayer Rd.
West Point, NY 10996
845-446-4731; www.thethayerhotel
.com
Sunday brunch is a special treat.

EVENTS

January: Wedding anniversary of George and Martha Washington, Washington's Headquarters, Newburgh; 845-562-1195; www.nysparks.com
February: General Washington's winter encampment, New Windsor cantonment, Vails Gate; 845-561-1765; www.friendsof palisades.org
George Washington's birthday celebration, Washington's Headquarters, Newburgh; 845-562-1195; www.nysparks.com
April: Revolutionary War encampment, New Windsor cantonment, Vails Gate; 845-561-1765; www.nysparks.com
May: 18th-century cooking, Fort Decker, Port Jervis; 845-856-2375; www.minisink .org
July: A Revolutionary celebration, Knox's Headquarters, Vails Gate; 845-561-5498; www.friendsofpalisades.org
Living history: Declaring independence, New Windsor cantonment, Vails Gate; 845-561-1765; www.friendsofpalisades .org
Henry Knox's birthday celebration, Knox's Headquarters, New Windsor; 845-561-5498; www.nysparks.com
September: American Heritage Festival, Kenridge Farm, Cornwall; 845-534-5506; www.museumhudsonhighlands.org
October: Twin Forts Day, Bear Mountain State Park; 845-786-2701; www.nysparks .com
December: Washington's Headquarters by candlelight, Washington's Headquarters, Newburgh; 845-562-1195; www.nysparks .com

INFORMATION

ORANGE COUNTY TOURISM
30 Matthews St., Goshen, NY 10924
800-762-8687;
www.orangetourism.org

PUTNAM COUNTY

Back on the east side of the Hudson, Putnam County offers rolling hills, green meadows, lakes, reservoirs, and ponds. George Washington ordered north and south redoubts—defensive fortifications—built on mountains in the Hudson

On September 25, 1780, Washington had a date to meet Benedict Arnold at Beverly, his home and headquarters in Garrison, for breakfast. But on his way Washington decided to inspect the redoubts and fortifications at West Point. At the same time Arnold got word that British major John André had been captured in Westchester. André had the plans to capture West Point in his boot. So Arnold hurriedly rode his horse to the river and got his boatman to row him to a waiting British ship. If Washington had not chosen to inspect the fortifications on the way and been on time to meet Arnold, the escape likely would not have been possible.

Highlands, and these are preserved today. Redoubts were also built above Garrison.

If you choose to walk to the south redoubt, you will find walls, the parapets of the batteries, and the stone foundations of huts. The land is owned by the Garrison school district. To reach the trailhead, head west between US 9 and NY 92 on Snake Hill Road; turn south on the driveway at #135 and veer left at the fork to a small parking lot. The trail to the left will take you to the south redoubt in about twenty minutes. To reach the north redoubt on land owned by the Open Space Institute, take the trail straight out of the parking lot and turn left when it meets another trail, another hike of about twenty minutes.

GARRISON

HISTORICAL SITES and MUSEUMS
Boscobel Restoration (845-265-3638; www.boscobel.org), 1601 NY 9D (across the river from West Point). Open Apr.–Oct. Boscobel was begun in 1804 by States Morris Dyckman. The name Boscobel was taken from a home of the same name in Shropshire, England. Charles II had hidden inside an oak tree in the forest of Boscobel in 1651 following his defeat by Cromwell. Dyckman had two pieces of wood from the "Royal Oak" made into two snuffboxes, which are on display in the house. He died in 1806, and his wife, Elizabeth, finished the house.

In the early 1950s the house had fallen into disrepair and was slated for the wrecking crew when it was purchased for $35. People in the area dismantled the house and stored the pieces in their barns until it could be rebuilt. Lila Acheson Wallace of the Reader's Digest generously financed the reconstruction. The house was completely restored and refurnished with as much accuracy as could be obtained from old records. The dining room contains silver belonging to the Dyckman family. Note the unusual wineglass coolers and the washstand that was available for travelers who wanted to clean up before dinner. The center hall of the house is so large that it was frequently used for dancing. The living room is set up for tea; afterward the tea table would be moved so the guests could play parlor games. The next

The Hudson River viewed from Garrison.

room is a more casual living room; look for the barrel organ. Downstairs in the museum area is a collection of decorative arts and memorabilia. Look for the snuff box in blue and gold. Ask about Boscobel's special candlelit tours if you are going to be in the area during the evening.

LODGING IN PUTNAM COUNTY

THE BIRD & BOTTLE INN
1123 Old Albany Post Rd./Route 9
Garrison, NY 10524
845-424-2333; www.thebirdandbottle inn.com
The inn dates from 1761 and has been recently restored. Guest rooms have antique bed frames, and chests add to the colonial flavor. 4 guest rooms.

HUDSON HOUSE INN
2 Main St.
Cold Spring, NY 10516
845-265-9355; www.hudsonhouseinn .com
This 1832 building is right on the water. It is the second oldest inn continually operating in New York. 12 guest rooms.

PIG HILL INN
73 Main St.
Cold Spring, NY 10516
845-265-9247; www.pighillinn.com
This redbrick B&B dates to the mid-1800s. 9 guest rooms, many with woodburning stoves.

RESTAURANTS IN PUTNAM COUNTY

THE BIRD & BOTTLE INN
1123 Old Albany Post Rd./Route 9
Garrison, NY 10524
845-424-2333; www.thebirdandbottle inn.com
New American cuisine is offered.

BRASSERIE LE BOUCHON
76 Main St.
Cold Spring, NY 10516
845-265-7676
French cuisine is created with local ingredients.

CATHRYN'S TUSCAN GRILL
91 Main St.
Cold Spring, NY 10516
845-265-5582; www.tuscangrill.com
Sunday champagne brunch is a specialty.

HUDSON HOUSE RESTAURANT
2 Main St.
Cold Spring, NY 10516; 845-265-9355
www.hudsonhouseinn.com
The River Room overlooks the Hudson

River, Storm King Mountain, and West Point. Half Moon Tavern serves a casual menu.

PLUMBUSH INN
1656 NY 9D
Cold Spring, NY 10516
845-265-3904; www.plumbushinn.net
Rustic American fare is offered in the inn or in the greenhouse atrium.

INFORMATION

PUTNAM VISITORS BUREAU
110 Old US 6, Carmel, NY 10512.
800-470-4854 or 845-225-0381;
www.visitputnam.org

Mid-Hudson

The Mid-Hudson region includes the counties of Dutchess, Ulster, Greene, and Columbia.

DUTCHESS COUNTY

Dutchess County offers eight hundred square miles of rolling, picturesque countryside on the east side of the Hudson midway between New York City and Albany. The county has prepared seven scenic tours, with suggestions for stops at historic sites. Call 800-445-3131 for your copy.

The county was named for the duchess of York, who became Queen Mary of England.

BEACON

Beacon was named to commemorate the historic beacon fires that signaled the Revolutionary armies on British movements. In the 1800s Beacon became "the hat-making capital of the U.S." There were fifty hat factories in the town.

Today the Hudson Highlands State Park, which stretches to the south, is a popular destination, with twenty-five miles of hiking trails and views of the Hudson River.

HISTORICAL SITES *and* MUSEUMS

Madame Brett Homestead (845-831-6533), 50 Van Nydeck Ave. Open Apr.–Dec., second Sat. of each month and by appointment. Dating from 1709, this is the oldest homestead in Dutchess County. There are 17 rooms containing furnish-

ings, porcelain, paintings, books, and tools. It has been owned by seven generations of the Brett family. Don't miss the restored Dutch garden.

Mount Gulian Historic Site (845-831-8172; www.mountgulian.org), 145
Sterling St. Open May–Oct., Wed.–Fri. and Sun.; Nov., Wed.–Fri. This reconstructed 18th-century Dutch homestead has a 1740s Dutch barn. It was the home
of the Verplanck family and during the Revolutionary War served as headquarters
for General von Steuben.

FISHKILL

Fishkill was settled in 1714. The "kill" part of the name is the Dutch word for
"stream." The New York Congress and the Committee of Safety for New York met
here. It is well known for Bannerman Castle, which you can now visit.

HISTORICAL SITES *and* MUSEUMS

Van Wyck Homestead Museum (845-896-9560; www.vanwyckhomestead.com),
US 9 off I-84. Open weekends Memorial Day–Oct. and by appointment. The
house dates from 1732, when it was built by Cornelius Van Wyck. It was a Revolutionary War headquarters from 1777 onward. The episode of Enoch Crosby, a
British double agent, ended with his trial in the house. James Fenimore Cooper
may have been inspired by this story when he wrote *The Spy*. The house has 18th-
century portraits of local residents as well as a genealogical library.

RHINEBECK

The Center for Performing Arts at Rhinebeck offers plays, dance, concerts, stage
readings, and workshops (845-876-3088; www.centerforperformingarts.org). The
Old Rhinebeck Aerodrome Museum offers vintage aviation and automobiles (845-
752-3200; www.oldrhinebeck.org).

HISTORICAL SITES *and* MUSEUMS

Museum of Rhinebeck History (845-876-4902 or 845-871-1798; www
.rhinebeckmuseum.com), 7015 US 9. Open Jun.–Oct., Sat.–Sun., Wed. by
appointment. The 1798 Quitman House offers local history exhibits, including
some from colonial and Revolutionary War periods.

ANNANDALE-ON-HUDSON

HISTORICAL SITES *and* MUSEUMS

Montgomery Place Historic Estate (845-758-5461; www.HudsonValley.org),
River Rd., County Route 103. Open weekends May–Oct. Janet Livingston Montgomery, the wife of General Richard Montgomery, lived here after the death of
her husband, who was killed in the New Year's Eve assault on Quebec in 1775. It

Bannerman Castle (845-831-6346; www.BannermanCastle.org). Although this site is out of our era, we can't resist including it. Travels on the railroad down the Hudson take you right by this amazing ruin in the middle of the river. The Scottish-style castle dates from the early 1900s. Frank Bannerman used it to store his military warehouse, including explosives; he had bought supplies and was selling them. The Indians believed that the island was haunted. Perhaps the wind howling through gave that impression. Now it is possible to take a cruise around the island on the Pride of the Hudson and also take a guided tour of the island. Call 845-220-2120 for reservations.

is filled with family pieces, including Gilbert Stuart portraits, chandeliers, china, and books. Horse-drawn carriages, featuring beautiful Percherons, often appear at Montgomery Place. The gardens were developed by Violetta White Delafield after visiting Italy every winter and bringing back ideas. She became a nationally recognized expert in ikebana, the art of Japanese flower arranging.

LODGING IN DUTCHESS COUNTY

BEEKMAN ARMS
6387 Mill St.
Rhinebeck, NY 12572
845-876-7077; www.beekman
delamaterinn.com
The oldest continuously operating inn in the United States dates from 1766. The ambiance is old-fashioned with modern conveniences. 73 guest rooms.

BELVEDERE MANSION
10 Old Route 9
Staatsburg, NY 12580
845-889-8000; www.belvedere
mansion.com
A neoclassical mansion, a carriage house, and two lodges overlook the Hudson River and Catskill Mountains. 35 guest rooms.

BYKENHULLE HOUSE B&B
21 Bykenhulle Rd.
Hopewell Junction, NY 12533
845-242-3260; www.bykenhullehouse
.com
This house is on the National Historic Register. There are a number of fireplaces in the house. 5 guest rooms.

DELAMATER HOUSE
25 Garden St.
Rhinebeck, NY 12572
845-876-7077; www.beekman
delamaterinn.com
This house is part of the Beekman Arms complex, which offers 73 rooms. The Delamater House dates from 1844 and has 7 guest rooms.

HIDEAWAY SUITES
439 Lake Dr.
Rhinebeck, NY 12572
845-266-5673; www.ehideawaysuites
.com
Guests have seclusion in the woods, yet are close to Rhinebeck. 3 suites and 3 guest rooms.

INN AT BULLIS HALL
88 Hunns Lake Rd.
Bangall (Stanfordville), NY 12506
845-868-1665; www.bullishall.com
This Greek-revival mansion dates from 1832 and maintains an English country house atmosphere. 5 guest rooms.

INN AT THE FALLS
50 Red Oaks Mill Rd.
Poughkeepsie, NY 12603
845-462-5770; www.innatthefalls.com
An atrium overlooks the water, and the
sound of the tumbling falls at night is
soothing. 36 guest rooms.

LAKEHOUSE INN
41 Shelly Hill Rd.
Stanfordville, NY 12581
845-266-8093; www.lakehouseinn.com
This getaway retreat is in the woods on a
lake. Each room is decorated with antiques
and its own theme. 7 guest rooms.

LE CHAMBORD INN
2737 NY 52
Hopewell Junction, NY 12533
845-221-1941; www.lechambord.com
This 1863 mansion features Oriental rugs,
original paintings, and crystal chandeliers.
25 guest rooms.

OLD DROVERS INN
196 E. Duncan Hill Rd.
Dover Plains, NY 12522
845-832-9311; www.olddroversinn
.com
This 1750 building once hosted cattle
drovers on their way with their livestock to
New York City. 5 guest rooms.

RED HOOK INN
7460 S. Broadway
Red Hook, NY 12571
845-758-8445; www.theredhookinn
.com
The inn dates from 1842 and is filled with
Victorian furnishings. 6 guest rooms.

TROUTBECK INN
515 Leedsville Rd.
Amenia, NY 12501
845-373-9681; www.troutbeck.com
This English country estate was popular
with literary personalities during the
1920s. 42 guest rooms.

VERANDA HOUSE
6487 Montgomery St.
Rhinebeck, NY 12572
845-876-4133; www.verandahouse
.com
Once a farmhouse and then a parsonage,
this antiques-filled house dates from 1842.
5 guest rooms.

RESTAURANTS IN DUTCHESS COUNTY

CULINARY INSTITUTE OF AMERICA
US 9
Hyde Park, NY 12538
845-471-6608; www.ciachef.edu/
restaurants
Restaurants include American Bounty,
Apple Pie Bakery, Caterina de' Medici,
Escoffier, and St. Andrew's Café. Students
prepare and serve meals; reservations are
suggested.

LE PETIT BISTRO
8 E. Market St.
Rhinebeck, NY 12572
845-876-7400; www.lepetitbistro.com
French cuisine is offered with nightly specials on a blackboard.

LE CHAMBORD
2737 Route 52
Rhinebeck, NY 12572
845-221-1941; www.lechambord.com
French cuisine is prepared with fresh local
ingredients.

OLD DROVERS INN
196 E. Duncan Hill Rd.
Dover Plains, NY 12522
845-832-9311; www.olddroversinn
.com
Cheddar cheese soup is a specialty as well
as colonial-style dishes.

ROASTED GARLIC AT THE RED HOOK INN
7460 S. Broadway
Red Hook, NY 12571
845-758-8445; www.theredhookinn
.com

Guests can dine in the dining room or in the bar.

**TRAPHAGEN RESTAURANT
AT BEEKMAN ARMS**
6387 Mill St.
Rhinebeck, NY 12572
845-876-1766; www.beekman
delamaterinn.com
American cuisine with a colonial flair is served.

EVENTS

February/March: Colonial puppetry art program, Van Wyck Homestead Museum, Fishkill; 845-896-9560; www.hudsonriver valley.com. Children learn about the heroes and heroines of Fishkill during the Revolutionary War.
June: Annual colonial dinner, Mount Gulian Historic Site, Beacon; 845-831-8172; www.mountgulian.org

INFORMATION

DUTCHESS COUNTY TOURISM
3 Neptune Rd., Poughkeepsie, NY 12601
800-445-3131 or 845-463-4000; www.dutchesstourism.com

ULSTER COUNTY

Esopus Indians lived in the area for centuries before Henry Hudson sailed up the river in 1609. A group of Huguenots (French Protestants) bought 40,000 acres of land from them and settled the New Paltz patent. They built stone houses that still stand on Huguenot Street in New Paltz.

NEW PALTZ

The town is lucky to have a collection of original buildings and their contents that take you from birth of the Huguenots in France to their burial in the local cemetery across the road. In 1677 the heads of twelve families signed a treaty with the Esopus Indians for 39,683 acres. Four months later Governor Andros issued a patent for the lands, named a township, and in 1678 the twelve families arrived to settle.

Under their leader, Abraham Hasbrouck, the group set up a unique form of government called the "Duzine," or "Rule of the Elders." One representative from each of the twelve families was elected to the Duzine.

Indians advised the families to build on high ground because the river sometimes flooded the valley; the families settled on what is now

The New Paltz settlers had originally come from Lille and Calais, France. As Huguenot refugees from Catholic persecution in France, they had subsequently lived near Speyer and Mannheim, Germany, in the Rheinland-Pfalz, and so named their new town New Paltz. "Huguenot" may have been derived from the Flemish Huis Genooten, which means "house fellowship," since the people met in homes to study the Bible and pray.

Huguenot Street. The settlers lived in log cabins until 1692, when they had enough means to build homes like those they had in France.

Although the original homes had one room with a cellar kitchen and attic above, they added on other rooms to create the larger homes we see today. Descendants of each of the original twelve families still maintain an interest in the houses; they have contributed some of the original furniture passed down through generations.

HISTORICAL SITES *and* MUSEUMS

Huguenot Street (845-255-1660; www.huguenotstreet.org), 18 Broadhead Ave. Open May–Oct., Tue.–Sun. Call for off-season appointment. We were lucky enough to have a tour with a descendant of the original settlers.

The **Jean Hasbrouck House** has his initials carved in stone to the left of the door. In the living room the table is covered with a rug or tapestry, a dulcimer stands in the corner, and a snodnose lamp (very early brass oil lamp) perches on the desk. The kitchen contains furnishings that were in the family before 1700. A large Dutch *kaas* (cupboard) has several Delft spice jars on top. Hudson Valley rush-bottom chairs are typical of the area. A collection of pewter ware and a variety of cooking utensils are displayed.

> There is a bar in the Hasbrouck House that has a little picket fence on top. Were the pickets there so that patrons could not lean on their elbows too long as they imbibed? No, clean glasses were placed on them to dry.

Upstairs in the attic you will see a beehive chimney, a loom, and an exhibit on the production of linen from flax. Don't miss the store in the house, which has a variety of goods common to the period.

A large stone monument in the street lists the names of the original patentees. This boulder was brought down from the mountains on a sledge. The cemetery contains the graves of all the patentees and their wives. Look for the stone with primitive angels done by a local stonecutter. One gives the first letter of each word in the epitaph.

ULSTER PARK

HISTORICAL SITES *and* MUSEUMS

Klyne-Esopus Historical Society Museum (845-338-8109; www.klyneesopus museum.org), 764 US 9W. Open Fri.–Tue., mid-May to the first week in Dec. The museum is housed in an 1827 Dutch Reformed Church established in 1791. The building was constructed with handmade bricks and hand-hewn beams. Exhibits include information on the Esopus community from 3000 BC to the present.

A stone monument in New Paltz lists the original patentees.

HURLEY

HISTORICAL SITES and MUSEUMS

Hurley Heritage Society Museum (845-338-1661; www.hurleyheritagesociety
.org), 52 Main St. Open Sat.–Sun., May–Oct. The museum offers displays on the
town of Hurley. Ask for a brochure on a walking tour of the historic district, which
includes homes dating from the 1670s.

KINGSTON

The original settlement, called Esopus, was built within a stockade for protection,
but the thatched-roofed houses were easily burned by Indians in 1663. The next
houses were built of local limestone between 1670 and 1750. The rural Flemish
style, originally a single room with a grain storage loft above, is also found in New
Paltz. Just before the Revolution the residents began to build square, two-story
town houses. The area is still referred to as the Stockade District.

HISTORICAL SITES and MUSEUMS

Kingston Heritage Area Visitor Center (800-331-1518 or 845-331-7517;
www.ci.kingston.ny.us), 20 Broadway (Rondout) and 308 Clinton Ave. (Stockade). Open year-round, Mon.–Fri.; weekends May–Oct. There are many stone
houses to see in the Stockade District. Ask for information.

    Senate House State Historic Site (845-338-2786; www.ci.kingston.ny.us),
312 Fair St. Open Apr.–Oct., Mon, Wed., Sat., Sun. This was the site of the first
New York State Senate meeting. The house had been built by Wessel Ten Broeck
and overlooked the Esopus Creek. Abraham Van Gaasbeek owned the house in
1777 when Kingston served as the capital of New York. The first meeting in his
house was on Sep. 9, 1777. By Oct. 7, however, the Senate was moved to Poughkeepsie.

    The museum contains the largest collection of paintings by John Vanderlyn,
who was a native of Kingston. Vanderlyn studied under Gilbert Stuart and made
copies of Stuart's famous George and Martha Washington portraits. Aaron Burr
offered to become his patron and sent him to study in France. Look for a painting entitled *Ariadne Asleep and Abandoned by Theseus on the Island of Naxos.* Another

---

HUDSON RIVER Cruises

✱ The *Rip Van Winkle*, Rondout
Landing on Broadway, offers
cruises to see several lighthouses
and some of the Hudson River mansions. Call 845-340-4700 or 800-

843-7472. The sloop *Clearwater*
offers cruises with stops at a number of towns. She is moored at 112
Market St., Poughkeepsie. Call
845-454-7673.

favorite of many viewers is the portrait of Mrs. John R. Livingston, in which a mirror catches her profile.

Hudson River Maritime Museum (845-338-0071; www.hrmm.org), 50 Rondout Landing. Open May–Oct. As maritime aficionados we love wandering around maritime museums. This one is especially appealing. We have watched Pete Seeger, featured in a video presentation, as he enjoys singing "Sailing Down My Golden River."

The museum has a number of boats on display from a variety of eras. You will see the *Matilda*, an 1899 steam tug, sitting in her cradle. She was retired in 1969 as the last operating commercial steam tugboat in North America. The boatbuilding shop here is the place to watch the restoration of recent acquisitions.

LODGING IN ULSTER COUNTY

CAPTAIN SCHOONMAKER'S B&B
913 NY 213
High Falls, NY 12440
845-687-7946; www.captainschoon
makers.com
This 1760 stone house and its guest room balconies overlook Coxingkill stream. 5 guest rooms.

DEPUY CANAL HOUSE INN
NY 213
High Falls, NY 12440
845-687-7700; www.depuycanalhouse
.net
This 1797 stone house has stone fireplaces and wide-plank floorboards. It was used by the lock master of the D&H Canal, next to the house. 5 guest rooms.

MOHONK MOUNTAIN HOUSE
1000 Mountain Rest Rd.
New Paltz, NY 12561
800-772-6646; www.mohonk.com
Dating from 1869, this historic hotel is set on a spectacular lake with a cliff on the other side—the view is unforgettable. 251 guest rooms.

RESTAURANTS IN ULSTER COUNTY

DEPUY CANAL HOUSE
NY 213
High Falls, NY 12440
845-687-7778; www.depuycanalhouse
.net
New American cuisine featuring Hudson Valley produce. Chefs on Fire is a bistro in the downstairs wine cellar for lighter fare.

LOCUST TREE
215 Huguenot St.
New Paltz, NY 12561
845-255-7888; www.locusttree.com
Dinner in this 18th-century house is offered in the dining rooms featuring northern European dishes or in the tavern for lighter fare.

INFORMATION

ULSTER COUNTY TOURISM
10 Westbrook Lane, Kingston, NY 12401
800-342-5826; www.ulstertourism.info

GREENE COUNTY

Greene County has been captured on canvas by the Hudson River School of artists. We head for exhibitions of their work featured by many art museums in the country. For those of you who are also intrigued by these paintings, the Thomas Cole

National Historic Site (518-943-7465; www.thomascole.org), at 218 Spring St., Catskill, NY 12414, offers a map and directions so you can follow the Hudson River School Art Trail. Call 800-355-2287 x5 for a brochure.

CATSKILL

Native Americans thought Henry Hudson's *Half Moon* was a large swan as it sailed past in 1609. Dutch settlers came in 1651 and named their home "Hop-O-Nose." One of them, Eldert Cruyf, could throw a stone 100 yards and was called "Eldert the Thrower." Catskill dates from 1773. The mouth of Catskill Creek formed a port, and people began shipping wheat out in the late 18th century. Today the Catskill Forest Preserve is popular for hiking and also offers three rivers for fishing.

HISTORICAL SITES *and* MUSEUMS
Thomas Cole National Historic Site (518-943-7465; www.thomascole.org), 218 Spring St. Open May 1–Oct. 31, Fri.–Sun. Although this house is just a tad beyond our time period for this book, we want to include it. Dating from 1815, the house has galleries of paintings and prints. Cole possessions and period furnishings are here.

COXSACKIE

The town was named after the Indian word for "hoot of an owl." The Dutch arrived in the late 1600s and were the primary residents until 1790. The village has a fine collection of colonial and Victorian houses to stroll by. Views from Riverside Park include the Hudson River and the distant Berkshire Hills in Massachusetts.

HISTORICAL SITES *and* MUSEUMS
Want to see a thirteen-sided barn? There's one at the **Bronck House** (518-731-6490; www.gchistory.org), 90 County Rt. 42. Open Memorial Day weekend to Oct. 15, Wed.–Sun. It was owned by Pieter Bronck in 1663; other buildings on the property date from 1685 and 1738. This was a working farm in the Bronck family for eight generations.

Inside, period furnishings fill the house, as well as an art collection featuring works by Thomas Cole, John Frederick Kensett, Ezra Ames, Richard Hubbard, Benjamin Stone, and Ammi Phillips. The unusual thirteen-sided barn with center-pole construction houses a collection of horse-drawn vehicles.

LODGING IN GREENE COUNTY

ALBERGO ALLEGRIA
43 NY 296
Windham, NY 12496
518-734-5560; www.albergousa.com
The house dates from 1876 and features stained-glass windows, a cathedral ceiling, and Tiffany lamps. 21 guest rooms.

BAVARIAN MANOR COUNTRY INN
866 Mountain Ave.
Purling, NY 12470
518-622-3261;
www.bavarianmanor.com
The inn dates from 1865 and is family run.
The property's 100 acres includes a lake.
18 guest rooms.

CHRISTMAN'S WINDHAM HOUSE
5742 NY 23
Windham, NY 12496
518-734-4230;
www.windhamhouse.com
This Greek-revival inn dates from 1805. 49
guest rooms.

POINT LOOKOUT MOUNTAIN INN
NY 23
East Windham, NY 12439
518-734-3381;
www.pointlookoutinn.com
This inn on the Mohican Trail is famous for
its five-state view. Guests can have a "raid
the refrigerator" breakfast. 14 guest
rooms.

WINTER CLOVE INN
Winter Clove Rd.
Round Top, NY 12473
518-622-3267; www.winterclove.com
The inn is has been family run for 150
years. It adjoins the Catskill Forest Preserve.
49 guest rooms.

RESTAURANTS IN GREENE COUNTY

BAVARIAN MANOR
866 Mountain Ave.
Purling, NY 12470
518-622-3261;
www.bavarianmanor.com
German/American cuisine is featured.

CHALET FONDUE
NY 296
Windham, NY 12496
518-734-4650; www.prattmuseum.com
Swiss/German/American cuisine is on the
menu.

VICTORIAN ROSE AT POINT LOOKOUT MOUNTAIN INN
NY 23
East Windham, NY 12439
518-734-3381;
www.pointlookoutinn.com
Chefs here are trained at the Culinary Institute of America.

EVENTS

October: Reenactment of the British arriving at Kingston Point, Forsyth Park,
Kingston; 800-331-1518; www.ulster
tourism.info; held every other year.

INFORMATION

GREEN COUNTY TOURISM
Exit 21, I-90, Cairo, NY 12413
800-355-CATS, 800-781-4492, 518-622-
0086; www.greenetourism.com

COLUMBIA COUNTY

If you can't get the song about Route 66 out of your mind, try driving it in Columbia County. You're guaranteed to slow down and watch the scenery up and down
hills. The state road now follows what was once the route of old turnpikes such as
Union turnpike from Hudson to New Lebanon. It dates from 1801. Mileposts
were made of white stone to mark the distance. The route winds through villages
with historic homes and beside streams and creeks.

GERMANTOWN

HISTORICAL SITES and MUSEUMS

Clermont State Historic Site (518-537-4240; www.friendofclermont.org), 1 Clermont Ave., Germantown, NY 12526. Open Apr. 1–Oct. 31, Tue.–Sun. This was the ancestral home of Chancellor Robert R. Livingston, one of the drafters of the Declaration of Independence. His great-great-grandfather of the same name was born in Scotland in 1654, spent years in Holland, and arrived in America in 1673. In 1686 Governor Dongan granted him a manor of 160,000 acres along the Hudson. As lord of the manor, Livingston the elder had full control of both the land and his tenants, and he also had a seat in the colonial Legislature. The British burned the manor house in 1777, but it was rebuilt with the same Georgian architecture; in the 1870s a French-style roof was added.

The rooms are furnished with family pieces, period furniture, and family portraits. Two French pieces are a crystal chandelier dating from 1804 and a balloon clock patterned after the first hydrogen balloon in Paris in 1783.

The gardens are stunning, with roses in the English garden and black locust trees planted by the Livingstons.

HUDSON

Shades of Nantucket! Raids on the Massachusetts island during the Revolution bothered the residents. In 1783 Seth and Tom Jenkins, worrying that the British would vanquish Nantucket in another attempt to regain control of the colonies, moved west to find another home. They chose Hudson as a site, thinking it was far enough up a navigable river to be safe, and moved there lock, stock, and barrel in their whaling ships, with a number of other families. Some lived on board ship while their houses were being constructed.

Although Hudson is 120 miles from the sea, whaling became its major industry. The new residents built up a number of the businesses they knew, including, of course, shipbuilding, a distillery, a sperm oil works, and a sail loft. The War of 1812 resulted in the demise of much of their industry. As France and England were locked in a worldwide struggle, both seized American ships, and Hudson skippers lost their money and their ships.

Now Hudson is a paradise for those who love to prowl among antique shops. And for a fine view of the Catskills, sit on a bench on Parade Hill at the foot of Warren Street.

HISTORICAL SITES and MUSEUMS

Olana State Historic Site (518-828-0135; www.olana.org), 5720 NY 9G, Hudson, NY 12534. Open Apr.–Jun., Wed.–Sun.; Jan.–Mar., Sat.–Sun. Although Olana, built in 1870, is beyond our time period, we want to include it as a major and very favorite destination. Set on a bluff 500 feet above the Hudson, this home looks out of place with its Persian-style exterior. But it is a treat to visit. Frederic Edwin Church, a painter of the Hudson River School, studied with Thomas Cole and painted amazing landscapes with a fine depiction of light. The views he had from his home must have been inspiring indeed. He wrote: "About one hour this side of Albany is the center of the world. I own it."

One of Hudson's whalers had an amazing story to tell after his whaleboat was stove in by a whale. The whale took Marshall Jenkins in its mouth and submerged. When the whale came up for air, his mouth opened and Jenkins came out!

Church and his wife, Isabel, planned the home with his pencil sketches and then color sketches. It took 20 years to build. It is decorated with Persian rugs, pottery, china, and many paintings. He collected 17th-century masters and also painted scenes from his Olana.

KINDERHOOK

As Henry Hudson sailed his ship along the Hudson in 1609, he noticed that a group of Mohican Indian children had gathered to stare at his ship. He named the place Kinderhook, or "Children's Corner." The eighth president of the United States, Martin Van Buren, known as "Old Kinderhook," was born, died, and is buried here.

HISTORICAL SITES *and* MUSEUMS
Luykas Van Alen House (518-758-9265; www.cchsny.org), NY 9H, Kinderhook, NY 12106. Open Memorial Day to Labor Day, Thu.–Sun. It may have been inhabited by the model for one of Washington Irving's characters, Katrina Van Tassel. The 1737 house, built of red brick, reflects typical Dutch architecture, with steep gables and separate outside doors for each room. A collection of Delft and Hudson Valley paintings is on display.

Lindenwald, the Martin Van Buren National Historic Site (518-758-9689; www.nps.gov/mava), 1013 Old Post Rd., Kinderhook, NY 12106. Open mid-May–Oct., daily. The house was finished in 1797 by ancestors of President Martin Van Buren. Lindenwald was renovated by Van Buren after his retirement. Following his death the house changed hands several times. The National Park Service has now restored it to the time of Van Buren's occupancy.

OLD CHATHAM

HISTORICAL SITES *and* MUSEUMS
The Shaker Museum and Library (518-794-9100; www.smandl.org), 88 Shaker Museum Rd., Old Chatham, NY 12136. Open end of May to end of Oct., Wed.–Mon. This site preserves the history of a community founded by Mother

Ann Lee in 1774. They lived by the Millennial Laws that prescribed celibacy, separate schools for boys and girls, and prohibited ownership of property.

If you've ever been attracted to the elegance of simplicity, Shaker products will blow your mind. And they are ingenious, too. Who else would have designed a chair that you could tilt back without scratching the polished floor? Or the first washing machine that would wash laundry at different temperatures? They also created the circular saw and a seed-sorting machine. Perhaps they even invented the homely but essential clothespin!

The Shakers were respected for the high quality of their furniture and products. This museum has exhibits of Shaker furniture, a blacksmith shop, a schoolroom, a collection of tools, nine rooms containing furnishings of that era, and a crafts gallery.

NEW LEBANON

HISTORICAL SITES *and* MUSEUMS
Mount Lebanon Shaker Village (518-794-9500) The site has been purchased by Old Chatham Shaker Museum and is not open on a regular basis. However, you can see it by appointment, and some special events are held here. A private boarding school occupies some of the Shaker buildings.

LODGING IN COLUMBIA COUNTY

INN AT THE SHAKER MILL FARM
NY 22
Canaan, NY 12029
518-794-9345; www.shakermillfarminn
.com
This restored 1824 Shaker gristmill is by a stream and waterfall. 20 guest rooms.

INN AT SILVER MAPLE FARM
NY 295
Canaan, NY 12029
518-781-3600; www.silvermaplefarm
.com
The 1870 barn has been converted but still has exposed beams and wide-board floor planks. A waterfall is within hearing distance. 11 guest rooms.

RESTAURANTS IN COLUMBIA COUNTY

MARIO'S RESTAURANT
NY 22 and US 20
New Lebanon, NY
518-794-9495
Northern Italian cuisine in an attractive mountain setting.

INFORMATION

COLUMBIA COUNTY TOURISM
401 State St., Hudson, NY 12534
800-724-1846 or 518-828-3375;
www.columbiacountyny.org

Capital District/Saratoga/Glens Falls

The Capital District includes the area surrounding Albany, the capital of New York. The Hudson and Mohawk Rivers merge here and provided a crossroads for early settlers. Warring parties vied for possession of the area during colonial wars and the Revolution because it was a strategic site with navigable water in several directions.

When Henry Hudson first sailed up the river, he ran aground south of the site of Albany and sent boats ahead to explore. A trading post dates from 1614 near Albany. Fort Orange was built by the Dutch in 1624. Rensselaer, on the eastern side of the river, dates from 1630, when it was named Rensselaerswyck as the patroonship of Kiliaen Van Rensselaer. Fort Crailo was built in 1705.

Schenectady was home to the Mohawk Indians, of the Iroquois confederacy. The Dutch arrived and settled in 1661 and built a stockade. At one point the sentries guarding it were fake—just snowmen! French and Indians attacked with ease in the infamous 1690 massacre.

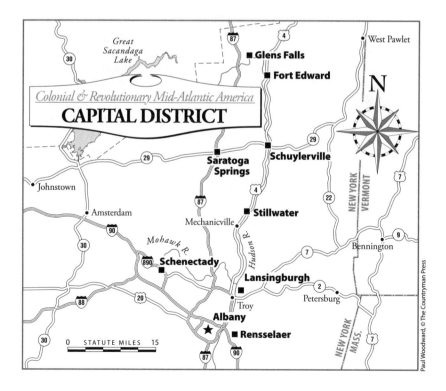

RENSSELAER COUNTY

The county was part of Rensselaerwyck, bought from the Mohawk and Mohican Indians in 1630. By 1683 it was part of Albany County. In 1772 Albany County was divided among several counties, including some in Vermont, and in 1791 Rensselaer County split from Albany County.

Today the eastern boundary of Rensselaer County meets southern Vermont and northwestern Massachusetts. The county covers 665 square miles, and the land is level and flat along the Hudson River, rising into the Rensselaer plateau and on to the Taconic range to the east. Berlin Mountain, at 2,818 feet above sea level, is the highest point in the county.

RENSSELAER

HISTORICAL SITES *and* MUSEUMS

Fort Crailo (518-463-8738; www.npsparks.state.ny.us), 9½ Riverside Ave. Open mid-Apr.–Oct., Wed.–Sun. Fort Crailo is a brick manor house on the east bank of the Hudson. It dates from the beginning of the 18th century, when it was built by Hendrick Van Rensselaer, grandson of the patroon. The name came from the family estate in the Netherlands; Crailo means "crows' wood." In 1740 additions were made, with more changes in the early 19th century.

The newborn Continental Army had its cantonment in the field here in June 1775, and this was the headquarters for General Schuyler during the Revolution. Today the fort contains the Museum of Dutch Culture in the Hudson Valley—a good place to learn about Dutch settlements and provide focus for the colonial era in the area. Some pieces of furniture are on display, including a cradle from the early 1700s.

Bennington Battlefield (518-279-1155; www.nysparks.state.ny.us/parks), NY 67, Hoosick Falls, 12090. Open May 1–Labor Day. Drive up to the top of the hill, where you will find a bronze topographical map of the battlefield, which lies in New York State, although the battle was named for the nearby Vermont town. Markers indicate battlefield positions, including those of Colonel Nichol's New Hampshire Regiment and Colonel Herrick's Vermont Rangers. Each of the present-day states that supplied militia—Vermont, Massachusetts, New Hampshire, and New York—has a stone monument.

It may be that the words to "Yankee Doodle" were written at Fort Crailo in 1758. The writer makes fun of colonial militia who were sent to reinforce General Abercrombie's invasion of Fort Ticonderoga in 1758.

INFORMATION

RENSSELAER COUNTY TOURISM
518-270-2958; www.rensco.com

ALBANY COUNTY

Albany County is the hub of east central New York. The original Dutch West India Company settlement, known as Fort Orange, dates from 1624. Forty years later the English arrived, and the county was established in 1683. As the parent county for a large part of the state, it once included present-day Schoharie, Schenectady, Saratoga, Rensselaer, and Greene Counties.

Albany was important as the head of navigation on the Hudson and the gateway to the Mohawk Valley as well as points north. It is still a transportation hub for the region, and the city of Albany has been the state capital since 1777.

ALBANY

HISTORICAL SITES *and* MUSEUMS

New York State Museum (518-474-5877; www.nysm.nysed.gov), Empire State Plaza, Madison Ave. Open daily. "Native Peoples of New York" is a favorite exhibit. Dioramas picture people living in a settlement at Lamoka Lake in the Finger Lakes area. The "three sisters" (corn, beans, and squash) diorama shows people working in their cornfields. The tattoos on the only male figure in the group were copied from a 1710 painting of a Mohawk who came to the court of Queen Anne in England. The Mohawk longhouse is 60 feet long. As you approach the longhouse you will see a Mohawk astride the beams working on the roof. Inside you will distinguish a family of children, teenagers, and adults engaged in various activities.

The "Ancient Life of New York City" explores colonial commerce from 1700 to 1800. It focuses on the area of what is now South Street Seaport, where boxes and barrels stand ready to be loaded on ships.

New York State Archives (518-474-8955; www.archives@nysed.gov), Empire State Plaza, Madison Ave. Open daily. History buffs now have the chance to see original documents from colonial and Revolutionary War days on the 11th floor of the New York State Museum building. You can see the papers that British spy John André was carrying when he was captured. The document was folded into twelfths to fit into his boot. Besides papers the department also saves artifacts. A pistol and a sword owned by George Washington are there. Some of the papers have scorch marks following a fire in 1911. Anyone who wants to see specific items not on display will need to register with a government photo ID and complete a form in the office on the 11th floor.

Philip Van Rensselaer built **Cherry Hill** in 1787 (518-434-4791; www.his toriccherryhill.org), 523½ S. Pearl St. Open Feb.–Dec., Tue.–Sun. Fortunately, because the house had never been sold outside the family, much of the personal belongings and clothing were saved. Five generations of the family lived here from 1787 to 1963. If you're thinking of cleaning out your attic, remember this family who never threw anything away, to the benefit of all of us.

Visitors enter the house through an orientation room, where diagrams of the

One of the Cherry Hill bedrooms was the scene of a murder. A member of the family, Elsie Lansing Whipple, had a love affair with a hired hand, Jesse Strang, and conspired to meet him in various places at home as well as in taverns. Jesse came in through a window and shot Elsie's husband, John Whipple—a crime for which he was hanged.

family tree outline the sequence of those who lived here. Philip and Maria Van Rensselaer were the first to do so, beginning in 1787. They were merchant farmers who also owned a town house on North Pearl Street; they had 13 children.

A tour of the house begins in the front hall, where there are several family portraits, including one that was used for target practice by children armed with bows and arrows—it was successfully restored. In the parlor stands a fire screen in queen stitch created by Arriet Van Rensselaer.

Herbert Rankin, a descendant who taught at Princeton, died in 1918 on a ship heading for Europe. He had his portrait painted in 1894 as a child. He was wearing leather leggings and a velvet suit. The portrait still hangs in the parlor, and sometimes the garments are also on display.

Schuyler Mansion (518-434-0834; www.nysparks.state.ny.us), 32 Catherine St. Open mid-Apr.–Oct., Wed.–Sun. Also open Tue. in June, July, and Aug.

The Schuyler Mansion is also called "The Pastures"; the two acres of lawns and gardens affirm the name. The house, high on a hill, once had a view of the river. Philip Schuyler built his home in 1761. He came from a prominent local family and distinguished himself during the French and Indian War.

George Washington visited here, as did Benjamin Franklin, Benedict Arnold, Baron von Steuben, Comte de Rochambeau, and even General Burgoyne. This last guest may seem surprising, because he had ordered Schuyler's country house near Saratoga to be burned during the crucial battles in 1777. Nevertheless, the defeated British general was a prisoner who was treated as a guest in the house.

Three of the five Schuyler daughters eloped because their parents reportedly did not approve of their choices. William Kennedy, in his *O Albany!* reported that some of the daughters eloped out of the windows on the second floor. Elizabeth married Alexander Hamilton in the formal parlor in 1780.

The house is furnished with period furniture, including some from the Schuyler family, Chinese export porcelain, Delftware, and English glassware.

Ten Broeck Mansion (518-436-9826; www.tenbroeck.org), 9 Ten Broeck Place. Open May–Dec., Thu.–Fri. This mansion dates from 1797, when it was built for General Abraham Ten Broeck and his wife, Elizabeth Van Rensselaer. They had lost their previous home to fire and were happy to build a larger, more elegant house. He had a distinguished career, serving as a delegate to the Second Continental Congress in 1775. Ten Broeck was in charge of the New York State militia at Saratoga in 1777. He was mayor of Albany and a member of the New York State Senate from 1779 to 1783.

Want to see a tomahawk's grisly evidence? Look for the gash on the stair rail, which may have been made by an Indian tomahawk. Tories tried to kidnap Schuyler during the Revolution, but he got word of their plot and was able to hire guards to thwart the attack. Legend reports that one of Schuyler's daughters had run downstairs to grab her baby sister from the cradle and was on her way back up with the baby when an Indian tomahawk was thrown at her and gashed the stair rail.

Theodore Olcott bought the house in 1848 and called it Arbor Hill, which is also the name of the surrounding area. He made many improvements, among them adding second-floor bathrooms with marble tops on the sink and bathtub. The Olcott family lived in the house for a century and gave it to the Albany County Historical Association in 1948.

The dining room fireplace contains Belgian marble, and the china is a rose medallion pattern. Three grandfather clocks stand in the hall and living room. They were also called "coffin clocks," because a person could be buried in one.

Cherry Hill in Albany.

LANSINGBURGH

Lansingburgh was established in 1771, and its residents were active in river commerce. Herman Melville lived here for a time from 1838. He embarked on his first sea voyage and published his first tale while a Lansingburgh resident. Melville Park is on the banks of the Hudson, on the site of the shipyard of Richard Hanford.

HISTORICAL SITES *and* MUSEUMS

The Lansingburgh Historical Society (518-235-3501 or 518-235-7647), 2 114th St. The society is headquartered in a wood-frame house with a brick facade, constructed in 1786 by merchant Stephen Gorham. He was the first postmaster. Next-door stands a two-story Dutch house dating from 1772. It was built by Abraham K. Van Vleck and was later the home of author-inventor Horatio Gates Spafford. The collections include maps, photographs, diaries, and records of the town.

LODGING

DESMOND HOTEL
660 Albany-Shaker Rd., Albany, NY 12211
800-448-3500, 518-869-8100;
www.desmondhotelsalbany.com
Colonial-themed courtyard areas and flowers blooming year-round. 323 guest rooms.

CENTURY HOUSE
997 New Loudon Rd. (US 9), Latham, NY 12047
888-674-6873, 518-785-0931;
www.thecenturyhouse.com
The hotel has a colonial theme. Some units have kitchens. 68 guest rooms.

MORGAN STATE HOUSE
393 State St.
Albany, NY 12210
518-427-6063, 888-427-6063;
www.statehouse.com
Dating from the 19th century, the main brownstone row house mansion has been restored with rich cherry woodwork. It was once home to Alice Morgan Wright, an artist and suffragette. 18 guest rooms.

RESTAURANTS

JACK'S OYSTER HOUSE
42 State St., Albany, NY 12207
518-465-8854;
www.jacksoysterhouse.com
Seafood is a specialty.

LA SERRE
14 Green St., Albany, NY 12207
518-463-6056
French and Continental dining in downtown Albany in an 1829 building.

NICOLE'S BISTRO AT THE QUACKENBUSH HOUSE
25 Quackenbush Square, Albany, NY 12207
518-465-1111; www.nicolesbistro.com
The restaurant is in a converted 18th-century home, the oldest intact building in Albany.

CENTURY HOUSE RESTAURANT
997 New Loudon Rd., Latham, NY 12047
888-674-6873, 518-785-0931;
www.thecenturyhouse.com
The restaurant offers regional American cuisine.

DESMOND HOTEL
660 Albany-Shaker Rd., Albany, NY
12211
800-448-3500, 518-869-8100;
www.desmondhotelsalbany.com
Scrimshaw offers fine dining, Simpson's is
casual.

EVENTS

May: Tulip festival, beginning with the
scrubbing of State Street by costumed
Dutch settlers; 518-434-2032;
www.albanyevents.org
June: Old Songs Festival of traditional
music and dance, Altamont Fairgrounds;
518-765-2815; www.oldsongs.org
July: Corn festival celebrations, Iroquois

Indian Museum, Howes Cave; 518-296-
8949; www.iroquoismuseum.org
July: Independence Day, Schuyler Mansion
State Historic Site; 518-434-0834;
nysparks.state.ny.us
September: Tours of the replica of Henry
Hudson's *Half Moon*; 518-434-0405;
www.albany.org

INFORMATION

**ALBANY COUNTY CONVENTION AND
VISITORS BUREAU**
25 Quackenbush Square, Albany, NY
12207
800-258-3582 or 518-434-1217;
www.albany.org

SCHENECTADY COUNTY AND SCHENECTADY

Algonquian Indians first lived on the land that is now Schenectady; then the Iroquois battled their way to the site. In 1661 Arendt Van Curler bought 128 square miles from the Indians and banded together with fifteen other families to form a patroonship, where they built homes within a stockade for protection against the French and Indians. The 1662 stockade is bounded by State, Front, and Ferry Streets and Washington Avenue. By 1690 there were 80 houses and 400 persons living in the stockade.

On February 8, 1690, the people in the stockade were unaware of danger that was imminent. During January, 114 Frenchmen and 96 Indians began an arduous trek by snowshoe from Montreal to Albany. But the Indians preferred to attack Schenectady instead of Albany. At a fork in the road (now Schuylerville), the choice was made and they turned toward Schenectady. When they were within six miles of the stockade they stopped and talked with four squaws living in a bark hut who told them all they needed to know. Advance scouts found that there were only two sentries and . . . both of them were snowmen! They reached the stockade, found a gate open, and sneaked around the houses in silence until a "single hideous and horrendous war whoop" broke the news to the inhabitants. At the given signal every cottage was attacked simultaneously. Every household was invaded, and no distinction of age or sex saved the miserable people from the tomahawk. Then commenced the *noche triste;* the bad night of horrors, slaughter, and burning. Sixty persons were killed, twenty-seven were taken captive, and many others died from the cold after their homes were burned. Prudently, the few survivors built the King's Fort after the massacre, where they lived along with their Mohawk allies.

HISTORICAL SITES *and* MUSEUMS

Take some time and visit the **Schenectady County Historical Society** (518-374-0263; www.schist.org), 32 Washington St. Open Mon.–Sat. The society maintains a museum of exhibits from the area, a library, a genealogical collection, and a collection of many documents. We were fascinated with the paintings of the stockade hanging on the walls.

Don't miss the "senility cradle" used for John Sanders II who was born in 1757. Visitors may be interested in the needlework collection complete with pincushions, lace, and Dutch bobbin lace from the 17th century. Toys and dolls are on display from several centuries. There's a "Liberty flag" and arms of the Revolutionary War upstairs. Indian artifacts include arrowheads, a 1720 ax head, Iroquois dolls, and a bead bag. The society also conducts a "walkabout" of the Stockade district every September.

One house has a tablet as follows: "Oldest house in City built before 1700 by Hendrick Brouwer, a fur trader, who died here 1707. Sold 1799, to James Rosa, Superintendent of Mohawk and Hudson Railroad, 1831." Hendrick's wife was Maritie Borsboom, and they were married two years after the massacre. The house passed on to several sons and grandsons also named Hendrick. A grandson of the first Hendrick served in the Revolutionary War as a member of the Albany County militia. James Rosa, who bought the house in 1825, was descended from Heymense Rosa, who came to the New World on the *Spotted Cow* in 1661. The house is not open except during special house tours, but it is lovely to look at from the outside. Now that we've told you about one home in the Stockade, see if you can find out about others!

LODGING

GLEN SANDERS MANSION
One Glen Ave., Scotia, NY 12302
518-374-7262; www.glensanders
mansion.com
Alexander Glen built his original home in 1658, then another and added on rooms to the second building. 22 guest rooms.

RESTAURANTS

GLEN SANDERS MANSION
One Glen Ave., Scotia, NY 12302
518-374-7262; www.glensanders
mansion.com
The restaurant offers a Continental menu.

EVENTS

September: The annual Stockade walkabout includes tours of historic homes, churches, and public buildings, plus Waterfront Faire activities; 518-377-9430; www.historicstockade.com

INFORMATION

CHAMBER OF SCHENECTADY COUNTY
800-962-8007, 518-372-5656;
www.sayschenectady.org

SARATOGA COUNTY

Just north of the Capital District lies Saratoga County, the scene of epochal events of the Revolutionary War. Violet Dunn wrote about the name in *Saratoga County Heritage:* "The fruitful hunting ground of the Iroquois Indians was called Sarachtogue, 'hillside of a great river' and 'place of the swift water.'"

Called the Carrying Place, the valleys where the Hudson River and the watershed of Lake George and Champlain meet was an early commercial and military highway. Explorers and traders passed through, and military campaigns crossed and recrossed. Many historians regard the Battle of Saratoga in 1777—actually two separate engagements—when General Burgoyne's army was defeated, as the turning point of the Revolution.

SARATOGA SPRINGS

Less than 10 miles west of the Saratoga battlefield is Saratoga Springs, the "Queen of the Spas," located on top of a liquid gold mine. During the glacial era streams deep in the earth picked up minerals that formed natural gases, which escaped in the form of springs and geysers. Iroquois Indians joined the forest animals in drinking from these bubbling, saline sources because they believed the waters had powerful medicinal effects. In 1767 the Iroquois carried Sir William Johnson, the British superintendent of Indian affairs, on a litter to Saratoga to cure his gout with the miraculous waters.

General Philip Schuyler made a road from his home in Schuylerville to High Rock Spring here. He pitched a tent and stayed several weeks. The next year he built a house for his family, and they used it as a summer place.

George Washington was another who visited Saratoga Springs to partake of the waters. In 1783, while Washington was waiting for the peace treaty, General Schuyler took him to High Rock Spring. Washington wanted to buy land there, but it was not available.

In 1787 Alexander Bryan built a house, and in the early 1800s he erected another stone and rough log house, which still stands today. It is now a restaurant called the Olde Bryan Inn.

Bryan came with his parents from Acadia, in Nova Scotia. They were one of the families in the "dispersion" forcibly carried out by the British. If you have read Longfellow's *Evangeline,* you will remember the story. The residents refused to sign allegiance to the King of England, and so the men and boys were herded into the church, then marched to waiting ships that took them away. The women and girls, as well as old people and children, were left to fend for themselves and later sailed on other ships. Many of them never saw their loved ones again.

Bryan's tavern was the meeting place for both sides during the Revolution. He was very skillful in receiving confidences and, as a Patriot, divulging them privately when necessary.

As the waters continued to bring visitors to Saratoga Springs in the 19th century, it became a fashionable resort for the wealthy with other entertainments, especially horse racing and gambling. Its flat track is the oldest venue for thoroughbreds in the country and the home of the National Museum of Racing. In the 20th century Skidmore College was founded, Saratoga Spa State Park was built, and the Saratoga Performing Arts Center was created. For the past several decades the town has boomed, regaining some of its old elegance and attracting many new residents. Today in Saratoga Springs you can drink the water from one of several fountains, buy bottled mineral water, or bathe in one of the bathhouses that are open to the public. Take it from us—the baths will relax you to the utmost.

Architecture in Saratoga Springs ranges from the Greek revival of the early 1800s, through the Gothic revival of 1830 to 1855, to the Victorian.

HISTORICAL SITES *and* MUSEUMS

Saratoga Springs Visitor Center (518-587-3241; www.saratoga.org), 297 Broadway. Open year-round, daily. Located in a trolley station for the Hudson Valley Railroad, the visitor center has arched windows and columns that provide a neoclassical touch. If you are here in the spring, the flowering trees in front provide color and fragrance. At one time trolleys ran to Glens Falls, Schenectady, and Kaydeross Park at Saratoga Lake, and around the east side of Saratoga. Brass chandeliers, chestnut seats, and the trolley platform remain. On the facade two bas-relief murals show the surrender of General Burgoyne in 1777 and Sir William Johnson at High Rock Spring.

By 1941 the name "Drink Hall" was a reality, as the state offered a choice of bottled mineral water. For ideal results one should imbibe Hawthorn in the morning, Coesa before dinner, and Geyser during the evening.

New York State Military Museum (518-226-0991; www.dmna.state.ny.us), 61 Lake Ave. Open Tue.–Sun. This new museum has a permanent exhibit entitled "Battleground for Freedom—New York during the Revolutionary War." Well over a hundred military engagements occurred on New York soil, more than in any other state. Displays feature Continental uniforms, muskets, swords, and other military pieces.

Sir William Johnson took the Indians' advice and tried the Saratoga Springs waters for his gout.

LODGING

THE ADELPHI HOTEL
365 Broadway, Saratoga Springs, NY 12866
800-860-4086, 518-587-4688; www.adelphihotel.com
Built in 1877, the Adelphi was part of the social life of the summer season in Saratoga. 39 guest rooms.

BATCHELLER MANSION INN
20 Circular St., Saratoga Springs, NY 12866
800-616-7012, 518-584-7012; www.batchellermansioninn.com
George Batcheller built this high-Victorian home in 1873. 9 guest rooms.

GIDEON PUTNAM HOTEL
24 Gideon Putnam Rd., Saratoga Springs, NY 12866
800-732-1560, 518-584-3000; www.gideonputnam.com
This 1930 building is in Saratoga Spa State Park. It is very popular for Sunday brunch. 120 guest rooms.

LONGFELLOWS HOTEL
500 Union Ave., Saratoga Springs, NY 12866
518-587-0108; www.longfellows.com
This inn, conference center, and restaurant was created from two 1915 dairy barns. 50 guest rooms.

UNION GABLES
55 Union Ave., Saratoga Springs, NY 12866
800-398-1558, 518-584-1558; www.uniongables.com
This Queen Anne mansion from 1901 was recently restored. 11 guest rooms.

RESTAURANTS

HATTIE'S
45 Phila St., Saratoga Springs, NY 12866
518-584-4790; www.hattiesrestaurant.com
Established in 1938, Hattie's is a local institution, serving southern cuisine.

LILLIAN'S
408 Broadway, Saratoga Springs, NY 12866
518-587-7766; www.lilliansrestaurant.com
Named for actress Lillian Russell, who summered in Saratoga, this restaurant is downtown.

LONGFELLOWS
500 Union Ave., Saratoga Springs, NY 12866
518-587-0108; www.longfellows.com
Dining is enhanced by fireplaces and an indoor waterfall.

OLDE BRYAN INN
123 Maple Ave., Saratoga Springs, NY 12866
518-587-2990; www.oldebryaninn.com
Established in 1773, the tavern and inn here were operated by Revolutionary War hero Alexander Bryan.

EVENTS

May: Heritage Day; 518-587-3241; www.saratoga.org

STILLWATER

HISTORICAL SITES *and* MUSEUMS

One of the key sites to visit for Revolutionary War lore is **Saratoga National Historical Park** (518-664-9821; www.nps.gov/sara) 648 NY 32, about 10 miles southeast of Saratoga Springs and 8 miles south of Schuylerville on US 4. Open

"Corking the bottle" refers to springing a trap to seal the fate of the British army. On October 12 John Stark crossed the river, and the next day he established an encampment in the gap between the river and what is now called Stark's Knob. On October 13 Burgoyne's German troops wrote: "The rebels had now entirely enclosed us, and had placed a post of observation on a height on our right flank . . . [they] had now made an uninterrupted chain of communication around our army."

year-round, daily. The visitor center has a new film, a museum, and a special lecture series available on topics such as "Archaeology at the Saratoga Battlefield." And you can watch 18th-century crafts demonstrated by guides in period costume.

The battles that are regarded as the turning point of the Revolution took place here during the fall of 1777, when American troops under the command of General Horatio Gates forced the surrender of the invading army of General John Burgoyne. Benedict Arnold attacked the British at Freeman's Farm on September 19 and was relieved of his command by Gates, for refusing to wait.

Arnold stayed near his troops, however, and reappeared in his general's uniform on October 7, riding his white horse at the head of his men. His courage enabled the Americans to break through the British lines and take two key redoubts. Arnold fell wounded in one of the assaults. The day became a major defeat for Burgoyne.

Burgoyne's army was demoralized, hungry, and outnumbered. Having lost 1,200 men, Burgoyne retreated to Schuylerville in a downpour, with his troops slogging through the mud.

Burgoyne established his headquarters in the Schuyler house and negotiated a qualified surrender. He insisted on the "Convention of Saratoga," an agreement that allowed his 5,700 remaining men to leave with "honors of war" intact and return to Britain (although Congress reneged on the deal). On October 17 Burgoyne's men stacked their weapons in a meadow along Fish Kill Creek. When news of Burgoyne's defeat arrived in France, it helped sway the decision by the French to join the war on the side of the Americans.

A firsthand account from a document written by Henry Jolly, a member of Colonel Daniel Morgan's rifle regiment (from The Battlements, a publication of the Friends of Saratoga Battlefield, summer 2002): "We then marched out . . . General Arnold moved on with his brave Yankees and attacked the British Grenadiers and drove them from their cannon . . . Colonel Morgan and his riflemen descended like a torrent upon the right wing of the British army and though I believe I have been at least 15 times engaged with the enemy, I have never seen so great a carnage, in so short a time, by the same number of men engaged. . . . I was within a few paces of General Arnold when he fell, his leg broken and his horse killed."

The Neilson farm at Bemis Heights on the Saratoga battlefield in Stillwater.

A visit to the Saratoga National Historical Park brings these events alive. After viewing the film *Something More at Stake,* take a look at the dioramas and the displays of artifacts from the Revolutionary era.

Visitors can take a self-guided tour of the battlefield on foot, by car, by bicycle, or on cross-country skis in winter. Along the route you will see markers for Freeman Farm, the American river fortifications, Chatfield Farm, Barber's wheatfield, the Balcarres redoubt, Breymann's redoubt, and Burgoyne's headquarters.

EVENTS AT SARATOGA NATIONAL HISTORICAL PARK

518-664-9821; www.nps.gov/sara
January: Frost Faire, with snow-tubing the "big hill," horse-drawn carriages, bonfire, refreshments
February: PBS "Liberty's Kids" series with park rangers, free gifts
March: "Remember the Ladies" tea and stories of women at Saratoga
April: Annual March for Parks
May: 18th-century British army "Field Day and Spring Training" encampment
July 4: Reading of Declaration of Independence and citizenship ceremony
July: Children's series—four programs every Thursday at the Schuyler house
August: Noontime concert series every Tuesday
18th-Century Day at General Philip Schuyler House
September: Annual anniversary encampment and Stillwater heritage weekend
October: Candlelight tour of Schuyler house

SCHUYLERVILLE

Schuylerville has been undergoing a renovation on the main street. New businesses have been opening their doors, offering books and gifts.

HISTORICAL SITES *and* MUSEUMS

Visitor Center at Fort Hardy–Schuyler's Canal Park (518-695-4159), 35 Spring St. Open Apr.–Nov., Wed.–Sun. The visitor center is located where the "surrender tree" still stands on the field on which Burgoyne's army laid down its arms. The date was Oct. 17, 1777. Fort Hardy, once on this site, was a supply depot for the upper Hudson and Champlain Valley.

The center has a new exhibit on the siege following the battles of Saratoga. For seven days Burgoyne's beaten troops took refuge in a fortified camp at the siege field. The Americans had about 20,000 men surrounding the fewer than 6,000 British and German troops.

General Philip Schuyler House (518-664-9821; www.nps.gov/sara), US 4, on the southern edge of Schuylerville. Open mid-June–Labor Day, Wed.–Sun. General Schuyler lived in this pleasant estate setting; the original house was burned by the British but rebuilt in 1777 after the victory. Although he and his wife, the former Catherine Van Rensselaer, lived in Albany, he needed a home near Saratoga. Schuyler was a prominent politician, statesman, businessman, and leader. His business interests included logging, farming, milling, and flax production. He transported his goods on his own sloops and a schooner down the Hudson to Albany, and goods from his estate reached as far as the Caribbean.

Apart from its military uses, the house represents a whole era in which military and political figures were primarily attached to the cultivation of land and rural peace. Schuyler wrote, "My hobby horse has long been a country life; I dismounted once with reluctance, and now saddle him again with a very considerable share of satisfaction, and hope to canter him on to the end of the journey of life."

The front door lock with its enormous key is one to admire. The front room contains original Schuyler wallpaper. A teacup given by George Washington is displayed. Also Schuyler's cane—he had gout from the age of 15. The dining room features a portrait of Catherine Schuyler. Note the wide chairs—very handy for the wide dresses of the day.

✺ Champlain Canal Tour Boats (518-695-5496, 518-695-5609; www.champlaincanaltours.com), Canal House, On the Towpath, Schuylerville, NY 12871. For the chance to see some of the waterways colonials traveled as well as view the site of the Battle of Saratoga from the river along which Burgoyne marched, take a boat tour. You can choose a tour of several hours, a day, or two days. The vessels cruise back and forth from Waterford to Stillwater to Whitehall.

Saratoga Monument (518-664-0921; www.nps.gov/sara), Burgoyne St. Open Memorial Day–Labor Day. On the hill above Schuylerville a granite obelisk reaches into the sky. It memorializes Burgoyne's surrender. Walk all around the base to observe statues of Gates, Schuyler, and Colonel Daniel Morgan, and an empty niche meant for Benedict Arnold, had he not become a traitor.

Climb 188 steps to a viewing platform at the top. Along the way, on the first two levels, you will see bronze relief tablets on the walls. In addition to the surrender, they illustrate local Revolutionary War scenes such as the murder of Jane McCrae—a celebrated incident that helped rally resistance against Burgoyne's invasion (see below)—and General Schuyler's wife setting fire to fields of grain to keep them from the enemy.

LODGING

THE DOVEGATE INN
184 Broad St., Schuylerville, NY 12871
518-695-3699; www.dovegateinn.com
This Federal-style home on the main street
has been restored. 3 guest rooms.

RESTAURANTS

RANDY'S AT THE DOVEGATE INN
184 Broad St., Schuylerville, NY 12871
518-695-6095; www.dovegateinn.com
This popular restaurant serves traditional
American cuisine with an international
influence for lunch and dinner. Reservations are appreciated.

INFORMATION

SARATOGA COUNTY CHAMBER OF COMMERCE
28 Clinton St., Saratoga Springs, NY
12866
800-526-8970, 518-584-3255;
www.saratoga.org

SCHUYLERVILLE AREA CHAMBER OF COMMERCE
P.O. Box 19, Schuylerville, NY 12871
518-695-5268; www.schuylervillearea
chamber.org

REGIONAL INFORMATION

800-732-8259, 518-434-1217;
www.capital-saratoga.org

*The Saratoga Monument commemo-
rating the battle stands on a hill above
Schuylerville.*

Washington County

Lying between the east shores of the Hudson River and Lake George and the Vermont border, Washington County is largely pleasant, rolling farmland in the south, with spurs of the Adirondacks and the South Bay of Lake Champlain jutting into its northern section. Filled with attractive old houses that look like they belong in Vermont, it is home to both active dairy farmers and gentleman farmers migrating from the cities.

Fort Edward

A short way down the Hudson from Glens Falls, Fort Edward has been popular with visitors and locals alike who come to revisit the history of the area. The railroad also stops in town on an infrequent schedule.

HISTORICAL SITES *and* MUSEUMS

If you've ever had a yen to become involved in an archaeological dig, you can do it in Fort Edward. Luckily, Rogers Island, the site of the 1755 Fort Lyman, later renamed Fort Edward, was left undisturbed for many years. No one built on the land, and the Hudson River flooded, spreading sand to cover existing foundations. In addition, the river was dredged in the early part of the 20th century, and the dredged material was placed on top of the barracks section of the island. All this helped protect the centuries of remains underground.

In 1991 Dr. David Starbuck began excavation on Rogers Island, offering an

DIGGING *into* HISTORY

Archaeologists, scholars, volunteers, students, and interested people look for digs all over the world, and some people plan their vacations around dig schedules. We've watched them in Europe and the U.S., carefully scraping, sweeping, and straining bits of earth in the hopes of finding something that has lain there for centuries. Grubby hands and clothes are nothing compared to the ecstatic joy on a beaming face of one who has scored.

Why do people take such pleasure in this? A dig site promises to yield something because people have lived there and they leave traces of their lives behind. Their forgotten leavings provide some of the answers to a fascinating puzzle. And there's the challenge of figuring out where to dig, based on research and lucky guesses.

For more information on digs, contact the **Rogers Island Visitor Center** (518-747-3693; www.rogersisland.org), 11 Rogers Island Dr. Open summer, Wed.–Sun. The center offers exhibits on local history through the Revolutionary War.

archaeological field study in the summer. Volunteers sign up from all over the country for the chance to work in this program. Part of the fun of this endeavor is the chance to work with others keenly interested in archaeology, to share experiences and listen to lectures.

When we visited, every square excavated hole had someone in it—scraping with a small trowel into a dustpan, then carefully pouring earth into a bucket for later screening. Gentleness is the answer in a project like this. Any piece that turned up was carefully wrapped in a paper towel, placed in a photo canister, and then into a brown bag. Information for the lab was then written on the bag with black marker: the date, place, quadrants, layer number, trench number, and name.

Look toward the river, past pleasure boats cruising by, to imagine 18th-century soldiers hauling boats out at the "Great Carrying Place." The Hudson loops to the west at Glens Falls, and boats coming upriver that wished to proceed northward had to be pulled out here and portaged overland to Lake George and Lake Champlain.

The barracks area has been allowed to become overgrown to protect artifacts and historical data still preserved underground. British soldiers lived in large barracks as long as 300 feet. Some officers, provincial soldiers, and Rogers' Rangers often lived in small huts.

One of the discovered huts was framed by wooden planks with hand-wrought nails and two fireplaces. Soldiers lost or dropped items in and around the hut: Lead pieces from their bullets, coins, a silver shoe buckle, nails, and stoneware have been found. Outside the hut a valuable "midden" or trash dump yielded all sorts of items such as musket balls, buttons, a Spanish coin, pottery, animal bones, and two pig skulls. In addition, excavators found a Native American layer with arrowheads and spear points that could date back to 2000 BC.

Old maps show a hospital near the end of the island. It is said that 892 men were placed there to die of smallpox. Duncan Campbell of the Black Watch regiment was in the hospital—no doubt along with many of his comrades—after he was wounded in the arm on July 8, 1758, in Abercrombie's futile attack at Ticonderoga. He died on July 17 and is now buried in Union Cemetery in Fort Edward. He lies next to Jane McCrea, who was scalped near Fort Edward on July 26, 1777, while on her way to meet her fiancé, a British officer.

The Fort Edward Historical Association is located in **Old Fort House Museum** (518-747-9600; www.oldforthouse.com), 29 Broadway. Open June 1–Labor Day, daily; Sep.–Oct., Tue.-Sun. The museum has a collection of books containing information on Jane McCrea, a piece of her shawl, a number of objects made from the wood of the tree near where she died, an 1834 print of her scalping, and a large painting of the scene of her death. Dr. Asa Fitch collected information on Jane McCrea from a number of settlers in the area.

The Old Fort House dates from 1772 and is one of the oldest frame buildings in this area. During the Revolutionary War both sides used the house as a headquarters. Benedict Arnold, Henry Knox, and John Burgoyne all lived in the house

The MURDER of JANE McCREA

✳ There are many accounts of the death of Jane McCrea, who lived with her brother John McCrea on the west bank of the river several miles below Fort Edward. She was engaged to a Loyalist officer, David Jones, who was serving with Burgoyne's approaching army. In hopes of joining him at the British camp, she went to the home of a Mrs. McNeil. Some say that the two ladies were sewing outside near the house when a group of American soldiers approached, then musket shots were heard, and the Americans ran by with Indians right behind them.

The women went into the house and down a trap door into the cellar, along with a young man. Indians raised the trap door and hauled everyone out by their hair. Jane was placed on a horse (sent for her from David Jones) by Indians who thought they would get a reward for bringing her to the camp. Another group of Indians came along, and in a tussle over the bridle of her horse one of the Indians shot her. Several accounts say that she was scalped and left beside a pine tree. It appears that Tories buried Jane and later she was moved to the State Street Cemetery, then to the Union Cemetery.

In spite of the irony that Jane McCrea was trying to join an enemy officer, her death proved to be a powerful recruiting tool for the rebels. As news of her brutal murder spread through the countryside, men flocked to join the American forces that surrounded and defeated Burgoyne at Saratoga.

Modern technology has allowed a team of archaeologists led by Dr. Starbuck to exhume the remains of Jane McCrea and Sarah McNeil, after consultation with living relatives. Each woman was then given a proper burial in her own grave instead of together. Their graves are in Union Cemetery.

at different times, and George Washington had dinner here in July 1783. An entry in a ledger lists his bill at $10.

The Historical Association displays artifacts from the colonial period up to the present day. Pieces from the colonial period were unearthed in the early 1900s by people digging to build their homes. Cases contain spades, hinges, axes, wedges, hooks, iron rings, a claw hammer, various size cannonballs, a bullet mold, buckshot, a French musket, lock flints, a powder horn, a compass case, ice creepers, and more. We were fascinated by the collection of commemorative spoons, including one given by Dr. Little with a pill on the bowl of the spoon.

Baldwin Barn now contains a gallery and gift shop.

EVENTS

September: French and Indian War encampment, Rogers Island Visitor Center, Fort Edward; 518-747-3693; www.rogersisland.org

WHITEHALL

Whitehall was settled in 1759 by Captain Philip Skene and thirty more British families. In his honor it was named Skenesborough. During the Revolution, Skene provided lumber and iron for the construction of boats to delay the British, who were in the process of assembling their own fleet to move down Lake Champlain from Canada. In early 1776 Congress ordered Thomas Gates, Benedict Arnold, and Philip Schuyler to provide vessels for the "Navy." Signs in Whitehall designate the town as the "Birthplace of the U.S. Navy; Arnold's Valcour fleet built in summer of 1776, in Skenesborough Harbor, now Whitehall." Many other places claim the same fame: Machias, Maine; Marblehead, Massachusetts; Beverly, Massachusetts; and Providence, Rhode Island, to name a few.

Today you can take a Carillon Cruise (802-897-5331) from the dock at Skenesborough Museum. Narration on the Revolutionary War and the War of 1812 brings that era to life. Whitehall regained importance as a shipping port with the opening in 1916 of the Champlain Canal, a 63-mile link that created an uninterrupted waterway from New York City to the St. Lawrence River.

HISTORICAL SITES *and* MUSEUMS

Skenesborough Museum (518-499-1155 x0716), Skenesborough Dr. Open mid-Jun.–Labor Day, daily; Labor Day–mid-Oct., Sat.–Sun. You can't miss the museum's main exhibit, a 16-foot diorama of the 1776 shipyard where Arnold directed the building of the fleet. A number of vessels are lined up on the shore, in process of construction. The home and businesses of the founder of Whitehall, Philip Skene, are represented as well.

Head into a larger room, which has a collection of models of ships that were on the lake from 1776 to 1812. Models include Arnold's flagship *Philadelphia,* which was built on this site and raised from the bottom of the lake in 1935; it's now in the Smithsonian in Washington.

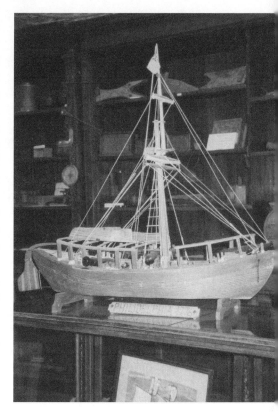

A model of Benedict Arnold's gunboat Philadelphia at the Skenesborough Museum in Whitehall.

There's a boat for children to play in, complete with a carved wooden sailor man-
ning the vessel.

Upstairs is a mannequin of Henry Francisco sitting on a rattan seat. The plac-
ard claims that he lived for 134 years, 4 months, and 25 days. He was born in
France in 1686 and died in Whitehall in 1820. Francisco fought in the Battle of
Saratoga. In 1819 Professor Benjamin Silliman of Yale University arrived in Whitehall to meet the oldest man in America; he wrote about Francisco in his *New England Galaxy.*

INFORMATION

FORT EDWARD CHAMBER OF COMMERCE
P.O. Box 267, Fort Edward, NY 12828
518-747-3000; www.rogersisland.org

LAKES TO LOCKS PASSAGE
814 Bridge Rd., Crown Point, NY 12928
518-597-9660; www.lakestolocks.com

WARREN COUNTY

In 1683 Warren County was part of Albany County. Dr. Joseph Warren, the
county's namesake, was a Patriot killed at the Battle of Bunker Hill in the Revolutionary War. The county includes a variety of topography, ranging from the
Hudson River valley to the southern Adirondacks, as well as all but a tiny fraction
of Lake George. Apart from the city of Glens Falls and the adjoining town of
Queensbury, it lies entirely within the six-million-acre Adirondack Park, a landscape of wooded mountains and clear lakes with scattered settlements.

GLENS FALLS

In 1760 a group of Connecticut residents applied for a land patent along the Upper
Hudson, and in 1762 it was approved and named Queensbury to honor the queen
of England. It was then sold to Abraham Wing and a group of Quakers, who settled there in 1763. George Washington came through the area in 1783 and stopped

at Butler Brook, near Halfway Brook. In 1788 the name of Wing's Falls was changed to Glens Falls for Colonel Johannes Glen, who had a summer cottage near the falls. Some say that he won the title to the city in a poker game.

Glens Falls was named "Chepontuc" by the Indians, which means "a hard place to get around." They had to carry their canoes around the rushing waters of the sixty-foot falls. Cooper's Cave, a setting in James Fenimore Cooper's *The Last of the Mohicans*, is located under the bridge, now called Cooper's Cave Bridge, to South Glens Falls. Cooper made famous a number of fictional characters, including Hawkeye, Chingachgook, and Uncas.

> The story inside the cave: "A spectral-looking figure stalked from out the darkness behind the scout, and seizing a blazing brand, held it towards the farther extremity of their place of retreat. Alice uttered a faint shriek, and even Cora rose to her feet, as this appalling object moved into the light, but a single word from Heyward calmed them, with the assurance it was only their attendant, Chingachgook . . ."

A viewing platform for the cave has recently opened at the South Glens Falls end of the bridge. Friends remember going into the cave when they were youngsters, but that is not possible now.

Today Glens Falls is a pleasant city with a large park for recreation. Its downtown is being revitalized with shops, restaurants, and condominiums. Because it prospered as a lumbering and paper milling center during the 19th century, it has many fine homes, a major hospital, and important cultural institutions, including the renowned Hyde Collection.

HISTORICAL SITES *and* MUSEUMS

The **Warren County Historical Society** (518-743-0734; www.warrencounty historicalsociety.org), 195 Sunnyside Rd., Queensbury, NY 12804. Open Tue. and Thu., or by appointment. Glass showcases exhibit material on the French and Indian War, along with artifacts such as a tomahawk and cannonball. The society offers a lecture series on current topics. Its members are celebrating the 250th anniversary of the French and Indian War (1754–63.)

The **Hyde Collection** (518-792-1761; www.hydecollection.org), 161 Warren St. Open Tue.–Sun. The original building, once the home of Louis and Charlotte Hyde, looks like a 17th-century Florentine villa. Like their friend Isabella Stewart Gardner in Boston, the Hydes traveled widely in Europe and built their home to house collections of furniture and art. The museum's collection includes a number of European and American masters from the 16th, 17th, and 18th centuries. A 1989 addition expanded gallery space for contemporary exhibits, concerts, and programs. A favorite exhibit recently was a collection of original paintings featuring Lake George.

The **Chapman Historical Museum** (518-793-2826; www.chapmanmuseum

HEARTLAND *of the* IROQUOIS

One evening at the Warren County Historical Society we were treated to lectures by reenactors dressed in Indian clothing and armed with clubs, tomahawks, and guns. Indians were excellent woodsmen who taught the rangers how to live and fight in the woods. Michael Dickinson, a Mohican reenactor, spoke of the need to preserve Native American culture. Gary Roberts, an Iroquoian reenactor, described each tribe in the Iroquois federation, beginning with the Mohawks, called the Keepers of the Eastern Door; the Senecas were Keepers of the Western Door. In between these tribes lived the Oneida, Onondaga, and the Cayugas. It was a matrilineal society that revered the clan mother, who selected the chiefs. Women owned the fields and the longhouse. Information was passed down the generations orally, and games trained the mind to remember. Wampum carried words—a message would be woven into a belt. It was not used for money by the Indians, but was by the Dutch traders.

.org), 348 Glen St. Open Tue.–Sat. The museum offers local-history exhibits as well as an extensive collection of Seneca Ray Stoddard's photographs. Stoddard was a prolific photographer and writer whose work created interest in the Adirondacks and helped lead to the founding of the Adirondack Park. The Victorian DeLong House has been restored and decorated in the period. History exhibits are featured in two galleries. The gift shop offers quality items for sale.

Cooper's Cave (518-793-1455; www.cityofglensfalls.com), south end of the Cooper's Cave Bridge, River St. in South Glens Falls. James Fenimore Cooper's novel *The Last of the Mohicans* described the cave as a hiding place. There is a sign directing you to the parking lot. Walk down a ramp to the observation deck. You can see the entrance to the cave but cannot go inside. (A painting in the lobby of the Queensbury Hotel in town will give you an idea of what it looks like inside.) There are a number of historical panels to read on the deck.

LODGING

MANOR INN
514 Glen St., Glens Falls, NY 12801
518-793-2699; www.the-manor-inn.net
The home is decorated with family heirlooms. 4 guest rooms.

QUEENSBURY HOTEL
88 Ridge St., Glens Falls, NY 12801
800-554-4526, 518-792-1122;
www.queensburyhotel.com
In downtown Glens Fall across from the park. Don't miss the painting in the lobby of Cooper's Cave from *The Last of the Mohicans*. 125 guest rooms.

RESTAURANTS

AIMIE'S DINNER & MOVIE
190 Glen St., Glens Falls, NY 12801
518-792-8181; www.aimiesdinnerand
movie.com
Watch a movie while enjoying dinner.

DAVIDSON BROTHERS
184 Glen St., Glens Falls, NY 12801
518-743-9026; www.davidsonbrothers
.com
This microbrewery offers pub fare.

GARDEN ON THE PARK
88 Ridge St., Glens Falls, NY 12801
518-792-1121; www.queensbury
hotel.com
This restaurant is in the Queensbury Hotel.

FIDDLEHEADS
21 Ridge St., Glens Falls, NY 12801
518-793-5789
The owner-chef prepares upscale cuisine.

THE ADIRONDACKS

A six-million-acre area of mountains interspersed with lakes, the Adirondacks were once in danger of being spoiled by reckless clear-cutting as lumber and paper mills harvested increasing quantities of timber. But because the Adirondacks had also become a prime tourist area after the Civil War, these practices were opposed by wilderness guides and hoteliers in the villages. Seneca Ray Stoddard, a guidebook writer and leading American photographer in the 1880s and 1890s, devoted much of his work to Adirondack landscapes. His lantern slide lecture to the New York Assembly on February 25, 1892, supported legislation that created the Adirondack Park two months later.

LAKE GEORGE

James Caldwell was the founder of what is now the town of Lake George. He received 1,595 acres because of his role in the Revolutionary War. Caldwell brought his family from Albany in 1787 and settled here. From a forest the area became a hamlet and finally a resort. The town of Caldwell was incorporated in March 1810. In 1903 Caldwell became a village, and in 1962 the name was changed to Lake George.

Although the town is now a popular tourist destination full of shops and restaurants, those of us who live here savor the lake and striking views from all sides. The lake is 32 miles long, 1 to 3 miles wide, and reaches depths of 200 feet; it is surrounded by mountains that rise as much as 2,000 feet above the water on both shores. Its extraordinary beauty is enhanced by 172 islands, many of them up in the "narrows" where people can come by boat and camp on attractive sites. Long before lake conservation became accepted, the Lake George Association was founded in 1885 to preserve the lake's clear waters and protect its shores, and many residents still use the water for drinking.

The lake has long been popular as a summer resort, with many hotels and mansions. Over the years, many have burned down. The Sagamore Hotel in Bolton opened in 1883, burned, and its successor was completed in 1894. In 1914 it

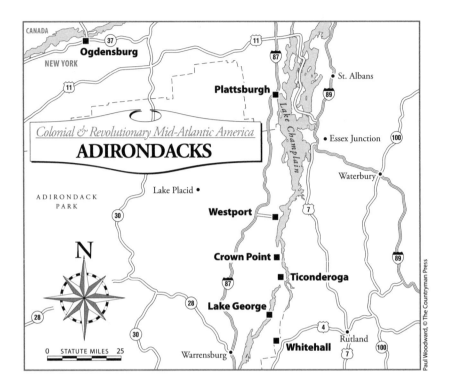

burned again, and the current structure rose in 1930. It has been renovated several times and is a grand hotel again.

A number of mansions sat on the western shore, which was dubbed "Millionaires Row." A few still stand, and some of the docks and boathouses remain. Steamboats were a means of transportation, and many of them now sit on the bottom of the lake.

Lake TOURS

You can still take lake tours and hear some of the stories of the old days by cruising on modern vessels: **Lake George Shoreline Cruises** (518-668-4644; www.lakegeorgeshoreline.com); **Lake George Steamboat Company** (518-668-5777; www.lake georgesteamboat.com); the **Morgan at the Sagamore** (518-644-9400; www.sagamore.com). Van tours of the area are also available. Call **Overlook Tours Inc.** (518-793-9290; www.overlooktours .com)

BATTLE OF LAKE GEORGE

The Battle of Lake George was the only British-American victory of 1755. Both the British and the French wanted control of the water route to Canada. General William Johnson arrived in late August at the southern end of the lake that the French had named St. Sacrement—which he promptly renamed Lake George, in honor of his king. On September 8 a large party of Johnson's men was ambushed during what became known as the Bloody Morning Scout. Both King Hendrick, the chief of a Mohawk group allied with the English, and Colonel Ephraim Williams, leading Johnson's troops, died. The French pursued the survivors and pressed the attack against Johnson's main army, but the provincials managed to repulse them. The French commander, Baron Dieskau, was severely wounded and captured.

Some of the stunning bronze monuments in Battlefied Park (see below) were recently rededicated. The Johnson/Hendrick monument depicts King Hendrick showing William Johnson that he should not divide his troops before the battle. Hendrick is giving Johnson arrows bunched together to signify strength in numbers.

Another monument shows an Indian drinking from a spring; it is a memorial to the Indians who once freely roamed the region. As many as fifty Native American tribes fought in the August 1757 siege of Fort William Henry, later built on the site. A replica of the fort stands there today.

A new obelisk honoring Ephraim Williams, who was killed on the Bloody Morning Scout, has been installed on US 9 near Bloody Pond. Williams was a benefactor of Williams College, in Williamstown in northwestern Massachusetts.

The 250th anniversary reenactment of the Battle of Lake George took place on September 16–18, 2005. We were free to wander through the camps and speak with reenactors about their camp life in the 1750s. All were in period dress, and they were busy preparing meals, making garments, cleaning guns, and playing 18th-century music. The battle was staged on two days at 2 P.M.

French and Indian War reenactors restage the Battle of Lake George.

Bloody Pond is so named because two hundred French Canadians and Indians were killed there and thrown into the water after being ambushed by colonists on their way to aid the forces at Lake George late on the day of the battle.

FORT GEORGE

HISTORICAL SITES *and* MUSEUMS

As the mist rolled into the head of Lake George, we peered into the fog rising from the water as if we were looking for a French bateau or Indian canoe to emerge. Walking for a couple of miles along the waterfront and into the **Lake George Battlefield Park** in the early morning makes the varied past of this magnificent lake come alive.

You can also imagine it easily while hiking the Tongue Mountain Trail or sailing through the wilderness area of the lake at night during the annual Ticonderoga Race. The spectacular topography around the lake is matched by an extremely varied and interesting human history. Physical reminders of that history remain, both in objects along the shore and in sunken bateaux and wrecked steamboats on the bottom. All you need is an observant eye to fire your imagination.

General Jeffrey Amherst began work on **Fort George** in 1759 and completed two or three acres of foundation within three weeks. A provincial officer reported that a month later "the Walls [are] about 14 Feet thick Built of Stone & Lime." In 1767 someone reported that Fort George was a "redoubt amounting to 12 guns, about 200 yards from shore, and some barracks." Although more work was done during the Revolutionary War, only one bastion was ever completed.

Fort George is located on high ground and is now buried in the woods that have overgrown the cleared land in Lake George Battlefield Park. The stones from the fortifications remain today, and visitors can clamber up the high side and look out over the park. (Please don't move or remove any of the stones, as this is a historic site for everyone to enjoy.)

During the 1760s Fort George was used as an artillery depot. The radeau *Invincible* (a radeau was a kind of fortified raft) carried munitions to Fort George. Troops and provisions rode on the *Snow Shoe,* a large vessel to transport soldiers.

In July of 1775 Philip Schuyler came to Fort George, where he was shocked to find the garrison in disorder. He cleaned it up and set regulations before leaving for Ticonderoga, which had been seized by Ethan Allen and Benedict Arnold in the opening weeks of the Revolution. Schuyler also built vessels on Lake George to be used during the invasion into Canada as well as to defend the lakes against British invasion.

Fort George again saw action in 1780 as a British and Indian raiding force under Major Christopher Carleton took Fort Ann, 10 miles to the east, raided Saratoga, and then came north again to the Fort Edward–Fort George military road. Captain John Chipman and 60 Vermonters held Fort George until they heard reports of Indian snipers near Bloody Pond, whereupon Captain Thomas Sill and 48 men went out after them. They ran right into Carleton's men, who fired upon them, and only 13 escaped. With just 25 men left to stand against more than 10 times as many in Carleton's force, Chipman was forced to surrender the fort, which was then burned. Carleton proceeded to collect all the boats he could find. He loaded them with cannon and as many prisoners as he could cram aboard, and the rest had to walk north along Rogers' Road.

FORT WILLIAM HENRY

Fort William Henry (518-668-5471; www.fortwilliamhenry.com), US 9. Open May–Oct. daily. The site of Fort William Henry, on a 50-foot bluff looking up the lake to the narrows, is still one of the most spectacular views in the world. Nomadic tribes passed through the area from 3500 BC on and left some evidence of their residence. Hunters came around 3000 BC and left pointed weapons. Refinements were made in the spears, knives, and other weapons left by people called Laurentians. By 1000 BC the Woodland people used bows and arrows and made earthenware. They had entered the agricultural age and left remains of both corn and beans. Later Indian settlements date from the colonial period, beginning in 1600. Artifacts include a lot of brass pieces and arrows mixed in with artillery from the fort.

Following the Battle of Lake George on September 8, 1755, William Johnson began to build a fort at the head of the lake. Trees were felled to construct walls for

Cannon fire can still be heard at Fort William Henry.

the fort. Soldiers dug powder magazines underground, as well as other rooms for storage. On November 13, 1755, the British flag first flew over the fort, which Johnson named William Henry for King George II's grandson.

Fort William Henry was designed to act as a base for an invasion northward, to take Fort Carillon at Ticonderoga and Fort St. Frédéric at Crown Point. It was also supposed to guard the region between Lake George and the Hudson River to discourage French attack.

The Marquis de Montcalm, the French commander in Canada, moved against the fort in the summer of 1757. Montcalm had a total of 8,000 French regular troops, Canadians, and Indians, who proceeded by boat and on foot down the west side of the lake and laid siege to the fort in August. Colonel George Monro, the fort's commander, failed to receive reinforcements from Fort Edward, and after six days of bombardment chose to surrender. Munro's men had permission to leave with "honors of war," their personal possessions, and head for Fort Edward.

What happened next, the infamous massacre of Lake George, has been detailed by both sides. Rum may have been at the heart of the matter, but what the Indians were really thinking is conjectural. Several historians feel that they resented being told to obey orders as slaves rather than being consulted before the siege. They were also eager to capture prisoners and to take what they could for themselves. They felt they had a right to pillage the fort and the entrenched camp. After all, they had paddled a thousand miles to fight for trophies that were their only pay.

A war whoop became their signal to attack. Ensign John Mayhem, whose name coincidentally matched the action, called it a "hell whoop" in a poem he wrote seven months later. Munro had been leery of whether Montcalm's Indians would honor the terms of surrender and so ordered that the rum supply be destroyed. However, this was not done, and the Indians helped themselves before they attacked and scalped the wounded lying in their rooms. A French escort had been provided for the surviving women, children, and soldiers as they walked to Fort Edward, but the bloodthirsty Indians attacked them as well, scalping all who could not escape. They forced open locked trunks left by the soldiers and put on British uniforms. Unfortunately for them, they also dug up recent graves in the cemetery to scalp those who had died of smallpox. They later paid the price for their greed. Montcalm, in despair at his inability to control the Indians, set fire to the fort after removing all the artillery from inside and loading it onto boats.

The following year General Abercrombie arrived to build a settlement for his army around the charred site of Fort William Henry, as he prepared to attack Fort Carillon at Ticonderoga. Two decades later, during the Revolution, troops from both sides camped inside the site. In 1783 General George Washington visited

VIEW of 18TH-CENTURY WARFARE

When we visited, a single shot was fired from the 18-pound cannon located on the bastion facing Lake George. Heads swiveled all along Beach Road as the sound reached the shore. We covered ears as we stood near the cannon. An interpreter explained the firing procedure to our group as another guide placed powder down in the barrel. He tamped it down, lit the fuse, and the blast followed in a few seconds. This demonstration is one of the most popular features of the museum.

Men in the 1750s could lose their hearing after repeated doses of cannon firing. Cannons could recoil as much as five feet, requiring a crew of eight to push them back into the port. We also had a chance to see a mobile field cannon, which was moved around on large wheels by the men.

Demonstrations in the Fort William Henry museum bring alive some of the military activity that once was crucial to the fort's survival. The musket fire demonstration was especially instructive, with its rich association of phrases we still use— "lock, stock and barrel," "go off half cocked," and "flash in the pan." The effective range of muskets was anywhere from 150 to 800 yards. Surprisingly, each side used different tactics, which affected their accuracy when firing. The British were used to linear tactics, advancing in a line in their bright red uniforms and concentrating their fire. The colonists, both English and Canadian, and the Indians were more accustomed to firing at objects, such as deer, so perhaps were more likely to hit the mark.

the site. It is said that he shook his head at reminders of the poignant scenes enacted there.

Today, visitors to the reconstructed Fort William Henry will experience the four demonstrations that make it come alive, then wander in the courtyard where there is a well perhaps containing a payroll of gold and silver—or the bodies of soldiers. Who knows? A crypt once held the bones of soldiers, most of them victims of diseases such as smallpox. A number of skeletons that had been displayed for years were reinterred in a respectful ceremony in 1993.

Walk down into the dungeon where soldiers were imprisoned. There is a model of a prisoner in a tiny cell, the pillory, and a guard room. A fireplace from 1755 is still there. A long ramp leads from the courtyard down into the underground powder magazine where kegs of black powder were stored. Curtains of leather were hung there and kept wet to defuse sparks.

The buildings lining the courtyard contain museum exhibits. The James Fenimore Cooper exhibits are in the West Barracks. Walk up the steps to see living areas of soldiers as they were in 1755. The North Barracks and East Barracks house more of the collection. Don't miss a display of illustrator Jack Binder's work; his original paintings here include a collection of military figures from the 1750s.

The **Lake George Historical Association** (518-668-5044; www.lakegeorge historical.org), 290 Canada St. Open mid-May–mid-Oct. Please phone for hours. Dating to 1895, when it was housed in a spare classroom in the Union School building, the museum now resides in the Old Court House and Jail. Historical displays include artifacts collected from the wars fought in this area. Look for the French and Indian War 12-pound cannonball with a fleur-de-lis on it. We were especially fascinated by the stories of historic boats still underwater in Lake George.

The **Lake George Submerged Heritage Preserve** (518-668-3352. This phone number is for the Department of Environmental Conservation dive booth located inside the building at the Million Dollar Beach. Divers need to register in the booth with a current dive card and

A bateau with swivel gun awaits action at Lake George.

advanced certification). DEC offers divers the chance to visit, and not touch, the *Land Tortoise*.

The *Land Tortoise*, a 1758 floating gun battery, was discovered by Joseph Zarzynski and a group that became known as Batteaux Below Inc. The vessel sat on the bottom of the lake for 250 years, preserved by the cold water. It is 52 feet long and can be seen in a 57-minute DVD documentary (a preview is available on the Internet: www.thelostradeau.com). Advanced divers must sign in and be assigned a time slot to dive to the radeau. It is a deep, cold-water dive, and a safety/decompression stop is recommended.

In addition, seven bateaux, the sunken fleet of 1758, were found along the east shore off Wiawaka; they are on the National Register of Historic Places. We asked Joe to dive in our cove, a perfect place to hide bateaux, but none was found.

LODGING

BOATHOUSE B&B
44 Sagamore Rd., Bolton Landing, NY 12814
518-644-2554; www.boathousebb.com
This B&B is really in a boathouse—with a view. It was the summer home of George Reiss, winner and defender of the Gold Cup races held on Lake George in 1933, 1934, and 1935. 7 guest rooms.

CANOE ISLAND LODGE
3820 Lake Shore Dr., Diamond Point, NY 12824
518-668-5592; www.canoeislandlodge.com
This family-run resort is right on the lake. It offers swimming, water-skiing, barbecues on an island, sailing, and tennis. 65 guest rooms.

COPPERFIELD INN
307 Main St., North Creek, NY 12853
800-424-9910, 518-251-2500;
www.copperfieldinn.com
This inn is convenient for both winter and summer sports. 31 guest rooms.

FORT WILLIAM HENRY RESORT
48 Canada St., Lake George, NY 12845
800-234-0267, 518-668-3081;
www.fortwilliamhenry.com
The recently expanded hotel overlooks Lake George. 195 guest rooms.

FERN LODGE
46 Fiddlehead Bay Rd., Chestertown, NY 12817
518-494-7238; www.thefernlodge
Luxury lodgings, Adirondack style. 3 guest rooms.

FRIENDS LAKE INN
963 Friends Lake Rd., Chestertown, NY 12817
518-494-4751; www.friendslake.com
This luxury country inn dates from the 1860s. 17 guest rooms.

GARNET HILL LODGE
13th Lake Rd., North River, NY 12856
518-251-2444; www.garnet-hill.com
Named for the garnet mine nearby, the lodge was built in 1936 as a residence for miners. 30 guest rooms in the lodge and surrounding buildings.

THE LAMPLIGHT INN
231 Lake Ave., Lake Luzerne, NY 12846
800-262-4668, 518-696-5294;
www.lamplightinn.com
The house dates from 1890. The Great
Room has 12-foot beamed ceilings. Additional houses on the property are available
for families or couples. 15 guest rooms.

MERRILL MAGEE HOUSE
3 Hudson St., Warrensburg, NY 12885
888-664-4661, 518-623-2449;
www.merrillmageehouse.com
The 19th-century Greek-revival main
house and additional buildings are set in
gardens and lawns. Don't miss Arabella in
the bathtub! 10 guest rooms.

RUAH B&B
9221 Lake Shore Dr., Hague, NY 12836
800-224-7549, 518-543-8816;
www.ruahbb.com
This 1900 home was built by Henry Waltrous, a prankster who created the Lake
George monster hoax. The house has Victorian furnishings and large windows looking out on the lake and gardens. 4 guest
rooms.

THE SAGAMORE
110 Sagamore Rd., Bolton Landing, NY
12814
866-385-6221, 518-644-9400; www
.thesagamore.com
Opening in 1883, this luxury resort is set
on its own private island and offers sailing,
golf, and other recreation. 350 guest
rooms.

RESTAURANTS

THE ALGONQUIN
4770 Lake Shore Dr., Bolton Landing,
NY 12814
518-644-9442
The Algonquin is right on the lake with
docks available.

THE CHERRY TOMATO
Bay Rd. and NY149, Lake George, NY
12845
518-798-2982; www.thecherrytomato
.com
Italian and American fare with wood-fired
pizza oven.

COPPERFIELD INN
307 Main St., North Creek, NY 12853
518-251-2500; www.copperfieldinn
.com
Trapper's Tavern and Gardens are the two
restaurants at this inn.

EAST COVE
Beach Rd. and NY 9L, Lake George, NY
12845
518-668-5265; www.eastcove.com
Casual dining in a log building; Sunday
brunch is a specialty.

GARNET HILL LODGE
13th Lake Rd., North River, NY12856
518-251-2444; www.garnet-hill.com
A full menu is available in a rustic setting
with view.

INN AT ERLOWEST
3178 Lake Shore Dr., Lake George, NY
12845
518-668-5928; www.theinnaterlowest
.com
Gourmet dining in a 19th-century stone
mansion.

FRIEND'S LAKE INN
963 Friends Lake Rd., Chestertown, NY
12817
518-494-4751; www.friendslake.com
New American cuisine with an award-winning wine list.

GEORGE'S PLACE FOR STEAK & SEAFOOD
3857 NY 9L, Lake George, NY 12845
518-668-5482
Early-bird specials with Tiffany lamps everywhere.

GRIST MILL ON THE SCHROON
100 River St., Warrensburg, NY 12885
518-623-8005; www.menumart.com/gristmill
American cuisine beside a rushing river.

LOG JAM
1484 US 9
Routes 9 & 149, Lake George, NY 12845
518-798-1155; /www.logjamrestaurant.com
A rustic cabin with a great salad bar.

MARIO'S RESTAURANT
429 Canada St., Lake George, NY 12845
518-668-2665; www.marioslakegeorge.com
Italian fare right on the main street.

MERRILL MAGEE HOUSE
3 Hudson St., Warrensburg, NY 12885
518-623-2449; www.merrillmagee house.com
This historic home offers two dining rooms and a tavern featuring "upscale affordable dining."

MONTCALM
1415 US 9, Lake George, NY 12845
518-793-6601; menumart.com/montcalm
Classic American entrees as well as lighter fare, in a log-cabin setting.

RIDGE TERRACE
2172 Ridge Rd., Lake George, NY 12845
518-656-9274
A log cabin restaurant in the pines.

THE SAGAMORE
110 Sagamore Rd., Bolton Landing, NY 12814
518-743-6110; www.thesagamore.com
A number of restaurants here include the Sagamore Dining Room, Mister Brown's Pub, the Club Grill, Trillium bis, the Veranda, and a boat, the *Morgan*.

SHORELINE
2 Kurosaka La., Lake George, NY 12845
518-668-4644; www.lakegeorgeshore line.com
Located right on the water with views of the cruise ships.

A TASTE OF POLAND
375 Canada St., Lake George, NY 12845
518-668-4386
A homey European setting for Polish and American cuisine.

INFORMATION

WARREN COUNTY DEPARTMENT OF TOURISM
1340 US 9, Lake George, NY 12845
800-365-1050, 518-761-6366; www.visitlakegeorge.com

ADIRONDACK REGIONAL CHAMBERS OF COMMERCE
5 Warren St., Glens Falls, NY 12801
888-516-7247, 518-798-1761;
www.adirondackchamber.org

LAKE GEORGE REGIONAL CHAMBER OF COMMERCE
2176 State Route 9, Lake George, NY 12845
800-705-0059, 518-668-5755;
www.lakegeorgechamber.com

Essex County

The name was taken from the English county of Essex. It was originally part of Albany County. Like other counties along Lake George and Lake Champlain, it is rich with Revolutionary history. With the exception of Lake Placid nestled among the high peaks of the Adirondacks, its attractive towns line the western shore of Lake Champlain, originally as working ports and now as tourist destinations. We were at first amused at the designation of part of that shore as the "Adirondack coast" until we drove between Westport and Willsboro and then saw cliffs along the same stretch from the water. Here the mountains do seem to meet the lake.

Ticonderoga

HISTORICAL SITES *and* MUSEUMS
Fort Ticonderoga (518-585-2821; www.fort-ticonderoga.org), 30 Fort Ticonderoga Rd. Open May–Oct. During the early stages of the French and Indian War in 1755, Robert Rogers watched the building of Fort Carillon from a little distance away. Its name may have been a corrupted version of Carrion, a fur trader who served with the French in a small fort at the site in the 1660s. Later, in British hands, the fort was renamed Ticonderoga, the Indian word quite accurately describing "the land between two great waters." In 1757 Rogers and his rangers sneaked within range and managed to kill a number of cattle. He left a note on the horns of one of the cattle: "I am obliged to you, sir, for the repose you have allowed me to take. I thank you for the fresh meat you have sent me. I will take care of my prisoners. I request you to present my compliments to the Marquis de Montcalm."

Montcalm, who had been given command of the French army in Canada the year before, used Ticonderoga as a staging area for his successful attack on Fort William Henry in July 1757.

Smarting from that bitter defeat and its grisly aftermath, the British under General James Abercrombie mounted in July 1758 the largest amphibious operation yet seen in America, with 15,000 troops embarked in 900 bateaux, 135 whaleboats, and 3 small radeaux. The armada proceeded from Fort William Henry, stretching out to six miles. An advance unit led by Major Robert Rogers and George Viscount Howe, the field commander of the invasion, by accident met a French reconnaissance party returning to the fort. In the fighting that followed, Howe was shot through the heart and instantly killed. He had been a favorite among the troops, and his loss disheartened the British and contributed to the blunders in strategy and tactics that followed.

Now faced with a field command he was unprepared for, Abercrombie hesitated for a day and a half, allowing Montcalm to prepare an effective defense on a ridge about a half-mile in front of the fort. It consisted of an abatis of logs eight to nine feet high stretching a third of a mile, with sharpened tree branches pointing toward the enemy. Fearing that replacements would arrive to reinforce Montcalm's

You can still hear the fife and drums at Fort Ticonderoga.

outnumbered 3,000 troops, Abercrombie ordered an immediate attack without bringing up his cannon to breach the abatis, sending wave after wave of troops with muskets and bayonets against the withering fire of sheltered defenders. When the seventh and last assault was repelled early that evening, the British had suffered more than 1,900 casualties against about 400 for the French.

During the assaults, the Black Watch of the 42nd Highlanders were especially tenacious. Some of them pushed their way past the abatis of trees to engage the enemy directly, but 647 were felled by bayonets and bullets. It is said that one courageous piper continued to play after he had lost his leg. The King's Royal Rifle Corps also fought valiantly before Abercrombie belatedly decided to retreat. Montcalm's two successive victories at Fort William Henry and Fort Carillon, at opposite ends of Lake George, marked the apex of French success during the war.

After the debacle, British forces attacked Fort Carillon once more a year later, in July 1759, this time under the command of Lord Jeffery Amherst. His armada had embarked 11,000 troops, split between British regulars and provincials. The French commander of Carillon, General Bourlamaque, had orders from Governor Vaudreuil to abandon the fort and fall back to Crown Point, which he did with 2,600 troops. He left 400 men behind to harass the British advance with artillery fire, delaying them for several days before blowing up the fort. Amherst promptly set about quelling fires and rebuilding the fort to continue his campaign on Lake Champlain.

Between the French and Indian War and the beginning of the Revolution, this strategic fort—now named Ticonderoga—decayed significantly and was only lightly manned by the British. It became a focus of conflict again through a bold stroke by Ethan Allen. He was leader of the Green Mountain Boys, a group of settlers in what is now Vermont who formed initially to protect their land grants from New Hampshire governor Benning Wentworth against counter-claims by New

Yorkers. Allen and his men, joined by Colonel Benedict Arnold of Connecticut, captured Fort Ticonderoga in a surprise raid on May 10, 1775. Because there were few boats, only 83 men and some officers had been ferried across to a site north of the fort by daybreak.

Allen realized that he could not wait for more and so began the charge. "My party who followed me into the fort, I formed on the parade in such a manner as to face the two barracks which faced each other. The garrison being asleep, (except the sentries) we gave three huzzas which greatly surprised them." Allen then ran up the steps and pounded on the door of the commanding officer, Captain Delaplace, ordering him to surrender the fort. A legend claims that he yelled, "Come out, you damned old rat!"

The following November, Colonel Henry Knox led an expedition to retrieve Ticonderoga's guns for use in the siege of Boston. Arriving at the fort in early December, Knox faced a 300-mile journey dragging heavy artillery across thin ice, through deep snow and mud, across mountains, and through unsettled territory, much of it roadless. He arrived outside Boston near the end of January with 58 mortars and cannon. General Washington soon had them in place, and shortly afterward the British abandoned Boston. (Read more about this story in our *Visitor's Guide to Colonial & Revolutionary New England*.)

The fort again played a critical role in stopping Sir Guy Carleton's advance down Lake Champlain in the fall of 1776. Carleton intended to reach Albany and winter there, as part of the British strategy of dividing New England from the rest of the colonies. Carleton had been delayed for much of the summer by the existence of Benedict Arnold's fleet, which he defeated at Valcour Island on October 11; he then faced a different obstacle at Ticonderoga on October 28. Some 13,000 American militiamen had fortified Mount Independence across from Ticonderoga and laid a log boom across this choke point in the lake, just a quarter-mile wide. Given the deteriorating weather and the 18th-century habit of not fighting in winter, Carleton turned back to Canada and began planning the same campaign for the following year.

When a British force of 8,000 men came down the lake the next summer under General John Burgoyne, both Ticonderoga and Mount Independence were much more lightly defended. General Arthur St. Clair had only 2,500 men to control the choke point, and he abandoned Ticonderoga when the British managed to place artillery on the nearby commanding heights of Mount Defiance.

In the years following Burgoyne's ill-fated campaign, Ticonderoga would see visits by a number of prominent patriots, including Washington and Jefferson. Afterward it went into decline, until it was purchased by William Ferris Pell in 1820. He built a summer home, Beaumont, which was destroyed in a fire, then he built the Pavilion in 1826, and it is still there. Stephen Pell played in the fort ruins as a child and found a tinderbox, which he cherished for years and now is a part of the museum collection. The Pell family restored the fort and oversaw the excavation of artifacts. The museum opened in 1909. President Taft, along with the ambassadors of France and England, the governors of New York and Vermont, and other distinguished guests, attended this event.

Excavations at the site have yielded firearms, buttons, pottery, china, cutlery, cannonballs, grapeshot, axes, sword blades, keys, and more. Visitors may walk through the museum and armory to see these artifacts, as well as an impressive collection of arms and uniforms and other military artifacts, including a blunderbuss used by Ethan Allen!

A colorful diorama features the Black Watch at Ticonderoga with their red jackets and kilts. The Black Watch collection includes a sporren, clay pipes, a broadsword, highland pistol, buttons, bagpipe ferules that go around the pipes, and a camp ax. Visitors can also see George Washington's spurs, swords belonging to Israel Putnam, Arthur St. Clair, and Alexander Hamilton, toy soldiers that belonged to Montcalm as a child, and a punch bowl that belonged to Sir William Johnson. An original American flag, possibly made by Betsy Ross, is also there. The library contains letters, diaries, papers, and books from the period.

From the Place d'Armes, or central parade ground, visitors can walk into the cellar of the East Barracks to see two gigantic ovens that once baked bread for the entire fort. The West Barracks contains an armory in its cellar. Guns are displayed within the time periods of their use. Swords are also in the collection.

Activities at the fort include cannon firings, fife and drum performances, reenactments, and a tattoo in the summer. The cannons on display along the south

---

Don't miss the silver bullet with a real history. Sir Henry Clinton had given this hollow bullet with instructions inside to a messenger on his way to Burgoyne. As he was captured, the messenger swallowed the bullet, and he refused to take an emetic until his captors threatened to "rip his bellie" to get it. He disgorged it, swallowed it again, and was forced to disgorge it for the second time. After all of that he was hanged as a spy.

curtain wall include British and French pieces, as well as some late 17th-century and early 18th-century Spanish models. The fort also sponsors conferences, including an annual gathering of French and Indian War scholars.

Be sure to check the daily schedule of events. We have taken our grandchildren several times and have been lucky to enjoy a fife and drum performance with colorful military uniforms on the parade ground.

You can stroll or drive down to the King's Garden, which has taken on new life after lying in ruins for years. In 1755 a garrison garden was planted to feed the troops. It resembled the kind of formal garden the French were familiar with at home and was used during both the French and Indian War and the Revolution. A bronze statue of Diana stands in the center of a pool.

EVENTS

June: Grand encampment of the French and Indian War; 518-585-2821; www.fort-ticonderoga.org
July: Commemoration of the battle of Fort Carillon; 518-585-2821; www.fort-ticonderoga.org
September: Revolutionary war encampment and battle reenactment; 518-585-2821; www.fort-ticonderoga.org

INFORMATION

TICONDEROGA AREA CHAMBER OF COMMERCE
518-585-6619;
www.ticonderogany.com

LAKE CHAMPLAIN VISITORS CENTER
94 Montcalm St., Suite 1
Ticonderoga, NY 12883
518-585-6619; www.lakechamplainregion.com

CROWN POINT

Besides the state historic site, you may want to visit Penfield Homestead Museum, which is beyond our period of time but an interesting museum; it's in the Ironville Historic District (518-597-3804; www.penfieldmuseum.org).

HISTORICAL SITES and MUSEUMS
Crown Point State Historic Site (518-597-3666; www.lakechamplainregion.com), 739 Bridge Rd. Open mid-May–Oct., Wed.–Mon. Crown Point, where Lake Champlain narrows to one-quarter of a mile, was an obvious choke point in the struggle for military control of the waterway. Fort St. Frédéric was built here by the French in 1734. The French razed it before leaving. The British began construction of massive Fort Crown Point in 1759, which they never finished. In 1773 the wooden fort at the site burned down.

The Green Mountain Boys, led by Colonel Seth Warner, captured Crown Point in 1775, lost control, gained the fort back, and finally left for the last time in 1777 as General Burgoyne entered New York.

There are self-guided tours and an orientation film. Take a walk outside and climb up to the bastions for a wonderful view of the lake as well as the fort.

The ruins of the massive British fortress at Crown Point overlook Lake Champlain.

The **Champlain Memorial Lighthouse** (518-597-3603) stands just south of the Champlain Bridge. You can see it when crossing the bridge either way. It dates from 1858 and in 1912 was proclaimed a memorial to Samuel de Champlain. August Rodin created the bas-relief "La Belle France."

EVENTS

August: French and Indian War encampment; 518-597-3666; www.lakechamplain region.com

WESTPORT

The town of Westport has a long history dating back to the colonial era. In 1764 William Gilliland was granted 2,300 acres, which he named Bessboro for his daughter. Edward Raymond built a home here in 1770, then a sawmill and a gristmill. His sawmill produced timber for Benedict Arnold's fleet. The settlement was destroyed in 1777 as British garrisons retreated northward after Burgoyne's defeat at Saratoga.

Land just south of the village was resettled in 1785 by Major Hezekiah Barber, and by 1790 ferries ran across the lake from Rock Harbor to Basin Harbor and from Barber's Point to Arnold's Bay. A decade later John Halstead, heading a group of developers, surveyed the village and built its first house and tavern.

Today you can also attend the Depot Theatre in the restored train station (518-

962-4449; www.depottheatre.org). The *Philomena D* offers boat tours (800-626-0342) on Lake Champlain, a great way to appreciate the rugged cliffs along sections of the western shore.

LODGING

ALL TUCKED INN
53 S. Main St./NY 22, Westport, NY 12993
518-962-4400; alltuckedinn.com
This inn has a very comfortable common room. 9 guest rooms.

INN ON THE LIBRARY LAWN
1234 Stevenson Rd., Westport, NY 12993
888-577-7748, 518-962-8666;
www.theinnonthelibrarylawn.com
This Victorian inn overlooks the lake. 10 guest rooms.

THE VICTORIAN LADY
6447 Main St., Westport, NY 12993
877-829-7128; 518-962-2345
An elegant setting with modern conveniences. 5 rooms.

WESTPORT HOTEL
6691 Main St., Westport, NY 12993
518-962-4501; www.thewestport hotel.com
This hotel has stenciled walls and a popular dining room. 10 guest rooms.

LAKE PLACID

A diversion inland between Westport and Plattsburgh will take you to Lake Placid. It is off our historical itinerary but offers much to do and see, including all the Olympic sites.

LODGING

LAKE PLACID LODGE
Whiteface Inn Rd., Lake Placid, NY 12946
877-523-2700; 518-523-2700;
www.lakeplacidlodge.com
This inn, dating to 1895, was once an Adirondack camp. Renovations after a disastrous fire currently include 12 cabins and a dining room; the main building is scheduled to reopen for 2008.

MIRROR LAKE INN
5 Mirror Lake Dr., Lake Placid, NY 12946
518-523-2544; www.mirrorlakeinn.com
In January 1988 a fire destroyed the entire 105-year-old main building; an 1895 grandfather clock and the grand piano were saved from the fire to grace the new building. 128 guest rooms.

CLINTON COUNTY

The Battle of Valcour Island began offshore, a few miles below the present-day site of Plattsburgh, on Oct. 11, 1776, with an aftermath trailing down Lake Champlain for several days. The Americans were under the command of Benedict Arnold, who had built his little navy in Whitehall, at the head of the lake, during the summer. They were clearly outnumbered and outgunned when the British fleet sailed into Valcour Bay, and Arnold's small fleet suffered both heavy damage and many casualties.

At the end of the day the American officers agreed to retreat to Crown Point, and Arnold managed to slip his surviving vessels along the shoreline past the British line in dense fog. Although most of the fleet was later destroyed or abandoned, this holding action prevented the British from moving down the lake, part of their strategy of splitting New England from the rest of the colonies.

PLATTSBURGH

Plattsburgh was settled shortly after the Revolution, in 1785, by Zephaniah Platt. This settlement played a key role in defending American territory as a British fleet moved into Lake Champlain during the War of 1812. Although it is not clear that the British wanted to repeat the invasion strategy down the lake of previous wars, they did intend to establish a base at Plattsburgh for naval control of the lake. Just as there was a shipbuilding race on Lake Ontario by the British at Kingston and the Americans at Sackets Harbor, another occurred as both sides hurriedly built fleets in shipyards at Ile aux Noix and Vergennes. The two fleets would meet on September 11, 1814—after negotiations to end the war had already started in Ghent—in the largest and bloodiest naval action ever fought on Lake Champlain.

On that morning two evenly matched fleets led by Master Commandant Thomas MacDonough on board the 143-foot *Saratoga* and Captain George Downie on board the 146-foot *Confiance* pounded away at each other at close range, causing enormous damage and 110 American and 170 British casualties. Downie was killed and the *Confiance* eventually surrendered. The Battle of Plattsburgh Bay was a major setback for the British.

In the 20th century Plattsburgh

The Lake Champlain Maritime Museum has been working for some time to map the underwater artifact scatter at the site of the Battle of Valcour Island. In 2006, 100 Revolutionary War artifacts were recovered. They include shot, shells, eyeglasses, and a small sword. To date over 227,500 square feet of the battlefield have been explored. In 1997, during a side-scan survey of the lake bottom, Art Cohn, director of the museum, discovered the wreck of the gondola *Spitfire*, sitting upright on the bottom in excellent condition.

A mural in City Hall features a rooster standing on a cannon. A British shot shattered a chicken coop on the deck of the *Saratoga,* freeing a gamecock that jumped up on a gun, clapped its wings, and crowed lustily. The men on board laughed and cheered, and then Macdonough fired the first American shot from one of the long guns and the battle was joined. The rooster standing on a cannon was seen as a good omen for American success.

was home to an Air Force base, the closure of which caused great apprehension, although the buildings have since been put to good use for museums and housing. You can take the *Spirit of Plattsburgh* for a scenic tour on Lake Champlain (518-566-7447; www.soea.com).

HISTORICAL SITES *and* MUSEUMS

Battle of Plattsburgh Association (518-566-1814; www.battleofplattsburgh.org), 31 Washington Rd. Open Tue.–Sat. You can light up some of the action of the Battle of Plattsburgh with buttons in a large diorama. There is a model of the *Saratoga,* a full-rigged ship of 143 feet overall, 35 feet in beam, and a shallow draft for versatility in lake waters. Commodore Thomas Macdonough commanded her in the battle. The association has received a drum that was used in the battle.

Clinton County Historical Museum (518-561-0340; www.clintoncounty historical.org), 3 Cumberland Ave. Open Tue.–Fri. Both the 1814 Battle of Plattsburgh and the 1776 Battle of Valcour Island are featured military exhibits. Walking sticks made from the salvaged timbers of the *Royal Savage,* which burned off Valcour Island, are on display. The museum will be moving to the former Air Force base in the near future.

Kent-Delord House (518-561-1035), 17 Cumberland Ave. Open May–Dec., Tue.–Sat., noon–4. The 1797 house was taken over by British officers before the 1814 battle but is more memorable as an index of the region's social history. The British left behind an oak tea chest, and it remained in the possession of the family until a Delord granddaughter, Fanny, died in 1913.

LODGING

POINT AU ROCHE LODGE AND B&B
463 Point Au Roche Rd., Plattsburgh, NY 12901
518-563-8714; www.pointauroche lodge.com
This property is next to Point Roche State Park, where there are 12 miles of hiking trails and a beach. 8 guest rooms.

THE INN AT SMITHFIELD
446 SR 3, Plattsburgh, NY 12901
800-243-4656 or 518-561-7750;
www.bestwestern.com
The inn is just off of the highway and convenient to downtown Plattsburgh. There is an indoor heated pool. 118 guest rooms.

The 1797 Kent-Delord House in Plattsburgh.

RESTAURANTS

ANTHONY'S RESTAURANT & BISTRO
NY 3, Plattsburgh, NY 12901
518-561-6420
This 150-year-old farmhouse is the setting for a variety of cuisine including Continental and American.

BUTCHER BLOCK STEAK & SEAFOOD
15 Booth Dr., Plattsburgh, NY 12901
518-563-0920
The restaurant is rustic, and the name describes the food.

EVENTS

September: The Battle of Plattsburgh; 518-563-4375; www.battleofplatts burgh.com

INFORMATION

PLATTSBURGH NORTH COUNTRY CHAMBER OF COMMERCE
7061 US 9, Plattsburgh, NY 12901
518-563-1000; www.northcountry chamber.com

OGDENSBURG

Ogdensburg, in St. Lawrence County, is on the St. Lawrence River in far north–central New York. You can't miss the Ogdensburg-Prescott International Bridge, which arches 125 feet above the river at the center.

A French fort, La Présentation (315-393-3620; www.fortlapresentation.net), Light House Point, was founded in 1749 by Abbé François Picquet. It was also a mission, trading post, and school. The location, on the point of land where the Oswegatchie River joins the St. Lawrence, was to provide a barrier preventing English access to the St. Lawrence River, as well as a base from which to raid English settlements in New York and Pennsylvania. The fort was destroyed by the time the British occupied the site in 1760. They built Fort Oswegatchie on the ruins of La Présentation, which was turned over to Samuel Ogden in 1796. In 1817 the settlement was incorporated as Ogdensburgh.

Plaques give visitors the story of Ogdensburg's early history. A legal battle has forced Exxon to clean up the contaminated area on the site of Fort La Présentation by early 2007. Drawings are in the works for a replica fort, which should be finished by 2010.

The **Frederic Remington Art Museum** (315-393-2425; www.fredericrem ington.org.), 303 Washington St. Open May–Oct., Mon.–Sun. This museum is beyond our era but is well worth a trip from anywhere. Original sculpture and paintings are on display. The priceless collection includes bronzes, watercolors, oil paintings, and many sketches. Mementos from Remington's travels also are here. Remington lived on Hamilton Street for eight years and grew up during the time when horses were used all over town—carriage horses, work horses, racing horses, saddle horses, and fire horses. No wonder he chose to draw and sculpt horses. You will also see his tools and pieces from his home.

EVENTS

July: Founder's Day Weekend, Fort La Présentation; 315-393-3620; www.fortlapresentation.net

INFORMATION

Ogdensburg Chamber of Commerce, 315-393-3620

CENTRAL LEATHERSTOCKING REGION

Sometimes regarded as the heartland of New York State, the Mohawk Valley was the site of French and Indian War activity and nearly 100 battles during the Revolution. These historic sites remind future generations that our liberty did not come easily but was achieved by the raw courage of our ancestors, who were often isolated in remote areas. As you travel you will be in the footsteps of men of both Loyalist and Patriot persuasions, Mohawks and Oneidas, as well as Palatine German, Dutch, and Highland Scots settlers. Joseph Brant, a Mohawk sachem who had been befriended by Sir William Johnson, and other Loyalists conducted raids on Patriot villages, towns, and farms in the Mohawk Valley from 1775 to 1781. To retaliate against this constant harassment, Washington dispatched General John Sullivan with 4,000 troops to destroy the villages of the Six Nations (apart from the Oneidas, who had sided with the Americans) in 1779.

The Mohawk River begins just north of Rome and cuts a path through the Allegheny Plateau. During the colonial and Revolutionary eras, the Oswego River, Oneida Lake, and the Mohawk River provided a water route from Lake Ontario to the Hudson River, with a portage at Fort Stanwix (Rome). Later the Erie Canal was built along the route (now part of the New York Canal System), connecting Lake Erie with the Hudson River at Cohoes.

Mohawk Indians lived here as "Keepers of the Eastern Door." These aggressive members of the Iroquois confederacy occupied the central part of New York State, eastward to the vicinity of Lakes Champlain and George. Many of them prospered by farming their fertile land.

Hiawatha, a 16th-century Mohawk chief, was a founder of the Iroquois confederacy. The five original nations of the confederacy—Mohawks, Oneidas, Onondagas, Cayugas, and Senecas—raised corn, tobacco, and vegetables. (The Tuscaroras later joined the confederacy, making it the Six Nations.) They also made sugar and syrup from maple trees.

As fur trade grew, the Mohawk Valley absorbed increasing numbers of men transporting pelts by canoes, bateaux, and barges. German settlers arrived in the 1720s, building sturdy stone houses as a deterrent against fire during Indian raids. In 1755, at the outset of the French and Indian War, the British built a series of forts to control activity along the crucial route.

In the summer of 1777, following an abortive invasion down Lake Champlain the previous year, the British again tried to stop the American rebellion by separating New England from the rest of the colonies. Their plan was to capture the Mohawk and Hudson-Champlain waterways. Burgoyne came south from Canada and Barry St. Leger marched eastward from Lake Ontario, while Howe was to come north along the Hudson. The plan went awry when Burgoyne was defeated at Saratoga and St. Leger was turned back at Fort Stanwix, and Howe moved in another direction to engage Washington in Pennsylvania. During St. Leger's offensive, the British and Loyalists struck out against Patriots in the Mohawk Valley, many of whom were killed or driven out as refugees.

The 1784 Treaty of Fort Stanwix changed the valley for the next two hundred years. Patriots benefited from extensive land redistribution.

Dutch, German, and British settlers had arrived in this area during the early 1700s. "The Noses" is the place where there is a natural break in the Appalachian Mountains. This area provided an important east-west axis for travel during the colonial and Revolutionary eras and afterward.

FORT JOHNSON

Sir William Johnson, one of the most fascinating characters of the 18th century, was England's superintendent of all Indian affairs in the northern colonies.

HISTORICAL SITES *and* MUSEUMS
Old Fort Johnson (518-843-0300; www.oldfortjohnson.org), NY 5. Open May 15–Oct. 15, Wed.–Sun. This 1749 stone building was home to William Johnson. Displays feature his role in the French and Indian War. His close relations with the Mohawks and other eastern Indian tribes led to their support in war. The

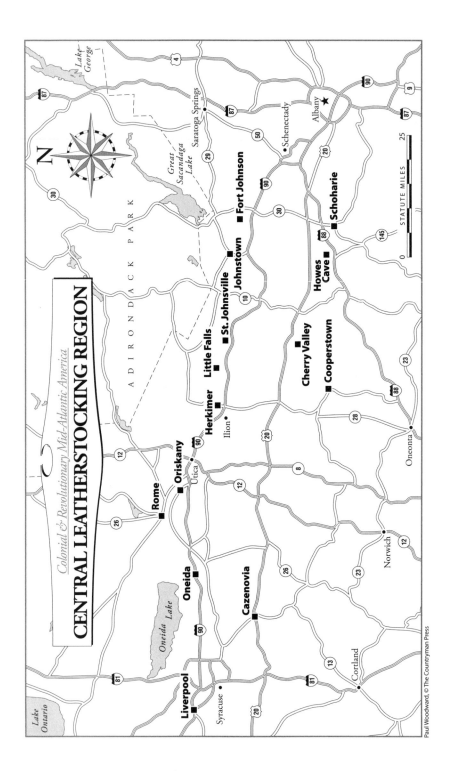

Colonial & Revolutionary Mid-Atlantic America

CENTRAL LEATHERSTOCKING REGION

Paul Woodward, © The Countryman Press

> ❋ Molly Brant was mistress of Fort Johnson from 1759 to 1763. She was a
> Christian Mohawk Indian who came to live with William Johnson in 1759,
> the year his wife died. She had eight children with him, providing and fighting
> for the lost inheritance after William Johnson died. Her brother Joseph Brant,
> also known as Thayendanegea, was one of the most influential Indian leaders of
> the 18th century.
>
> Molly was a strong woman who spoke her mind and was helpful to Sir
> William in his management of Indian affairs. She was proud of her Iroquois her-
> itage and also fit into the white community, entertaining guests in their home
> and receiving notes after a visit: "My Love to Molly & thanks for her good Break-
> fast," and "Sorry I did not take Leave of Miss Molly . . ."

building is the home of the Montgomery County Historical Society. Original family furnishings are here.

EVENTS

July: Colonial Days; 518-843-0300

JOHNSTOWN

Johnstown and nearby Gloversville have been centers for glove making for a long time.

HISTORICAL SITES *and* MUSEUMS

Johnson Hall State Historic Site (518-762-8712; www.nysparks.com/sites), Hall Ave. Open May 15–Oct. 15, Wed.–Sat. 10–5, Sun. 1–5. This 1763 Georgian home belonged to William Johnson, British superintendent of Indian affairs before the Revolution. After his death his son, John Johnson, lived in the home.

Molly Brant and William Johnson moved to this home in 1763, and Molly continued to welcome guests, manage her family of eight children, and provide the link between Sir William and his Indian allies. It was recorded that ". . . One word from her goes farther with them than a thousd. From any White Man . . ."

Sir William died in 1774, and Molly and their children moved to her native village of Canajoharie. She established a trading business until William's estate was settled. Then they moved to Fort Niagara and then to Carleton Island in the St. Lawrence River and finally to Kingston, Ontario, where she died in 1796.

EVENTS

June: 18th-century market fair; 518-762-8712

St. Johnsville

The Dutch settled here in the mid-1600s and then the Palatine Germans, who arrived as refugees from their war-torn homeland on the Rhine River in Germany.

HISTORICAL SITES *and* MUSEUMS
Fort Klock Historic Restoration (518-568-7779; www.fortklock.com), NY 5. Open Memorial Day–mid-Oct, Tue.–Sun. This 1750 trading post and farmhouse was built by Johannes Klock. The building has walls two feet thick and it sits on rock. The complex includes a blacksmith shop, schoolhouse, Dutch-style barn, and herb garden. It was used for refuge during the French and Indian War. On Oct. 19, 1780, the Battle of Klock's Field was fought west of the home.

Herkimer

The Mohawk Indians lived here until 1720, when Palatine Germans arrived as the first white settlers. They farmed the land successfully, and by 1800 they had developed cheese production.

You can spend some time in the region digging for "Herkimer diamonds," which are really quartz crystals (800-562-0897; www.herkimerdiamond.com).

Little Falls

The Iroquois called this place Little Falls to distinguish it from the big falls on the river, to the east in Cohoes. Lock 17 on the Erie Canal here drops forty feet. Historic Canal Place includes two stone mill buildings that have been restored for use as shops and restaurants.

HISTORICAL SITES *and* MUSEUMS
Herkimer Home State Historic Site (315-823-0398; www.nysparks.com/sites), 200 NY 169. Open mid-May–June 30 and Sep.–Oct., Wed.–Sun.; July–Aug., Tue.–Sat. General Nicholas Herkimer sat up against a tree, continuing to direct a battle after suffering a grievous injury in the Battle of Oriskany. Herkimer's bravery even while mortally wounded continued during the six hours of the battle. He was then carried to his home, his leg was amputated, and he died soon afterward.

The home went to his brother George, then nephew John, and then various owners out of the family before New York State took it over in 1913. Today a video relates the story of the family, of how Johan Jost Herchheimer came from the German Palatinate in 1725 and settled south of the Mohawk. His eldest son, Nicholas, built a farmstead here in 1752 and later built the Georgian mansion you see today. During the French and Indian War Nicholas Herkimer was captain of militia, then commissioned as brigadier general, commander of the county's militia.

The office in the house is now set up with games such as checkers, dominoes, and dice ready for play, along with quill pens and a secretary. The items belonging to the general include a heart-shaped pipe box.

Mrs. Herkimer entertained in the parlor, serving tea English style; she locked her tea container, as it was valuable. Herkimer married twice, both times to women named Maria, the first an aunt to the second.

INFORMATION

HERKIMER COUNTY CHAMBER OF COMMERCE
28 W. Main St., Herkimer, NY 13407
315-866-7820; www.herkimercountychamber.com

ROME

Rome was originally called "the carrying place" by the Indians. Right in what is now the center of town was one of the most important portages in colonial times, connecting the Great Lakes with the Hudson River.

Today, in addition to the fort we list here, Rome is also home to **Erie Canal Village**, a re-creation of an 1840 village (315-337-3999; www.eriecanalvillage.net). The Rome Sports Hall of Fame (315-339-9038) offers all sorts of sports memorabilia.

The home of General Nicholas Herkimer in Little Falls.

What is a "sally port?" Forts like Stanwix sometimes contained a narrow passageway in the "backdoor" area, from which men could sally out to get necessary water from a nearby creek or other source.

HISTORICAL SITES *and* MUSEUMS

Fort Stanwix National Monument (315-336-2090; www.nps.gov/fost), 112 E. Park St. Open Apr.–Dec., daily. The fort was built in 1758 during the French and Indian War, then abandoned until 1776, when American soldiers under General John Stanwix rebuilt it. As you look at this star-shaped structure, you can imagine those inside using a pattern of crossfire to mow down attackers. A sentry from the Third New York Regiment, which was a colonial unit, is stationed at the drawbridge where visitors enter.

At the visitors center you can watch a film recounting the 21-day siege by the British and Loyalists in August 1777. By withstanding the siege, the defenders, under Colonel Peter Gansevoort, delayed British general Barry St. Leger and prevented him from reinforcing General Burgoyne at the Battle of Saratoga.

Walk inside the fort to see the officers' quarters; the men's quarters, where as many as 10 men would sleep in a platform bed; the surgeon's day room, where soldiers would go for possible amputation, bleeding, or quarantine; and the museum, which houses a number of artifacts found during archaeological digs. You will hear the cannons boom on weekends.

ORISKANY

Can you imagine anyone continuing to direct a battle while sitting under a tree with a shattered leg? Herkimer did it! **Oriskany Battlefield** (315-768-7224), 7801 NY 69, was the scene of one of the bloodiest battles of the Revolution, on August 6, 1777. British general Barry St. Leger, who intended to travel from Oswego down the Mohawk Valley to join up with General Burgoyne near Albany, found a strong Patriot force when he got to Fort Stanwix, then commanded by Colonel Peter Gansevoort. The resulting siege continued without resolution for three weeks.

Brigadier General Nicholas Herkimer gathered 800 Tryon County militia and set off to relieve Fort Stanwix. St. Leger sent Loyalist troops, including Mohawk Indians under Joseph Brant, to ambush them. General Herkimer's horse was shot and his leg was shattered. He continued to direct the battle while sitting under a beech tree, resting on his saddle and smoking his pipe. The battle ended inconclusively, though the Patriot side had been badly mauled. General Herkimer traveled by raft down the Mohawk River; his leg was amputated

Colonel Peter Gansevoort, who commanded Fort Stanwix during the British siege, was the grandfather of author Herman Melville.

when he reached home in Little Falls, and he died 11 days later. The Oriskany Monument marks the site of the battle.

EVENTS

July: Reading of the Declaration of Independence. Fort Stanwix, 315-336-2090; www.nps.gov/fost
August: The Siege Begins. Fort Stanwix, 315-336-2090; www.nps.gov/fost
November: Revolutionary War living history weekend, wintering at the fort.

Fort Stanwix, 315-336-2090; www.nps.gov/fost

INFORMATION

ROME CHAMBER OF COMMERCE
139 W. Dominick St., Rome, NY 13440
315-337-1700; www.romechamber.com

ONEIDA

Oneida is halfway between Syracuse and Utica near Oneida Lake.

HISTORICAL SITES *and* MUSEUMS

Shakowi Cultural Center (315-829-8801; www.oneida-nation.net/shakowi/), 5 Territory Rd. Open daily. The center houses the Oneida Indian Nation's collection of artifacts and artwork. The building was made of white pine without a single nail. Lectures, workshops, and performances are given here.

MOHAWK VALLEY LODGING

INN BY THE MILL
1679 Mill Rd., Saint Johnsville, NY 13452-3911
866-568-2388, 518-568-2388; www.innbythemill.com
The 1835 stone gristmill was once part of the Underground Railroad. The 1894 Mill Guest House and Cliffside guest cottages overlook waterfalls and the gorge. 5 guest rooms.

PUTNAM MANOR HOUSE
112 W. German St., Herkimer, NY 13350
315-866-6738; www.cnybb.com/putnam.htm
This ivy-covered brick mansion dates from the early 1900s. 5 guest rooms.

ROSEMONT INN B&B
1423 Genesee St., Utica, NY 13501
866-353-4907, 315-790-9315;
rosemontinnbb.com
This Italianate Victorian mansion, completed in 1870, is in the downtown historic district. Rockers await on the porch. 7 guest rooms.

HOTEL UTICA
102 Lafayette St., Utica, NY 13502
315-724-7829; www.hotelutica.com
This downtown 1912 hotel has been thoroughly restored and unobtrusively updated. 114 guest rooms.

RESTAURANTS

BEARDSLEE CASTLE
123 Old State Rd., Little Falls, NY 13365
800-487-5861, 315-823-3000; www.beardsleecastle.com
In a 19th-century replica of an Irish castle, the cuisine is American with a Mediterranean flair. A wood-burning grill provides special flavor.

FENIMORE COOPER COUNTRY

J ames Fenimore Cooper, the region's most celebrated resident, was famed for his Leatherstocking Tales, or series of novels, including *The Last of the Mohicans* and *The Deerslayer.* "Leatherstocking" refers to the woodsmen who wore leather leggings to protect themselves from branches and thorns when making their way through the forest.

SCHOHARIE

Schoharie was settled in 1712. Today there are several destinations besides the historical sites. The Schoharie Valley Railroad Museum offers local train history (518-295-7505; www.midtelnet/scha).

HISTORICAL SITES *and* MUSEUMS
Old Stone Fort (518-295-7192; www.theoldstonefort.org), 145 Fort Rd. Open May–Oct., Tue.–Sun.; July–Aug. also open Mon. This 1772 Dutch Reformed Church was stockaded during the Revolution. You can also see a 1760 Palatine German house and an 18th-century Dutch barn. The fort was attacked in 1780 by forces led by Sir John Johnson and Chief Joseph Brant.

EVENTS
October: Stone Fort Days/History Fair; 518-295-7292; www.theoldstonefort.org

HOWES CAVE

Caverns make this area fascinating, and you can explore them on an underground tour.

HISTORICAL SITES *and* MUSEUMS
Iroquois Indian Museum (518-296-8949; www.iroquoismuseum.org), Caverns Rd. Open Apr.–Dec., Tue.–Sun. The museum is housed in a modern structure that depicts the great longhouses of the Iroquois. Inside visitors will find out about the religion, government, and life of the Iroquois. Displays include an eagle pipe, wampum beads, corn-husk dolls, a Mohawk pot from the 1600s, and gourd rattles.

The archaeology collection of tools displays points that were sharp and used for arrows, darts, or spears. From the Early Iroquois period, from 900–1300, you'll see an effigy pipe, points, mortars and pestles, and pottery. After contact with Europeans, the Iroquois acquired objects such as the 1787 English musket, brass pots, shot, and powder horns you'll see here.

Lester Howe discovered the caverns in 1842. With only the light from his oil lamp, Howe forced himself to crawl and slide farther in on each visit, until he finally reached a large underground lake. Undaunted, he carried in materials to build a raft. On the other side of the lake, he found stalactites, stalagmites, and a variety of grotesque stone shapes.

Downstairs, children can make corn-husk dolls, match furs, identify points, create songs, play games, and engage in other activities.

Howe Caverns (518-296-8900; www.howcaverns.com), NY 7. Open daily. Although this place is neither colonial nor Revolutionary, we could not leave this natural wonder out. The 80-minute guided tour takes you down into the prehistoric caverns for a walk on brick walkways and a boat ride. Bring a jacket, as the temperature is 52 degrees.

CHERRY VALLEY

Cherry Valley is a quiet village a few miles east of Otsego Lake, just south of US 20. It was settled by John Lindesay in 1738. Two years later Samuel Dunlop brought seven Scotch-Irish families from New Hampshire to settle here.

In 1778 a regiment of Tories under Captain Walter Butler and seven hundred Indians under Mohawk chief Joseph Brant attacked the residents. A stone monument honors the victims of the notorious massacre.

HISTORICAL SITES *and* MUSEUMS
Cherry Valley Museum (607-264-3303 or 3098; www.cherryvalleymuseum.org), 49 Main St. Open Memorial Day–Oct. 15. The museum collections include memorabilia, period furnishings, and clothing. There is a diorama of the Cherry Valley Massacre.

INFORMATION
CHERRY VALLEY CHAMBER OF COMMERCE
44 Main St., Cherry Valley, NY 13320
607-264-3755; www.cherryvalleyny.com

COOPERSTOWN

James Fenimore Cooper, born in 1789, watched his father build the settlement of Cooperstown. William Cooper was determined to make life easier for residents who suffered with the short growing season. He built a grain storehouse, a potash factory, and ten frame houses. People brought in their maple syrup and ashes, trading them for grain.

James grew up in wilderness carved out of the forest. The places he knew later figured in his writing. His fictional hero Natty Bumppo was also known as Leatherstocking and Hawkeye.

> Mrs. Cooper refused to leave her civilized life in New Jersey, so her husband had servants pick her up in her chair and move her to Cooperstown in 1790, along with one-year-old James.

HISTORICAL SITES and MUSEUMS

Farmers' Museum (607-547-1450 or 1500; www.farmersmuseum.org), NY 80. Open mid-May–Columbus Day, Tue.–Sun.; Apr. 1–mid-May, and day after Columbus Day–Oct. 31, Tues.–Sat. This museum illustrates a typical village during the period of 1790 to 1860. The village consists of 12 buildings. The main barn contains displays depicting the hardships of families as they struggled to plant and reap crops. In contrast, they also had fun on skates, sleds, and even carousel horses.

The Cardiff Giant, a 10-foot-long gypsum statue found in 1869, was originally thought to be a petrified prehistoric man. The hoax was created by George Hull.

Upstairs in the textile loft, you can watch spinning and weaving. As you walk around the village you'll notice wonderful aromas, which probably come from the kitchen at Lippitt Homestead, where guides are preparing food.

Fenimore Art Museum (607-547-1400; www.fenimoreartmuseum.org), NY 80, across from the Farmers' Museum. Open late Apr.–May and Oct.–Dec., Tue.–Sun.; June–Sep., daily. The museum houses a collection of Native American and American art in a lovely setting on Otsego Lake. The Great Hall has special pieces of the American Indian communities from the Northwest Coast, Alaska, California, the Southwest, Plains and Prairies, and Northeast Woodlands. The Thaw Collection of North American Indian Art is magnificent. There's also a Mohawk bark house, a reproduction of an 18th-century Indian hunting and fishing camp.

Cooperstown has many other attractions, including the Glimmerglass Opera, Glimmerglass State Park, and, of course, the Baseball Hall of Fame.

INFORMATION

COOPERSTOWN CHAMBER OF COMMERCE
31 Chestnut St., Cooperstown, NY 13326
607-547-9983; www.cooperstownchamber.org

CAZENOVIA

John Lincklaen, a land agent for the Holland Land Company, settled here in 1793. Chittenango Falls State Park is popular for camping, hiking, fishing, and picnicking beside the 167-foot waterfall. Football in its U.S. form is claimed to have been invented by a native, Gerrit Smith Miller, in 1860.

HISTORICAL SITES *and* MUSEUMS

Lorenzo State Historic Site (315-655-3200; www.lorenzony.org), 17 Rippleton Rd. Open May–Oct., Wed.–Sun. This 1807 house was home to John Lincklaen, founder of Cazenovia. Original furnishings are still in the house. It overlooks Cazenovia Lake, and there are formal gardens to wander through.

LEATHERSTOCKING REGION LODGING

BRAE LOCH INN
5 Albany St., Cazenovia, NY 13035
315-655-3431; www.braelochinn.com
A bit of Scotland in an estate built in 1805. 12 guest rooms.

INN AT COOPERSTOWN
16 Chestnut St., Cooperstown, NY 13326
800-437-6303, 607-547-5756; www.innatcooperstown.com
In the historic district, this Second Empire mansion dates from 1874. 17 guest rooms.

LINCKLAEN HOUSE
79 Albany St., Cazenovia, NY 13035
315-655-3561; lincklaenhouse.com
Dating from 1835, the house features Williamsburg chandeliers and Delft tiles. 23 guest rooms.

THE OTESAGA RESORT
60 Lake St., Cooperstown, NY 13326
800-348-6222, 607-547-9931; www.otesaga.com
The imposing 1910 building has great views of the lake. 135 guest rooms.

FINGER LAKES

The Finger Lakes region is one of wine and water—vineyards and eleven long, slender, and deep lakes left by departing glaciers. Waterfalls and gorges complete a water ambience of scenic splendor interspersed by high rolling hills that resemble huge ocean swells. The Iroquois believed that the Great Spirit placed his hand on this region and left behind his fingerprints.

The lakes at the heart of the region still retain their Indian names: Canandaigua, Keuka, Seneca, Cayuga, Owasco, and Skaneateles. The tribes of the Iroquois lived in the area, from the Mohawks in the east to the Senecas in the west. The Iroquois observed the "Great Binding Law" allowing free speech, religious freedom, and the right to defend themselves. Women ruled the groups, with the clan mothers selecting the chiefs. Women also owned the fields and longhouses. A man who married would move to his wife's longhouse.

You can travel up or down each lake to enjoy views and sample wines, or choose to journey from town to town along NY 5 and US 20, with briefer dips south along the shores.

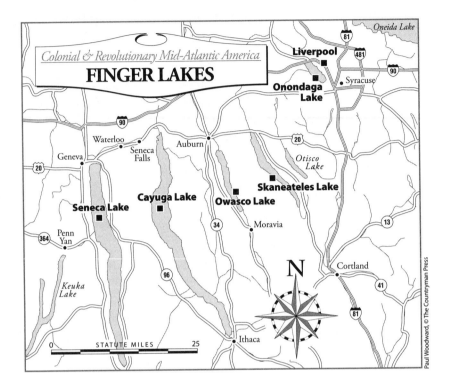

ONONDAGA LAKE

In 1656 the Jesuits founded a mission here, called Saint Marie de Gannentaha, but it was abandoned after two years. The Indians had discovered salt on this site; later, in the 17th century, Father LeMoyne discovered a salt spring, which led to the development of the salt industry in Syracuse.

LIVERPOOL

Liverpool is located on Onondaga Lake in the Syracuse metro area.

HISTORICAL SITES *and* MUSEUMS
Sainte Marie among the Iroquois (315-453-6768), Onondaga Lake Pkwy. Open early May–Labor Day, Mon., Wed., and Fri.–Sun.; after Labor Day–early Oct., Sat.–Sun. Sainte Marie is a living-history museum on the site of a 1657 mission. In 1639 Jesuits came from Quebec to the area, but their first mission burned. In 1656 some 50 Frenchmen left Quebec for Onondaga, where they built another mission, Sainte Marie de Gannentaha (the Indian word for the lake). They had been invited by the Iroquois to leave Quebec and found a permanent settlement

so that they could travel to nearby villages to teach Christianity. They traveled in four canoes of Algonquian pattern and four of Iroquois, plus two other boats for shooting the rapids. They worked for about two years, building a stockade, chapel, workhouse, garden, and barn. Within 20 months it was abandoned after the Onondagas warned them to leave.

Today, visitors will see a reconstructed mission depicting the year 1656. Costumed interpreters speak from the 17th century. One of them told us that they expected to serve in the mission for life; they worked very hard and were tired enough to sleep when the sun went down. Another said that he became ordained two years ago and then came to the New World. The blacksmith was at work with his bellows; he described his journey along the St. Lawrence River, down small rivers and through portages before he arrived at the mission. The carpenter was making a wooden shoe called a sabot, as well as wooden nails and trunnels—"tree nails" or pegs. As he worked we talked with him and found that he viewed the Dutch as heretics who spread lies among the Iroquois.

Someone was cooking over the fire in the huge fireplace; he especially liked eating the flesh of a beaver, which swam like a fish. The mercenary, or soldier, enjoyed hunting and fishing as well as working with wood and did not believe in being idle. He hunted deer, elk, wild cows (moose), squirrels, rabbits, and beaver. Some of them talked about leaving as they felt uneasy. Programs are presented throughout the year.

Onondaga Lake Park (315-453-6712 or 315-451-7275; www.onondaga-countypark.com), Onondaga Pkwy. The park includes the original salt spring and the Jesuit well. The Salt Museum has a replica of a salt boiling block. (See description of Sainte Marie among the Iroquois on previous page.)

SKANEATELES LAKE

Farmers arrived in the area during the late 1700s. William Seward thought Skaneateles Lake the "most beautiful body of water in the world." The village is also a boating center, not only for the lake but for the New York State Canal System.

BOAT *Tours*

Mid-Lakes Navigation Co. (800-545-4318, 315-685-8500; www.midlakesnav.com), 11 Jordan St. Open May–Oct. Sightseeing cruises of varying lengths on Skaneateles Lake and the Erie Canal provide the chance to enjoy the area by water. Two- and three-day cruises are also available. In fact, anyone fascinated by canal trips should look into this company's cruises, which head west to Buffalo, east to Albany, and continue north to Whitehall, lasting several days.

Owasco Lake

The first settler in Auburn was Colonel John Hardenbergh, who arrived in 1793. He was a surveyor and Revolutionary War hero. Auburn is noted for its historic houses, mostly from the Civil War period.

HISTORICAL SITES *and* MUSEUMS
Ward O'Hara Agricultural Museum (315-252-7644 or 5009; www.cayuganet .org/agmuseum), 6880 E. Lake Rd. Open mid-May–mid-Sep., daily. The farm dates from the early 1800s to early 1900s. Buildings include a general store, creamery, blacksmith shop, veterinarian's office, and kitchen.

Cayuga Lake

Aurora was the site of the Cayuga Indian village of Deawondote. General John Sullivan's army destroyed it in 1779.

In 1788 John Harris built a log cabin and started three ferry lines across the lake. By 1800 the Cayuga Bridge was completed. By 1857 it was abandoned, but a few of the old pilings are still visible.

Seneca Lake

Geneva, at the northern end of Seneca Lake, contains a series of stately homes overlooking the lake. It is also the home of Hobart and William Smith Colleges.

HISTORICAL SITES *and* MUSEUMS
Geneva Historical Society–Prouty-Chew House and Museum (315-789-5151; www.genevahistoricalsociety.com), 543 S. Main St. Open year-round. The 1829 home in the historic district contains period furnishings and local history exhibits.

Canandaigua Lake

The town of Canandaigua stands on the site of the Seneca Indian village Kan-an-dar-gue. It was destroyed by General John Sullivan in 1779.

HISTORICAL SITES *and* MUSEUMS
Ontario County Historical Society (585-394-4975; www.ochs.org), 55 N. Main St. Open year-round, Mon.–Sat. 10–4:30, Wed. 10–9. The research library offers genealogical information, and there are exhibits on local and regional history.

FINGER LAKES LODGING

BELHURST CASTLE
4069 NY 14, Geneva, NY 14456
315-781-0201; www.belhurstcastle
.com
The castle dates from 1885 and contains handsome stained-glass windows. 34 guest rooms.

GENEVA ON THE LAKE
1001 Lochland Rd., Geneva, NY 11456
315-789-7190; www.genevaonthe
lake.com
This Italian Renaissance–style villa is set on 10 acres of gardens and woods. 29 guest rooms.

HOBBIT HOLLOW FARM
3061 W. Lake Rd., Skaneateles, NY 13156
800-473-3796, 315-685-2791;
hobbithollow.com
Lake, meadow, and vineyard views from a colonial-style farmhouse set on 320 acres. 5 guest rooms.

MORGAN-SAMUELS INN
2920 Smith Rd., Canandaigua, NY 14424
585-394-9232; www.morgansamuels
inn.com
This 1810 English-style mansion is set on 46 acres. 6 guest rooms.

PACKWOOD HOUSE
14 W. Genesee St., Skaneateles, NY 13152
877-225-9663, 315-217-8100;
www.packwoodhouse.com
Lakefront terraces are available at this contemporary hotel. 19 guest rooms.

THE SHERWOOD INN
26 W. Genesee St., Skaneateles, NY 13152
800-374-3796, 315-685-3405;
www.thesherwoodinn.com
This former stagecoach stop, dating from 1807, is in the village downtown. 24 guest rooms.

RESTAURANTS

DOUG'S FISH FRY
8 Jordan St., Skaneateles, NY 13152
315-685-3288; www.dougsfishfry.com
/skaneateles.htm
This hole-in-the-wall place is very popular, with fish fried just right.

THE KREBS
53 W. Genesee St., Skaneateles, NY 13152
315-685-5714; www.thekrebs.com
For more than a century, the Krebs trademark traditional meal has been served here.

SHERWOOD INN DINING ROOM
26 W. Genesee St., Skaneateles, NY 13152
800-374-3796, 315-685-3405;
www.thesherwoodinn.com
Diners have a view of the lake and enjoy tavern fare of all kinds.

REGIONAL INFORMATION

FINGER LAKES TOURISM ALLIANCE
309 Lake St., Penn Yan, NY 14527
800-530-7488, 315-536-7488; www
.fingerlakes.org

WESTERN NEW YORK/GREATER NIAGARA

Several sites fall within the Revolutionary era, including the Genesee Country Museum at Mumford, Letchworth Park at Castile, and Fort Niagara at Youngstown.

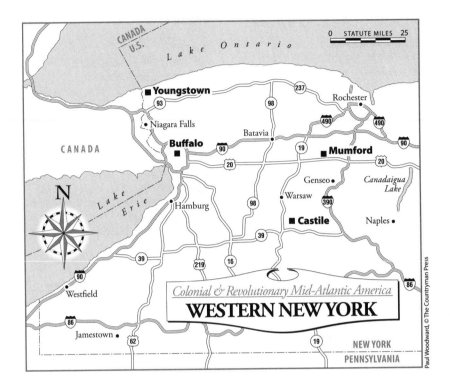

The map, labeled "Colonial & Revolutionary Mid-Atlantic America / WESTERN NEW YORK," shows cities including Youngstown, Niagara Falls, Buffalo, Batavia, Rochester, Mumford, Genseo, Warsaw, Castile, Hamburg, Westfield, Jamestown, Naples, and Canadaigua Lake, along with Lake Ontario and Lake Erie. Credit: Paul Woodward, © The Countryman Press

MUMFORD

HISTORICAL SITES *and* MUSEUMS

Genesee Country Village and Museum (585-538-6822; www.gcv.org), 1410 Flint Hill Rd. Open May–Oct., Tue.–Sun.; July–Labor Day, daily. You can see 68 historic buildings and 13 heirloom gardens, including a sculpture garden, a carriage museum, and the country's premier gallery of wildlife and sporting art. You'll see demonstrations of 17 trades and crafts and can hike on five miles of interpretive trails that wind through 175 acres of meadows, fields, woods, and wetlands.

The earliest house in the village dates from 1797. Amherst Humphrey had a 10-room "framed" house that was grander than most of the log houses in the area. There were fireplaces to heat the two front rooms, plus a large fireplace in the kitchen. The Humphreys raised four boys and five girls in the house. A costumed weaver works at the treadle loom.

In contrast, the Pioneer's Cabin, dating from 1810, was a one-room log cabin owned by Nicholas Hetchler that held his entire family, including 13 children. When we visited, carrot, onion, and watercress soup was in the works. Out in the barn we stopped to see three tiny piglets.

LODGING

GENESEE COUNTRY INN
948 George St., Mumford, NY 14511
585-538-2500, 800-697-8297;
www.geneseecountryinn.com
The building dates from the 1800s and
was a plaster and paper mill. 10 guest
rooms.

RESTAURANTS

RICHARDSON'S CANAL HOUSE
1474 Marsh Rd., Pittsford, NY 14534
585-248-5000; www.richardsoncanal
house.net
Built as a public house in 1818.

CASTILE

HISTORICAL SITES *and* MUSEUMS

Letchworth State Park (585-493-3600; www.letchworth.com). Open Apr.–Oct.,
daily; Dec.–Feb., Sat.–Sun. In Letchworth State Park the Genesee River roars,
tumbles, and plunges over three spectacular waterfalls, and every year the river cuts
deeper into surrounding cliffs. Some are 600 feet high. So it's not surprising that
this section of the river has been dubbed the "Grand Canyon of the East." The
William Pryor Letchworth Pioneer and Indian Museum (585-493-2760) offers
displays of local artifacts. Open mid-May–mid-Oct., 10–5 daily.

LODGING

GLEN IRIS INN
7 Letchworth State Park, Castile, NY
14427
585-493-2622; www.glenirisinn.com
This former country estate overlooks the
Middle Falls of the Genesee River and the
gorge. 16 guest rooms.

BUFFALO

Buffalo has a wealth of museums to visit, including the famous Albright-Knox Art
Gallery (716-882-8700; www.albrightknox.org). The Theodore Roosevelt Inau-
gural National Historic Site was the site of his inauguration in 1901 (716-884-
0095; www.nps.gov/thri). The Allentown district is beyond our time period but
an interesting place to wander, shop, and dine (716-881-1024).

HISTORICAL SITES *and* MUSEUMS

Buffalo and Erie County Historical Society (716-873-9644; www.bechs.org),
25 Nottingham Court. Open Wed.–Sat. Exhibits include a Native American scene
depicting Indian life inside the longhouse and the village. Both permanent and
changing exhibits illustrate the cultural history of the area.

The statue of Mary Jemison in Letchworth State Park.

"The WHITE WOMAN of the GENESEE"

The story of Mary Jemison reflects the changing human habitation of the land during the turbulent last half of the 18th century. Mary was born on a ship as her family emigrated from Ireland. In 1758, when she was 15, she and her family were taken captive by Senecas. Other family members were killed, but she was adopted by the Senecas and came to the Genesee Valley with her husband and her children.

Because the Senecas were siding with the British and raiding pioneer settlements, General Washington ordered an expedition to destroy Indian villages on this frontier. Mary took her children and went to Gardeau Flats (now in the park) in 1779. The Big Tree Treaty of 1797 gave Mary her own reservation land of 18,000 acres, where she raised her family. In 1831 Mary moved to the Buffalo Creek Reservation, where she lived until her death in 1833.

William Letchworth brought her body back to the Genesee Valley, erected a monument over her grave with a statue of Mary and her oldest son, Thomas, on her back. She appears as the young girl who first went to live with the Senecas, dressed in Indian clothing.

LODGING

ASA RANSOM HOUSE COUNTRY INN
10529 Main St., Clarence, NY 10529
716-759-2315; www.asaransom.com
The oldest part of the inn dates from1853; Asa Ransom built a gristmill here in 1803, the first in Erie County. 9 guest rooms.

THE ROYCROFT INN
40 S. Grove St., East Aurora, NY 14052
716-652-5552; www.roycroftinn.com
This 1905 mansion has both original and reproduction furniture from the Roycroft Arts and Crafts movement. 29 guest rooms.

RESTAURANTS

ASA RANSOM HOUSE COUNTRY INN
10529 Main St., Clarence, NY 10529
716-759-2315; www.asaransom.com
Popular country cuisine flavored with herbs from the inn's gardens.

ROYCROFT INN DINING ROOM
40 S. Grove St., East Aurora, NY 14052
716-652-5552; www.roycroftinn.com
Outdoor dining in warm weather or overlooking the courtyard garden.

Youngstown

HISTORICAL SITES *and* MUSEUMS

Fort Niagara State Park, Old Fort Niagara
(716-745-7611; www.oldfortniagara.org).
Open year-round, daily. Fort Niagara was built
by the French in 1726. The fort was very active
during the French and Indian War, the American Revolution, and the War of 1812.

A self-guided tour takes you to the provisions storehouse, powder magazine, Dauphin
battery, Gate of the Five Nations (a good place
from which to view the mist above Niagara Falls
on a clear day), the south redoubt, 18-pounder
battery, land defenses, north redoubt, and around to the "French Castle." The castle, restored to its mid-18th-century style, shows how the officers and men lived
in those days. Major Robert Rogers (of Rogers' Rangers fame) was imprisoned in
the castle at one time. Stop to see the well that was used from 1726 until 1812. It
was sealed at that time and reopened in 1927.

> Some say that the headless ghost of a murdered French officer still searches for his head. He sometimes sits on the edge of the well at midnight and rises when the moon is full to continue his search.

EVENTS

May: Niagara's soldiers through the ages, Fort Niagara; 716-745-7611;
www.oldfortniagara.org
July: French and Indian War reenactment, Fort Niagara; 716-745-7611;
www.oldfortniagara.org

Barracks at Fort Niagara.

Current Information

DEPARTMENT OF ECONOMIC DEVELOPMENT
Division of Tourism
30 S. Pearl St.
Albany, NY 12245
800-225-5697; www.iloveny.com

Pennsylvania

Historical Introduction
to the
Pennsylvania Colony

our decades before the Quakers arrived in Pennsylvania, the broad Delaware River had attracted other European traders and colonists. One can imagine the astonishment in the minds of the Swedish settlers of New Sweden as their new governor, Johan Printz, arrived on shore in 1643. Pieter de Vries wrote that he was "A man of brave size, who weighed over four hundred pounds." He was heavy with muscle and bone, not fat. The Indians called him affectionately "Big Guts" or "Big Tub." John Winthrop reported that Printz was an experienced professional man with ideas "furious and passionate" who went after his projects vigorously.

Printz built his two-story, glass-windowed home on Tinicum Island, near the present site of Philadelphia, then added a gristmill and a church. He was aggressive in making changes, such as substituting the planting of tobacco as a cash crop instead of corn, which could be purchased from the Indians. Printz set about eliminating English settlers as he allied himself with the Dutch. He built forts on Delaware Bay and on the Schuylkill River to maintain control of traders and Indians on the waterways.

Wars in Europe resulted in neglect of New Sweden, and the Swedish Crown did not send ships with necessary supplies for years. The colony ran out of goods used for bartering with the Indians. Immigration ceased, and Printz decided to return to Sweden.

Peter Stuyvesant, the director of Dutch New Netherland, had made life miserable for Printz and continued to harass the new director of New Sweden, Johan Rising. With reinforcements from Amsterdam in 1655, Stuyvesant sent a force of seven ships and 700 men to invade New Sweden. The settlements were easily

---

Overleaf: Independence Hall, the cradle of American independence.

overpowered and became part of New Netherland until the British took over that colony in 1664.

William Penn and the Quakers

William Penn was born in London in 1644, son of Admiral Sir William Penn, an eminent naval leader in the Dutch wars. While managing his father's estates in Ireland as a young man, he became interested in George Fox's version of Christianity then spreading in Ireland and Wales. Fox believed that every man and woman could discover an inner light, the holy spirit within themselves, and live a godly life according to its dictates. The problem for Quakers came in their rejection of established religion, their unwillingness to join militias and bear arms, their refusal to swear oaths on Bibles, and not incidentally their habit of wearing plain black dress that made them easily identifiable. During the Restoration no fewer than 15,000 of them were imprisoned for their convictions, and many were martyred.

When Penn left the Church of England to become a Quaker, Lady Penn reported that the admiral "had intended to make William a great man, but the boy would not hearken." William was imprisoned for his publicly expressed religious convictions—he produced no fewer than forty-two books and pamphlets—four times during seven years of his young manhood. While in prison he wrote *No Cross, No Crown,* his most famous essay on the principles of Quakerism, and tracts on the irrationality of persecuting Quakers.

When he was out of prison and engaging in political action on behalf of the Quakers, Penn sensed that little change was likely in England and turned his attention to proposing a colony in America. In 1681 he petitioned King Charles II for land, even though he knew that the king could refuse his request because he was a Quaker. But Penn was also an insider, since his father had introduced him to the king and the king's brother James, Duke of York (later James II), and he knew a number of other prominent Tories. Penn and Charles II had been friends since they were young, and Penn kept up the friendship in spite of disagreements on the extent of royal power in the colonies and on religion.

> Later Penn wrote that "the government at home was glad to be rid of us [Quakers] at so cheap a rate as a little parchment to be practiced in a desert three thousand miles off."

In the end, Charles, who wanted to repay his 16,000-pound debt to Penn's father, who had died in 1670, granted Penn 45,000 square miles in the territory between Maryland and New York. The charter of Pennsylvania was signed by the king in 1681 and named in honor of Penn's father as Penn's Woods, or Pennsylvania. Penn was required to pay two beaver skins to Windsor Castle on the first of January every year. It was the largest grant ever made to an individual in the colonies.

Penn chose his cousin William Markham as deputy governor of the province and sent him ahead to plan the settlement. Now officially the proprietor, Penn reached newly plotted Philadelphia on the ship *Welcome* in 1682.

Framing a Government

Perhaps no American colony was so assiduous as Pennsylvania in framing and revising its terms of government. Unlike the Puritan colonies or royal colonies that began with certain fixed assumptions, Penn had enough latitude in his proprietary charter to create a pattern of individual liberty and religious toleration. His 1682 "Frame of Government" professed freedom for its people: "Any Government is free to the People under it where the Laws rule, and the People are a Party to those Laws." A council was elected by the freeholders, men who owned fifty acres of land and cultivated part of it or paid local taxes. They drew up laws with the governor and sent them to a popular assembly, which could approve, reject, or amend them but not propose new legislation. The Privy Council in London approved laws made in Pennsylvania. In contrast to Massachusetts and Connecticut, there was to be no established church, no mandatory tithes, no persecution based on "religious persuasion."

But as soon as the Frame of Government was put into practice, some parts of it proved unworkable. The council was too large to be effective, the assembly resented its inability to initiate legislation, and the influence and privileges of the wealthy Quakers who had helped Penn finance the colony raised the ire of their poorer brethren. Some of these problems were addressed in the revised charter produced by the second assembly in 1683, but others persisted, including dissatisfaction from the lower counties (which later became Delaware) about their status, and about handling of property. At one point Penn was exasperated enough to write, "For the love of God, me, and the poor country be not so governmentish, so noisy, and open, in your dissatisfactions." And the Quakers caused him trouble as they refused to bear arms or pay taxes for defense. Penn agreed with them on not using arms for aggression but felt that defense was reasonable and necessary.

Many of these problems were addressed when Penn signed the new Charter

---

PENNSYLVANIA *Time Line*

1609	**1643**	**1681**	**1682**
Pennsylvania claimed by the Dutch after Henry Hudson's visit to Delaware Bay	Finns and Swedes settle on Tinicum Island in the Delaware River	England's King Charles II grants a proprietary charter to William Penn	English Quakers arrive, then Welsh Quakers and Dutch Quakers, continuing until 1720; Penn makes first visit to Pennsylvania and summons a General Assembly

of Privileges in 1701, just as he was leaving for England after his second stay in Pennsylvania. He was not happy with many of its provisions, which overturned his original principles of government, but he acceded because it was supported by a preponderance of the assembly. This new constitution provided for a unicameral assembly—the only one in British colonies—of four men from each county to be elected yearly by the freemen. The governor and his advisory council made up the executive branch. The assembly constituted the legislative branch, and the judicial branch consisted of judges and officers elected within each county. This system remained in force until the constitution for an independent commonwealth replaced it in 1776.

A Haven for Immigrants

From the outset, Penn's colony provided a haven not only for persecuted Quakers but also for a mélange of other religious dissidents, including Moravians, Mennonites and their splinter group, the Amish. Settlers arrived from England, Wales, Ireland, Holland, and Germany. As a result of this influx, and amity with surrounding Indian tribes, the colony grew rapidly and Philadelphia became the most populous city in America.

The Quakers who left their homelands to escape religious persecution remained the dominant religious and political group in the colony. In Britain many Quakers had refused to take advantage of the Toleration Act of 1689, because it required

Penn appealed to potential settlers by reporting, "the Air is sweet and clear, the Heavens serene, like the South-parts of France, rarely Overcast . . . . Of Fowl of the Land there is Turkey (Forty and Fifty Pound weight) which is very great; Phesants, Heath-Birds, Pidgeons and Partridges in abundance." Passengers would pay "six pounds per head for masters and their wives, five pounds for each servant, and fifty shillings for each child under ten, suckling children traveling free." Each passenger could ship one chest free and additional freight at forty shillings per ton. Land was to be granted outright, except for a small quitrent reserved for the security of the title.

1683	1684	1699	1701	1708
Second assembly revises First Frame of Government	Penn returns to England	Penn begins second visit to Pennsylvania	Penn completes a new constitution, the Charter of Privileges, before sailing for England	Germans arrive, then Swiss until 1750

> ✳ Thomas Penn, the proprietor who lived in Pennsylvania from 1732 to 1741,
> observed: "This province has for some years been the asylum of the dis-
> tressed Protestants of the Palatine, and other parts of Germany, and I believe it
> may with truth be said that the present flourishing condition of it is in a great
> measure owing to the industry of these people; and should any discouragement
> divert them from coming hither, it may well be apprehended that the value of
> your lands will fall, and your advances to wealth be much slower; for it is not
> altogether the goodness of the soil, but the number and industry of the people
> that make a flourishing country."

taking an oath of allegiance to the Crown, and taking oaths of any kind was against Quaker principles. The industrious Quakers were pleased to find a peaceful life in Pennsylvania that allowed them to prosper and worship openly. Dutch Quakers arrived in 1682 and settled in Germantown. Germans arrived in 1708 and continued streaming in until 1750. Wars had devastated their lands, with armies looting and destroying villages and crops.

In 1714 the group of Mennonites called Amish arrived in Berks County. Such religious groups had been persecuted by Protestants as well as Catholics in Europe, but they were welcomed in Pennsylvania. Moravians arrived from Poland, Hungary, and Moravia, and some moved north to found the town of Bethlehem.

The Scotch-Irish immigration began in 1717 and continued until 1776, when they numbered about one-fourth of Pennsylvania's population. Many of them had come because of religious persecution. Later, some arrived because of "rack-renting," which occurred when landlords raised rents as long leases expired; many of these people had lost their homes. They tended to settle on the northern and western frontiers, and some were squatters on Indian land.

Acquiring Indian Land

The major tribes inhabiting the land granted to William Penn were the Delawares (Lenni-Lenape) in the Delaware River basin, the Susquehannocks (also called Conestogas) along the river of the same name, and the Shawnees in the Wyoming

PENNSYLVANIA *Time Line*

1717	**1737**	**1754**
Scotch-Irish arrive until 1776	In the "Walking Purchase," Penn's heirs acquire dubious rights to more than a million acres of Indian lands in eastern Pennsylvania	Purchase of land from the Six Nations includes most of the land west of the Susquehanna; George Washington defeated at Fort Necessity as French and Indian War begins

and Ohio Valleys. Penn did not settle any of his land until the Indians had been paid for it. The determination of Quaker settlers to live amicably with their Indian neighbors prevailed during the early years of the colony and contributed to its rapid growth and prosperity. Later land dealings with the Indians, however, were not so scrupulous. Superficially, all of Pennsylvania except for the northwestern third had been bought by 1768, and the rest of the land was purchased in 1784 and 1789. Yet it is questionable that the Iroquois confederation had any right to sell land they did not live on but merely controlled through conquering vassal tribes. Decades before the final purchases, the initial amity that Pitt had established eroded, finally bursting into rebellion and brutal warfare in 1763.

The French and Indian War

Indian troubles had not been of special concern to most Pennsylvanians, apart from those on the frontier who were directly affected by the presence of French forces and allied Indians nearby. Most Quakers were against involvement in any war. When Benjamin Franklin told them that they would have to give up their religious principles to the extent of passing a militia bill, some chose to withhold their votes. The militia bill of 1755 did not change much, and in fact the Privy Council vetoed it much later. However, its passage did diminish Quaker power in the colony. Militia groups were quickly formed and stockades built for defense, as well as blockhouses at five-mile intervals in between the stockades where families could find some protection in time of need.

Fears of war were justified. Tension had been building for years over rival French and British claims in the Ohio country beyond the frontier. Virginia merchants, in competition with Pennsylvanians, also had vital commercial interests in the region. In 1753 Virginia's royal governor, Robert Dinwiddie, had sent soldiers to build a fort at the fork where the Monongahela and Allegheny rivers flow together to form the Ohio. The small Virginia contingent had been easily driven off by a much larger French force, which then built Fort Duquesne at this strategic spot. On his way to the area with a small force in 1754, a Virginia colonel by the name of George Washington attacked a French encampment led by the Sieur de Jumonville, who was killed in the encounter—an incident that ignited what became

---

1755
General Edward Braddock's army, on its way to attack Fort Duquesne, ambushed and defeated by French and Indian forces

1758
General John Forbes's army takes Fort Duquesne and renames it Fort Pitt; Treaty of Easton settles all land disputes between settlers and Indians except "Walking Purchase"

1763
Most forts in western Pennsylvania fall during Pontiac's Rebellion; royal proclamation forbids colonial settlement west of the mountains

> ✳ When dealing with the Delawares for more land in 1737, colonial adminis-
> trators based their offer on a 1680 document of doubtful authenticity. It
> recorded a promise to sell Indian land beginning between the junction of the
> Delaware and Lehigh rivers "as far west as a man could walk in a day and a
> half." When the Delawares agreed to honor it, Provincial Secretary James Logan
> hired three runners and set them out on a prepared trail. Only one completed
> the course, traveling seventy miles, but that garnered 1.2 million acres in north-
> eastern Pennsylvania for the proprietorship. Feeling that they had been cheated,
> the Delawares fought the deal unsuccessfully for two decades before moving
> westward.

known in the colonies as the French and Indian War, though the conflict soon
spread around the world. To fend off a counterattack from a larger force led by
Jumonville's brother, Washington hastily built and defended the barricades of Fort
Necessity before he was forced to surrender and allowed to retire.

The following year Washington joined British general Edward Braddock's
campaign to capture Fort Duquesne, which involved building a road across the
mountains to transport 2,400 men and their artillery for the attack. Before Braddock reached the fort, a French and Indian ambush in the woods caught his army
by surprise and mauled it badly, with 900 casualties. The remnant retreated in a
rout, and Braddock died on the road he had struggled to build. Success in secur-
ing the fort would not come until 1758, when General John Forbes led 6,000
British and colonial soldiers to attack it. He cut a new road to get there, only to
find that the French had abandoned and demolished the fort. Forbes then built
Fort Pitt on an adjoining site to control the region.

Frontier Troubles

At the end of the French and Indian War, simmering Indian discontent along the
western frontiers of the Mid-Atlantic colonies turned violent in Pontiac's Rebellion. Incited by Chief Pontiac of the Ottawas, Indian groups attacked British forts
stretching along the frontier from northern Michigan to western Virginia. In

---

PENNSYLVANIA *Time Line*

1768	**1774**	**1776**
Indian Treaty "to pur-chase land south of a line crossing the province diagonally from the northeast corner to the southwest corner"	First Continental Congress meets in Philadelphia	Declaration of Independence adopted and read in Philadelphia; new state con-stitution replaces Penn proprietary; Washington crosses the Delaware and defeats Hessians at Trenton; Congress temporarily retreats to Baltimore

essence it was a protest against unabated incursions on Indian lands and broken promises that British forts would be dismantled at the end of the war and white settlers removed. In western Pennsylvania all the small posts that had been built along the frontier during the French and Indian War to protect settlers fell to raids from Delawares and Shawnees, and many men, women, and children living on isolated farms were brutally murdered and mutilated. During the summer of 1763 only Fort Pitt and a handful of other posts withstood a siege. Colonel Henry Bouquet's defeat of Indians who had ambushed him at Bushy Run in August brought a temporary lull in raids.

Reaction soon set in among the frontier settlers, mostly Scotch-Irish Presbyterians who thought the Quaker authorities in southeastern Pennsylvania were not doing enough to protect them. In December fifty armed men attacked friendly Indians, the remnants of the Conestoga tribe, in what became known as the Conestoga massacre, first killing several in the cabins of a settlement, then with larger force breaking into a Lancaster workhouse where the survivors had been sheltered temporarily and murdering them. As authorities sought to protect other vulnerable Indian groups by moving them to Philadelphia, western anger mounted, and hundreds of rebels nicknamed the "Paxton Boys" marched toward the city, which had hurriedly formed a militia to defend itself. When the mob reached Germantown, a delegation from the council and assembly that included its leader, Benjamin Franklin, met them and persuaded them to present their grievances to the assembly.

As Indian attacks resumed on the frontier in 1764, Governor John Penn took stronger action, declaring rebelling Indians enemies who could be pursued and killed. By the end of the year, British forces and militias had brought the rebellion to an end, but sporadic threats recurred throughout the remainder of the century until the tribes had migrated westward.

Debates and Decisions in Philadelphia

As Parliament persisted in its efforts to make its colonies help repay the hefty debts of the French and Indian War and the continuing cost of maintaining troops, American resistance and anger increased. A succession of taxes—the Sugar Act of

1777	**1778**	**1780**	**1781**
Washington fails to stop British invasion in battles at Brandywine and Germantown; General William Howe occupies Philadelphia; Second Continental Congress adopts Articles of Confederation and sends them to states for ratification	British evacuate Philadelphia and meet Washington's army at the Battle of Monmouth	Pennsylvania passes first emancipation law, banning slavery for children born in the state	Articles of Confederation ratified; Cornwallis surrenders to American and French forces at Yorktown

1763, the broader Stamp Act of 1765, the Townshend Acts of 1766, and the explosive Tea Act of 1773—collectively affected merchants, lawyers, shopkeepers, printers, and a whole range of other Americans directly. When the colonies reacted with destructive "tea parties," Parliament responded in 1774 with intransigence, closing the port of Boston, passing the so-called Intolerable Acts and the Quebec Act that stripped western lands from colonial control.

The response was almost inevitable, and Philadelphia became its center for a variety of reasons. The colonies, disparate in so many ways, needed to combine forces to mount an effective opposition. Previous attempts had been evanescent, like Benjamin Franklin's plan at the Albany Congress in 1754 for a limited union to defend the northern colonies against the French—a plan ignored by the colonial assemblies—or the Stamp Act Congress in New York City in 1765, which had accomplished its goal when the act was repealed. Now the incursions on what colonists regarded as their rights had become cumulative and more serious, requiring a new gathering of representative leaders. Philadelphia, conveniently located between northern and southern colonies in an era when transportation was slow and painful, was an obvious choice. As America's largest and most prosperous city, it also had a long tradition of freedom from royal interference, lively political debate, and a heritage in publishing that made it a marketplace for ideas.

The story of the First Continental Congress in the fall of 1774 and its successor gathered in the following spring has been told, retold, and mythologized so frequently that repeating its outlines would be superfluous here. But it is worth noting that our knowledge of the outcome often obscures the complexity of the process. The preponderance of opinion among the delegates moved only slowly and erratically toward embracing total independence and might not have reached that point if not for the hard line taken by Lord North and the harsh actions of George III. For example, the Declaration of Rights adopted in the fall of 1774 did not object to Parliament's regulation of external commerce, and the Olive Branch Petition sent to the king in the summer of 1775 envisioned "a happy and permanent reconciliation"—a somewhat anomalous gesture while George Washington's newly minted Continental Army was besieging British troops in Boston.

PENNSYLVANIA *Time Line*

1783	**1787**	**1788**	**1789**	**1790**
Treaty of Paris formally ends Revolutionary War	Constitutional Convention in Philadelphia drafts and adopts Constitution	United States Constitution ratified	Washington inaugurated as first president	Federal capital begins moving from New York City to Philadelphia

The king ignored the petition and declared the colonies to be in rebellion. In December Parliament passed the Prohibitory Act, which laid an embargo on American trade and authorized the seizure of American ships. Thomas Paine's inflammatory *Common Sense* openly argued for total independence in January of 1776, yet resistance to that final separation persisted throughout the spring among moderate delegates from the Mid-Atlantic states, especially Pennsylvania. Then Richard Henry Lee from Virginia presented a resolution in early June calling for independence, foreign alliances, and a confederation of colonies. The process of drafting, revising, and adopting the Declaration of Independence had begun.

Battles for Independence

To combat American independence, British strategists planned three lines of attack. First they wanted to seize and hold New York and Philadelphia. Second, they planned to take control of the Champlain-Hudson corridor, which would seal off New England. Third, they would capture the South. Pennsylvania became an important part of this line of attack in 1777. After routing the Continental Army at the Battle of Long Island, British forces occupied New York in September 1776, then spent the winter in New Jersey on the way to Philadelphia. In the summer of 1777 General Howe abandoned his role in helping to seal off New England, passing it on to General Clinton, and chose to confront Washington in Pennsylvania.

Howe's force sailed for the Chesapeake to mount an invasion of Philadelphia from the south, landing in Maryland in August and marching northward with 15,000 troops. Washington, with 11,000 men, established a line to stop him along flooded Brandywine Creek, and a major battle followed on September 11. Howe was able to cross the creek with part of his force in a flanking movement to get behind Washington's position, while another part faced it directly, finally forcing the Americans to retreat. Another loss occurred on September 20 in Paoli, when Americans sent to attack the British rear guard were surprised in camp at night by a bloody bayonet charge. British troops reached the streets of Philadelphia three days later, and on September 26 Howe formally took possession of

1794	1796	1800	1814	1813
Washington and Hamilton lead 13,000 federal troops to suppress the Whisky Rebellion in western Pennsylvania; Jay Treaty avoids war with Great Britain	Washington publishes Farewell Address establishing precedent of two-term limit on presidency	Federal capital moves from Philadelphia to Washington	British invade and burn Washington but fail to get past Fort McHenry in Baltimore	Battle of Lake Erie

the city, where he and his officers were welcomed by many wealthy Tories. Washington's final attempt to dislodge him by attacking the troops barracked in Germantown faltered when reinforcements under General Cornwallis arrived from the city.

Patriots had already removed important government records and the Liberty Bell by the time Howe marched into Philadelphia. Congress moved to Lancaster and later York, while Washington and his troops settled in Valley Forge to endure a winter of terrible privations and suffering. But by March they were better clothed and fed and undergoing training under Baron von Steuben, who was able to transform a diverse group of citizens into well-disciplined soldiers. In the spring of 1778, an unintended consequence of Howe's decision to move toward Philadelphia rather than up the Hudson the previous summer forced the evacuation of the city. The American victory at Saratoga and Benjamin Franklin's subsequent success in gaining a French alliance had resulted in French ships and troops sailing to blockade Delaware Bay, making the British occupation untenable. General Clinton replaced Howe, and the British left Philadelphia, heading for New York. Washington followed and engaged them in the important but indecisive Battle of Monmouth in New Jersey. The major battles in Pennsylvania were over, but Pennsylvania Tories and Indians teamed up for raids along the northern and western frontiers that lasted until 1782.

The Aftermath

When Congress returned to Philadelphia after the evacuation, it continued to operate under the Articles of Confederation that had been adopted in 1777, even though they were not ratified until 1781, largely because rights to western lands had not been settled. Having survived its own debates and confrontations over adopting the new state constitution, and proud of its role in establishing a new nation, Philadelphia continued as the center of state and national political life through most of the remaining years of the century. Flaws in the Articles of Confederation that were primarily reactions to the excesses of British rule, especially weak executive power and lack of the ability to raise taxes, brought fifty-five delegates from twelve states (not including Rhode Island) back to Philadelphia for the Constitutional Convention in May of 1787. The constitution that they debated and hammered out in compromises throughout the hot Philadelphia summer was adopted in September and finally ratified by the required number of states in June of the following year.

In 1790 the federal capital moved from New York to Philadelphia, and the city remained the center of U.S. political life until 1800. That turbulent decade for the infant nation saw successive scares of imminent war with Britain and then France, the controversial Jay Treaty with Britain, the military suppression of the Whiskey Rebellion, and the transformation of Revolutionary leaders into party men, Federalists and Republicans. That change led to the nasty political campaign between Adams and Jefferson, one of the bitterest in American history.

Regions *to* Explore

PHILADELPHIA

Philadelphia earned its claim to be "birthplace of a nation" and remains the centerpiece of the state for those seeking to recapture some physical sense of the colonial and revolutionary eras. Unlike New York, where most major buildings of those eras have been demolished, or Boston, where they are often overshadowed by nearby skyscrapers, those in Philadelphia have the good fortune to stand in a section of the city undisturbed by major development. Luckily, the center of the city gradually migrated westward, away from the settlement near the river that William Penn's agents laid out. Part of this section of the city has been set aside as a National Historical Park, and much of the rest has been restored under stringent historical preservation guidelines. As a result of these efforts you can visit the scenes of major events in the original buildings and sense the ambience of early Philadelphia by walking the streets of whole neighborhoods. For those interested in colonial architecture, it is a feast for the eyes.

Beyond the major buildings in Independence Park, there are cobblestones to walk on, sidewalk cafés where you can rest your feet, and historic inns and taverns for a meal. Neighborhoods include Society Hill, Germantown, and Fairmont Park, with more sprinkled around just outside the city.

Society Hill is situated between Front Street, Seventh Street, Walnut Street, and Lombard Street. It was originally named for the Free Society of Traders. William Penn chartered this company to promote land development. Today many restored 18th-century homes remain, alongside modern structures.

Germantown is in northwest Philadelphia. The area was settled by both German and Dutch people. Some of the houses are recognized by their Dutch doors.

Fairmount Park is on both sides of the Schuylkill River. People are enthusiastic about enjoying the paths, bicycle route, horse trails, and roads. The park was founded in 1812, and the Centennial Exposition of 1876 took place here. A number of historic houses remain, including Cedar Grove, Laurel Hill, Mount Pleasant, Strawberry Mansion, Sweetbriar Mansion, and Woodford Mansion.

From its founding, Philadelphia grew into a major center of culture as well as

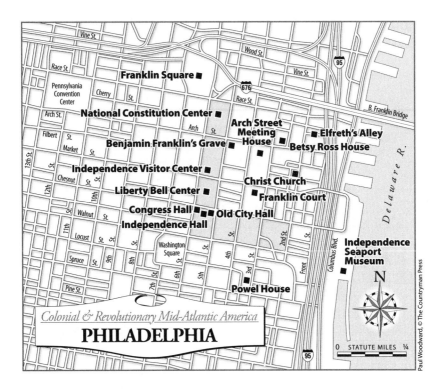

Colonial & Revolutionary Mid-Atlantic America
PHILADELPHIA

politics, and most visitors will want to sample at least some of this artistic, theatrical, musical, and literary wealth. Museums include the Philadelphia Museum of Art, the Rodin Museum, the Franklin Institute, Independence Seaport, the Mummers Museum, Rosenbach Museum and Library, and the Please Touch Museum, to name but a few. Festivals are held on Penn's Landing, and the Kimmel Center for the Performing Arts offers ballet, opera, concerts, and theater. Whenever we visit, we run out of time to enjoy the city's lively cultural life, as well as it explosion in fine cuisine during the last decade.

HISTORICAL SITES *and* MUSEUMS
Today's visitors can take a walking tour of the "most historic square in America," in **Independence National Historic Park** (215-965-2305; www.nps.gov/inde), Sixth and Market Sts. Open daily. The visitor center offers a film, *Independence,* for orientation, and park rangers can advise you on your choice of tour. Free, timed tickets are available and required for tours of Independence Hall. Entrance to Congress Hall, Independence Hall, Old City Hall, and the Liberty Bell Center require security screening.

The **Liberty Bell Center** (215-965-2305; www.nps.gov/inde), Sixth and Market Sts. Open daily, with extended hours in summer. The phrase "Let freedom ring" echoes through American history, and the Liberty Bell, so named by abolitionists in 1835, has long been a national icon. Most bells remain fixed in place, yet the flawed but treasured Liberty Bell has been almost endlessly peripatetic. Perhaps now it has found a permanent home in the Liberty Bell Center.

Records in January 1750 list the need for a steeple superstructure as a "suitable place thereon for hanging a bell." The arrival of the bell was to coincide with the 50th anniversary of William Penn's Charter of Privileges, which ensured freedom of faith for the citizens of Pennsylvania colony.

When British general Howe invaded Philadelphia during the Revolution, this bell, along with others, was hustled out through Quakertown (where one of our ancestors harbored it briefly) and then to Allentown, where it stayed until June 1778. It was placed in the tower until 1846, then moved several more times until the U.S. bicentennial year, 1976, when it was moved into its present pavilion. It stands alone in front of a large window that frames Independence Hall outside. This movable bell deserves a rest!

Independence Hall (215-965-2305; www.nps.gov/inde), Chestnut St. between 5th and 6th Sts. Built as the Pennsylvania State House in 1732, Independence Hall became the site of major decisions establishing the United States. Here the Second Continental Congress met, and here George Washington was appointed commander in chief of the Continental Army. The Declaration of Independence and the Articles of Confederation were adopted here, and the end of the Revolutionary War was announced here.

The "Rising Sun" chair in the Assembly Room was used by George Washing-

In 1751 the bell was ordered through the colonial agent. The specifications read: "Get us a good bell, of about two thousand pounds weight, the cost of which we presume may amount to one hundred pounds sterling, or perhaps with the charges something [more] . . . Let the bell be cast by the best workmen, and examined carefully before it is shipped. . . ." The bell arrived aboard the vessel *Myrtilla,* but as luck would have it, the bell cracked the first time it was rung. The bell was recast in 1752; because the tone was not ideal, they recast it again.

The Liberty Bell.

If you are driving from a distance and want to be sure to have a timed ticket, you can phone the National Park Service at 800-967-2283 for a reservation. You are advised to be in line 30 to 40 minutes in advance of your time to go through security.

ton in 1779. Look for the silver inkstand on his desk, used by signers of the Declaration of Independence and the Constitution.

As you tour Independence Hall and the other colonial sites, think of the oppressions by the Crown that led to the appropriate name, Independence Hall. Taxes imposed from London, including the Stamp Act, angered those who lived in Pennsylvania. Legal documents, newspapers, and almanacs all required the payment of a tax. To avoid it, those who printed almanacs published the 1766 version in mid-1765.

Joseph Galloway, a prominent spokesman who supported the act, reported, "No business can be legally transacted, no lawsuits prosecuted, no vessels sail, no securities for money taken." Lawyers who believed the law to be unconstitutional took matters into their own hands and decided not to use stamps. Merchants agreed to refuse British goods. The Stamp Act was repealed in 1766, as Franklin appeared in Parliament to soften the American viewpoint. He said that Americans objected to taxes because they were "forced upon the people without their consent, if not laid by their own representatives."

In 1767 the Townshend Acts became law. Taxes were to be collected on imported glass, lead, paint, paper, and tea. This money was supposed to pay for British officials living in America, but in fact more officials were needed simply to enforce the rules. By 1770 the Townshend taxes had been dropped except on tea. Parliament rescinded the export tea tax in 1773, and at the same time the East India Company decided to sell surplus tea at bargain rates. The colonials in Philadelphia were suspicious and printed sheets from "The Philadelphia Committee on Tarring and Feathering." When the expected tea ship, the *Polly*, with Captain Ayres at the helm, arrived in Chester, he was escorted to a town meeting, where it became obvious that he was to sail his unloaded ship out of the bay.

In 1774, when the First Continental Congress met in Philadelphia, the colonists agreed to a trade boycott, to be enforced by the Continental Association. Volunteers kept track of merchants, warehouses, and ship cargoes, reporting on any suspicious imports. The Second Continental Congress met in 1775 and asked Pennsylvania for six companies of riflemen to travel to Boston to join the siege that had developed after the fights at Lexington and Concord. A Pennsylvania navy was formed, and defenses were built along the Delaware River.

A number of the signers of the Declaration of Independence were well aware they would be hanged as traitors if the Revolution failed.

In 1776 Thomas Paine produced his *Com-*

mon Sense, which argued eloquently for independence. He wanted Americans to replace the monarchy with a republic.

The Pennsylvania Constitution of 1776 gave independence to the colonists. It continued the rights that had become traditional in the colony, including freedom of religion, as well as the unicameral legislature. The new constitution maintained the requirement of a Christian oath for officeholders but made it more latitudinarian, or tolerant of different doctrines, which created controversy. The most significant change was eliminating property and financial requirements for voting, a broadening of the electorate that alarmed business and professional classes.

Benjamin Franklin is the most influential patriot associated with Philadelphia during the Revolution. He came to town from Boston in 1723 and within five years had bought a printing business, then a newspaper, the *Pennsylvania Gazette,* and at the age of 27 began to publish *Poor Richard's Almanac.*

Franklin's house was in the process of construction in 1764 when he was called back to London. His wife, Deborah, stayed behind to oversee the construction, which progressed with many difficulties. Franklin did not return for 10 years, and Deborah died just before he arrived.

The next year he was sent by Congress to France, along with Silas Deane and Arthur Lee, to try to persuade the French to sign treaties with America. He settled into a house in Paris and was sought after by the court of Louis XVI and Marie Antoinette. Franklin, who already had an international reputation as a scientist and inventor, was respected and loved abroad. He knew how to maintain good relations with the French and did so quietly without badgering them. In February 1778, two Franco-American treaties were signed. The first recognized American independence and provided for commercial relationships between the two countries. The second was a defensive alliance, in case Britain declared war on France. Both France and the United

Paine wrote, "O ye that love mankind! Ye that dare oppose not only the tyranny, but also the tyrant, stand forth! . . . how a race of men came into the world so exalted above the rest, and distinguished like some new species, is worth inquiring into, and whether they are the means of happiness or of misery to mankind."

Poor Richard provided pithy quotes galore:

"People of good sense, I have since observed, seldom fall in disputation, except lawyers and university men."

"Wise and good men are the strength of a state: much more so than riches or arms."

"Good sense is a thing all need, few have, and none think they lack."

"To lengthen thy life, lessen thy meals."

"Be mindful of the past."

"Wherever Liberty shines, there people will naturally flock to bask themselves in its beams."

> **How many statues of Benjamin Franklin can you find in the city?** There's one at the Benjamin Franklin National Memorial at the Franklin Institute, another at Franklin Court, along with the ghost of his home. A third is at his grave in the Christ Church Burial Ground.

States would not sign a separate peace but would both continue to fight until Britain agreed to American independence.

Franklin Court (215-965-2305), 316–322 Market St., is the site of his home, which was razed in 1812. Open daily. The National Park Service has conducted archaeological digs to uncover the foundations. Today a "ghost" or "skeleton" sculpture stands to show the outlines of the home. Visitors can visit the restored office of his grandson's newspaper and see demonstrations of 18th-century printing and bookbinding. There is also a colonial post office where you can buy commemorative stamps.

From the courtyard take a ramp into an underground museum. Look for the telephone "hotline," where you can dial Franklin's friends both in America and Europe to hear them tell stories about him.

HISTORIC TOURS

Tours of the historic area include "The Liberty Tale," by Historic Philadelphia Inc., 215-629-5801.

More HISTORIC SITES *to* VISIT

American Swedish Historical Museum (215-389-1776), 1900 Pattison Ave. Open Tue.–Sun. The museum has 12 permanent galleries and a research library offering the history of Swedish residents dating from 1638, when the New Sweden colony was established.

Arch Street Meeting House (215-627-2667), 320 Arch St. Open Mon.–Sat. The 1804 building is used for Quaker gatherings. William Penn granted the land in 1693 for a graveyard, but it is used for worship and society business. The house can seat 1,000. Exhibits detail the history of the Friends.

Betsy Ross House (215-686-1252; www.betsyrosshouse.org), 239 Arch St. Open Memorial Day–Labor Day daily; Tue.–Sun. the rest of year. Visit the home of Betsy Ross, who may have made the first American flag in 1776. This 1740 brick house is furnished with period pieces. Some of them belonged to Betsy Ross. Betsy and her third husband, John Claypoole, rest in the garden.

Christ Church (215-922-1696; www.oldchristchurch.org), Second and Market Sts. Open daily. Dr. John Kearsley designed the church in the style of Christopher Wren. Fifteen signers of the Declaration of Independence worshiped here. The 1727 building has one of the oldest Palladian windows in the country. You will see brass plaques identifying the pews used by Benjamin Franklin, Betsy Ross, and George Washington. The font used to baptize William Penn in 1644 in London is here.

Loxley Court, one block west of the Betsy Ross house, was the site of Benjamin Franklin's kite experiment. He used a kite made of a silk handkerchief and two crossed cedar sticks, with a key tied to his end of the silk kite string. A wire from the key went into a Leyden jar. Apparently the key came from the door of Benjamin Loxley's house. Franklin's son William was told to run with the kite during a lightning storm. The charge in the storm cloud traveled down to the key, which sparked when Franklin touched it with his hand. This was the first proof of electricity in lightning. Franklin was fortunate he was not electrocuted.

Benjamin Franklin and four other signers of the Declaration of Independence are buried in Christ Church Burial Ground. You can toss a penny on Benjamin Franklin's grave for good luck.

Cliveden (215-848-1777; www.cliveden.org), 6401 Germantown Ave. Open Apr.–Dec., Thu.–Sun. This house was built from 1763 to 1767 for Pennsylvania chief justice Benjamin Chew. It was constructed by a local mason and carpenter using local stone. Its design reflects English homes of the period, including a Doric frontispiece and pediment and five urns on the front of the roof. Family portraits are hung in the house, and the furnishings are Philadelphia pieces of the 18th and 19th centuries.

Scars from the 1777 Battle of Germantown are still visible. The American advance had gone well until some troops began firing on each other in dense fog. Then this stone house proved an impregnable fortress, with up to 100 British troops shooting at the American advance from its windows. General Henry Knox convinced Washington that the house should not be left behind and brought up cannon to bombard its walls; the cannonballs simply bounced off, and 75 Americans were killed trying to storm it. The decision not to bypass the house may have cost Washington the battle, with a loss of about 1,000 casualties.

Elfreth's Alley (215-574-0560; www.elfrethsalley .org), 126 Elfreth's Alley. Elfreth's Alley Museum is open Mar.–Oct., Tue.–Sun.; rest of the year Thu.–Sun. This 15-foot-wide alley between Second and Front Streets is the oldest continuously inhabited street in Philadelphia. It opened between 1702 and 1704. The 33 homes range from two to three and a half stories. All are privately owned and, aside from the museum at number 126, are open only on Elfreth's Alley Days in June.

Elfreth's Alley, between Second and Front Streets.

Society Hill is a historic district near the Delaware River restored by the residents. It was named for the Free Society of Traders from London. William Penn granted the society a charter in 1681 for 20,000 acres. Some of the earliest brick homes were those of John Palmer and Joseph Wharton at 117 and 119 Lombard Street. They date from 1743. Walk on the cobblestone streets past Georgian and Federal houses lighted by Franklin lamps. Within the district **Head House Square** was originally a marketplace dating to 1745. Now renovated, it is a redbrick collection of shops and restaurants.

Tomb of the Unknown Soldier of the American Revolution stands in Washington Square. It is a monument with a statue of George Washington and the flags of the original 13 colonies. Soldiers and victims of the yellow fever epidemic of 1793 were buried on this land.

Hill-Physick-Keith House (215-925-2251, 215-925-7866; www.philaland marks.org), 321 S. Fourth St. Open Thu.–Sun. Henry Hill, a wine merchant and legislator, built the house in 1786. The fanlight over the front door is stunning. Dr. Philip Syng Physick lived here beginning in 1815; he was called the "father of American surgery."

Powel House (215-627-0364; www.philalandmarks.org), 224 S. Third St. Open Thu.–Sun. The house was built for Charles Stedman in 1765 and was later home to Samuel Powel, mayor of Philadelphia. Samuel and Elizabeth Powel bought the home in 1769. The Powels entertained George Washington, Benjamin Franklin, and John Adams, among many others. A tour will take you upstairs to the rococo ballroom. Martha and George Washington celebrated an anniversary here in 1779. Washington saw the pretzel-back chairs in the house and had two dozen made for himself. He gave a set of china in the dining room to the Powels.

Grumblethorpe (215-925-2251; www.philalandmarks.org), 5267 Germantown Ave. Open Thu.–Sun. The house was built by John Wister. British major general James Agnew used the house as headquarters during the Battle of Germantown. Daughter Sally Wister spent part of her life in the Foulke mansion in Penllyn, Pennsylvania. While there she wrote a journal entitled "A True Narrative, Being a Quaker Maiden's Account of Her Experiences with Officers of the Continental Army." This journal is addressed to a school friend, Deborah Norris, who lived in the Norris mansion adjoining the State House in Philadelphia. Wister wrote as interesting events crowded one upon another and declared, "I shall hang up my pen until something offers worth relating."

Deshler-Morris House (215-596-1748), 5442 Germantown Ave. Open Apr.–Dec., Tue.–Sun. David Deshler built the house in 1772. Sir William Howe took it for his headquarters after the Battle of Germantown in 1777. President Washington used it during the hot summers of 1793 and 1794.

Stenton (215-329-7312; www.stenton.org), 4601 N. 18th St. Open Tue.–Sat. James Logan, William Penn's secretary, built the house in 1728. He had good rapport with the Indians, who sometimes visited him and camped here. The house is furnished with William and Mary and Queen Anne pieces.

EPIDEMIC OF 1793

✵ Washington was among 20,000 residents who fled Philadelphia's confined streets and alleys during the late summer of 1793 as the capital city suffered the largest yellow fever epidemic in American history. He explained his move in these words: "As Mrs. Washington was unwilling to leave me surrounded by the malignant fever which prevailed, I could not think of hazarding her and the Children any longer by my continuance in the city, the house in which we lived being, in a manner, blockaded, by the disorder." Dr. Benjamin Rush, a signer of the Declaration of Independence, had discovered the first case on August 5 and many more in following weeks, and he urged all "that can move, to quit the city."

Among those who stayed, panic destroyed normal relationships, even those between parents and children, as the toll of the fearful disease rose, ultimately killing somewhere between 4,000 and 5,000 residents before the first frost stemmed the epidemic. The mass migration of more than a third of a city populated by 55,000 brought business to a halt and created great economic hardship. The black population, who some believed were immune, stayed to tend the sick and were much lauded for that service, but 240 of them also died.

National Constitution Center (215-409-6600; www.constitutioncenter.org), 525 Arch St. Open daily. This fairly new museum has gotten rave reviews. It is the first museum dedicated to the U.S. Constitution. You will see a multimedia presentation and then wander through the 100 interactive exhibits. Live performances by actors give life to the story of the Constitution. You can be sworn in as a president and sign a copy of the Constitution. Don't miss the dramatic section almost alive with life-size statues of our founding fathers.

Independence Seaport Museum (215-413-8613, 215-925-5439; www.philly seaport.org), 211 S. Columbus Blvd. Open daily. This museum reveals the maritime heritage of the Delaware River, Delaware Bay, and its tributaries. Exhibits begin with "Once upon the Delaware," reminders of 1682 and William Penn. This exhibit is in prints and photographs. John Barry, an Irish immigrant who became a hero of the Continental Navy and is often called the father of the U.S. Navy, is represented here. Other important figures of the day included Steven Decatur, a naval officer who destroyed the captured U.S. frigate *Philadelphia* in the harbor of Tripoli; shipbuilder and designer

✵ Heard of a busybody? Some homes have this contraption attached to their second-story windows. Several mirrors are angled so that the resident can look down to the front door. You can see who is knocking without being observed!

Joshua Humphreys, whose most famous vessel was the *USS Constitution;* and John Fitch, who invented a steamboat that made a trial voyage on the Delaware River in 1787.

LODGING

ALEXANDER INN
301 S. 12th St., Philadelphia, PA 19107
877-ALEX-INN, 215-923-3535;
www.alexanderinn.com
This boutique hotel has been recently renovated. Dating from 1900, the brick building is right in Center City. 48 guest rooms.

INDEPENDENCE PARK INN
235 Chestnut St., Philadelphia, PA 19106
800-528-1234, 215-922-4443;
www.independenceparkhotel.com
This building dates from 1856 and is in the historic district. Breakfast is served in the glass-enclosed courtyard. 36 guest rooms.

THE LATHAM HOTEL
135 S. 17th St., Philadelphia, PA 19103
877-LATHAM1, 215-563-7474;
www.lathamhotel.com
A boutique hotel, the Latham is in the heart of downtown and has an elegant European style. 139 guest rooms.

PARK HYATT PHILADELPHIA AT THE BELLEVUE
Broad and Walnut Sts., Philadelphia, PA 19102
215-893-1234; www.parkphiladelphia.hyatt.com
This historic French Renaissance–style hotel is in the historic district, and has been renovated since its earlier Bellevue days. 172 guest rooms.

THOMAS BOND HOUSE
129 S. Second St., Philadelphia, PA 19106
800-845-2663, 215-923-8523;
www.winston-salem-inn.com/philadelphia
This 1769 Georgian home, once the residence of a Philadelphia physician, is in Independence National Historical Park. 12 guest rooms.

RESTAURANTS

CITY TAVERN
138 S. 2nd St., Philadelphia, PA 19106
215-413-1443; www.citytavern.com
The original City Tavern began serving in 1773; this re-creation serves 18th-century fare with atmosphere.

DOWNEY'S RESTAURANT
526 S. Front St., Philadelphia, PA 19147
215-625-9500; www.downeysrestaurant.com
This Irish pub overlooks the Penn's Landing waterfront.

FORK306
Market St., Philadelphia, PA 19106
215-625-9425;
www.forkrestaurant.com
Diners can enjoy the open kitchen at this stylish bistro.

FOUNTAIN RESTAURANT IN FOUR SEASONS HOTEL
1 Logan Square, Philadelphia, PA 19103
215-963-1500; www.fourseasons.com/philadelphia
This elegant dining room overlooks Swann Fountain.

MOSHULU
401 S. Columbus Blvd., Penn's Landing, Philadelphia, PA 19106
215-923-2500; www.moshulu.com
This 1904 square rigger is the largest four-masted sailing ship in the world still afloat, now a popular restaurant.

EVENTS

July: Let Freedom Ring, Liberty Bell Center; 215-965-2305
December: Deck the Alley, Elfreth's Alley; 215-574-0560

INFORMATION

PHILADELPHIA CONVENTION & VISITORS BUREAU
1700 Market St., Philadelphia, PA 19103
800-225-5745; www.pcvb.org

PHILADELPHIA AND THE COUNTRYSIDE
30 S. 17th St., Philadelphia, PA 19103
888-GOPHILA; www.gophila.com

INDEPENDENCE VISITOR CENTER
6th and Market Sts., Philadelphia, PA 19106
800-537-7676; www.independence visitorcenter.com

SOUTHEASTERN PENNSYLVANIA

The countryside and suburbs surrounding Philadelphia are filled with many additional historical sites to visit. As more immigrants came to escape religious persecution, ethnic villages sprang up in the eastern section of Pennsylvania. The Brandywine Valley attracted settlers and was later the site of important Revolutionary War battles. On the other side of Philadelphia, in Bucks County, settlements grew along the Delaware River, and some of the old mansions are there still.

BRANDYWINE VALLEY

William Penn founded the area as one of his first named counties, Chester. Since 1789 the area has been divided into Chester County and Delaware County. The Brandywine River (or Creek) curves through West Chester and Chadds Ford and down into Delaware, joining the Delaware River at Wilmington.

CHADDS FORD

Chadds Ford started life as a river crossing. It is still a small center, with shops and restaurants.

HISTORICAL SITES *and* MUSEUMS

Brandywine Battlefield Park (610-459-3342; www.ushistory.org/brandwine), 1491 Baltimore Park. Open Mar.–Nov., Tue.–Sun.; Thu.–Sun. the rest of the year. This park is the site of an important battle between George Washington's soldiers and the British in September 1777. The visitor center offers a video narration and exhibits on the battle. There are two houses to visit within the park.

General William Howe was eager to take Philadelphia and expected that Wash-

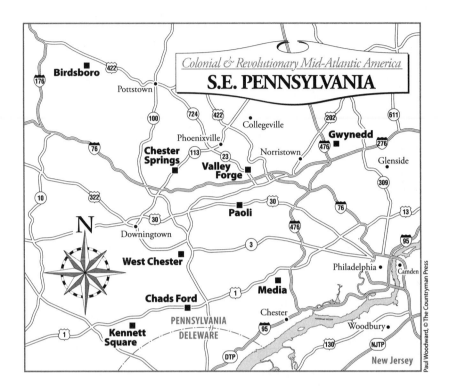

Colonial & Revolutionary Mid-Atlantic America
S.E. PENNSYLVANIA

ington's troops would try to stop him along the Delaware River. So he decided to transport his army by ship around Cape Charles, Virginia, and up the Chesapeake Bay to Head of Elk in Maryland, about 40 miles southwest of Philadelphia.

Before the battle Washington's men were stationed along the east side of Brandywine Creek from Pyle's Ford, south of Chadds Ford, to Buffington's Ford toward the north. Under cover of fog the British began marching toward the American troops, pausing for a wine party at Jeffery's Ford on the way.

Unfortunately, Washington did not receive enough accurate information about troop movements, and a British flanking attack drove the Americans back. The Americans fought valiantly and were able to slow the British advance but eventually suffered defeat. Although victorious, British General William Howe was not able to crush the Americans completely. Washington told Congress, "Notwithstanding the misfortune of the day, I am happy to find the troops in good spirits; and I hope another time we shall compensate for the losses now sustained."

Although Quakers remained neutral on military matters, they maintained cordial relations with the Revolutionary effort. Two prominent Quakers opened their homes to General Washington and his aide, the Marquis de Lafayette. Both homes are in the park.

You can visit the farmhouse, owned by **Gideon Gilpin**, used by Lafayette. The house was built in three sections; the oldest dates from the last days of the 17th century. It is half-timbered with rubble construction. After the battle the British destroyed Gilpin's property, but he later petitioned the court for a license to run a tavern in his home. The carriage used by Lafayette is also here.

The claim for losses filed by Gilpin follows: 10 milch cows, 1 yoke of oxen, 48 sheep, 28 swine, 12 tons of hay, 230 bushels of wheat, 50 pounds of bacon, 1 history book, 1 gun.

Next door stands a reconstruction of the house used by General Washington, owned by **Benjamin Ring**. Washington stayed there for two nights before the battle. He held a council of war with his generals in the Ring house on September 9 to make plans. The house stood a mile from Chadds Ford.

Chadds Ford Historical Society (610-388-7376; www.chaddsfordhistory.org), Creek Rd. Open May–Sep., daily. The society bought and restored two historic houses, and they are open to the public.

The **John Chad House** (610-388-7376; www.voicenet.com/-cfhs), Creek Rd., across from the historical society, dates from 1725 when John Wyeth Jr. built it for him. In 1729 he married Elizabeth Richardson. By 1731 he was running a tavern and also a ferry service across the Brandywine. Chadds Ford was named for him; Elizabeth lived in the house for over 60 years after he died in 1760.

Elizabeth Chad may have watched the battle from her attic window in the west end of the house. She hid her silver spoons every day in her pocket.

Today the house is operated as a living-history museum, with guides in colonial dress. The kitchen is used for baking breads and biscuits. The cook preheats the oven and then puts her hand in to gauge the heat; when she can't keep it in, it is ready for the bread. Crafts are demonstrated in the parlor.

The **Barns-Brinton House** (610-388-7376; www.voicenet.com/-cfhs), 1736 Creek Rd., was built by blacksmith William Barns in 1714. He saw the need for a tavern on "Ye Great Road to Nottingham," which was a road between Philadelphia and Maryland. This brick building has patterned gables and Flemish bond brickwork. The family slept on one side, and the other contained a barroom and sleeping for travelers.

James Brinton bought the house; he was the grandson of William Brinton, who built the 1704 House in West Chester. The house still retains the two sides: public rooms and tavernkeeper's quarters. Guides in colonial dress welcome visitors and describe tavern life in the 18th century and demonstrate crafts of the period.

The **William Brinton 1704 House** (610-399-0913; www.brintonfamily.org), 1435 Oakland Rd., West Chester. This home resembles English medieval style.

The 1704 Brinton House at the Chester County Historical Society.

It has 27 leaded-glass windows. There is an indoor bread-baking oven. The house was renovated with the help of the John Hill Brinton diary. The Brinton Association of America has furnished the house with pieces similar to those that would have been there in 1704.

Brandywine River Museum (610-388-2700; www.brandywinemuseum.org), US 1. Open daily. Although this museum is not in our time period, it is the lifeblood of the Wyeth family, and few visitors bypass the work of this amazing family on a trip to the Brandywine Valley. The museum is housed in Hoffman's Mill, a gristmill constructed in 1864. When it faced extinction at auction in 1967, local residents formed the Brandywine Conservancy, to buy the mill. The group then spearheaded a funding program to restore the building and turn the interior into a sparkling new art gallery.

The new wing is striking, with its twin turrets and glass tower. Large windows provide views of the river from several different angles. Take a look at the remarkable lighting, which allows the natural light to focus on the paintings and statues in the gallery.

In our many trips to the Brandywine Valley we have always focused on the Wyeths and recently had dinner with the only Wyeth grandchild, Victoria. She gives tours at the museum and after every tour meets with her grandfather to consult on her commentary. She changes her lectures to capture his passion and love for his work. Almost every day he says, "I'm going paintin', Vic."

The museum features paintings by three generations of Wyeths. N.C. Wyeth, a noted illustrator, moved to the Brandywine Valley in 1902 and raised a family of five talented children. Andrew Wyeth, the youngest of his children, is one of the best known American painters, and his son, Jamie Wyeth, continues the family heritage. When we were there Jamie strolled into the museum to buy a book, and no one bothered him.

"Who do you think you are, Andrew Wyeth?" the policeman growled at the man painting on a country road in Chadds Ford. He was. His granddaughter, Victoria Wyeth, filled in the story: The astonished policeman had red cones placed around the artist that day so he could continue to paint undisturbed.

Recently the museum opened two more Wyeth sites. One is the N.C. Wyeth studio, where the father worked and began giving Andrew art lessons when he was five years old. The Palladian window sheds light on his possessions just as he left them. The Kuerner Farm, where Andrew and Karl Kuerner used to sit on a bench made of two buckets and a board, drink hard cider, and talk, is also open. An easel by the window holds a painting of the sun coming through that window captured by Andrew. Don't miss the Wyeths!

By the hearth in the Brinton House.

KENNETT SQUARE

Kennett Square offers shops and restaurants, plus a booming industry of mushrooms. It is called the "mushroom capital of the world." They grow quietly inside buildings in town. Stop in the Mushroom Cap (610-444-8484) for mushroom sampling, fresh mushrooms, mushroom cookbooks, marinated mushrooms, and gifts.

Longwood Gardens (610-388-1000; www.longwoodgardens.org), US 1. Open Apr.–Oct., daily, also Tue., Fri., Sat. evenings June–Aug. William Penn originally sold this land to George Peirce in 1700. His son Joshua built a log cabin in 1709 and cleared land for a working farm. Joshua also built the brick farmhouse in 1730. By 1798 Joshua's twin 32-year-old grandsons were planting trees and studying them in the Quaker tradition as a way of understanding the Almighty. As this horticultural family passed the land down through the decades, the garden grew and an arboretum was developed. In 1906 Pierre S. du Pont bought the estate and 203 acres of the famous gardens.

As the du Ponts traveled abroad, they developed ideas to use at home, including the special features of English, French, and Italian gardens. The outdoor gardens are set beside two lakes, with fountains bursting forth among formal gardens and forests with tall trees for accent. You can stroll through 350 acres and see an astounding 14,000 varieties of species. Pierre du Pont took great pleasure in designing the system for the fountains and waterfalls, which are illuminated with colored lights and sometimes enhanced by fireworks as well.

The Peirce–du Pont House is open to the public. Exhibits describe the horticultural development of Longwood Gardens.

The du Ponts' Longwood Gardens include an arboretum and fountains.

WEST CHESTER

HISTORICAL SITES and MUSEUMS

Chester County Historical Society (610-692-4800; www.chestercohistorical
.org), 225 N. High St. Open May 1–Oct. 1, Tue., Thu., Sat. William Brinton
the elder arrived with his wife, Ann Bagley Brinton, in 1684. They probably lived
in a lean-to, then received a patent for 456 acres. His son, William Brinton the
younger, built the stone house in 1704. The house features 27 leaded casement
windows, raised hearths, and an indoor bake oven. A colonial herb garden blooms
outside.

MEDIA

This living-history museum will give you a taste of what life was like in rural colonial Pennsylvania.

HISTORICAL SITES and MUSEUMS

Colonial Pennsylvania Plantation (610-566-1725; www.delcohistory.org/colo-
nial plantation), Ridley Creek State Park. Open mid-Apr.–mid Nov., weekends.
Interpreters in period dress express the lives of the Pratt family who lived on the
farm for three generations; members of the family farmed here for over 250 years.
Interpreters may be baking bread, carding wool, planting crops, or mending fences.
Behind the fences are farm animals of the period.

PAOLI

The so-called Paoli Massacre happened after Washington's retreat from Brandywine, as General Anthony Wayne's Pennsylvania division was encamped behind
the British lines near Paoli tavern (actually in neighboring Malvern). Paoli was
Wayne's hometown. The British caught Wayne by surprise in a midnight bayonet charge. Most of the Pennsylvanians escaped, including Wayne, but the 53
corpses found were mangled by bayonets.

Outside our time period but nice to visit is the **Wharton Esherick Studio**
(610-644-5822), 2049 Waynesborough Rd. Esherick was known as the dean of
American craftsmen, and his studio includes paintings, woodcuts, ceramics, sculpture, and furniture. Don't miss the desk with a toggle "boomerang" mechanism
to open the doors, drawers, and top. A row of coat pegs caricatures each of his
workmen.

HISTORICAL SITES and MUSEUMS

There are a number of stories about "Mad" Anthony Wayne, who may have gotten his nickname from a soldier furious after being imprisoned in the guardhouse
for being drunk—or from his tenacity and daring in battle. One of Wayne's most

Wayne said to Washington, "Give the order, sir, and I will lay siege to Hell!" Washington replied, "Take Stony Point first." And Wayne was victorious at Stony Point on the Hudson River in 1779.

famous military exploits was leading a successful midnight attack on Stony Point in July 1779, with unloaded muskets and fixed bayonets to maintain silence.

Historic Waynesborough (215-925-2251 or 610-647-1779; www.easttown.org/waynes borough.html), 2049 Waynesborough Rd. Open mid-March–Dec. This 18th-century house was home to General Anthony Wayne. His grandfather purchased the land, and Wayne was born in the house. He became a Revolutionary War hero who served with George Washington and the Marquis de Lafayette. He led the Pennsylvania line in the battles of Brandywine and Germantown, stayed in the Valley Forge encampment, and fought at Monmouth.

Wayne retired to the house after the Revolution, but in 1792 President Washington called him to serve as major general and commander in chief of the "Legion of the United States" against Indians in the Northwest Territory. Wayne won a signal victory at the Battle of Fallen Timbers. He died at Fort Presque Isle (Erie) in 1796 on his way home to Waynesborough. Seven generations of the Wayne family lived here until 1965.

This Georgian home was constructed in three sections from native stone quarried on the property. It has a center passage, with the earlier wing and a later wing attached. The house has been restored to its 18th-century appearance, as well as containing pieces from Federal, Victorian, and colonial revival periods. The collections include a copy of the general's own map from the Paoli Massacre.

General "Mad" Anthony Wayne was born and lived in Waynesborough, in Paoli.

CHESTER SPRINGS

This was once a colonial-period health resort. Ruins of the first military hospital in America are here. The hospital dates from 1777, and it was the chief medical facility for the Valley Forge encampment. It was also the site of an 18th-century mineral water spa.

The Landscape school for the Pennsylvania Academy of the Fine Arts and a movie studio are here. Patty Duke, Robert Lansing, Lee Meriwether, and Steve McQueen started their film careers in the studio.

HISTORICAL SITES *and* MUSEUMS
Historic Yellow Springs (610-827-7414;www.yellowsprings.org), 1685 Art School Rd. Open Mon.–Fri. Tours are available with advanced reservations. This 18th- and 19th-century village is the site of the only Revolutionary War hospital commissioned by the Continental Congress. The grounds are open for self-guided tours.

VALLEY FORGE

HISTORICAL SITES *and* MUSEUMS
Valley Forge National Historical Park (610-783-1099; www.nps.gov/vafo), 1400 N. Outer Line Dr., King of Prussia, PA 19406. Open daily.

If you want to see where George Washington really did sleep, go into the visitor center. His canvas tent, 53 feet in circumference, was used as both office and bedroom. There is a film for orientation, plus displays including a time line of important dates. Tours are given on weekends from the visitor center.

If Washington had had his way, the troops would have spent that winter of 1777–78 in Wilmington, Delaware, where equipment and supplies could be brought by water and the men could be housed comfortably. The Pennsylvania legislature, however, demanded that the troops remain out in the country to prevent British foraging parties from ransacking homes and villages. Washington responded to the legislature that it was easy from their vantage point in their warm and comfortable homes to send his men out into the cold, seemingly with little pity. Washington knew what the men's misery would be.

Accounts written by men on the march to Valley Forge describe the snow and cold, the lack of food, and their fatigue and utter despair. As Washington rode beside a group who were without shoes, he asked the colonel why he had not provided them and was told that the supplies had run out. When they arrived at Valley Forge, they were too tired to put up tents and slept by their campfires. The 12,000 Continental Army soldiers felt cold winds howling around them as they prepared for winter. The Schuylkill River froze a few days after they arrived, and the snow was six inches deep. Yet the next day was proclaimed Thanksgiving. Each man received half a gill of rice with a little vinegar to ward off scurvy.

Firing a field piece at Valley Forge.

The winter encampment was supposed to rest the troops, encourage them to stay the winter, and then train them. The men built log houses 14 to 16 feet in length and half as wide, with a fireplace and bunks. As the winter progressed, many men died and many more deserted and returned home.

The man responsible for training the troops was Friedrich von Steuben, once a member of the elite general staff of Frederick the Great of Prussia. He worked directly with the men, drilling them from dawn to dusk, marching, loading muskets, and charging against imaginary redcoats. The men learned military arts and the value of discipline. What's more, they gained confidence from their new skills, which raised their morale.

You can choose to take a bus tour or drive around the route following a map. You will first see the Muhlenberg Brigade, where the militia defended the outer line of the area. The Memorial Arch is dedicated to the patience and fidelity of the soldiers who remained in Valley Forge. Not far away, General Anthony Wayne's statue is made of bronze; he is seated on a horse fac-

> ✦ A local resident told us a story about Wayne. On his way home from fighting Indians in the Northwest Territory, Wayne died and was buried in Erie. His son, Isaac, traveled there years later to bring home his father's remains. Because the roads were very bumpy, the bones kept falling out of the box. So every January 1, Wayne's ghost gets on his horse Nancy and goes out looking for his bones.

ing in the direction of his own home in Chester County.

The **Isaac Potts House** was Washington's headquarters. Now furnished with period pieces, the house is open to the public. It was built by a Quaker family, and Washington rented it from them. Martha Washington lived here with her husband through that hard winter, along with about 20 military aides and servants.

Possibly the first recorded mention of the game of baseball dates from 1778. A soldier in Washington's army at Valley Forge wrote in his diary that they played a game of "base" that day.

The **Dewees House** (homestead of some of our ancestors) and adjacent huts for his life guards are also in this particular group of buildings. Visitors can explore the sites of earthworks where cannons were emplaced. Artillery Park contains a concentration of cannon; artillery was stored there ready for use. Washington Memorial Chapel contains stained-glass windows tracing the founding of our country. The bell tower features a 58-bell carillon.

BIRDSBORO

HISTORICAL SITES *and* MUSEUMS
Hopewell Furnace (610-582-8773; www.nps.gov/hofu), 2 Mark Bird Lane. Open daily. Mark Bird developed Hopewell Furnace in 1771 on French Creek. Four essential natural resources made the location a good one for an iron furnace: fast-flowing water to turn the waterwheel and provide mechanical power for the bel-

A reconstructed log house at the Valley Forge encampment.

FORTUNES of a FURNACE

The subsequent history of the furnace that was so essential to the Continental Army provides a capsule view of rapidly evolving technology in America. A number of other owners tried to make the furnace profitable, but by 1808 it was closed again. In 1816 it was fired up once more because the iron industry was booming. By 1820 there were more than 150 employees, and the village was thriving.

Five years later the Schuylkill Canal opened, so the wagons bringing in raw materials and carrying out finished products did not need to travel as far. The canal increased the range for Hopewell products to New York and Boston. In 1838 the Reading Railroad further increased the customers for Hopewell. But as the middle of the century approached, new technologies for iron-making began to make older furnaces obsolete. In 1853 Hopewell built an anthracite furnace, but the operation finally was closed in 1883.

lows; a supply of limestone; many hardwood trees to be cut and burned into charcoal to fuel the furnace; and easily mined iron ore deposits near the surface. Mr. Bird paid his employees good wages, and they were happy to live here.

During the Revolution the furnace produced cannon, shot, and shells. Bird commanded the second battalion of Berks County Militia and also bought uniforms, tents, and provisions for 300 men. During the hard winter of 1778 he sent a thousand barrels of flour down the Schuylkill River to Valley Forge to feed Washington's starving men.

Unfortunately, Bird fell deeper and deeper into debt during the war, and in 1788 he lost Hopewell Furnace.

The visitor center offers an audiovisual presentation and exhibits of tools and original iron castings made here. The "Big House" was the center of activity for the village; sometimes 30 people lived here, along with the ironmaster and his family. The villagers gathered in the house for parties, marriages, deaths, and other occasions. Because the village was so remote, visitors were always invited to stay overnight.

The ironmaster himself was a key figure in the community. He had to be an expert in personnel, technology, production, and transportation, as well as a salesman, expeditor, currency expert, marketing analyst, credit manager, bill collector, purchasing agent, investment counselor, and bookkeeper. This heavy load was shared with the company clerk, who also lived in the Big House. The clerk spent most of his time in the village store, where he was the storekeeper and the furnace paymaster.

Most village workers were not paid in cash, but instead they charged their purchases against their earnings, an early example of the company towns that developed as America became industrialized. Many of the men who worked in Hopewell were skilled workers, including the founder, who was responsible for producing high-quality iron; the molder, who poured the liquid iron into molds; and the blacksmith, who made mine and furnace tools and repaired the machinery. Unskilled labor included the woodcutters, colliers, and miners. Men worked in 12-hour shifts to tend the furnace when it was in blast.

As you walk around the village, you will see a demonstration of the charcoal-making process, which shows all of the layers added to the conical pile. Walk into the furnace building, look at the giant waterwheel, and listen to its slap-slap-slap as it turns. You can also visit tenant houses, barns, the blacksmith shop, and office store.

GWYNEDD

Like many families in America, ours has deep roots in the colonial era. Edward and Eleanor Foulke emigrated in 1698 from Bala, Wales, sailing on the *Robert and Elizabeth* from Liverpool with their nine children. Although forty-five passengers died during the eleven weeks at sea, the Foulke family survived intact and arrived safely in Philadelphia. Edward bought land from William Penn sixteen miles from Philadelphia in the township named Gwynedd, or North Wales.

In 1898 a bicentennial reunion was held in the Friends Meeting House in Gwynedd, and over 500 descendants of Edward and Eleanor Foulke attended to celebrate the 200th anniversary of their ancestors' arrival in America. They visited the site of the original house, which is near Penllyn Station, and also the grave of Edward Foulke outside the Meeting House.

In 1998 we attended the reunion to celebrate the 300th anniversary of the family in America. We had a wonderful four days of meeting 800 cousins, looked at an exhibition of family artifacts, participated in computer research into family lines, attended seminars including ours on travel in Wales, enjoyed Welsh folk dancing, had a Welsh tea, attended Quaker meeting at the Friends Meeting House, found the grave of Edward Foulke in the churchyard, and took a special tour of Foulke sites in the area. They included the home of Hugh Foulke, who built a log home in 1730 in Quakertown. Liberty Hall was where the Liberty Bell was hidden for a time. The Burgess-Foulke House contains a rush-seat rocking chair that belonged to Edward and Eleanor.

HISTORICAL SITES *and* MUSEUMS
The **Burgess Foulke House** (215-536-3298), 26 N. Main St., Quakertown, PA 18951. The house is open for visitors year-round. Please phone for days. As Foulke descendants we enjoyed speaking with Nancy Roberts of the Quakertown Historical Society. She is married to Donald Roberts, whose ancestors came at the same time as the Foulkes. Edward Roberts had married Mary Bolton, descended from a lord in England. The Roberts and Foulkes intermarried. Looking back at our ancestors is great!

LODGING

BRANDYWINE RIVER HOTEL
1609 Baltimore Pike, Chadds Ford, PA 19317
800-274-9644, 610-388-1200;
www.brandywineriverhotel.com
The hotel is in a historic colonial area next to museums, gardens, and shops. 40 guest rooms.

THE PENNSBURY INN B&B
883 Baltimore Pike, Chadds Ford, PA 19317
610-388-1435; www.pennsburyinn.com
The original dwelling dates from 1714. It was built of Brandywine blue granite rubble stone. 7 guest rooms.

SWEETWATER FARM B&B
50 Sweetwater Rd., Glen Mills, PA 19342
610-459-4711; www.sweetwater farmbb.com
The manor house dates from the 18th century and is set on 50 acres. 14 guest rooms.

WILLIAM PENN INN
1017 DeKalb Pike, Gwynedd, PA 19436
215-699-9272; www.williampenninn .com.
Dating from 1714, this is the oldest continuously operated country inn in Pennsylvania.

KENNETT HOUSE B&B
503 W. State St., Kennett Square, PA19348
800-820-9592, 610-444-9592;
www.kennetthouse.com
The house dates from 1910 and features chestnut and rosewood woodwork. 4 guest rooms.

RESTAURANTS

DILWORTHTOWN INN
1390 Old Wilmington Pike, West Chester, PA 19382
610-399-1390;
www.dilworthtown.com
The 1758 building and additions have been restored to gracious colonial atmosphere on three floors.

THE GABLES AT CHADDS FORD
423 Baltimore Pike, Chadds Ford, PA 19317
610-388-7700; www.thegablesat chaddsford.com
This converted 1800s dairy farm offers American cuisine with French and Asian influences.

HANK'S PLACE
US 1 and PA 100, Chadds Ford, PA 19317
610-388-7061
This restaurant is a favorite hangout of Andrew Wyeth.

EVENTS

May: French Alliance Day, Valley Forge National Historical Park; 610-783-1077; www.nps.gov/vafo/
June: March-Out, Valley Forge National Historical Park; 610-783-1077; www.nps.gov/vafo/
September: Brandywine battlefield reenactment; 610-459-3342; www.ushistory.org/brandywine

INFORMATION

BRANDYWINE CONFERENCE AND VISITORS BUREAU
1 Beaver Valley Rd., Chadds Ford, PA, 19317
800-343-3983; www.brandywine country.com

CHESTER COUNTY CONFERENCE AND VISITORS CENTER
17 Wilmont Mews, West Chester, PA, 19382
800-228-9933; www.brandywine valley.com

VALLEY FORGE CONVENTION AND VISITORS BUREAU
600 W. Germantown Pike, Suite 130, Plymouth Meeting, PA 19462
610-834-1550; www.valleyforge.org

NORTH OF PHILADELPHIA / BUCKS COUNTY

For over three centuries Bucks County has been significant in American history. You can stand on the spot where William Penn built his summer mansion and in many other colonial settlements along the Delaware River.

FALLSINGTON

This historic village has been well preserved and includes pre-Revolutionary, Federal, and Victorian buildings. The square is very attractive, with three Friends meetinghouses. Maps and guided tours are available.

HISTORICAL SITES *and* MUSEUMS
Visitors enjoy strolling around **Historic Fallsington** (215-295-6567; www.his toricfallsington.org), 4 Yardley Ave. Open Mar. 15–Nov. 15, Wed.–Sun. Guided tours are given mid-May–mid Oct., Tue.–Sat. During the winter, tours are by

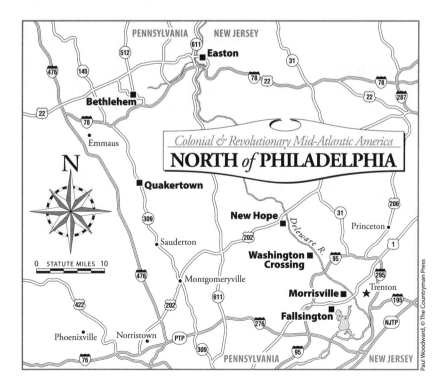

appointment. Some of the houses date back 300 years and are lived in by descendants of the first settlers.

The **Burgess-Lippincott House** dates from 1780; Allen Lippincott lived here from 1809 onward. Look at the handsome doorway. Inside, there is a carved fireplace and a stairway with a wall-banister.

The 1685 **Moon-Williamson House** is one of the oldest houses in Pennsylvania still standing on its site. Samuel Moon, a joiner and carpenter, built the house. He also made Windsor chairs. The furnishings are primitive.

The **Falls Friends Meeting House** was first built in 1690. It was abandoned and fell into ruin. The second meetinghouse, built in 1728, has a gambrel roof. The third, dating from 1789, is now a community center, and the fourth meetinghouse dates from 1841 and is still in use.

Two fieldstones on the **Schoolmaster's House** bear the date 1758. The Falls Friends Meeting House believed in education for their children and so built this house. It is not open.

EVENTS

October: Historic Fallsington Day. The houses are open, and there are craft displays and entertainment; 215-295-6567

MORRISVILLE

HISTORICAL SITES *and* MUSEUMS

Pennsbury Manor (215-946-0400; www.pennsburymanor.org), 400 Pennsbury Memorial Rd. Open Tue.–Sun. This site was chosen by William Penn for his home from the 23 million acres granted to him for the colony of Pennsylvania. Although the land had been given by King Charles II of England, Penn instructed William Markham, his secretary, to buy it from King Sepassing of the Delaware Indians. William Penn met with three tribes—the Lenni-Lenape, the Mingoes, and the Shawnees—to consummate this "Great Treaty of Friendship" in 1682.

James Harrison began to build the house in 1683, carrying on correspondence with Penn, who had returned to England. Penn moved into the house in 1700 with his second wife, Hannah, newborn son, John, and 21-year-old daughter, Letitia.

The Penns traveled between Pennsbury Manor and Philadelphia on their own 27-foot river barge—a five-hour trip with six oarsmen, a coxswain, and a boatswain. A replica of the English barge is on display.

Pennsbury required a large staff to provide a smoothly run household, tend the gardens, and operate the entire plantation. Crops included corn, wheat, barley, vegetables, and fruits. The plantation made its own cider and beer. Penn's gardens were laid out in a geometric pattern.

The original house was destroyed, but the present buildings were reconstructed according to old records. Rooms are furnished with period pieces; one armchair belonged to William Penn.

WASHINGTON CROSSING

HISTORICAL SITES *and* MUSEUMS

Washington Crossing (215-493-4076; www.ushistory.org/washingtoncrossing), 1112 River Rd. Open Tue.–Sun. This is a spot where history comes alive. George Washington was worried about his men, many of whom were ill, badly clothed, and exhausted after the long retreat across New Jersey in the closing days of 1776. After so many defeats, Washington wanted a psychological victory to cheer his men and convince skeptical congressmen that the cause of independence was not lost. That cause had reached a critical moment, with "the enemy in the Heart of our Country, the currency inflating, enlistments expiring, the disaffected daily increasing, and public sentiment at a stand," in General Nathanael Greene's words. Greene had written to John Hancock on December 21 requesting more authority for Washington, knowing that the army's effectiveness had been severely hampered by the need to get permission from Congress for every important military decision. Congress responded by granting Washington field authority for the conduct of the war for a period of six months, subject to congressional review, on December 27, just a day after the victory at Trenton.

It was not customary in the 18th century to fight battles during the dead of winter because of extra difficulties in moving troops and artillery. But Washington was aware that the British line, spread in clusters along the New Jersey side of the Delaware, was especially vulnerable in December as a result of independent raids by militia groups. Those initiatives grew out of the brutal behavior of foraging British and Hessian soldiers, who not only took residents' food but also plundered their houses and sometimes raped their daughters. The population's resentment produced spontaneous "risings" in the occupied territories, as well as raids encouraged by Washington to gather intelligence about enemy positions. Coping with this harassment put extra strain on the British and Hessian troops, and especially on Colonel Johann Rall's garrison at Trenton. When Washington's attacking force was finally discerned through the wind-driven snow on the morning of December 26, the defenders were not drunk—as the legend would have it—but exhausted from constant alerts through much of the month.

The **Thompson-Neely House**, dating from 1702, was the site of meetings in preparation for the Delaware crossing. No matter how opportune might be an attack partially shielded by a howling nor'easter, getting all his troops and artillery across the river at night presented Washington with difficulties that might have proved insuperable. As he crossed, Washington was four hours behind his projected timetable and even considered calling off the attack.

Fortunately, he had men who were experienced in handling boats; only the

WASHINGTON'S *Weather*

The Delaware crossing became the third stroke of good fortune that partially salvaged an otherwise dismal year of defeats for Washington. Success in all three depended upon a familiar storm pattern on the East Coast—the three-day nor'easter. In March Washington had succeeded in getting the guns Henry Knox had dragged all the way from Ticonderoga to Dorchester Heights, where they commanded the British position in Boston. General Howe ordered an attack on the heights and began to send troops in transports when a fierce nor'easter set in and scattered the operation; the next day, with the storm still raging, Howe decided to evacuate Boston.

Again, at the end of August when Washington had lost the Battle of Long Island to General Howe's overwhelming forces and was trapped at Brooklyn Heights, he was in danger of losing the entire Continental Army and perhaps the war. When a strong nor'easter set in, it was his turn to evacuate—under its cover, if the timing was right. The same strong northeast winds that kept the British fleet from beating up into the East River to block his escape made the crossing to Manhattan too rough to get boats loaded with troops across. But when that wind died about 11 o'clock on the night of August 29 and was replaced by moderate breeze from the southwest, Washington was able to start his mass evacuation, but not complete it before dawn. Then came the final stroke of luck that would continue his concealment: a thick fog that did not lift until his last boats reached Manhattan about 7 AM.

So the nor'easter that provided cover for the crossing to attack Trenton rounded out a year when the weather seemed to take sides for the Americans at three crucial moments.

weather could defeat his daring plan to surprise the British at Trenton on Christmas Day. If the river froze, all would be lost, for the ice would block boats but not be thick enough to support troops, horses, and heavy equipment.

On Christmas Day 1776 the password among the troops was "Victory or Death" as they prepared to advance into a dark, gray, ice-strewn river. As they walked toward the boats 200 yards north of McConkey's Ferry, men without adequate shoes left blood on the snow. Many of the men were terrified because they could not swim. They started embarking at 6 PM to ensure that the six-hour crossing for the whole attack force would be completed in the dark. The weather turned from snow to sleet, slowing their progress through the ice floes, and only two of Washington's four attack forces at the northern crossing made it, while those farther south were blocked by ice jams.

After the northern forces had landed and marched halfway to Trenton, Washington divided his men into two groups, with John Sullivan leading them to the right and Nathanael Greene to the left. Sleet and snow were falling, but the men followed orders to advance into Trenton in two directions. The Hessians were caught off guard at 8 AM but quickly assembled and resisted fiercely, staging two counterattacks. When they were surrounded and Colonel Rall received a wound that proved fatal, his remaining officers decided to surrender an hour after the battle started. Washington had regained the confidence of his men by this bold attack, and news of the victory restored hope for the ultimate success of the Revolution.

A reenactment of this crossing is held at 1 PM on December 25 every year. Visitors shiver as they imagine the pain of that night. You can see the famous painting *Washington Crossing the Delaware,* by Emanuel Leutze, in the **Washington Crossing Memorial Building**. The **McConkey Ferry Inn** has been restored; George Washington is thought to have had dinner there before crossing.

Three and a half miles up the road, you will come to the Thompson's Mill section of the park, which includes Thompson's Mill Barn, which has been restored. Soldiers' graves are also there.

NEW HOPE

The charming town of New Hope is known for its barge canal. You can take a trip past one garden after another, homes and studios of local residents, ducks quacking at one another. It is also one of the favorite places for antique hunters—you may not find anything from the colonial era, but then again, you might.

HISTORICAL SITES *and* MUSEUMS

The **Van Sant House**, Mechanic St., dates from 1743. It was peppered by a British shelling in 1776; grapeshot can still be seen in the attic walls.

The **Parry Mansion**, Main and Ferry Sts., was built in 1784 by Benjamin Parry, a wealthy lumber mill owner; it is open for visitors. The New Hope Historical Society (215-862-5652; www.newhopehistoricalsociety.org) has restored this stone house and furnished the rooms in different styles, including the 1775–1800 period.

LODGING

AARON BURR HOUSE B&B
80 W. Bridge St., New Hope, PA 18938
215-862-2343; www.aaronburrhouse
.com
This B&B dates from 1873. Some of the rooms have fireplaces. 8 guest rooms.

CENTRE BRIDGE INN
2998 N. River Rd., New Hope, PA 18938
215-862-9139; www.centrebridgeinn
.com
River views are abundant and the guest rooms have colonial furnishings. 10 guest rooms.

EIGHTEEN SEVENTY WEDGWOOD B&B INN
111 W. Bridge St., New Hope, PA 18938
215-862-2570; www.wedgwoodinn
.com
Built in 1870 over the ruins of an earlier structure where General William Alexander, Lord Stirling, encamped in December 1776. 10 guest rooms.

EVERMAY ON-THE-DELAWARE
889 River Rd., Erwinna, PA 18920
877-864-2365, 610-294-9100;
www.evermay.com
This historic country inn dates from the
1700s. Afternoon tea is served. 17 guest
rooms.

GOLDEN PHEASANT INN ON THE DELAWARE
763 River Rd., Erwinna, PA 18920
800-830-4474, 610-294-9595;
www.goldenpheasant.com
This 1857 fieldstone inn is on the National
Register of Historic Places; accommodations have river views. 6 guest rooms.

HOTEL DU VILLAGE
2535 N. River Rd., New Hope, PA 18938
215-862-9911; www.hotelduvillage
.com
This 1907 estate was once a private girls'
school. Country French cuisine is served.
20 guest rooms.

THE MANSION INN
9 S. Main St., New Hope, PA 18938
215-862-1231; www.themansioninn
.com
The ornate mansion dates from 1865.
7 guest rooms.

PINEAPPLE HILL INN
1324 River Rd., New Hope, PA 18938
888-866-8404, 215-862-1790;
www.pineapplehill.com
This restored 18th-century manor house is
near Washington Crossing. 9 guest rooms.

RESTAURANTS

CENTRE BRIDGE INN
2998 N. River Rd., New Hope
215-862-2048; www.centrebridgeinn
.com
Guests can dine in the main dining room
or on the brick terrace. The menu changes
seasonally.

LA BONNE AUBERGE
1 Rittenhouse Circle, New Hope, PA
18938
215-862-2462; www.bonneauberge
.com
Dinner is served in an 18th-century farmhouse. Classic French cuisine.

THE MANSION INN
9 S. Main St., New Hope
215-862-1231; www.themansioninn
.com
The 1865 Victorian inn offers Continental
fare.

EVENTS

December: Washington crossing the
Delaware, 215-493-4076

INFORMATION

BUCKS COUNTY CONFERENCE & VISITORS BUREAU
3207 Street Rd., Bensalem, PA 19020
800-836-2825; www.buckscounty.travel

NEW HOPE VISITOR CENTER
1 W. Mechanic St., New Hope, PA
18938
215-862-5030; www.newhopevisitors
center.org

BETHLEHEM

HISTORICAL SITES *and* MUSEUMS
Bethlehem Moravian Museum (610-867-0173), 66 W. Church St. Open
Thu.–Sun. The town was founded on December 24, 1741, when Count Nicholas
Ludwig von Zinzendorf celebrated a communion service with a group of newly
arrived Moravian settlers in their first house. The Moravians' Protestant religion

began with Jan Hus during the 15th century in Bohemia, and they came to America to spread the gospel to the Indians. The Moravians brought their traditions with them, and lighted advent stars with 26 points beam from almost every front porch during December. We attended a memorable concert that combined voice, organs, woodwinds, strings, and brasses.

Traditionally, on December 1 the city is suddenly illuminated on the north side with thousands of white lights on trees and on the south side with colored lights. An 81-foot-high star gleams from the top of South Mountain. Guides in Moravian dress lead tours through the historic district.

Moravian community "putzes" are assembled by volunteers who arrange the tiny wooden and ceramic figures, gather pine boughs, and crawl under the stage to install the lighting prior to the Christmas season. These miniature nativity scenes include both sound and light. Visitors enter a darkened and quiet room, waiting for the first spotlight to appear on a scene, and voices describe the nativity story as one scene after another is illuminated. It is a moving experience.

The Gemein Haus, which is the oldest building in town, was built in 1742 and held all 56 settlers. The original concept of the church was its communal plan—all worked for the church and lived in separate "choirs" according to sex and age. By 1800 this plan became superfluous as families chose to build their own homes.

The Gemein Haus is now the Moravian Museum. Saal Hall, the original place of worship, is within the house; services were conducted two or three times every day. A 1530 Nuremberg Bible is on display. The room that Count Zinzendorf stayed in is here, complete with a brown leather chair and ornate black wrought-iron hinges on the door. Quilts, such as one by "Christine," were made from scratch as the Moravians sheered the sheep, dyed, carded, and spun the wool, and wove the cloth. The music room contains an old flute, trombones with their cases, and a serpentine wooden horn covered with leather with fish skin in between.

The Old Chapel, the second place of worship in Bethlehem, dates from 1751. Movable wooden benches provided flexibility for the congregation. An open Bible stands on a table where Indians were baptized. Our guide explained the significance of ribbons on caps: Red was for little girls, burgundy for teens, pink for those confirmed, blue for married women, and white for widowed women. All wore a gray jacket, gray skirt, gray woolen cloak, and white apron.

Private residences include the Sisters' House, dating from 1744, where single women lived and worked, and the Widows' House. The Brethren's House, dating from 1748, where single men lived, is part of Moravian College's music department.

LODGING

HISTORIC HOTEL BETHLEHEM
437 Main St., Bethlehem, PA 18018
800-607-BETH, 610-625-5000;
www.hotelbethlehem.com
Dating from 1922, the hotel is in the
Moravian historic district. 128 guest
rooms.

THE SAYRE MANSION
250 Wyandotte St., Bethlehem, PA
18015
877-345-9019; www.sayremansion.com
The mansion dates from 1858; the landscaping includes centuries-old trees. 18
guest rooms.

RESTAURANTS

INN OF THE FALCON
1740 Seidersville Rd., Bethlehem 18015
610-868-6505; www.innofthefalcon
.com
This 1790 stone colonial tavern offers
American and Continental cuisine.

INFORMATION

**LEHIGH VALLEY CONVENTION AND
VISITORS BUREAU**
840 Hamilton St., Suite 200, Allentown,
PA 18101
800-747-0561; www.lehighvalleypa
.org

EASTON

Easton is located at the confluence of the Delaware and Lehigh Rivers and the Morris Canal. It became an industrial center in the early 19th century. Today the **Two Rivers Landing** building at 30 Centre Square is home to a visitor center focusing on the history of the canal transportation system, the Crayola Factory, and the National Canal Museum.

Thomas Penn, the son of William Penn, and Benjamin Eastburn surveyed the "Thousand Acre Tract" in 1736. The new town there was named Easton. In the middle of the century it became a meeting place to resolve land disputes between colonists and Indians, a situation further complicated by incursions of Connecticut settlers on land claimed by the Penns. At the Albany Conference in 1754, both colonies had purchased land from the Indians. Quaker pacifists took the lead in establishing these conferences at Easton, an initiative that annoyed colonial officials. At the third conference, in 1758, Teedyuscung, leader of the Delawares, agreed to a settlement of all disputes other than the fraudulent Walking Purchase, as long as their hunting grounds in the Wyoming Valley were preserved. After his death in 1763 that fragile peace collapsed in the frontier raids of Pontiac's Rebellion.

On July 8, 1776, the Declaration of Independence was read in Easton's Centre Square. The town still has a number of buildings that date to the 18th century.

HISTORICAL SITES *and* MUSEUMS

Bachmann Tavern (610-250-6600), City Hall, 1 S. Third St. Bachmann Tavern has 70 percent of the original structure. The upper windows are original. As the oldest building in the city, it served as a tavern and residence of George Taylor, a signer of the Declaration of Independence. George Washington and Ben Franklin visited the tavern. It also served as a courtroom until the original courthouse was built. The building was being restored, but work has stopped. Visitors can see the outside of this historic building.

The First United Church of Christ (610-258-3361), N. Third and Church Sts. The church dates from 1775 and became a hospital during the Revolution. It was the site of the Indian Treaty Conference in 1777.

Northampton County Courthouse, Centre Square. Although the first court proceedings were held in taverns, this building dates from 1752.

Northampton County Museum 610-253-1222), Ferry and Fourth Sts. This Historical and Genealogical Society has collections on early history plus primitive 18th- and 19th-century paintings of local scenes.

Parson Taylor House (610-252-2435), S. Fourth and Ferry Sts. William Parsons built his house in 1757. Later George Taylor, signer of the Declaration of Independence, lived here.

Trinity Episcopal Church (610-253-0792), Spring Garden and Sitgreaves Sts. Services were held in homes until 1798, when Samuel Sitgreaves donated the land for the church. If you like reading stones, the graveyard is one to stroll.

EVENTS

July: Reading of the Declaration of Independence in Easton; 610-250-6600
December: Moravian putz, Bethlehem; 610-867-0173

PENNSYLVANIA DUTCH COUNTRY

The "Dutch" does not refer to Holland but rather to Deutsch—German. The Pennsylvania Dutch region in Lancaster County contains a pocket of living history that does not need to be re-created because, at least in rural areas, it never disappeared. Beginning in 1727 the Amish, also known as the "plain people," emigrated from Europe to find freedom from persecution. They are well known for their superior farming techniques. The typical farmer tills about sixty acres of grain, alfalfa, corn, and tobacco using horse-drawn equipment. Any profits are put right back into the farm, because frugality is a virtue espoused by the Amish.

Because the Amish were persecuted in Germany, they don't wear anything suggestive of military clothing. They do not wear buttons, because military uniforms have brass buttons, and pockets are removed from their shirts. They wear suspenders (belts are considered too modern), black shoes, and broad-brimmed hats. Men may grow a beard after they are married.

Small girls can have buttons and dresses in blue, green, or purple (or pink, under age six). Women wear the same-colored dresses with a black apron. Single girls wear a white apron on Sundays. Women's dresses are fastened with about thirty pins. When they marry, they take off the white aprons and do not wear them again until they die. When someone in the family dies, they wear black dresses. Women part their hair in the middle and pull it back into a bun, covering the hair with a white organdy prayer veil or a black bonnet. Children may play with dolls as long as certain restrictions are observed. In earlier days dolls did not have faces; now, commercially made dolls are acceptable if the original clothing is replaced by Amish clothing.

As you drive past their farms, you will see that there are no electric lines leading into their homes—and they don't own telephones.

Within each Amish house is a room reserved for church services. The services take place from 8 AM until noon, using the Martin Luther Bible as well as the King James version. Interpretation of the Bible is literal; Amish accept the words of the Bible by faith. Families in the district take turns having services in their homes. The meal is provided by the host family and consists of sandwiches, salads, and hot coffee. Men and boys eat first, women and girls afterward.

The Amish do not believe in infant baptism. They wait until the child is at least fourteen to ensure that he or she understands the full meaning of commitment. Anyone may choose to leave the faith before that time, but if one chooses to leave after baptism, he or she is shunned for life by the community. The Amish believe in a close brotherhood and will gather to help one another when needed. In fact, they do not carry insurance against natural disasters. After tornadoes or

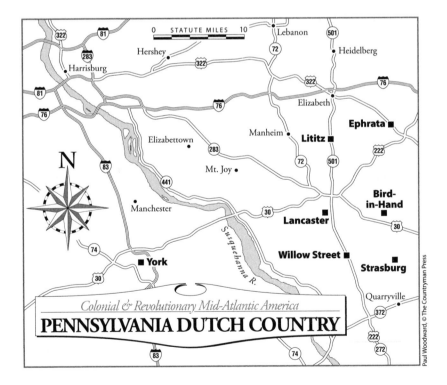

A common sight in Amish country.

floods, they will bring food to neighbors and get to work rebuilding their barns and houses.

Weddings are held in November on Tuesdays or Thursdays. November is the least busy month for the men, and Tuesdays or Thursdays are the least busy days for the women. The guests bring dishes of food to the wedding, but gifts are given later. The couple will spend the first night in the home of the bride's parents, then will honeymoon until March, spending one night with each of the wedding guests and receiving gifts at that time. They receive two wedding gifts from each guest. The man receives farming equipment or animals, and the woman gets something she can use in her home. In March they settle into their own house and farm, given to them by the groom's parents. The bride's parents give them furniture and perhaps a dairy herd.

LANCASTER

George Gibson became the first recorded settler in Lancaster when he opened a tavern there in 1721. James Hamilton sold building lots and included the proviso "new owners should make, erect, build, and finish on each and every lot, at their own cost and charge, a sufficient dwelling house, of the dimension of sixteen feet square at least, with a good chimney of brick or stone" within two years or the land would revert to Hamilton.

No motorist can be unaware of the buggies in this part of Pennsylvania because they have their own marked highway lane, but the uninitiated may miss the meaning of the type of black buggy they see. Unmarried Amish ride in an open "courting" buggy; no chaperone is needed, as anyone can see what is going on! Married couples have a closed buggy, designed in a rectangular shape with glass in front. Both types of buggies are graceful and well sprung, with contours fitted to the human body that no modern automobile can match.

The famous long rifle came into being in this frontier region as gunsmiths developed the Pennsylvania rifle. Some say that Martin Meylin may have bored the first rifled gun barrel in 1750 at his forge three miles south of Lancaster.

Lancastrians were loyal to the Crown, which had provided support against France in the French and Indian War. But as they realized the way the Crown was trying to run the American colonies without representation, their allegiance turned. After Lexington they supported the colonial cause, and companies of expert riflemen were organized.

During the Revolutionary War, American wounded were taken to the hospitals in Lancaster. The Moravians in Lititz and the Seventh Day Baptists at Ephrata tended to the wounded. Some British and Hessian prisoners were brought to Lancaster to keep them safe. The Continental Congress met in Lancaster for one day on September 27, 1777. They were careful to meet in places away from the British.

Today Lancaster still brings to mind the Amish traditions, including the popular farmers markets. Many homemade treats are for sale, including cheese, pretzels, and shoofly pie. As you travel on the roads you will see Amish buggies.

HISTORICAL SITES and MUSEUMS

Historic Rock Ford Plantation (717-392-7223; www.rockfordplantation.org), 881 Rockford Rd. Open Apr.–Oct., Thu.–Sun. Edward Hand, an Irishman, came to Lancaster to practice medicine in 1774. As a colonel in the Continental Army he became adjutant general to George Washington. Dating from 1792, this Federal brick mansion has four floors. Two pieces original to the Hand family are a mahogany Federal card table and a porcelain Chinese covered jar.

Lancaster also claims the origin of the Conestoga wagon. And the Conestoga horse was bred to pull it. Later, the Conestoga wagon became the familiar "prairie schooner" of the West.

The **Pennsylvania Dutch Convention and Visitors Bureau** (800-723-8824, 717-299-8901; www.padutchcountry.com), 501 Greenfield Ave., offers a film, *The Lancaster Experience*. It will help you to understand more about the Amish people and their way of life.

Lancaster Chamber of Commerce (717-397-3531), 100 S. Queen St. Interpreters in colonial costume will take you on a **Historic**

Lancaster Walking Tour (717-392-1776) to see homes, courtyards, churches, and hear about the people who lived or visited long ago. A 90-minute film precedes each tour.

If you want a glimpse into Amish life, visit the **Amish Country Homestead** (717-768-3600; www.amish experience.com), 3121 Old Philadelphia Pike (PA 340), Bird-in-Hand. Open Apr.–Nov., daily. Call Amish Country Tours (717-768-8400).

The Amish Farm and House (717-394-6185; www.amishfarmand house.com), 2395 US 30E, Lancaster. Open Apr.–Oct., daily. You will see animals on the farm and also a schoolhouse. Buggy rides are available. Whittling and quilting demonstrations take place here.

Hex signs still adorn a number of barns in the area. The Pennsylvania Dutch may have been simply decorating their barns, or superstition may have been involved. Eight-pointed stars were thought to symbolize perseverance, and six-pointers were called "witch's feet." Another theme was the trompe l'oeil "devil's door." The fake one was often at the end of a row of three real doors and painted to look like them. They say that witches flew into the fake one and then headed off to bother another farm.

Lancaster Central Market (717-291-4723), in Penn Square, is a wonderful place to look, buy, and people-watch. Open Tue., Fri., Sat. It is said to be the oldest operating market in the country. Andrew Hamilton arranged the land for this market in 1730, and in 1743 King George II proclaimed the site as the Central Market. You'll find fruits, vegetables, cheese, poultry, meat, seafood, and flowers—all ready for purchase.

An Amish bedroom.

The **Landis Valley Museum** (717-569-0401; www.landisvalleymuseum.org), 2451 Kissel Hill Rd. Open daily. Henry and George Landis pulled together the implements, tools, and furnishings of various eras and established them in appropriate buildings to create this museum of rural life and culture. The museum is divided into three chronological areas, covering the time span from the colonial era to the end of the 19th century.

The first area centers on a settler's farmstead of the 1750–1800 period. Visitors will see implements, tools, and furnishings of that era. It is a treat to stroll into this peaceful setting on a sunny day when the animals are out. The farm has a typical Pennsylvania "bank barn"; you get to the top level by walking up a bank at the back; the livestock live in the lower level. Walk into the settler's cabin to see a costumed guide engaged in weaving or some other task.

> ✳ If you happen to see a house with an iron representation of an Indian on it, that tells everyone that the owner indeed paid the Indians for the land.

The second area is built around a Federal farmstead depicting the 1815 period, with an adjoining "grandmother's house." The third area has been designed as a typical village crossroads of the 1825–1900 period. It includes craft buildings, a tavern, and a hotel. A group of women were quilting when we were there.

The museum offers seminars and workshops. Landis Valley Fair is held in early June; activities include life on the farm beginning in the 1760s, a 1700s military encampment, open- hearth cooking, and craft demonstrations. The Landis Valley Museum also has an unusual heirloom seed project with vegetable and flower seeds similar to those grown by the colonists. Gardeners learn how to harvest seeds from their own gardens as a "restoration" project. Many families have passed down seeds for generations.

The **Hans Herr House** (717-464-4438), 1849 Hans Herr Dr., south of town, dates from 1719. It is the oldest building in Lancaster County and also the oldest Mennonite meetinghouse in America. Andrew Wyeth is a descendant of Hans Herr, and you may have seen this medieval-style stone house in some of his paintings. The house has been restored and furnished. Costumed interpreters may be cooking at the gigantic fireplace, where pots hang from an iron crane. You'll see a collection of various utensils standing on the hearth, including a toaster, a waffle iron, and a roaster that was turned with a crank. Or maybe the cook will have trussed a chicken and hung it over the fire, to be twirled around whenever she goes by.

LITITZ

Lititz was settled in 1743 by Moravians who named it for their hometown in Bohemia. Nowadays Lititz is well know for soft pretzels. There is also a candy museum and store where hand-dipped candies are made.

There are two Mennonite cultures in America. One group left Switzerland and immigrated to Germantown, Pennsylvania, in 1683. The Amish left this group. A Dutch-Russian group immigrated to Kansas and Manitoba, Canada. They stress simple and separatist lifestyles.

The Moravians, called the Unity of the Brethren, began in 1457 in Moravia and Bohemia (now the Czech Republic). The group came to Savannah, Georgia, in 1735, then moved to Bethlehem, Pennsylvania, in 1741. They stress Christian unity and personal service.

HISTORICAL SITES *and* MUSEUMS

The **Lititz Moravian Archives and Museum** (717-626-8515), Church Square and Main St. Open Memorial Day–Labor Day. The Brothers' House dates from 1759. It was a hospital after the Battle of Brandywine.

Take a walk along Main Street to see 18th-century homes still lived in today. A brochure for a walking tour is available at the **Lititz Historical Foundation** in the **Johannes Mueller House** (717-627-4636), 137–39 E. Main St. The house dates from 1792 and is built of stone with an adjoining log cabin. Mueller's workshop was in the cabin.

EPHRATA

Ephrata is popular for a farmers market with both indoor and outdoor stands. It is open year-round. Factory outlets are also in town.

HISTORICAL SITES *and* MUSEUMS

Ephrata Cloister (717-733-6600; www.ephratacloister.org), 632 W. Main St. Open Mar.–Dec. daily, rest of the year Tue.–Sun. Ephrata Cloister was one of America's first communal societies. It was founded by Conrad Beissel, a German Seventh-Day Baptist, who gathered a group of celibate recluses, both male and female. Besides a male order and a female order, there was a third order, that of householders. These married men and women lived in the community, worshiped there, and supported the work of the cloister.

They believed in a life of simplicity and self-denial. Because they baptized converts in the river, they were sometimes called the "Seventh-Day Dunkers." These people were well known for their art, music, and calligraphy.

This group cultivated choral music known as Vorspiel, a kind of musical drama, still presented by performers to give visitors an idea of the way of life in this communal settlement.

Fraktur is a German script that has a thin shape, pointed ends, and bristling serifs, that is, the ends of the letter strokes. It can be seen on baptismal certificates, documents, and in songbooks, often colorfully illustrated with folk-art drawings.

They were also well known for their calligraphy called Fraktur. This term describes the 18th- and 19th-century colorfully painted or printed watercolor documents common in their German community. The letters in these documents look "fractured."

A number of original buildings still stand, including the Saal, or chapel. This is a five-story frame building with a steep gable roof and narrow slits for windows. Hand-illuminated German manuscripts are in the chapel. The Saron, or sisters' house, has 62 rooms; the sisters slept here on wooden benches with a wooden block for a pillow. The Almonry is a log house belonging to Conrad Beissel. This was where the poor came to receive food and clothing.

INFORMATION

PENNSYLVANIA DUTCH CONVENTION & VISITORS BUREAU
501 Greenfield Rd., Lancaster, PA 17601
800-723-8824 or 717-299-8901; www.padutchcountry.com

YORK

York calls itself the "factory tour capital of the world." Factories produce pretzels, dinnerware, and motorcycles, among other things. You can pick up a booklet of the tours offered at the Visitor Information Center.

Thomas Cookson plotted the city in 1741 and used the name and symbol, the white rose, from York, England.

During the fall of 1777, British troops were on the march to Philadelphia, inspiring members of the Continental Congress to flee west to a more secure place for conducting their affairs. They crossed the Susquehanna River and took lodgings in York. From September 30, 1777, to June 27, 1778, York was the national capital. It was here that the Continental Congress adopted the Articles of Confederation that provided a legal national government.

HISTORICAL SITES *and* MUSEUMS

The **Colonial Complex** includes the General Gates House, Golden Plough Tavern, Barnett Bobb Log House, and the Colonial Court House (717-845-2951; www.yorkheritage.org), 157 W. Market St. Open Tue.–Sat. The **Golden Plough Tavern** was built in the 1740s and retains a German style of architecture, with William and Mary period furniture. As you walk through the tavern, look for sections exposed to show the original construction. A settee from 1710 still has its original hide. The fireplace has a hole where hot coals could be pushed through to heat the next room. You will see the taproom, where the men sat smoking their pipes and drinking ale.

It has now been combined with the **General Gates House** so you can walk from one into the other. General Horatio Gates and his wife lived here in 1778. Some in Congress wanted to replace George Washington with Gates. This group was called the Conway Cabal. The house is remembered as the place where Lafayette prevented the ousting of Washington as commander in chief of the Continental Army. The toast he gave to Washington was the signal for the end of the plots to remove him.

The nearby **Barnett Bobb House** is a log house typical of the colonial period. Look for the furniture decorated with a quill dipped in paint and the chest that looks as if it were painted with a corncob.

The **Historical Society Museum** (717-848-1587; www.yorkheritage.org) is at 250 E. Market St. This museum offers information on York County from early days to the present.

> The guide will tell you about the "soul hole," which Germans believed was important to have in a house; should someone die, the soul could escape quickly and not be trapped in the house. Note the short bed that must have forced sleeping in a semi-sitting position; perhaps the prevalence of respiratory problems caused by dampness and cold made this position more comfortable.

LODGING

BIRD-IN-HAND FAMILY INN
2740 Old Philadelphia Pike,
Bird-in-Hand, PA 17505
800-665-8780; www.bird-in-hand.com
A family-style inn on 15 acres. 125 guest rooms.

BIRD-IN-HAND VILLAGE INN & SUITES
2695 Old Philadelphia Pike,
Bird-in-Hand, PA 17505
800-665-8780; www.bird-in-hand.com
Accommodations in four restored historic buildings. 24 guest rooms.

THE INNS AT DONECKERS
318–324 N. State St.
Ephrata, PA 17522
800-377-2206, 717-738-9502;
www.doneckers.com/inns
Three inns offer a variety of lodging: the Guest House, the 1777 House, and the Homestead. 31 guest rooms.

HISTORIC SMITHTON INN
900 W. Main St., Ephrata, PA 17522
877-755-4590, 717-733-6094; www
.historicsmithtoninn.com

This 1763 property was once a stagecoach inn, and features a fireplace in each of the 8 guest rooms.

THE E.J. BOWMAN HOUSE
2672 Lititz Pike, Lancaster, PA 17601
717-519-0808; www.ejbowmanhouse
.com
The house dates from the 1860s. Music is a part of each day; bring your instruments if you wish. 5 guest rooms.

O'FLAHERTY'S DINGELDEIN HOUSE
1105 E. King St., Lancaster, PA 17602
800-779-7765, 717-293-1723; www
.dingeldeinhouse.com
The house was built in 1910 in the Dutch colonial style, and is set amid trees and gardens. It was built for the Armstrong family. 6 guest rooms.

ROSE MANOR B&B
124 S. Linden St., Manheim, PA 17545
800-666-4932, 717-664-4932;
www.rosemanor.net
The home dates from 1905. There's a plant-filled conservatory where you can sip lemonade in summer. 5 guest rooms.

LEOLA VILLAGE INN & SUITES
38 Deborah Dr., Leola, PA 17540
717-656-7002; www.leolavillage.com
Some of the buildings date from 1873.
What was once a tobacco barn is now the
lobby. 61 guest rooms.

THE ALDEN HOUSE
62 E. Main St., Lititz, PA 17543
800-584-0753, 717-627-3363;
www.aldenhouse.com
The brick Federal-style house, built in
1850, is in the historic district. 5 guest
rooms.

THE GENERAL SUTTER INN
14 E. Main St., Lititz, PA 17543
717-626-2115; www.generalsutterinn
.com
The inn was founded in 1764 by the Moravian church. California pioneer John Sutter
arrived there to find a cure for his arthritis.
11 guest rooms.

CAMERON ESTATE INN
1855 Mansion Lane, Mount Joy,
PA 17552
888-422-6376, 717-492-0111;
www.cameronestateinn.com
The inn dates from 1805; the Cameron
family was prominent in the 19th century.
18 guest rooms.

AFTER EIGHT B&B
2942 Lincoln Highway East, Paradise,
PA 17562
888-314-3664, 717 687-3664;
www.aftereightbnb.com
This brick home was built in1818 and is
filled with antiques. 11 guest rooms.

CANDLELIGHT INN B&B
2574 Lincoln Highway East, Ronks, PA
17572
800-77-CANDLE, 717-299-6005;
www.candleinn.com

The home dates from the 1920s. Guest
rooms are decorated with Victorian
antiques. 7 guest rooms.

ROSE GARDEN B&B
1566 Lime Valley Rd., Strasburg, PA
17579
717-687-3651; www.rosegarden
bedandbreakfast.com
The house dates from 1869 and is furnished with Victorian pieces. 3 guest
rooms.

THE YORKTOWNE HOTEL
48 E. Market St., York, PA 17401
717-848-1111; www.yorktowne.com
The hotel dates from 1925. It is a National
Historic Landmark. 120 guest rooms.

RESTAURANTS

HAYDN ZUG'S
1987 State St., East Petersburg, PA
17520
717-569-5746; www.haydnzugs.com
A general store in the 19th century, this
restaurant offers a colonial atmosphere
and classic American cuisine.

THE RESTAURANT AT DONECKERS
333 N. State St., Ephrata, PA 17522
717-738-9501; www.doneckers.com/
restaurant
Innovative French and American cuisine
among art and antiques.

INFORMATION

**YORK COUNTY VISITORS
INFORMATION CENTER
YORK COUNTY CONVENTION
& VISITORS BUREAU**
1425 Eden Rd., York, PA 17402
888-858-YORK, 717-852-6006;
www.yorkpa.org

SOUTHERN PENNSYLVANIA

This area stretches from Bedford, where there is a living-history museum, to Carlisle, with its Hessian history, to Harrisburg and Cornwall.

BEDFORD

Bedford is known for its array of antique shops. Take a walking tour and you can't miss them.

Bedford was first settled by Robert Ray in 1751. Later it was renamed for the Duke of Bedford. The Espy House was George Washington's headquarters in 1794. He was on his way with troops to stop the Whiskey Rebellion, which arose when a group of farmers did not want to pay tax on whiskey. British general John Forbes traveled along the Forbes Road (now US 30) on his way to capture Fort Duquesne in the French and Indian War.

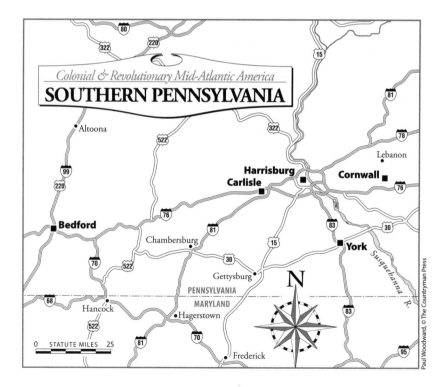

> Early settlers used what were called "lug bars" to hang pots over the fire in fireplace cooking. Colonial women were at risk for burns because eventually the wooden lug bars would dry out and break unexpectedly. Hearth cooking was created to solve this problem. Cooks pulled hot coals out onto the hearth, trivets were placed on the coals, and pots then set onto the trivets. (Information from Old Bedford Village)

Fort Bedford Museum (814-623-8192; www.bedfordcounty.net), Fort Bedford Dr. Open Memorial Day–Labor Day, daily. Native American artifacts as well as colonial pieces from the 1700s are on display. It is housed in a reproduction of an early blockhouse.

Old Bedford Village (814-623-1156; www.oldbedfordvillage.com), 220 Sawblade Rd. Open Memorial Day–Labor Day, Thu.–Tue. This is the reproduction of a village from 1750 to 1850, including some 35 buildings. Original log cabins, one-room schools, and other structures were moved from their sites and brought to the village. Visitors may smell freshly baked cookies from the bakery oven, watch a weaver, a blacksmith, a broom-maker, or a carpenter.

EVENTS

June: Militia Days, Old Bedford Village; 800-238-4347

CARLISLE

The U.S. Army War College is now at Carlisle Barracks. The buildings were once part of the Carlisle Indian School; Jim Thorpe, considered one of the greatest athletes of all times, went to the school.

Carlisle was settled about 1720, and a fort was built in 1758, during the French and Indian War. During the Revolution a line was drawn at High and Hanover Streets, where those loyal to the king were to walk. No one did.

Indian Pumpkin GRIDDLE CAKES
(from *Old Bedford Village Hearth Cooking* by Vi Laws)

1 cup yellow cornmeal	Mix the cornmeal, sugar, baking soda, and salt in large bowl. Add the pumpkin, water, and egg and mix well. Stir in the melted fat. Drop by heaping tbsp onto a greased, hot griddle and fry, turning once. Serve with maple syrup.
1 tbsp light brown sugar	
½ tsp salt	
½ tsp baking soda	
½ cup pumpkin	
⅓ cup water	
1 beaten egg	
2 tbsp browned butter	

HISTORICAL SITES
and MUSEUMS
Carlisle Barracks (717-245-3131; www
.carlisle.army.mil), on US 11 one mile north
of the city, was once a Revolutionary War
forge. In 1777 Hessian soldiers built the magazine there and used it to store gunpowder,
cannon shot, and small arms. Confederate
general J. E. B. Stuart's troops burned it just
before the Battle of Gettysburg. It was recon-

> Mary Hayes McCauley,
> said to be "Molly
> Pitcher," legendary for her
> fighting service in Washing-
> ton's army at the Battle of
> Monmouth, is buried in the
> Old Graveyard, where there
> is a monument for her.

structed in 1879 and served as the first nonreservation Indian school in the United
States. You will need to go through security with photo ID.

The **U.S. Army Heritage Education Center** (717-245-3700), 950 Soldiers
Drive, houses the **Hessian Powder Magazine Museum** (717-245-3971) Guardhouse Lane. Open late May–early Sep., daily 10–4.

HARRISBURG

French backwoodsman Étienne Brûlé first spotted this location in 1615 as he was
traveling on the Susquehanna River. In 1710 John Harris opened his trading post
here. John Harris Jr. provided ferry service across the river in 1753. He insisted
that the name of the town be changed from Louisbourg to Harrisburg, contingent on selling land to the legislature. Harrisburg became the state capital in 1812.

HISTORICAL SITES and MUSEUMS
John Harris / Simon Cameron Mansion, the **Dauphin County Historical Center** (717-233-3462; www.dauphincountyhistory.org), 219 S. Front St. Open
Mon.–Thu. The house was built by the founder of the city, John Harris, in 1766
and enlarged in 1863 by Simon Cameron. China and furniture on display date
from both owners. There is a collection of tall case clocks and also dolls.

Fort Hunter Mansion and Park (717-599-5751; www.forthunter.org), Front
St. Open Tue.–Sun. The mansion was built on the site of the 1756 Fort Hunter.

> "Hessians" was the all-purpose name for German mercenaries who fought
> on the side of the British during the Revolution, although not all of them
> were from Hesse. That small state in the center of what later became Germany
> had been invaded frequently in the almost incessant wars of the 17th and 18th
> centuries, and by the 1770s it had developed the largest army in Europe, highly
> professional and loyal. Parts of the army were often leased to other European
> countries to help support a state poor in resources and trade. Feared by the
> colonists, the Germans generally wore blue uniforms, had helmets with brass
> decoration, and often sported mustaches.

This stone house has a few pieces from the 18th century and more from the 19th century. Collections include costumes and toys. The fireplace is original.

The State Museum of Pennsylvania (717-787-4980; www.statemuseumpa .org), 300 North St. Open Tue.–Sun. The museum is housed in a circular six-story building, adjacent to the Capitol building. There are exhibits on Indian life, natural history, archaeology, geology, military history, antique cars and carriages, and period furnishings.

CORNWALL

Cornwall Iron Furnace (717-272-9711; www.cornwallironfurnace.org), 94 Rexmont Rd. Peter Grubb mined the Cornwall Ore Banks in the 1730s. Magnetite ore was mined for two more centuries. Grubb built the Cornwall Iron Furnace in 1742, and in 1798 Robert Coleman bought the furnace. The sandstone building has unusual pointed windows. It was constructed into the side of the hill, and the ore, limestone, and charcoal were poured into the furnace from the top. The visitor center has exhibits to describe the processes of iron making, charcoal making, and mining.

LODGING

PHEASANT FIELD B&B
150 Hickorytown Rd., Carlisle, PA 17013
877-258-0717, 717-258-0717;
www.pheasantfield.com
The brick farmhouse dates back 200 years, and was once a stop on the underground railroad. You may walk the Labyrinth across the road. 8 guest rooms.

RESTAURANTS

BOILING SPRINGS TAVERN
The Square, 1st and Front Sts., Boiling Springs, PA 170079
717-258-3614

The tavern was built in 1832 by Anheuser-Busch. This popular restaurant serves a variety of steak, seafood, and pasta dishes.

JEAN BONNET TAVERN
6048 Lincoln Hwy., Bedford, PA 15522
814-623-2250; www.jeanbonnettavern .com
Built in the 1760s, this tavern was owned by friends of William Penn and George Washington. Jean Bonnet bought it in 1779. The native stone walls, fireplaces, and exposed beams preserve the colonial atmosphere for lunch and dinner, with a light menu.

NORTHWESTERN PENNSYLVANIA

ERIE

The Erie Indians were the first inhabitants; the city is named after them. Wars in 1653 against the Seneca, Cayuga, and Onondaga and a pestilence destroyed the tribe. In 1753 Fort Presque Isle was built by a French military expedition. The

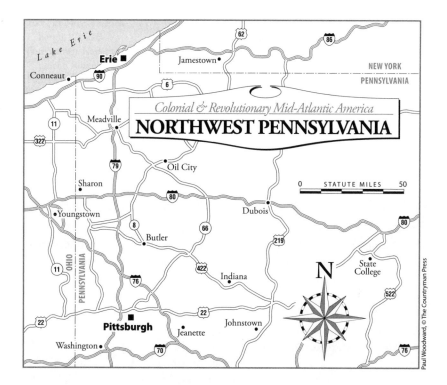

Colonial & Revolutionary Mid-Atlantic America

NORTHWEST PENNSYLVANIA

Paul Woodward, © The Countryman Press

French left in 1759, and the English rebuilt the fort. The English garrison was wiped out during Pontiac's Rebellion, and the fort was destroyed.

Indian troubles persisted after the Revolution, and in 1794 General Anthony Wayne succeeded in vanquishing the tribes during the Battle of Fallen Timbers (near present-day Toledo, Ohio). Settlers arrived, and Erie was founded in 1795.

Commander Oliver Hazard Perry supervised the building of ships in Erie during the War of 1812. The keels of the *Niagara* and the *Lawrence* were laid in March 1813, and the vessels were launched in June. On August 1 Perry undertook the task of floating the vessels across the sandbar at the entrance to the bay with the aid of "camels," or pumped-out tanks that provided extra buoyancy.

On September 10 Perry and his men, on board the *Lawrence,* challenged the British and engaged them in battle. The vessel was reduced to a hulk by British long guns, and Perry and his remaining men dashed by boat to the *Niagara;* from this ship Perry reattacked the battered British fleet and decisively won the Battle of Lake Erie.

Both the *Lawrence* and the *Niagara* were allowed to sink in Misery Bay after the battle. The *Lawrence* was raised in 1876 and, although she was not intact, was

> Perry wrote: "We have met the enemy and they are ours: Two ships, two Brigs, one Schooner and one Sloop."

taken to Philadelphia for the country's centennial celebration and finally burned in a fire that consumed the centennial buildings.

The *Niagara* was raised in 1913 for the centennial of the battle; she was towed to various ports on Lake Erie during that summer. She was brought back to Erie and remained in the water until the 1930s, when she was put into her cradle. Until September 1987 visitors could climb aboard the *Niagara* and look up to see the flag flying from the shrouds: "DONT GIVE UP THE SHIP."

In September 1987 the *Niagara* was completely dismantled, and salvageable pieces were stored. She was then rebuilt, using some of the original 1813 timbers. She was launched on September 10, 1988, and now is berthed next to the Erie Maritime Museum.

HISTORICAL SITES *and* MUSEUMS

Erie County Historical Society (814-454-1813) 417–19 State St. Open May–Sep., Tue.–Sat.; Wed.–Sat. the rest of the year. Exhibits focus on Erie County history from presettlement to today. We were amused to see the "doors" on the right side of the hall. There is nothing but plaster behind them! There is a model of Fort Presque Isle and relics from the fort. The Erie Society for Genealogical Research is located in the museum.

The Erie Maritime Museum (814-452-2744; www.brigniagara.org), 150 E. Front St. Open Apr.–Dec. daily. Please call for winter hours. The museum offers the story of the Battle of Lake Erie in multimedia and interactive exhibits. The history of the *Niagara* is here, and she is moored within yards of the museum when she is in port. A replica of the *Lawrence* offers the chance to enjoy hands-on experience with the mast, spars, and rigging. The *Wolverine,* the nation's first iron-hulled warship, has stories to tell of its previous life as the USS *Michigan.*

RESTAURANTS

PUFFERBELLY ON FRENCH STREET
414 French St., Erie, PA 16507
814-454-1557; www.thepufferbelly.com
In a former fire station, the restaurant is named for the steam pumpers and engines for firefighting in the late 1800s. The menu is creative with seasonal dishes.

INFORMATION

ERIE AREA CONVENTION AND VISITORS BUREAU
208 E. Bayfront Pkwy., Suite 103 Erie, PA 16507
800-524-ERIE, 814-454-7191; www.visiteriepa.com

SOUTHWESTERN PENNSYLVANIA

The land where the Allegheny and the Monongahela Rivers meet, also called the Forks of the Ohio, was a crucial spot during the French and Indian War. The triangle of land there is the apex of Pittsburgh's Golden Triangle. Both French and English considered "The Point" as a key to trade and settlement.

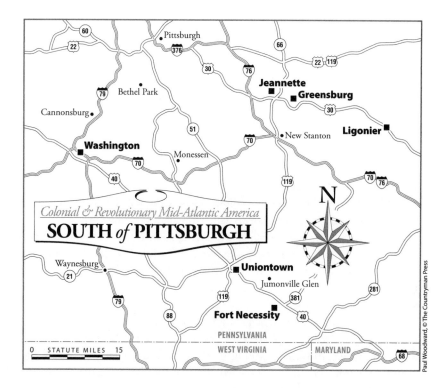

Colonial & Revolutionary Mid-Atlantic America
SOUTH of PITTSBURGH

In the 1740s William Trent, an English fur trader, built his trading post at the Forks. He traded with Indian tribes and became a wealthy man. In the early 1750s the French, in an effort to secure their prior claim to the country, began constructing a string of forts from Lake Erie southward. This alarmed Governor Robert Dinwiddie of Virginia, who, eager to protect Virginia's interests (and his own interests as a land speculator), sent an eight-man expedition under George Washington to warn the French to clear out. The French refused. In response, in 1753 Dinwiddie ordered construction of a fort at the Forks. Construction begin early in 1754, but only months later the English were driven out by the French, who began to build their own, bigger fort, called Duquesne, after the governor-general of New France.

Dinwiddie again dispatched young Washington, this time to help build a road to the Forks. You can follow in Washington's footsteps as he ventured forth. On May 28, 1754, the young Virginia colonel learned of a nearby party of French soldiers fifty miles south of the Forks. Washington talked with a friendly Seneca chief, Tanaghrisson, called the Half King, and they agreed to confront the French. As Washington and his men and the Indians approached the French camp, a shot was fired by an unknown man. Ten Frenchmen were killed in the ensuing fight,

The WAR That Made AMERICA

A PBS documentary, *The War That Made America,* premiered in early 2006. It was produced by WQED and French and Indian War 250 Inc. as a centerpiece of the 250th anniversary commemoration. Learn more at 412-392-2408; www.thewarthatmade america.org.

and Ensign Joseph Coulon de Villiers de Jumonville, the French officer in command, was taken prisoner. At some point, unexpectedly, the Half King walked up to Jumonville and split his skull open with a tomahawk, killing him.

Washington knew that the French would retaliate. On May 29 he ordered that a log palisade be built at Great Meadows to prepare for an attack. He named it Fort Necessity. Captain James Mackay arrived with 100 British soldiers on June 14, but Mackay and Washington argued about who would be in command. They finally agreed to share the job.

On June 28 a group of French left Fort Duquesne to attack the British. The French group was led by Captain Louis Coulon de Villiers, a brother of the murdered Jumonville. Instead of fighting Washington in the open, the French surrounded the stockade, and from the wooded hills they kept up a deadly fire as a steady rain fell. The defenders' weapons became wet, they began to run out of ammunition, and the trenches filled with water. A third of them were killed or wounded. Washington asked the French for terms of surrender. The fort was given up on July 4, and Washington's remaining men were allowed to leave. The French razed Fort Necessity and went back to Fort Duquesne.

The conflict quickly escalated. In 1755 the British government sent General Edward Braddock and 1,500 soldiers to take the Forks. But this was wilderness, and Braddock found it was not easy to build a road to get his cannon and heavy equipment, as well as troops, in a position to attack Fort Duquesne. Braddock's vanguard was ambushed by a group of French and Indians at Turtle Creek on July 9, 1755. The ensuing fight, known as the Battle of the Monongahela, became a debacle for the British. Two-thirds of Braddock's force were killed or wounded. Braddock himself was mortally wounded and died three days later during the retreat; he was buried in the middle of the road he built, to avoid exhumation and scalping by pursuing Indians. Washington, who served as an aide to the general, had two horses shot from under him during the fighting.

Britain declared war on France in 1756, and the Crown encouraged colonial involvement. Four battalions of Pennsylvania men were formed and called the Royal Americans. In 1758 William Pitt, who now oversaw the British war effort, sent Brigadier General John Forbes to plan an attack on Fort Duquesne. As Forbes's army neared the fort, they found that the French troops had exploded and abandoned it. Forbes ordered that a new fort be built of earth, stone, timber, and brick just east of the ruins of Fort Duquesne. He named the place "Pittsbourgh," to honor William Pitt; the fort was dubbed "Fort Pitt." With an area of more than seventeen acres, Fort Pitt became the center of British activity west of the Allegheny Mountains.

The Treaty of Paris, signed in 1763, ended the struggle between Britain and France for control of North America. The French, however, were not the only losers. Their Indian allies, and those of the British as well, now had to contend with a flood of new white settlements, as well as harsh new trade policies by the British, who no longer had to compete with France for the tribes' friendship. Ottawa Chief Pontiac was determined to seek revenge for his people, and in surprise attacks captured all the western forts except Pitt, Ligonier, Bedford, and Detroit. Many traders and settlers took refuge in Fort Pitt. Colonel Henry Bouquet was on his way with five hundred men to relieve Fort Pitt when Indians ambushed his expedition in August 1763. But he fought off the attackers, then turned the tables on the Indians in the Battle of Bushy Run.

The British victory at Bushy Run not only allowed Bouquet to relieve Fort Pitt, but also let the Indians know that they would not win. Pontiac's Rebellion caused a backlash against even the most peaceful Indians. In 1763 a vigilante group of Scotch-Irish called the "Paxton Boys" attacked a group of Conestoga Indians, many of them Christians, killing six of them. The rest of the Conestogas asked for protection, but the Paxton Boys broke into the workhouse in Lancaster and killed them also. Only intervention by Benjamin Franklin himself prevented further bloodshed when a mob of 500 Paxton Boys marched on Philadelphia, intending to kill Indians seeking shelter there.

The Proclamation of 1763 forbade settlers to live west of the mountains. This enraged the people who had chosen to live there, especially when they realized that the Indians they had been fighting were to have the land. By 1768 a new Indian treaty established a new boundary line, which kept the existing villages within the colony.

In October of 1772 hard-won Fort Pitt was sold to William Thompson and Alexander Ross for 50 pounds. John Connolly took the fort, rebuilt it, and called it Fort Dunmore, after Virginia's royal governor. Eventually Fort Pitt, under the leadership of General Edward Hand, became the western headquarters of the Continental Army. A peace treaty was signed with Native Americans at Pitt on September 17, 1778.

PITTSBURGH

Where was your town on the list when Pittsburgh was rated number 1 as a place to live by Rand-McNally? Let's give Pittsburgh a chance! It was once a grimy, smoky city, but in the late 1940s a countywide smoke-control program began to clear the air. In the 1950s Gateway Center and Point State Park were developed over the rubble of downtown gloom. Visually you will be amazed to discover the Gothic influence in the city—gargoyles, stained glass, arches, turrets, and pinnacles.

HISTORICAL SITES and MUSEUMS

Fort Pitt Museum, (412-281-9284; www.fortpittmuseum.com), 101 Commonwealth Plaza, Point State Park. Open Wed.–Sun. The museum is housed in the fort's re-created Monongahela bastion. On the outside you can see how Fort Pitt used earthworks and masonry for defense.

William Pitt Memorial Hall contains a circular display in its center with a large model of Fort Pitt and the Point as they looked in 1765. Pick up a telephone to hear the history of the fort. In 1772, when Fort Pitt was abandoned by the British, someone remarked, "The Americans will not submit to British parliament and they may now defend themselves."

The first floor has exhibits, scale models of the three successive French and Indian War forts at the Point, a reconstructed trader's cabin, displays of frontier life, and materials on early Pittsburgh. Head upstairs to see a new exhibit on the causes, events, and consequences of the struggle between England and France.

The **Fort Pitt Blockhouse**, built in 1764, has two rows of holes for firing on attackers. Colonel Henry Bouquet built it. Two tunnels led from it—one to the fort and the other to the Monongahela River. You can visit the blockhouse, the only remaining structure of Fort Pitt, located in **Point State Park**. Walk around the park to see some of the bastions and earthworks of the old fort.

Senator John Heinz Pittsburgh Regional History Center (412-454-6000; www.pghhistory.org), 1212 Smallman St. Open daily. This center is both a museum and a research facility. The history center, along with the Smithsonian Institution and the Canadian War Museum / Museum of Civilization, mounted a French and Indian War exhibit, which is currently traveling to other museums. It is called "Clash of Empires: The British, French & Indian War, 1754–1763." Among the exhibit's objects are the 1754 Treaty of Fort Necessity, the original surrender document signed by 22-year-old George Washington of the Virginia Regiment; the fork and knife from Washington's mess kit; ornate British and French swords; and guns, cannons, and Indian tomahawks.

Nine models, sculpted by Gerry Embleton, represent some of the real-life characters and incidents in the war. John Bush, an African American provincial soldier from Massachusetts, was known for his engraved powder horns. A French officer angry with his own inept superiors burns his own flag rather than surrender it to the British. Some of the exhibit will return as a permanent display.

LAUREL HIGHLANDS

The region in the Allegheny Mountains southeast of Pittsburgh has been dubbed the "Laurel Highlands" because of the prolific groves of mountain laurel growing there. The area is especially rich in historical sites from the French and Indian War.

Exhibits tell about Fort Necessity, where the French and Indian War began.

HISTORICAL SITES *and* MUSEUMS

Fort Necessity (724-329-5512; www.nps.gov/fone), US 40, Farmington. Open daily. The fort was the scene of George Washington's first military setback, in 1754. Virginia's governor Dinwiddie had sent Washington on a difficult assignment, with inadequate supplies of food, equipment, and weapons. In addition his men were inexperienced and discouraged. The attack at Jumonville Glen (see below) and the battle at Fort Necessity marked the beginning of the French and Indian War.

Visitors can tour a reconstructed stockade that encloses a storehouse. A slide presentation is useful for orientation. Exhibits include photographs, maps, and artifacts.

Braddock's Grave (724-329-5512; www.nps.gov/fone), US 40. The stone monument honors British general Edward Braddock. He was mortally wounded in the Battle of the Monongahela in July 1755 and died on the retreat. He was buried in an unmarked grave west of Fort Necessity.

Jumonville Glen (724-329-5512; www.nps.gov/fone), US 40, four miles west of the entrance gate to Fort Necessity. Turn onto Jumonville Rd. The entrance to Jumonville Glen is two miles north. Open daily Apr. 15–Nov. 15. This is the site where Washington's men and a group of Seneca Indians attacked a French scouting party from Fort Duquesne. French retaliation resulted in Washington's defeat at Fort Necessity.

FORT LIGONIER

General John Forbes ordered the construction of **Fort Ligonier** (724-238-9701; www.fortligonier.org), 216 S. Market St., Ligonier. Open May–Oct. 31, daily. Forbes intended that it serve as a base in the attack against the French. Today's full reconstruction of the 1758–66 fort contains barracks and a museum.

There are mannequins in the officers' mess building, the officers' quarters, and the supply room. In the Forbes hut John Forbes is lying on a cot suffering from an unknown disease. He stayed for Christmas and then went to Philadelphia, where he died on March 11, 1759.

Reenactments, encampments, craft demonstrations, and archaeological digs are held at the fort. Portraits include those of Sir John Ligonier, King George III, and Queen Charlotte.

BUSHY RUN

Bushy Run Battlefield (724-527-5584; www.bushyrunbattlefield.com), PA 993, Jeannette. Battlefield open Wed.–Sun. 9–5 year-round. This was the site of a battle in August 1763 between Shawnee, Delaware, Ottawa, Mingo, and other Indians and the British, led by Colonel Henry Bouquet, who was

A covered wagon at Fort Ligonier

Fort Ligonier is a full reconstruction of a French and Indian War frontier fort.

en route to relieve Fort Pitt during Pontiac's Rebellion. The Indians had severed the lines of communication between the frontier forts and the settlements. On August 4 the Indians attacked and the British retreated. The next day the Indians attacked again; Bouquet faked a retreat and encouraged the Indians to mount an attack on the south side of his defenses. But some of his men moved around through the valley to the east and suddenly fell upon the Indians, who then retreated. The battle marked the turning point in Pontiac's Rebellion and reopened the line of communication and supplies to Pitt. The museum contains exhibits relating the details of the battle.

The **Edge Hill Trail** is a walking path around the battlefield so that visitors can visualize the scene in 1763. Look at the trail markers as you make your way around. You may picnic here.

> German settlers brought over with them a dubious weather forecasting tradition that takes place on February 2, known as Groundhog Day. They claim that when the groundhog comes out of his den and sees his shadow there will be six more weeks of winter. Punxsutawney Phil is the designated groundhog who surfaces in Punxsutawney every year.

LODGING

TARA—A COUNTRY INN
2844 Lake Rd., Clark, PA 16113
800-782-2803; www.tara-inn.com
Built in 1854 as a private home, this inn offers a Gone With the Wind atmosphere. Formal gardens overlook Shenango Lake. 27 guest rooms.

BUHL MANSION GUESTHOUSE AND SPA
422 E. State St., Sharon, PA 16146
866-345-2845, 724-346-3046;
www.srinns.com/buhlmansion
The mansion dates from 1890; industrialist Frank Buhl built it as a castle for his wife. Guest rooms have fireplaces. 10 guest rooms.

MOUNTAIN VIEW INN
121 Village Dr., Greensburg, PA 15601
800-537-8709, 724-834-5300;
www.mountainviewinn.com
The inn dates from 1924 and features individually decorated rooms and landscaped grounds. 89 guest rooms.

THE INN ON NEGLEY
703 S. Negley Ave., Pittsburgh, PA 15232
412-661-0631; www.theinnsonnegley.com
The Victorian mansion, built in the late 1800s, is in the historic East End of Pittsburgh. 8 guest rooms.

OMNI WILLIAM PENN HOTEL
530 William Penn Place, Pittsburgh, PA 15219
412-281-7100; www.omniwilliampenn.com
The luxury hotel, built in 1916, has been restored to its original grand style. 596 guest rooms.

THE PRIORY
614 Pressley St., Pittsburgh, PA 15212
866-377-4679, 412-231-3338;
www.thepriory.com
Now an elegant European-style hotel, it was built in 1888 for Benedictine priests serving the church next door. 24 guest rooms.

EVENTS

March: Charter Day at Fort Pitt; 412-281-9284
July: Anniversary commemoration of the Battle of Fort Necessity; 724-329-5811
August: Re-enactment, Bushy Run; 724-527-5584
October: Fort Ligonier Days; 724-238-9701

INFORMATION

GREATER PITTSBURGH CONVENTION AND VISITORS BUREAU
425 Sixth Ave., Pittsburgh, PA 15219
800-359-0758, 412-281-7711; www.visitpittsburgh.com

Current Information

PENNSYLVANIA TOURISM OFFICE
400 North St., 4th Floor

Harrisburg, PA 17120
800-847-4872; www.visitpa.com

New Jersey

Historical Introduction
to the
New Jersey Colony

From the outset the New Jersey colony had to contend with the interests of its larger and more powerful neighbors, New York and Pennsylvania. It suffered the additional disadvantage of being cut in half through much of the colonial era, with lasting effects from a residue of competing interests after it was unified. At first it was part of an aggressive New Netherland and later New York, followed by years of competing land grants and shifting government control as proprietorships changed hands. The influence of Pennsylvania was more benign, but William Penn confirmed the bifurcation into East and West Jersey that interfered with settlement and political cooperation.

Lacking harbors that would generate major cities like New York and Philadelphia at its northeastern and southwestern borders, the colony remained largely agricultural. The gap between large landowners managing their holdings with deputies, and small farmers and townspeople, led to almost incessant fractious disputes between appointed officials and elected assemblies. Known for its mixed sympathies, especially at the beginning of the Revolution, New Jersey was slow in supporting and joining the Patriot cause. Nevertheless it was destined by geography to become a corridor for advancing and retreating armies, as well as the site of several major battles.

Early Explorers

Giovanni da Verrazano was commissioned to explore for Francis I of France in 1524. Verrazano was the first European to sail along much of the eastern coast of North America, including that of present-day New Jersey. He explored the shores

---

Overleaf: Molly Pitcher, the real Mary Hayes, became a legend at the Battle of Monmouth.

and harbors of New York, Long Island, Narragansett Bay, Maine, Delaware Bay, and perhaps Pamlico Sound on the Carolina coast.

Henry Hudson sailed the *Half Moon* into New York Bay in 1609 and anchored off Sandy Hook. Since the initial reception of the Indians had been friendly, his crew began to explore the New Jersey side of the bay along the Staten Island shore. After discovering Newark Bay, which they thought to be an open sea, his men turned back toward the ship. Two Indian canoes chased them, shot one of the sailors in the throat with an arrow and wounded two others. After dark Hudson's men were not able to find their ship and rowed back and forth until daybreak. Thus began the continually changing story of one of the greatest harbor complexes in the world.

Early Settlers under Various Flags

The Dutch West India Company followed the New Netherland Company as merchant-navigators continued to seek wealth through the flourishing fur trade. In 1620 Captain Cornelius May sailed for America in the *Blijde Boodschap* (Joyful Message) and explored Delaware Bay. He named Cape May for himself.

Two families and eight single men were the first Europeans to live in what was to become New Jersey, on Burlington Island in the Delaware River, but by 1630 these people had moved to New Amsterdam (New York). A few men lived in Fort Nassau, now the city of Gloucester across from Philadelphia. In fact, the company had trouble enticing any potential Dutch emigrants to move from their comfortable homes in the Netherlands.

The New Sweden Company was organized in 1633 in Sweden. Two ships, the *Kalmar Nyckel* and the *Fogel Grip,* arrived at the Delaware River in 1638. Storms had plagued the settlers on board for months, and they were happy to be on shore. Under a Swedish charter, Peter Minuit established a settlement on the Delaware, which included parts of present-day Pennsylvania, New Jersey, and Delaware.

The energetic Johan Printz arrived in the New Sweden colony in 1643 with two ships—*Fama* (Fawn) and *Svangen* (Swan). He ruled as governor from 1643 to 1653. Printz built Fort Elfsborg, also called "Mosquito Castle," on the eastern shore of the Delaware on the New Jersey side near present-day Salem. It was named after the Alvsborg Fortress near Gothenburg, Sweden. The fort was obliterated as the river changed its course.

The neighboring Dutch, who had earlier claimed much of the territory occupied by New Sweden, used military coercion to annex the settlements to New Netherland in 1655. Dutch governor Peter Stuyvesant was not popular with the original settlers, however, because he wanted to restrict their religious freedom.

Troubles under English Rule

Without warning, in August of 1664 four British warships anchored in Gravesend Bay and demanded the surrender of New Netherland within forty-eight hours. Realizing that they were ill prepared to defend Manhattan and dissatisfied with

> The Cornbury Ring, reputedly a bunch of unsavory characters, brought political corruption to the colony in a big way. Some of them had official posts, and pay, in both New York and New Jersey. Others were embezzlers and crafty land speculators. By 1707 most people had caught on to their tactics and wanted to get rid of the Cornbury Ring. The assembly compiled a list of grievances against Lord Cornbury—some called him a "detestable magot"—and he was recalled to England.

their government, the city's residents persuaded Peter Stuyvesant to surrender the colony, including its outposts across the Hudson and the former Swedish settlements on the Delaware. The new English governor, Richard Nicolls, soon set about granting lands that would eventually become part of New Jersey to new settlers, only to learn later that he had been trumped by the king's brother. King Charles II had given James, Duke of York, the land in between the Hudson and Delaware rivers, and James had in turn split it between Lord John Berkeley and Sir George Carteret—two courtiers who had accompanied him during exile in France. The two proprietors wanted more settlers and so granted land in exchange for annual fees called "quitrents," a traditional feudal substitute for services performed. Later they found it hard to collect the quitrents, as settlers struggled for independence from absentee landlords.

The name "Jersey" came from Carteret, the former governor of the Isle of Jersey in the English Channel, and the mistaken cartographic notion that the granted land was an island. Philip Carteret, the cousin of Sir George Carteret, was appointed the first governor of New Jersey. He proclaimed Elizabethtown as the capital and named it after George Carteret's wife.

In 1673 the Dutch recaptured New Netherland, but the Treaty of Westminster gave it back to the English in 1674. Lord Berkeley, in financial straits, had sold his land to a group of Quakers that included William Penn. This in effect split the colony into East and West Jersey, precipitating perpetual struggles for power in the two halves of the colony. In 1681 Penn and eleven other Quakers purchased East Jersey from the Carteret family, putting the colony back together under the

NEW JERSEY *Time Line*

1524	**1609**	**1620**	**1638**	**1665**
Giovanni da Verrazano arrives in New York Bay	Henry Hudson explores New York and Newark bays	Cornelius May explores Delaware Bay	Peter Minuit settles New Sweden on the Delaware River	Governor Nicolls of New York grants settlers New Jersey lands, while Duke of York splits same land between two proprietors

ownership of a large group of proprietors. The remainder of the century was filled with disputes between proprietors and settlers over land titles, rents, voting rights, and self-government, as well as power struggles with New York over control of East Jersey. In 1680 Philip Carteret was abducted and tried by Governor Andros of New York, and in 1681 he dissolved a legislature that threatened his constitutional authority. In the absence of consistent authority, many settlers longed for royal control, not anticipating that it might be equally chaotic.

The Cornbury Ring

Political conditions got worse rather than better after the turn of the century. After New Jersey became a royal colony in 1702, Queen Anne appointed her cousin Edward Hyde, Lord Cornbury, as governor. The first recorded bribe in New Jersey was delivered to Cornbury's home, with many more to follow as sycophants sought to curry favor with the new regime. In the politics of the colony he sided with the proprietors and found ingenious ways to defeat the antiproprietors—such as making them stand outdoors all day in winter weather before allowing them to vote. Cornbury later ignored both parties and put his own henchmen, the "Cornbury Ring," into power.

Inching toward Independence

With this long history of grievances against the Crown, it is somewhat surprising that in New Jersey, resentment against the imposition of new controls and taxes remained dormant in the years before the Revolution. But there were some reasons for New Jersey's moderation. Parliamentary measures that affected western land claims or maritime commerce excited Virginia planters and land speculators and Massachusetts merchants more than New Jersey farmers. But the Stamp Act of 1765 did catch the attention of townspeople because it placed heavy burdens on their ordinary business. Also, the disputes between large landowners and elected assemblies had tended to polarize groups sympathetic to the Crown and those opposed to its official machinations. Into that mix religion added passion, with militant Presbyterians advocating independence and Anglicans and Quakers resisting it for quite different reasons. As the Revolution approached, the colony's his-

1672	1674	1676	1681	1702
Duke of York cancels Nicolls land grants	Lord Berkeley sells his land to Quakers	William Penn confirms division between East and West Jersey	A dozen Quakers, including Penn, purchase East Jersey from the Carteret family	New Jersey becomes a royal colony under the administration of New York's governor, Lord Cornbury

tory of oppositions coalesced into new forms, and New Jersey became known for bitter conflict between Patriots and Loyalists.

The story of William Franklin, son of Benjamin Franklin, represents this internecine polarization. In one of the ironies of colonial and family history, as Benjamin Franklin abandoned his ambitions for authority in the British establishment and became a passionate Patriot, William converted to the Church of England and embraced Tory principles. He was governor of New Jersey during the crucial period, from the end of the French and Indian War in 1763 to the Declaration of Independence in 1776. William was successful in restraining an ambivalent assembly through 1775 and even persuaded it to pass resolutions calling for reconciliation. That was too much for Patriots, who arranged for his arrest in January of 1776. Franklin remained under house arrest until July, when he was deported to Connecticut as a prisoner of war. After being released, he sought haven in British-occupied New York. His sympathies remained with the Crown, even including emigration back to England in 1782.

The tide of political action had turned. The reluctance of the assembly was not mirrored in gatherings orchestrated by Patriots. New Brunswick had been the site of the first provincial congress held in 1774 to appoint delegates to the Continental Congress in Philadelphia. As that group was drafting the Declaration of Independence in 1776, the provincial congress had hurriedly created its own declaration and adopted a state constitution. That constitution allowed "all inhabitants of this Colony, of full age, who are worth fifty pounds proclamation money" to vote. More than a century of struggle for control of government between large and small landowners was over.

Ten Crucial Days

Once in the fray, the new state was occupied by British troops and battered incessantly as both sides struggled for control of the territory between New York and Philadelphia. Between the end of December 1776 and the first week in January 1777, a number of battles took place as the beleaguered Continental Army tried to halt the British advance toward Philadelphia. George Washington was at a disadvantage because the enlistments of most of his troops expired at the end of the

---

NEW JERSEY *Time Line*

1738	1774	1776	1777	1778
New Jersey is separated from New York, gets its own royal governor	College of New Jersey students burn tea in support of Boston	Washington crosses the Delaware and wins Battle of Trenton	Washington wins Battle of Princeton in January; Continental Army then winters at Morristown	Battle of Monmouth

---

year. Their spirits were also at low ebb because of cold and privation. Washington hoped for a victory to boost morale.

Crossing the Delaware with great difficulty on Christmas night, Washington took advantage of the concealment provided by a raging nor'easter to attack Trenton the next morning. Because of frequent raids by Patriot militias in the surrounding countryside, the Hessian garrison there had been on high alert for weeks, yet the exhausted defenders fought hard before capitulating. The Continental Army took 900 Hessian soldiers captive, along with their British supplies, and wisely retreated over the river. As a second battle for Trenton loomed, Washington faced 6,000 British regulars under General Cornwallis. Using cover of darkness to evacuate his troops—a trick he had successfully executed before to save his army after the Battle of Long Island—Washington and his men continued into enemy territory, where they again surprised and vanquished the British in the Battle of Princeton on January 3, 1777. Washington's call to his men was, "It's a fine fox chase, my boys!" After this victory the Continental Army moved north to Morristown for the winter, where troops lived in huts and suffered from cold, lack of food, and smallpox.

New Jersey was the site of another major battle on June 28, 1778. After a dreadful winter at Valley Forge, Washington followed the army evacuating Philadelphia under the command of Sir Henry Clinton while it was strung out over 12 miles in a line of 10,000 troops and 1,500 wagons. General Charles Lee, with 5,000 troops and militia, was to attack the British rear at Monmouth, and Washington was to follow. When Washington reached the action he found Lee's forces in confused retreat, and angrily took charge.

With Washington rallying and organizing his men, the battle continued without resolution throughout the day in 100-degree heat until dark. During the night the British resumed their march northward, to fight another day. One of the stories of that time was the heroism of "Molly Pitcher," the real Mary Hayes (McCauley). She had been carrying water to the men in her husband's gun crew. When he was overcome by the heat, she courageously stepped in to help fire his cannon.

New Jersey's last major battle during the Revolutionary War took place in

1783
Congress meets in Nassau Hall in Princeton; America and Britain sign peace treaty in Paris; Washington delivers farewell address

1787
New Jersey ratifies the U.S. Constitution

1789
New Jersey ratifies the Bill of Rights

1790
Trenton becomes the state capital

Springfield and Hobart Gap on June 6 and 7, 1780, when 6,000 German and British troops sought to destroy Washington's dwindling army in Morristown. Baron von Knyphausen tried to capture Hobart Gap so that he would be able to reach the Americans in Morristown, but outnumbered New Jersey regulars and militia were able to hold the high ground the first day. When reinforcements from Clinton's army arrived the next day, General Nathanael Greene's troops were able to thwart this direct attack on the Continental Army at Morristown.

Two of the attacking units at Springfield were Loyalist regiments, a sign of the continuing split loyalties that wracked New Jersey communities from the beginning to the end of the war. By the beginning of 1777 civilians of both persuasions were attacked by militias out of control after the collapse of stable government. To stop brutal marauding that resembled mob action and often pitted neighbor against neighbor to settle old scores, Robert Livingston, the first governor of the state, asked the legislature to create a council of safety to root out Loyalists and either convert or punish them. As president of the council, he was hated by Loyalists, suffered assassination attempts, and was said to sleep no more than two consecutive nights in any house. Yet he did succeed in restoring some civil order among a population filled with rancor.

In spite of its tangled responses during this era, New Jersey played a crucial role as a highway and battleground for major campaigns. During the Revolution the Continental Army had crossed and recrossed the state repeatedly. General Washington and his men spent two winters in Morristown and one at Middlebrook. Crucial battles were fought in Trenton, Princeton, Monmouth, and Springfield. After the British capitulation, the Continental Congress met in Princeton in 1783 and in Trenton in 1784. Trenton became the state capital in 1790.

Regions *to* Explore

THE DELAWARE RIVER AND BAY SETTLEMENTS
CENTRAL NEW JERSEY
NORTHERN NEW JERSEY

THE DELAWARE RIVER AND BAY SETTLEMENTS

The expansive reaches of the Delaware River and Bay first tempted explorers who thought this might be the beginning of the Northwest Passage to Asia. Later, the river and bay, with their network of tributaries, provided the needed water transport for colonial development.

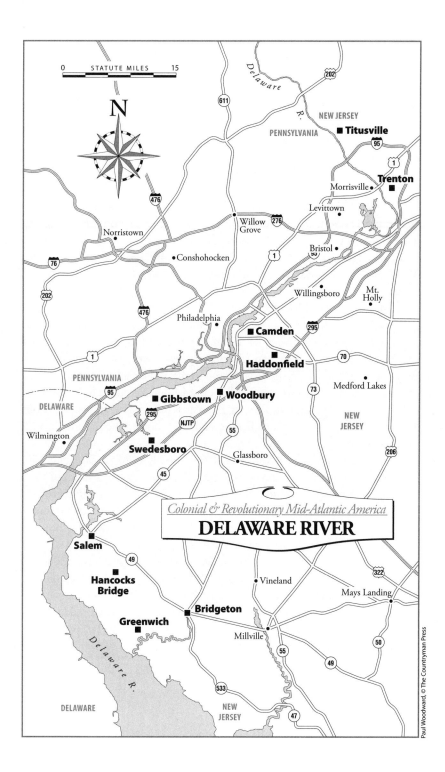

Colonial & Revolutionary Mid-Atlantic America
DELAWARE RIVER

0 STATUTE MILES 15

N

NEW JERSEY
PENNSYLVANIA

■ **Titusville**

■ **Trenton**
Morrisville •

Levittown •

Willow Grove •

Norristown •

• Conshohocken

Bristol •

Willingsboro •

Mt. Holly •

Philadelphia •

■ **Camden**

■ **Haddonfield**

Medford Lakes •

PENNSYLVANIA

■ **Gibbstown** ■ **Woodbury**

DELAWARE

NEW JERSEY

Wilmington •

■ **Swedesboro**

Glassboro •

■ **Salem**

■ **Hancocks Bridge**

• Vineland

Mays Landing •

■ **Bridgeton**

■ **Greenwich**

Millville •

Delaware R.

DELAWARE

NEW JERSEY

BRIDGETON

Lenni-Lenape Indians lived in the area and burned sections of the forest to clear farming land. Swedes and Finns arrived in 1638 and made use of these fields. The area was settled by Quakers in the late 17th century, and the city still retains an extensive historic district representing all succeeding eras. Within fifty years settlers built a bridge over Cohansey Creek and the town was called Bridgeton. Residents rang a liberty bell with vigor on July 4, 1776, when townspeople gathered to hear the Declaration of Independence read.

HISTORICAL SITES and MUSEUMS
Bridgeton Historical District and Downtown Bridgeton (856-455-3230; www.cityofbridgeton), 50 E. Broad St. The town retains a wealth of historical structures. Today people gravitate to **Dutch Neck Village** (856-451-2188), 97 Trench Rd., a mile southwest of Bridgeton, for the variety of antique and craft shops.

Old Broad Street Church (Jonathan Wood is chairman of the Friends of Old Broad Street Church and welcomes calls for tours of the church, 856-825-6993), Broad and Lawrence Sts. Many of the officers buried in the graveyard belonged to the Society of the Cincinnati. The society was organized at the end of the Revolutionary War by George Washington so that old friendships would not be forgotten. The Palladian window is like one at Mount Vernon. The "Seeing Eye of God" is above the window. There is a wineglass pulpit. The church dates from 1792 to 1795. Services are held here several times during the summer, as well as Thanksgiving.

New Sweden Farmstead Museum (856-455-3230 x280), in Bridgeton City Park, W. Commerce St. and Mayor Aitken Dr. Open mid-May–Labor Day, Sat.–Sun. The museum is noted for its replicas of 17th-century structures reflecting the Swedish culture of the people who lived here. You'll see a threshing barn, blacksmith shop, stable, sauna, smokehouse, and cabin. Hex signs were meant to make sure only good spirits came into the building.

The riverfront promenade in the park is the place to stroll on brick paths and rest on benches. Concerts and events are held here during the summer.

Woodruff Museum of Indian Artifacts (856-451-2620), in the Bridgeton Public Library, 150 E. Commerce St. Open Mon.–Sat. American Indian pieces were collected in a 30-mile radius of Bridgeton. They date from 10,000 to 8,000 BC, but more recent artifacts belonged to the Lenni-Lenape Indians and date from AD 700 to 1800.

INFORMATION

BRIDGETON CHAMBER OF COMMERCE
53 S. Laurel St., Bridgton, NJ 08302
856-455-1312; www.baccnj.com

GREENWICH

Greenwich is downstream on the Cohansey River, less than five miles from Delaware Bay. From 1695 to 1765 the royal governor authorized annual fairs to be held in Market Square. By 1701 Greenwich had become a thriving port. It was one of only three official ports of entry for New Jersey. Ships unloaded cargo here, and warehouses and merchants thrived.

New Jersey's only tea party took place in Greenwich in December 1774. Patriots in Indian disguise gathered on the square to burn tea snatched from the East India Company. This was one of five "tea parties" to protest British taxation. Visitors will see the **Tea Burners Monument** on Ye Greate St. and Market Lane.

Gibbon House (856-455-4055; www.cchistsoc.org), 960 Ye Greate St. Open Tue.–Sat. Nicholas Gibbon built his home in 1730. It looks like a London town house from the outside and is now the home of the **Cumberland County Historical Society**. The house contains 18th- and 19th-century furnishings, including rush-seated Ware chairs that were made by the Ware family up into the 1930s. Don't miss the 1650 **Swedish Granary**, a Swedish log cabin built by early settlers, just behind the Gibbon House.

HANCOCKS BRIDGE

This small town is in the far southwestern corner of the state, near the head of Delaware Bay, where the Delaware River swings northeastward toward Wilmington and Philadelphia.

HISTORICAL SITES *and* MUSEUMS
The 1734 **Hancock House** (856-935-4373; www.state.nj.us/dep/parksandforests), 3 Front St. Open Wed.–Sun. This was the site of a massacre during the Revolution. In 1778 Major John Graves Simcoe led a retaliatory raid on the town because its Quaker residents had supplied food to Washington's troops at Valley Forge. In a surprise attack, a British force of 300 killed 30 local militiamen who were sleeping here. Judge William Hancock, the homeowner, was also killed.

SALEM

The oldest village along the Delaware River, Salem was built on land bought by Quaker John Fenwick in 1675. Today Salem is a popular place for birding. History buffs enjoy seeing the colonial and Federal houses, although they are not open.

HISTORICAL SITES *and* MUSEUMS
To conclude the land purchase, Fenwick met the Lenne-Lenape (Delaware) Indians under the **Salem Oak**, estimated to be over 500 years old, in the **Friends Burying Ground**.

The **Salem County Historical Society** (856-935-5004; www.salemcounty historicalsociety.com) is at 79–83 Market St. Open Tue.–Sat. The society owns the 1721 **Alexander Grant House** there. If you are interested in genealogical research, visit the library in the house. Twenty-one rooms contain pieces from the colonial and Federal periods, and you will also see a colonial garden, a stone barn, and a law office dating from 1736.

INFORMATION

SALEM COUNTY CHAMBER OF COMMERCE
91A S. Virginia Ave., Carneys Point, NJ 08069
856-299-6699; salemnjchamber.homestead.com

SWEDESBORO

Swedish pioneers came from Christiana (Wilmington, Delaware) and built farms in Raccoon, now called Swedesboro. They sailed across the Delaware River to attend church in Christiana, until they built their own church on the banks of Raccoon Creek. Today the community is working on Trinity Square, which will be an interpretive park to tell the story of Swedesboro.

HISTORICAL SITES *and* MUSEUMS
"Old Swedes" Trinity Church (856-467-1227), 208 Kings Hwy. Open Mon.–Sat. The log cabin church was finished in 1703, and it was the first Swedish Lutheran Church in New Jersey. Although damaged during the Revolutionary War, it was rebuilt in 1784. The burial ground contains the graves of a number of Revolutionary War heroes and a former New Jersey governor.

GIBBSTOWN

Gibbstown is across the Delaware River from Chester, Pennsylvania.

HISTORICAL SITES *and* MUSEUMS
C. A. Nothnagle Log House (856-423-0916), 406 Swedesboro Rd. Hours are unscheduled. It is attached to the private home of Doris and Harry Rink, who give tours by appointment. The house is listed on the National Register of Historic Sites and is considered to be the oldest log cabin in the country. It is believed to date from around 1638. It was built without nails, and the rafters had no ridgepoles; the structure was held together by dovetails and trunnel pins. Bricks were probably brought from Sweden. The original earthen floor was covered by pine boards in 1730.

WOODBURY

Just across the Delaware from Philadelphia, Woodbury was occupied by the British in 1777, and General Charles Cornwallis made his quarters in the home of John Cooper, a member of the Continental Congress. Cooper was denounced for his patriotism by other pacifist Quaker friends. Continental Army cavalry hero "Light Horse" Harry Lee (the father of Robert E. Lee) stayed in Woodbury in 1779 during campaigns in south Jersey.

HISTORICAL SITES *and* MUSEUMS

Two miles west of US 130 on the riverfront, **Red Bank Battlefield Park** is the site of **Fort Mercer** on a strategically important bluff overlooking the river. Fort Mercer was one of three sites, along with Fort Mifflin and Billingsport, to serve as river defenses. The Americans hoped to keep the British from getting their supplies into Philadelphia, and a British attempt to clear the river led to the Battle of Red Bank. There, 400 American defenders drove off more than 1,200 attacking Hessians on October 22, 1777. They only evacuated the fort a month later when Cornwallis approached with an overwhelming force.

In the park you can visit the restored home of **Ann Whitall** (856-853-5120). Open Apr.–Sep., Wed., Sun. She reportedly sat calmly spinning wool during the battle. After a cannonball struck her house, she carried her spinning wheel to the basement and went right on spinning. When the battle was over she cared for the wounded from both sides in her home.

> Chevaux-de-frise were underwater obstructions made of large, rock-filled, pine-log boxes, with long poles tipped with iron spikes projecting from them at angles. They were sunk in the river channel, ready to impale an enemy ship coming upriver.

After the Revolutionary War, the Whitall family resumed working their plantation, which included orchards, livestock, a gristmill, a ferry, a shad fishery, and a smokehouse. James Whitall and his sons also worked with Philadelphia merchants.

Architecturally this house is typical of southern New Jersey structures beginning in 1748. Made of brick, it is two and a half stories with a gable roof. The ridge of the roof runs parallel to the river, with chimneys at either end. The west facade faces the river and was used as a business entrance. The east facade was for family use. The brickwork includes the initials of the owners (James and Ann) and the year (1748).

The stone kitchen was added during the third quarter of the 18th century and was connected to the house by a doorway from the common room. An herb garden outside the kitchen was kept for both culinary and medicinal use.

James Whitall's office is in the southwest corner, and a large common room, the center of life for the family, occupies the southeast corner of the house. Two parlors open off the hall, one used to entertain guests.

EVENTS

October: Eighteenth-century field day, Red Bank Park; 856-853-5120
December: Colonial Christmas open house, Red Bank Park; 856-853-5120

INFORMATION

GREATER WOODBURY CHAMBER OF COMMERCE
Kings Hwy., Woodbury, NJ 08096
856-845-4056; www.greaterwoodburychamber.com

HADDONFIELD

Haddonfield was founded by a woman, Elizabeth Haddon. Her father had no sons, so he sent his daughter from England in 1701 to develop his land. She built a house and gave herself in marriage to Quaker missionary John Estaugh. She asked him, and he accepted. Henry Wadsworth Longfellow wrote about this romance in "The Theologian's Tale" in *Tales of a Wayside Inn.*

Today Haddonfield is known for its paleontology sites as well as historic homes. It was the second municipality in New Jersey to organize a historical preservation district. Arrowheads and pottery shards were found by residents along the Cooper River, evidence of the Lenni-Lenape settlement there.

Today, besides visiting the dinosaur sculpture on Kings Highway across from Chestnut Street (see sidebar), you can head out Maple Avenue to the site where the fossil bones were found. There's a bench and two historic markers honoring the discovery. Eagle Scout Christopher Brees marked it in 1984; his father is the curator of the Hadrosaurus Park. The actual site is at the bottom of the ravine, which is in its wild state and not easily accessible.

HISTORICAL SITES *and* MUSEUMS

Indian King Tavern (856-429-6792; www.levins.com/tavern), 233 Kings Hwy. East. Open Wed.–Sat. Mathias Aspden built the tavern about 1750. The New Jersey Assembly met here on March 10, 1777. They approved the adoption of the great seal of New Jersey. On September they met again and enacted a law substituting the word "state" for "colony" in all commissions, writs, and indictments.

You can see the assembly room, a barroom, a keeping room, and a sleeping chamber. Dolley Madison may have slept in the bed in that room.

Greenfield Hall, the Historical Society of Haddonfield (856-429-7375), 343 Kings Hwy. East. Open Tue. and Thu. and the first Sun. of each month. The hall was built in 1841 on the foundation of an earlier 18th-century house. A collection of early American furniture, china, tools, and other pieces is on display.

> ✳ Happy Birthday, Haddie! Who is Haddie? It is a large bronze statue of the dinosaur *Hadrosaurus foulkii,* sculpted by John Giannotti and placed in Haddonfield in 2003.
>
> In 1838 William Hopkins uncovered large bones in a marl pit, at Hopkins Pond. William Foulke heard about them and in 1858 dug out the first full skeleton of a dinosaur found in North America, the most complete dinosaur skeleton in existence at the time. He noted that it had the anatomical features of both a lizard and a bird. It was classified as *Hadrosaurus* (sturdy lizard) *foulkii* (in honor of Foulke) and is now in the Philadelphia Academy of Natural Science.

LODGING

HADDONFIELD INN
44 West End Ave., Haddonfield, NJ 08033
800-269-0014, 856-428-2195; www.haddonfieldinn.com
The inn dates from the 1870s and features a turret and fireplaces in bedrooms. 9 guest rooms.

INFORMATION

HADDONFIELD INFORMATION CENTER
2 Kings Court, Haddonfield, NJ 08033
856-216-7253; www.haddonfieldnj.org.

CAMDEN

Camden got its start in 1681 when William Cooper began his ferryboat service across the Delaware River to Philadelphia. Today Camden is seeing a renaissance on its waterfront. Adventure Aquarium is a popular place, as is the battleship *New Jersey.*

HISTORICAL SITES *and* MUSEUMS

Pomona Hall (1726), on Park Boulevard at Euclid Avenue, was home to Cooper's descendants. The home is owned by the **Camden County Historical Society** (856-964-3333), 1900 Park Blvd. Open Sep.–July, Wed.–Fri. and Sun. Pomona Hall contains period furnishings and includes an adjacent library. Interpreters in period dress demonstrate activities. Open-hearth demonstrations are given once a month.

TRENTON

Trenton was settled in 1679. In 1714 William Trent, a Philadelphia merchant, bought 1,600 acres here and a mill. It came to be called Trent's Town. By 1776 Hessian troops were occupying the town, but when Washington crossed the Delaware eight miles upriver and attacked them, 900 of the Germans were captured in the first Battle of Trenton. Intelligence then reached Washington that the British general Cornwallis was gathering forces in Princeton to counterattack—

an army that eventually numbered about 9,000 regulars. Expiring enlistments in his own army threatened the loss of its best units by the end of December, but a bounty for reenlistment, along with Washington's personal persuasion, convinced them that the cause of liberty was at stake in the next month. On the night of the army's return to the Pennsylvania shore, Washington's staff reached a consensus that they should recross the Delaware to defend Trenton. That movement started on the morning of December 29 and proved even more difficult than the first crossing, because sections of the river were covered with ice too thin to support artillery and wagons. Yet by New Year's Eve Washington had assembled some 6,800 troops and established a plan of defensive positions overlooking a swollen creek at the southern edge of town.

On the morning of January 2 the long British line began slogging through deep mud on the road from Princeton to Trenton. It was slow going, especially for the guns and heavy wagons, and there were further delays as American pickets began to harass the British along the way at creeks that had to be forded. It was getting near sunset when the head of the line moved through the village of Trenton and began to form up on high ground facing Washington's gun emplacements and troops across Assunpink Creek. A series of attacks followed, first at the fords and then at the narrow bridge, as winter dusk settled in, but each advance was battered by Washington's artillery and musket fire. When it became dark and the attacks ceased, the bridge was piled with dead redcoats.

Cornwallis, who didn't like to fight in the dark, is reported to have remarked, "We've got the Old Fox safe now. We'll go over and bag him in the morning." That same evening Washington's staff reluctantly reached a similar assessment that defeat was probable if not inevitable the next day, with dire consequences for the just renewed Continental Army. The ice-choked Delaware blocked speedy retreat to Pennsylvania, so the conclusion was another of Washington's famous secret and silent night operations, a circling evacuation that headed east beyond British lines then turned north to attack now lightly defended Princeton. Helped by the cold night freeze that made roads more passable, Washington's army was within reach of Princeton by dawn. The Old Fox was not to be bagged that day.

Trenton became the state capital in 1790. The city has a number of historic districts from various eras. The Mill House Historic District runs from Mercer to Jackson Streets.

HISTORICAL SITES *and* MUSEUMS

New Jersey State Museum (609-292-6464; www.newjerseystatemuseum.org), 205 W. State St. Open Mon.–Sat. At this writing the museum is under renovation but should be fully open sometime in 2007. It will have three floors of exhibits on many topics, including history of the colonial and Revolutionary periods. You will see American Indian artifacts from the area, including the Cherokee, Nanticoke, Powhatan Renape, and Ramapo tribes. The highlight of the museum is the replica of Emmanuel Leutze's painting of Washington crossing the Delaware River by Robert Bruce Williams. It is hung in the auditorium.

New Jersey State House (609-633-2709), 125 W. State St. Open Mon.–Sat. A gold dome tops this 1792 building. You can see the 145-foot domed ceiling of the rotunda, the legislative chambers, the caucus rooms, and the governor's reception room. Portraits of New Jersey's early governors are surrounded by stained glass. Tours are given on the hour.

Old Barracks Museum (609-396-1776), Barrack St. Open daily. Built in 1758 for British soldiers during the French and Indian War, it later housed the Hessians before the Battle of Trenton. In 1777 it served as a Continental Army hospital. You will see the restored officers' quarters, soldiers' barrack rooms, and a hospital room.

The exhibit "Of War, Law, and the Third Amendment" describes the practice of forced quartering in America when soldiers stayed in people's houses uninvited. "The Battle of Trenton" exhibit includes period weapons and equipment. Interpreters in period dress take the parts of Trentonians of 1777 as they describe the battle. "Hail the Conquering Hero" is a celebration of Washington's entry into Trenton.

William Trent House (609-989-3027), 15 Market St. Open daily. William Trent built his home as a summer estate on the banks of the Delaware between 1716 and 1719. He emigrated from Scotland in 1682 and nine years later was one of the most successful businessmen in Philadelphia.

The drawing room contains three japanned pieces (coated with a black lacquer or enamel). The tea set from China does not have handles—they poured the tea into a saucer and drank from it. The library has an Elizabethan game box that allows one to play backgammon, tric-trac (a tic-tac-toe game), and chess.

The chandelier in the dining room has lift-off arms so that anyone could take one to light the way to a bedroom. Each bracket and arm was a little different, so they were numbered for replacement the next morning.

Trenton Battle Monument (609-737-0623), N. Broad and N. Warren Sts. and Brunswick and Pennington Aves. This Beaux Arts monument was designed by John Duncan. It is on the site where Washington placed his artillery for the Battle of Trenton.

RESTAURANTS

DIAMOND'S RIVERSIDE
1140 River Rd., West Trenton, NJ 08628
609-882-0303; www.diamondsriver side.us
Steak and seafood are specialties; a variety of other dishes are offered.

JOHN HENRY'S SEAFOOD RESTAURANT
2 Mifflin St., Trenton, NJ 08610
609-396-3083; www.johnhenrys seafood.com
This family restaurant offers fresh seafood in a Mediterranean setting.

JOE'S MILL HILL SALOON
300 S. Broad St.
609-394-7222
A neighborhood favorite in an 1850 building.

HISTORICAL SITES *and* MUSEUMS

Washington Crossing State Park (609-737-0623; www.state.nj.us/dep/forestry/parks), 355 Washington Crossing–Pennington Rd. Visitor Center and Ferry House open Wed.–Sun. year-round. Pennsylvania and New Jersey each honor Washington's December crossing of the Delaware. The Visitor Center offers audiovisual presentations, including the "Battles of Trenton and Princeton," filmed during the U.S. bicentennial. Also, the Harry Kels Swan Collection of Revolutionary War artifacts is on exhibit. Twelve interpretive themes begin with the "Prelude to the Revolution" (1758–73) and end with the "Results of the Revolution" (1781–83). Artifacts include letters, muskets, maps, and other items.

The **Johnson Ferry House** (609-737-2515) is where Washington and his officers talked about military strategy. Open Wed.—Sun. year-round. Period rooms are decorated as if the ferry keeper and his family had just stepped out. The **Nelson House**, at the landing on the Delaware, is small; a portion of it used to be a hotel, but the train knocked off some of the building. Open weekends, depending on the weather. Inside are brochures of the park and old photographs.

Howell Living History Farm (609-737-3299; www.howellfarm.com), 101 Hunter Rd. Open Feb.–Nov., Tue.–Fri. and Sun. Joseph Phillips bought 125 acres from the landholder, William Bryant, in 1732. The farm has been restored to its 1900–1910 appearance. Lots of animals live on the farm, which uses horses instead of tractors.

LODGING

CHIMNEY HILL ESTATE
207 Goat Hill Rd., Lambertville, NJ 08530
800-211-4667, 609-397-1516;
www.chimneyhillinn.com
This fieldstone inn, originally a farmhouse, dates from 1820. 12 guest rooms.

THE INN AT LAMBERTVILLE STATION
11 Bridge St., Lambertville, NJ 08530
609-397-4400; www.lambertville station.com
The train station dates from the 1800s; the inn rooms overlook the Delaware River. 45 guest rooms.

WOOLVERTON INN
6 Woolverton Rd., Stockton, NJ 08559
888-264-6648, 609-397-0802;
www.woolvertoninin.com

The stone manor house dates from 1792 and is set on 10 acres. 13 guest rooms.

CHESTNUT HILL ON THE DELAWARE
63 Church St., Milford, NJ 08848
888-333-2242, 908-995-9761;
www.chestnuthillnj.com
This 1860 mansion on the Delaware River has been restored to its Victorian appearance. 11 guest rooms.

RESTAURANTS

LAMBERTVILLE STATION RESTAURANT
11 Bridge St., Lambertville, NJ 08530
609-397-8300; www.lambertville station.com
The Riverside Room in this restored 19th-century train station offers a Sunday champagne buffet brunch; other dining areas and menus are also offered.

EVENTS

At Washington Crossing State Park;
609-737-0623; www.state.nj.us/dep/
parksandforests/parks/washcros.html
April: School of the soldier
May: State history fair
September: New Jersey Frontier Guard
encampment
December: Washington crossing the
Delaware

INFORMATION

**DELAWARE RIVER REGIONAL
TOURISM COUNCIL**
c/o South Jersey Tourism Corp.
One Port Center, 2 Riverside Dr.,
Suite 102, Camden, NJ 08103
856-757-9400;
www.visitsouthjersey.com

CENTRAL NEW JERSEY

PRINCETON

We have special feelings for Princeton, as one of us attended college there. Over the years since then we have driven to Princeton from anywhere remotely close to reminisce. We were both there in 1950 for the Dartmouth-Princeton game when a hurricane charged through, taking pieces of the stadium off. Commencement in 1952 was magical, followed by naval service in Japan, marriage in 1953, and fifty-four years later we are still loving life and travel. The rich historical sites in Princeton have filled our travel writing agenda and our travel guides for the last twenty-eight years.

Princeton was first called Stony Brook for a stream, then Prince's town in 1724, and finally Princeton. It was a stagecoach stop on the New York–Philadelphia turnpike.

Princeton was the site of an important American victory in the Revolution. "Bagging the fox" was the goal of British general Cornwallis, who considered himself the hunter, but Washington, the "fox," had more tricks in store.

Cornwallis, leaving some troops in Princeton, had hurried down to Trenton with about 9,000 men to bag Washington, who in turn sent parties to harass and slow the British on the mud-churned road south. On January 2 Cornwallis arrived in Trenton to find Washington waiting for him at Assunpink Creek near the middle of town. Failing in his initial attacks (the Second Battle of Trenton), and figuring he had his "fox" trapped, Cornwallis put off his major assault for the morning.

Washington had the chance he needed. As he had done at Long Island in 1776, he again kept his campfires burning and fooled the British into thinking he was digging in. Then, in the middle of the night, his army slipped around the enemy's positions, intending to make a dash for Princeton. As Washington and his men headed north over the country lanes, the muddy tracks that had slowed Cornwallis on his way south froze with a drop in temperature, so Washington's men were able to make more speed, even though they were exhausted.

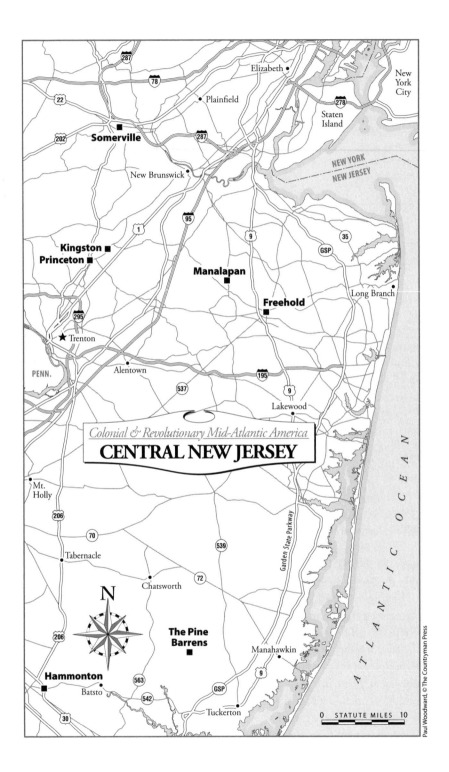

Elizabeth

New York City

Plainfield

Staten Island

287

78

22

202

287

Somerville

New Brunswick

NEW YORK
NEW JERSEY

95

1

9

35

GSP

Kingston

Princeton

Manalapan

Long Branch

Freehold

295

Trenton

PENN.

Alentown

537

195

9

Lakewood

Colonial & Revolutionary Mid-Atlantic America

CENTRAL NEW JERSEY

Mt. Holly

206

70

Tabernacle

539

Garden State Parkway

N

Chatsworth

72

The Pine Barrens

Manahawkin

9

Hammonton

Batsto

563

542

GSP

Tuckerton

30

ATLANTIC OCEAN

Paul Woodward, © The Countryman Press

0   STATUTE MILES   10

They arrived outside Princeton on January 3, 1777, and the battle quickly began. Ahead of the main body of troops, General Hugh Mercer's forces planned to demolish the wooden bridge across Stony Brook on the Kings Highway leading into town. There they encountered two British regiments left behind by Cornwallis and were forced to retreat to a position near the Thomas Clark House.

Washington's personal arrival on the scene turned the tide. "It's a fine fox chase, my boys!" was Washington's call to his men as they rode through British regiments and assured an American victory. He went on to capture the British headquarters at Nassau Hall, before moving his exhausted army north to winter quarters in Morristown. At the junction of Nassau, Mercer, and Stockton Streets, the marble Princeton Battlefield Monument stands tall, with a figure of Liberty encouraging Washington.

The Continental Congress met in Princeton from June to November 1783. In August of that year Washington stood in Nassau Hall to receive thanks.

Today Princeton still has a rural charm that fits the image of a small, Ivy League university town and has survived the astounding growth of high-tech research institutions and corporate headquarters in the surrounding countryside. As you drive into town from the north, west, or south, you will see one mansion after another, all beautifully landscaped with lush grounds, gigantic old trees, and seasonal flowers.

The university's campus, like that of Cambridge in England, has a sense of space and tranquillity that seems forever immune from the bustle of the town or the highway just one mile east. Many of the buildings also imitate those of Cambridge colleges like King's or Trinity, in the collegiate Gothic style with gray stone, or the redbrick newer parts of St. John's, interspersed with a few Victorian brownstones and Greek-revival buildings. Nassau Hall, built in 1756 and occupied by the British in 1777, is still the centerpiece of the campus as the site of the university administration and faculty meetings.

HISTORICAL SITES and MUSEUMS

Princeton University (609-258-1766), 110 College Rd. Open for tours; please call for days and times. It was founded as the College of New Jersey in 1746, when it trained Presbyterian ministers and teachers. The college moved into Nassau Hall in 1756. In 1768 the Reverend John Witherspoon, a Scotsman, became the first president. He was a member of the Continental Congress and a strong revolutionary. He signed the Declaration of Independence, stating that the country was "not only ripe for the measure but in danger of rotting for the want of it."

Princeton Historical Society (609-921-6748; www.princetonhistory.org), 158 Nassau St. Open Tue.–Sun. Bainbridge House was built in 1766 by Job Stockton. It was the birthplace of William Bainbridge, a commander of the USS *Constitution* ("Old Ironsides") during the War of 1812.

Two temporary exhibitions are mounted on the main floor every year, using pieces from the collection, including furniture, paintings, clothing, and household objects. Walking tours are offered on Sunday. Please phone for information.

Historic Morven (609-683-1514; www.historicmorven.org), 55 Stockton St. Open Wed.–Sun. Richard Stockton purchased large tracts of land, some of it from William Penn, in 1697. Stockton's grandson, also named Richard, a signer of the Declaration of Independence, built Morven, a Georgian mansion, between 1751 and 1759. The next grandson, Robert Field Stockton, became a commodore in the navy, fought in the War of 1812, and spent much of the family fortune building three elegant mansions in Princeton.

When we visited Morven during the 1980s, an archaeological dig turned up all sorts of artifacts and details on the original landscaping. They found an English Staffordshire plate dating to 1810, a pewter spoon, a handblown bottle, a porcelain statuette, and miniature children's toys, to name a few finds from various summer excavations. A renovation took place for many years, and now it is open and offers exhibits on New Jersey history.

Drumthwacket (609-683-0057; www.drumthwacket.com), 354 Stockton St. Open one day a week by appointment. In 1696 William Olden, a Quaker settler, bought the land and built the Olden House, which still stands here. In 1835 Charles Smith Olden built the central section of the mansion. Moses Taylor Pyne added to the mansion and gave it the Celtic name Drumthwacket, which means "wooded hill." The house is now the residence of the governor of New Jersey. It is furnished with pieces from the 18th and 19th centuries.

Past presidents come to life at Princeton.

Ceremonial silver pieces on the dining room table have nautical themes. The tall clock was made by a New Jersey cabinetmaker. Don't miss the inlaid knife box on the 1800 Edgarton buffet. "Jib" windows open on the bottom in the dining room. The painting in the parlor of George Washington was created after Charles Wilson Peale by the Peale school. The music room has two original Rembrandt Peale paintings. The library houses a collection of priceless books.

Thomas Clarke House, Princeton Battlefield State Park (609-921-0074), 500 Mercer Rd. Open Wed.–Sun. Thomas Clarke built his house in 1770. General Hugh Mercer of Pennsylvania fell mortally wounded with

Historic Drumthwacket is now the residence of the governor of New Jersey.

seven bayonet wounds at the Battle of Princeton and was carried here where he died. The house contains period furniture and Revolutionary War exhibits. Some of the pieces belonged to the Clarke family.

LODGING

INN AT GLENCAIRN
3301 Lawrenceville Rd., Princeton, NJ 08540
609-497-1737; www.innatglencairn .com
The renovated manor house dates from 1736. 5 guest rooms.

NASSAU INN
10 Palmer Square, Princeton, NJ 08542
800-862-7728, 609-921-7500; www .nassauinn.com
Established in 1756, the inn is in downtown Princetown and near the university. 203 guest rooms.

PEACOCK INN
20 Bayard Lane, Princeton, NJ 08540
609-924-1707; www.peacockinn.com
The mansion dates from 1775.

RESTAURANTS

LAHIERE'S RESTAURANT
5 Witherspoon St., Princeton, NJ 08542
609-921-2798; www.lahieres.com
The cuisine is contemporary American and European.

The Thomas Clarke House.

TERESA'S CAFÉ ITALIANO
23 Palmer Square East, Princeton, NJ 08542
609-921-1974; http://www.princeton chamber.org/images/gold.gif
Trattoria-style dining.

YANKEE DOODLE TAP ROOM IN NASSAU INN
10 Palmer Square, Princeton, NJ 08542
800-862-7728, 609-921-7500; www .nassauinn.com
This historic restaurant offers meals all day.

INFORMATION

PRINCETON CHAMBER OF COMMERCE
216 Rockingham Row, Princeton, NJ 08540
609-520-1776; www.princeton chamber.org

PRINCETON REGIONAL CHAMBER OF COMMERCE
9 Vandeventer Ave., Princeton, NJ 08542
609-924-1776; www.princeton chamber.org

KINGSTON

Kingston is just a few miles northeast of Princeton on NJ 27.

HISTORICAL SITES *and* MUSEUMS
Rockingham State Historic Site (609-683-7132), 84 Laurel Lane. Open Thu.–Sun. John Berrien bought the property about 1735. Rockingham was the last wartime headquarters of General Washington. The Washingtons and a small staff lived here from August 23 to November 10, 1783.

Washington used the Blue Room on the second floor as his study. It was here he wrote his Farewell Address to the Armies. Washington hosted many guests, including Hamilton, Jefferson, Madison, Robert Morris, John Witherspoon, Tom Paine, Richard Stockton, and Elias Boudinot. He put up a marquee on the lawn when there were too many visitors.

The building has moved three times, and we visited last just before the final move. It is now on 27 acres and has been restored and repainted. The rebuilt kitchen has red oak beams that are typical of those used in the 18th century.

SOMERVILLE

Somerville is about fifteen miles north of Princeton on US 206.

HISTORICAL SITES *and* MUSEUMS
Old Dutch Parsonage (908-725-1015), 65 Washington Place. Open Wed.–Sun. John Frelinghuysen built the home in 1751. He came from Amsterdam to serve three congregations of the Dutch Reformed Church. The parsonage was the birthplace of General Frederick Frelinghuysen, who became a member of Washington's staff during the Revolutionary War. The Reverend Jacob Hardenbergh lived here from 1756 to 1781. He founded Queens College, which became Rutgers University.

Wallace House State Historic Site (908-725-1015), 38 Washington Place. Open Wed.–Sun. John Wallace, a Philadelphia merchant, built the home in 1777 and called it Hope Farm. Washington used the house as his headquarters during the Middlebrook winter encampment from December 11, 1778, to June 3, 1779. Martha Washington joined her husband on February 5 and stayed through the spring.

MANALAPAN

HISTORICAL SITES *and* MUSEUMS
Monmouth Battlefield State Park (732-462-9616), 347 Freehold-Englishtown Rd. Open daily. The 1777 American victory at Saratoga and the entry of the French into the war on the American side set the stage. With the French navy offshore in early 1778, the British abandoned their occupation of Philadelphia and decided to regroup in New York.

Under the command of General Sir Henry Clinton, about 10,000 troops started across New Jersey, with a wagon train 12 miles long. Washington's army of about the same number, trained by General von Steuben at Valley Forge, left to intercept them.

They met at Monmouth. The long and crucial Battle of Monmouth took place in 100-degree heat on June 28, 1778. At dusk the fighting ceased, with 200 Americans and 300 British reported killed or missing. About half of those were from heat prostration. The Americans took a well-earned sleep to prepare for reengagement at dawn, but after a short rest the British continued their march to Sandy Hook and New York City.

Historians note that during the early years of the Revolution the larger British army had long hoped to fight the Americans in an open field and conquer them all at once—a strategy repeatedly thwarted by Washington's brilliant tactical decisions. At Monmouth the British had that chance, and failed. Thus, though the fighting was a draw, the result was considered both a military victory and a political triumph for the Americans.

Monmouth Battlefield has a visitor center with an audiovisual presentation and an electronic relief map so you can follow the route of the troops during the battle. An archaeological dig produced many artifacts such as musket balls, ramrod tips, pipe fragments, buttons, buckles, coins, a shoulder box, and a Charlevoix musket.

Craig House, dating from 1710, is on the grounds. It was built by Archibald Craig for his family of 11 children and used as a field hospital by the British during the battle. The Craigs hid their silverware in the well before leaving; the British drained the well and found the silver. When Mrs. Craig heard that the British were approaching her farm, she took her children and two slaves and fled by wagon.

Tennent Church, dating from 1751, stands on a hill overlooking the battlefield, and you can get your bearings here. The churchyard contains bodies of

Molly Pitcher being presented to George Washington on the field of battle at Monmouth.

The heroism of water carrier "Molly Pitcher," Mary Hayes McCauley, who took over firing her husband's cannon at Monmouth after he was overcome by the heat, is legendary. She was rewarded by her presentation to General Washington. Look for the marker at Molly Pitcher's well.

Americans who died in that battle. New headstones have replaced the old crumbly ones, including that of Captain Henry Fauntleroy of Virginia, felled by a cannonball on his twenty-second birthday.

FREEHOLD

HISTORICAL SITES *and* MUSEUMS
Covenhoven (732-462-1466), 150 W. Main St., Freehold. Open Tue., Thu., Sun. William and Elizabeth Covenhoven built their home in 1752. British general Sir Henry Clinton used the house as his headquarters before the Battle of Monmouth. The house has been restored and is open to visitors.

EVENTS
June: Battle of Monmouth reenactment; 732-462-9616

INFORMATION
WESTERN MONMOUTH CHAMBER OF COMMERCE
17 Broad St., Freehold, NJ 07728
732-462-3030; www.wmchamber.com

THE PINE BARRENS

In a state crisscrossed by constantly evolving transportation systems, as well as expanding commercial and suburban development, the Pine Barrens may be New Jersey's only "natural" museum of the past. Now protected and treasured for its canoeing, hiking, fishing and hunting, its rivers and woods were once scenes of considerable industrial activity.

If you've read John McPhee's *The Pine Barrens,* you will have some understanding about this part of New Jersey, which is so near a megalopolis and yet so isolated and rural.

HAMMONTON

HISTORICAL SITES *and* MUSEUMS

Batsto Village (609-561-3262), Wharton State Forest, County Rt. 542. Open daily 9-4. "Batsto" was derived from the Swedish word *batstu,* which means "bathing place." Charles Read built the **Batsto Furnace** in 1766; it was a major supplier of munitions during the Revolutionary War. The furnace also produced camp kettles and iron fastenings and fittings for artillery caissons, wagons, and ships.

Visitors can tour a restoration of the village that grew up around the ironworks. The 36-room **Ironmaster's House** (1766) belonged to Joseph Wharton, a financier from Philadelphia, who restored the house as a summer home. Inside, the house is fully furnished with period pieces.

Seventeen workers' homes are also open, and you may wonder why they are black. They were built of Jersey cedar clapboards that blacken with age and the weather. There's a sawmill, gristmill, and general store to visit, too. When you get to the horse barn, look at the vertical slots in the walls, which were designed for ventilation, to prevent hay inside from molding.

Workers' homes at Batsto Village.

> "Pineys," the people who live deep in the forest, have tales to tell about the "Witch of the Pine," Peggy Clevenger. They say that she could turn herself into a rabbit and that she had a treasure of gold. Residents also tell about various strange creatures inhabiting the forest, including the "Jersey Devil" that carried off farm and domestic animals and left cloven tracks behind.

Legends abound about the "pine robbers" who fled into the forest to safety. Some are based on historical fact, while others are embellished or fictional—believe what you will. One, Joe Mulliner, who was hanged in 1781, was the Robin Hood of the Pine Barrens. Apparently he was finally captured because he could not resist coming out of hiding to dance in a local tavern.

NORTHERN NEW JERSEY

MORRISTOWN

In an era when impassable roads and snow-laden fields made combat impossible, war stopped in winter. During the Revolution, British troops spent this lull in cities like New York and Philadelphia, while Americans who bivouacked in the wilderness suffered miserable cold and near starvation, once at Valley Forge and twice at Morristown.

Yet George Washington made a good choice when he marched his troops north to Morristown in January 1777, after brilliant victories at Trenton and Princeton. The Watchung Mountains provided a barrier against any possible British advance from New York City, and the position just west of the New York–Philadelphia track allowed him to easily counter any enemy movement. Because of these advantages, Washington again bivouacked in Morristown for the winter of 1779–80. The area was agricultural, so he knew his men would be fed. And there were furnaces and forges to meet the needs of his army.

Today Morristown has a number of museums to visit, including Fosterfields Living Historical Farm, Historic Speedwell, and the Morris Museum.

HISTORICAL SITES *and* MUSEUMS
Morristown National Historical Park (973-539-2085; www.nps.gov/morr), 30 Washington Place. Open daily. It was the first national historical park to be established in the United States and has three units. The **Ford Mansion** (973-539-2085 x210) 30 Washington Place, dates from 1772. Mrs. Jacob Ford Jr., a widow with four young children, offered her home to George and Martha Washington. Although many officers' wives and families chose to remain at home, Martha

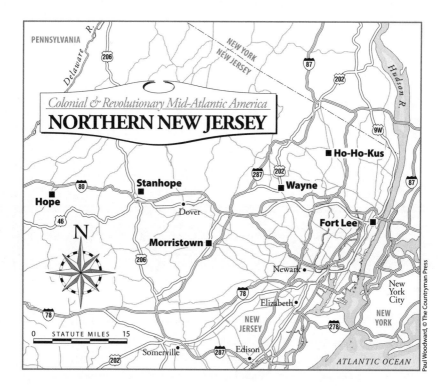

Colonial & Revolutionary Mid-Atlantic America
NORTHERN NEW JERSEY

Paul Woodward, © The Countryman Press

packed up and left Virginia to live with her husband during each winter. General and Mrs. Washington lived here during the winter of 1779–80, along with the owner.

Mrs. Ford was familiar with the army, as her husband had been a colonel in the New Jersey militia. This large house is furnished with Chippendale furniture. Upstairs General and Mrs. Washington's bedroom was on the right. Aides slept in another room but moved out when guests arrived. The Marquis de Lafayette used the room when he arrived in May.

Across the lawn the **Washington Headquarters Museum and Library** documents the history of the period with an orientation film, exhibits, and an extensive collection of books and manuscripts relating to the colonial era and the Revolution.

Fort Nonsense, on Washington Street, was built by Washington's soldiers during the first encampment in 1777 as a defense for supplies in town. According to the scuttlebutt of the time, probably apocryphal, Washington had his men build it just to keep them busy—therefore the name.

Jockey Hollow, the third unit of the park, is on Western Avenue five miles southwest of town and is the principal site of the later encampment. There the Continental Army spent the miserable winter of 1779–80, enduring a succession

George and Martha Washington lived in the Ford Mansion in the winter of 1779–80.

of blizzards. Now the five reconstructed huts represent the 1,200 that once filled the hollow.

There you can also see the **Wick House**, a restored farmhouse once occupied by Major General Arthur St. Clair, commander of the Pennsylvania line. The Wick family was prosperous, and their house reflected a comfortable lifestyle. The six-room house has been restored, and the rooms are divided as they might have been when St. Clair and two of his officers shared the quarters with the family. It is furnished with 18th-century-style pieces.

EVENTS

March: Reenactment of Washington's winter encampment; 973-539-2085
August: Colonial country fair; 973-539-2085

STANHOPE

Today you can also enjoy cycling, hiking, boating, canoeing, rafting, fishing, golf, and hiking in the area. Several parks and forests offer the chance to get out and enjoy nature.

HISTORICAL SITES *and* MUSEUMS

Waterloo Village (973-347-0900; www.waterloovillage.org), 525 Waterloo Rd. Open Memorial Day weekend to Labor Day, Wed.–Sun. The site was once an Indian meeting place and burial ground. Settlers had arrived by the mid-1740s. A Philadelphia company bought the land and built a four-fire, two-hammer forge, a gristmill, sawmill, and homes. Today there are 26 buildings to tour. Winakung is a re-creation of a 1625 Lenni-Lenape village complete with longhouses and dugout canoes. Demonstrations of crafts and gardening are held here.

LODGING

THE WHISTLING SWAN
110 Main St., Stanhope, NJ 07874
973-347-6369; www.whistlingswaninn.com
The home was built in 1905 and has been restored with Victorian decor and gardens. 9 guest rooms.

HOPE

Today Hope is a popular place for those who want to escape New York City on weekends. The town has historic buildings, antique shops, and crafts boutiques. Moravians from Bethlehem, Pennsylvania, settled here in 1769. A number of the original buildings survive, although many residents left for Pennsylvania in 1808.

"Jenny, jump!" was the cry by a father who saw Indians sneaking up on his little daughter. The town commemorates the incident, although no one knows all the story.

LODGING

THE INN AT MILLRACE POND
313 Johnsburg Rd., Hope, NJ 07844
800-746-6467, 908-459-4884; www.innatmillracepond.com
The inn consists of the gristmill from 1769, along with other historic buildings beside the millrace. 17 guest rooms.

Interior of one of the reconstructed army huts at Jockey Hollow in Morristown.

WAYNE

Wayne was a farming community until the railroad came through, enabling people to escape here from New York City on weekends. Some residents commute to the city.

HISTORICAL SITES *and* MUSEUMS
Dey Mansion (973-696-1776), 199 Totowa Rd. Open Wed.–Sun. Dirck Dey, a Dutch planter, built his Georgian home in the 1740s. General George Washington was invited by Theunis Dey to use it as his headquarters during the Revolutionary War. Washington lived here in July, October, and November of 1780. The Dey Mansion is headquarters of the Bergen County Militia, a reenactment group. You'll find a blacksmith shop, a plantation house, a family cemetery, and a formal garden on the property.

HO-HO-KUS

The name Ho-Ho-Kus derives from a Delaware Indian name. The town is now an affluent suburb of New York City.

HISTORICAL SITES *and* MUSEUMS
The Hermitage (201-445-8311), 335 N. Franklin Turnpike. Open Wed.–Sun.

Johannes Traphagen was the first owner of the Hermitage, arriving around 1743. Henry Lane, the next owner, built a stone house, barn, gristmill, sawmill, and planted an orchard. The stone house dates from the mid-18th century. James Prevost was another owner.

George Washington and his staff visited here often. Other visitors included James Madison, the Marquis de Lafayette, Alexander Hamilton, William Alexander (Lord Stirling), and Aaron Burr. Burr married the owner of the house, Theodosia Prevost.

James McHenry, Washington's secretary, wrote: "At Mrs. Prevost's we found some fair refugees from New York who were on a visit to the lady of the Hermitage. With them we talked and walked and laughed and danced and gallanted away the leisure hours of four days and four nights, and would have gallanted and danced and laughed and talked and walked with them till now had not the general given orders for our departure."

FORT LEE

Fort Lee has a beautiful location on the Hudson River palisades, across the George Washington Bridge from New York City. Film crews converged on the town and stayed until the mid-1920s. They moved to Hollywood, where winters are not cold.

HISTORICAL SITES *and* MUSEUMS

Fort Lee Historic Park (201-461-1776), Hudson Terrace. Open Wed.–Sun. The visitor center traces the history of Fort Lee during the Revolutionary War. George Washington chose this site on the palisades to defend New York City and the Hudson River. British warships could be easily spotted below. As the British were pushing American forces out of Manhattan and Westchester after the Battle of Long Island, General Cornwallis scaled the Palisades in a daring attack on Fort Lee in November 1776, and Washington ordered it abandoned to save the remnants of his army, which immediately began a long retreat across New Jersey.

Walking trails lead to overlooks featuring the New York skyline. You will walk by a reconstructed 18th-century soldiers' hut and gun batteries.

Current Information

NEW JERSEY COMMERCE AND ECONOMIC DEVELOPMENT
Office of Travel and Tourism
20 W. State St.
Trenton, NJ 08625
800-847-4865, 609-777-0885
www.newjerseycommerce.org/about_travel_tourism.shtml

Delaware

Historical Introduction
to the
Delaware Colony

The Dutch East India Company was eager to find a western route to its East India ports, where its agents bought silk, spices, and porcelain. The company hired English navigator Henry Hudson, who during his exploration sailed the Half Moon into Delaware Bay in August of 1609. He had hopes of finding the Northwest Passage to the Pacific but circled around and did not proceed farther because of shoals. But he did envision trade with the Native Americans as a lucrative possibility, and Dutch explorers and traders did follow to the region, which they claimed for their country. One of their most prized purchases was fur.

Hudson was followed by English sea captain Samuel Argall in 1610. Argall was blown off course and found the bay that he named after his governor, Lord De La Warr of Virginia. (Probably Lord De La Warr did not see the bay or any part of the state that bears his name.) Argall lived in Jamestown, Virginia, which had been settled in 1607. Dutchman Cornelius May arrived in 1620 and without a touch of modesty named the capes at the mouth of the bay Cape Cornelius and Cape May.

The Lenni-Lenape Indians in the area at first welcomed a group of some thirty Dutch settlers who left Hoorn in the Netherlands with Captain Peter Hayes on the *Walvis* (Whale.) They arrived at Cape Henlopen and established Zwaanendael (Lewes) in 1631. All the settlers were men, and their purpose was setting up a base for whaling. They were friendly with the Indians until one of the Indians took the coat of arms belonging to the Dutch. The Indians turned against the Dutch after a dispute over the theft, in which an Indian lost his life. The unlucky colonists were murdered by the Indians. Captain David Pietersen de Vries arrived

The Immanuel Episcopal Church in New Castle dates to 1703.

in 1632 to be the new leader of the colony and found it destroyed. However, with a key location at the mouth of the bay, Lewes was resettled in 1659. It became a favorite port in a storm for mariners, and ship owners built homes that had a view of the harbor and their vessels.

Swedes versus Dutch

The next settlers in Delaware were Swedish, and they arrived in 1638 on two ships, the *Kalmar Nyckel* (Key of Kalmar) and *Fogel Grip* (Griffin). Peter Minuit was at the helm as they landed, on about March 29. They chose to live at the site of present-day Wilmington, at "The Rocks" on the Christina River, where rocks had made a natural dock. They called their settlement New Sweden and built Fort Christina, named after the young queen of Sweden, whose father, King Gustavus Adolphus, had died in battle in 1632. She had become queen at the tender age of six.

Many of the first settlers were soldiers who knew how to defend themselves but not necessarily how to survive in the wilderness. But the next group of settlers included artisans to build ships and mills and farmers to grow tobacco. The artisans knew how to make utensils and construct log houses.

Johan Printz ruled New Sweden from 1643 to 1653. He had instructions to defend the colony, keep good relationships with the Indians, raise tobacco, make salt from ocean water, develop fishing, and keep silkworms, among other things. Above all, he was to make money for the company. An enormous man, he was called "Big Tub" by the Indians.

A new governor, Johan Rising, arrived in 1654 and soon after seized Fort

---

Peter Kalm, who visited Delaware years later, wrote: "The whole house consisted of one little room the door of which was so low that one was obliged to stoop in order to get in. As they brought no glass with them they were obliged to be content with little holes before which a moveable board was fastened. . . ."

DELAWARE *Time Line*

1609	1610	1631	1632	1638
Henry Hudson explores Delaware Bay and River	English sea captain Samuel Argall names the bay and river after Lord De La Warr, the governor of Virginia	Dutch settle at Zwaanendael (site of present-day Lewes)	Native Americans destroy settlement at Zwaanendael	Peter Minuit leads a group of Swedes to establish Fort Christina (Wilmington)

A strong and sometimes opinionated leader, Stuyvesant had little tolerance for dissent. His autocratic manner in New Netherland had brought some to complain that he expressed himself "in foul language better fitting the fish market than the council board." When Puritans from Long Island wanted to govern themselves, Stuyvesant retorted: "We derive our authority from God and the West India Company, not from the pleasure of a few ignorant subjects." Lutherans wanted to have a minister of their own choosing, but Stuyvesant forbade any form of worship other than the Dutch Reformed Church.

Casimir, which the Dutch—who claimed the same territory—had built three years earlier. Rising tried to get the colonists involved in planning ordinances to govern them, but before his efforts were recognized, Peter Stuyvesant arrived from New Amsterdam, seeking revenge for the seizure of Fort Casimir. Stuyvesant and his fleet of seven warships sailed up the river, easily overwhelmed the Swedish forts, and annexed the Delaware colony to New Netherland.

England Takes Over

The Delaware Bay region so hotly disputed between the Dutch and the Swedes was also claimed by England, on the basis of an early voyage by John Cabot (probably far to the north of Delaware Bay) and more recent explorations by Captain John Smith. In 1664 King Charles II, recently restored to the throne of England, awarded the land between the Connecticut and Delaware Rivers to his brother, the Duke of York. In that same year, with the English military takeover of New Netherland, the Delaware settlements became part of New York for nearly two decades (save for a brief Dutch resurgence). The English Quaker William Penn, who received his land grant for Pennsylvania from King Charles in 1682, was in addition granted Delaware by the Duke of York. But the Calverts of Maryland also thought they owned parts of Delaware, based on their charter of 1632, and in 1670 they had started making land grants to settlers. Penn and Lord Baltimore began arguing about the exact land controlled by Penn on the lower Delaware.

1643	**1651**	**1654**	**1655**	**1659**	**1664**
Johan Printz becomes governor of the New Sweden colony	Peter Stuyvesant builds Fort Casimir (New Castle)	New Sweden governor Johan Rising seizes Fort Casimir	The Dutch forcibly annex New Sweden, which becomes part of New Netherland	Lewes is founded	English take over New Netherland; Delaware becomes an English colony

Even though a court ruled in favor of Penn in 1685, disputes between their heirs continued throughout the 17th century and recurred sporadically in the 18th.

Even though the three Delaware counties—New Castle, Kent, and Sussex—were effectively under the political control of Pennsylvania, they remained restive. New Castle resented the rapid growth of Philadelphia as a rival port, and isolated colonists farther south along Delaware Bay feared that a pacifist Quaker government would not adequately protect them against privateer raids during King William's War—a fear confirmed when even Lewes was ransacked in 1697. The three counties felt underrepresented in the Pennsylvania government, and when a conference that Penn called in New Castle in 1700 ended in stalemate, they refused to attend further meetings and were granted a separate assembly to manage their own affairs. That anomalous relationship lasted until the Revolution, even though the Delaware counties shared the same governor with the rest of Pennsylvania.

Moving toward Independence

Although their status remained nebulous between competing charter claims, the three Delaware counties had a working independence throughout the first half of the 18th century in most matters, with only nominal supervision from Pennsylvania or the Crown. That sense of independence was severely jarred by the Stamp Act of 1765, especially because the Delaware counties, unlike those in Pennsylvania, had willingly contributed both money and men to support British troops in the recently concluded French and Indian War. Two young men, Caesar Rodney, a planter, and Thomas McKean, a lawyer, were sent to the Stamp Act Congress to express opposition to the act, and they also drafted a letter thanking George III when the act was repealed. But Parliament's repeated attempts at taxation stiffened resistance. The Townshend Acts inspired John Dickinson, a Pennsylvania lawyer and large landowner in Kent County, to write the influential *Letters from a farmer in Pennsylvania,* and the Tea Act of 1773 created large meetings in New Castle and Kent Counties in 1774, resulting in aid to Boston and a call for sending delegates to the First Continental Congress.

Like other colonies, Delaware organized militias and formed a Council of

DELAWARE *Time Line*

1682	1731	1764	1765	1776
The Duke of York transfers control of the Delaware colony to William Penn	Thomas Willing founds Willington, renamed Wilmington in 1739	Charles Mason and Jeremiah Dixon draw boundaries between Pennsylvania, Delaware, and Maryland	Caesar Rodney and Thomas McKean represent Delaware at the Stamp Act Congress	Delaware Assembly declares independence from England

The three Delaware delegates to the Continental Congress were split as the vote for the Declaration of Independence approached, with Thomas McKean and Caesar Rodney in favor and George Read opposed. But Rodney was away at the time, and McKean sent word to him to return, which he did on the stormy night of July 1, 1776, in time to vote the next day to assure Delaware's approval. Read finally joined the other two and signed the Declaration. A statue in Rodney Square, Wilmington, commemorates Rodney's ride.

Safety to coordinate them, but some in the three counties feared their vulnerability to attack from the sea and continued to oppose separation from Britain and changing the existing constitution. Such opposition was shown not only in words, but also took the form of minor insurrections against Patriots. Nevertheless, delegates to a constitutional convention in 1776 were able to modify the old constitution to shift power from the governor to the legislature, as many other colonies did, and create the independent state of Delaware.

For the most part, the military action of the Revolutionary War bypassed Delaware. The only battle on Delaware soil occurred at Cooch's Bridge on September 3, 1777, when Washington ordered General William Maxwell to harass General Howe's troops heading for Philadelphia. Shortly after that Wilmington was briefly occupied. Delaware's main contribution was its regiment in the Continental Army, famed for competence and valor. About 4,000 Delaware men enlisted for service, and they fought in all battles from Long Island to Yorktown.

Delaware First

When the Constitutional Convention met in Philadelphia in 1787, Delaware's delegates, worried about their lack of ports, control of commerce, and small population, supported changes in the Articles of Confederation that would secure the influence of the second-smallest state in the union. John Dickinson, one of the Delaware delegates, proposed the compromise that would solve the conflict between large and small states, a split in power allotting equal numbers from each state in

1777	1787	1798	1802	1813
Dover replaces New Castle as state capital	Delaware is the first state to ratify the new U.S. Constitution	British ship *DeBraak* sinks off Lewes	Du Pont company is founded	British squadron shells Lewes in last foreign attack against Delaware

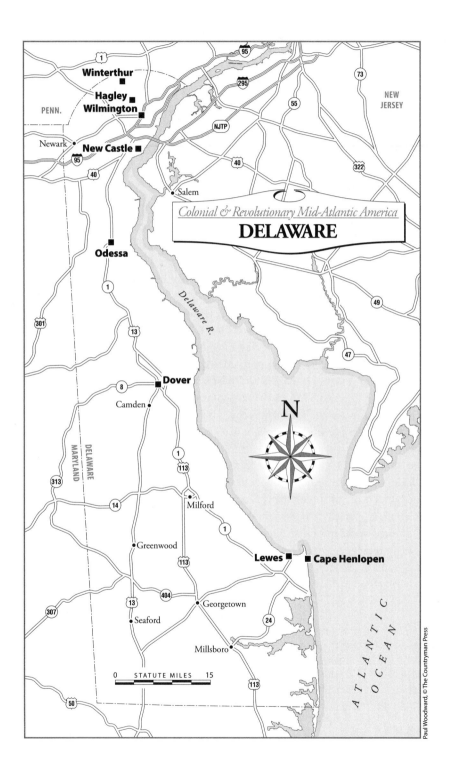

Colonial & Revolutionary Mid-Atlantic America
DELAWARE

Paul Woodward, © The Countryman Press

> ✻ Do you know why the state bird of Delaware is the "blue hen chicken"?
> During the Revolution one of the companies from Delaware was made up
> of soldiers from Kent County. Their leader was Captain John Caldwell, who
> owned gamecocks. The soldiers often had cockfights with the Kent County blue
> hen breed, which was known for fighting with determination. The company
> was also known for fighting with determination, and it came to be called "Cald-
> well's Gamecocks." Colonel John Haslet's First Delaware Regiment included
> some of these soldiers, and this regiment was called "The Blue Hens' Chickens."

the Senate and proportional representation in the lower house. Satisfied, Delaware
became the "First State"—its favorite name—by quickly ratifying the Constitution of the United States on December 7, 1787.

Regions *to* Explore

SOUTHERN DELAWARE
CENTRAL DELAWARE
NORTHERN DELAWARE

SOUTHERN DELAWARE

LEWES/CAPE HENLOPEN

Today this area bills itself as the place to enjoy "sand, surf, and serenity."
People come to sample the white-sand beaches, boardwalks, golf, fishing,
whale and dolphin watching, nature walks, cycling, and bird watching.
Sightseeing is a prime activity.

Located where Delaware Bay meets the Atlantic Ocean at Cape Henlopen,
Lewes not only has a number of historic sites dating to the 17th century, but also
both bay and ocean beaches for swimming. Boaters will find the Lewes-Rehoboth
Canal handy for easy access to the bay or the ocean. Docking is available within
walking distance of restaurants, shops, and lodging. Charter boats offer tours.
Cape Henlopen State Park has over 5,000 acres, including a saltwater lagoon (Gor-
dons Pond), and the Great Dune, which rises eighty feet above sea level. Walkers,
runners, cyclists, and skaters enjoy a two-mile paved trail.

Known as "the saltiest town in Delaware," Lewes was well known to ship captains, who could find shelter in bad weather behind the Delaware Breakwater. Delaware pilots have lived in town for at least 280 years. They know what an east wind can do.

Cape Henlopen is less than three miles east of town. The beach there was littered with more than 200 shipwrecks during the early years of our country. Pirate activity was also rampant, and stamped silver bars from their hauls might still be found.

The first colony of Dutch whalers in Lewes arrived in 1631. Thirty-two settlers were to build a brick dwelling and a wooden fence. The settlement was intended as a base for Atlantic Ocean whaling hunts. It was named Zwaanendael, or "Valley of the Swans." The settlement was obliterated by an Indian massacre in the year after its founding, but more settlers arrived in 1659.

In its early years Lewes was fair game for pirates. In 1698 French pirates laid siege to the town, then broke into every house and made off with family treasures. In 1708 pirates burned and sank three vessels off Cape Henlopen within four days, causing William Penn's secretary to write, "The coast begins to be intolerably infested."

Besides the peaceful-sounding "Valley of the Swans," Lewes was also called "Harlot's Creek" under the Dutch and "Whorekill" and "Deal" under the English. In 1680 the magistrates asked Governor Edmond Andros to consider "summe other name for the Whoorekill." William Penn finally named the town Lewes, after the town of the same name in Sussex, England.

HISTORICAL SITES *and* MUSEUMS
Visitors can take the Pilottown Road to see the **DeVries Monument and Fort Site**; the monument is on the site of the north bastion of the fort. Its inscription reads: "That Delaware Exists as a Separate Commonwealth is due to this Colony."

Take a look at **Zwaanendael Museum** (302-645-1148; www.delawarestate museums.org). Open Tue.–Sun. It is stunning, with a spectacular stair-step roof. You may wonder if you're in the Netherlands. In fact, the building is a replica of the town hall in Hoorn, Holland. It was constructed in 1931 to commemorate the 300th anniversary of the first settlement in Delaware.

Inside, the HMS *DeBraak* exhibit is exciting for those fascinated with nautical archaeology. She existed prior to 1781, when she sailed in Dutch naval operations from the North Sea to the Mediterranean. The British captured her in 1795, and the Admiralty converted her rig from a single-masted cutter to a two-masted brig-sloop.

When sailing off Cape Henlopen in 1798 the vessel sank, perhaps because she was "overmasted" and therefore top-heavy. After her discovery in 1984, the state of Delaware provided specialists to study her hull and artifacts.

Enter the salvors, the state of Delaware, and the National Trust for Historic Preservation. Sub-Sal Inc. of Reno, Nevada, had discovered the wreck and began recovery efforts under the supervision of a nautical archaeologist hired by the state.

The Zwaanendael Museum is a replica of the town hall in Hoorn, Holland.

CUTTERS *and* SMASHERS

The HMS *DeBraak* was originally a single-masted vessel called a cutter. These ships were able to move into shallow waters and also assist larger ships at sea. Her hull was covered with overlapping copper plates to keep marine organisms from demolishing the wooden bottom. A "kentledge," iron ballast bars, added weight below to provide stability. She carried two long guns that fired 6-pound projectiles and 14 guns, called smashers, that fired 24-pound projectiles. Her smashers were very destructive at short range.

The competing interests of gold seekers anxious to proceed quickly and hold down the costs of salvage would come into conflict with those of nautical archaeologists more concerned with maintaining and mapping the wreck site slowly and carefully.

The climax was described in testimony before Congress by J. Jackson Walter, then president of the National Trust for Historic Preservation, in 1987: "[The wreck was] lifted by cables without benefit of a proper cradle. . . . salvors ripped into the hull and dropped much of its content and interior onto the sea floor. . . . The salvor then employed a clamshell bucket to dump the remains of the vessel into a road construction rock sorter to sift for treasure."

Artifacts brought up included shot, musket balls, and spoons. Also recovered were barrel staves, barrel end pieces and hooping, and earthenware and stoneware jars and pots.

Other museum exhibits include a 1625 logbook, written by Robert Jewett, describing the bay as seen from the deck of Henry Hudson's *Half Moon*. Displays also tell about the lighthouse built in the 1760s. Made of granite, it stood almost 70 feet tall. On April 13, 1926, it toppled into the sea.

Look for the "merman" in a glass case, with the head and arms of a monkey and the tail of a fish. Such stuffed animals were known as devil fish and were displayed as oddities. Upstairs you'll see collections of coverlets, samplers, china, silver, models, dolls, doll cradles, accordions, puzzles, and a Dutch costume from Marken, Holland.

Next door, the **Fisher-Martin House** dates from 1730 (877-465-3937, 302-645-8073; www.beach-net.com/lewestour), 120 Kings Hwy. Open Memorial Day–Oct. 1, daily; fall–spring, Mon.–Fri. It was moved from Coolspring as part of the 350th anniversary festivities of the first settlement and now serves as a visitor center and home of the chamber of commerce. The house was owned in 1695 by Thomas Fisher and then left to his son Joshua, who charted Delaware Bay. The Martin family lived in this gambrel-roof house from 1736 until 1959.

The **Lewes Presbyterian Church** across the street was founded in 1692; it is the third building on the site. If you love strolling around old cemeteries looking at interesting headstones, try this one.

Several private houses not open to the public date from the colonial era, including the 1760 **Marvil House** at 124 Gills Neck Rd. Captain Richard Howard, a Delaware Bay and River pilot, built the house knowing he could watch for ships from the upper floors. Head along Market Street to 202 W. Third St. to see the late 18th-century **Metcalf House**, once a blacksmith shop. The **Daniel Nunez House**, at 208 W. Third St., was once an inn.

The **Lewes Historical Complex** (302-645-7670; www.historiclewes.org), 110 Shipcarpenter St., has 12 historic properties, including the Plank House, Burton-Ingraham House, Rabbit's Ferry House, Thompson Country Store, and the Old Doctor's Office. Open early May–mid-June, Sat.; mid-June–early Oct., daily; Jan. 1–early May and early-Oct.–Dec. 31 by appointment. Tickets are available at Ellegood House, Third St.

The **Rabbit's Ferry House** contains a small part of an 18th-century one-room farmhouse with a sleeping loft. The house has original cypress shingles, woodwork and fireplace paneling, and brick nogging in the walls. The larger section dates from the mid-18th century and has the original mantel, paneling, doors, chair rails, and window trim.

The **Hiram-Burton House** belonged to a member of Congress, Dr. Hiram Rodney Burton. He was also president of the Medical Society of Delaware. The house contains a reading room for those who want to learn more about Delaware history. The kitchen wing dates from the 18th century.

The **Cannonball House Marine Museum** dates from 1765. It was home to pilots for the *Bay & River Delaware, Gilbert McCracken,* and *David Rowland.* It was struck by a cannonball, and a replica of the cannonball still stands in the wall. The museum has models of sailing vessels, half models, sailors' art, lamps of the past, and the remains of an Indian dugout canoe that may be 400 years old.

The Plank House, in the Lewes Historical Complex.

The cannonball house in Lewes.

LODGING

THE BLUE WATER HOUSE
407 E. Market St., Lewes, DE 19958
800-493-2080, 302-645-7832;
www.lewes-beach.com
Caribbean colors and decor enliven this
B&B near the beach. 6 guest rooms.

GRIST MILL INN
19045 Robinsonville Rd., Lewes, DE
19958
302-645-6968;
www.hometown.aol.com/gristmill2
This Cape Cod–style inn dates from the
early 1900s, and offers bass fishing on the
premises. 2 guest rooms.

THE INN AT CANAL SQUARE
122 Market St., Lewes, DE 19958
888-644-1911, 302-644-3377;
www.theinnatcanalsquare.com

Most rooms in this inn on the waterfront
have a balcony overlooking the Lewes Harbor. 24 guest rooms.

JOHN PENROSE VIRDEN HOUSE B&B
217 Second St., Lewes, DE 19958
302-644-0217, 302-644-4401;
www.virdenhouse.com
This antiques-filled Victorian home is in the
historic district. Gardens surround the
house. 4 guest rooms.

ZWAANENDAEL INN
142 Second St., Lewes, DE 19958
800-824-8754, 302-645-6466;
www.zwaanendaelinn.com
This downtown inn with a European small-
hotel ambience dates from 1926 and is on
the National Historic Register. 23 guest
rooms.

In 1785 the *Faithful Steward* left Londonderry, Ireland, for Philadelphia. She carried 249 passengers, goods in her hold, and a large consignment of copper coins. When she went aground, her mainmast was cut away to lighten her. She got free but was unable to beat against a rising wind and gain sea room. She went aground again 20 miles south of Cape Henlopen, totally helpless in the huge seas of what may have been a hurricane.

Residents of Lewes were not able to reach her and watched lifeboats coming ashore empty because there was no way to get passengers into them. Eventually the ship broke up, and four out of every five persons on board drowned. Coins from her cargo began washing up a hundred years later, no doubt adding to coins from past shipwrecks.

RESTAURANTS

THE BUTTERY
Second Ave. and Savannah Rd.,
Lewes, DE 19958
302-645-7755; www.butteryrestaurant
.com
In a mansion in the heart of the historic district; try the jumbo lump crab cakes.

LIGHTHOUSE RESTAURANT
Savannah Rd. and Angler's Rd., Lewes,
DE 19958
302-645-6271; www.lighthouselewes
.com
The restaurant specializes in fresh, local seafood.

ROSE & CROWN
108 Second St., Lewes, DE 19958
302-645-2373
This restaurant and pub has and English flavor. Black Angus beef is a specialty.

INFORMATION

DELAWARE TOURISM OFFICE
99 Kings Hwy., Dover, DE 19901
866-284-7483;
www.visitdelaware.com, also
www.state.de.us/gic/facts/history

LEWES CHAMBER OF COMMERCE AND VISITORS BUREAU
120 Kings Hwy., Lewes, DE 19958
877-465-3937, 302-645-8073;
www.leweschamber.com

CENTRAL DELAWARE

Kent County might well be considered the first county in the United States, since Delaware became the first state when the legislature in Dover, the Kent County seat, took the lead in ratifying the U.S. Constitution.

The Bombay Hook National Wildlife Refuge offers 16,000 bird-friendly acres. This is a habitat for migrating and wintering ducks and geese. A twelve-mile auto route provides sights of many birds; there are also five walking tours along the route.

DOVER

Dover was originally proclaimed the seat of Kent County in 1683 by William Penn. In 1776 Caesar Rodney, a Continental Congress delegate, rode from Dover to Independence Hall in Philadelphia with only a few minutes to spare. He cast his vote and saved the day for independence!

Dover became the state capital after the British captured New Castle in 1777. The green, laid out by William Penn, was the site of public events. A portrait of King George III was burned there after the ratification of the Declaration of Independence.

Now you may see and hear some of the planes from Dover Air Force Base. The **Air Mobility Command Museum** (302-677-5938; www.amcmuseum.org), 1301 Heritage Rd., is open Tue.–Sat. While it is far from our time period, it is a major attraction in Dover. We walked through the museum to see a number of planes: a C-5 Galaxy, P-51D Mustang, B-17 Flying Fortress, C-17 Globemaster, C-47 Skytrain, and C-141 Starlifter.

HISTORICAL SITES *and* MUSEUMS

The **Old State House** (302-739-4266; www.destatemuseums.org), on the eastern side of the green at number 25, dates from 1792, but its bell was cast earlier, in 1763. Open Tue.–Sun. You'll see an 18th-century courtroom and legislative chamber, and a reconstructed geometrical staircase. There are two signs by the prisoner's dock; the red one was used to indicate a verdict of guilty and the white one for innocent. You can't miss a large portrait of George Washington in the Senate chamber. Guided tours are given.

 On the Dover green stood "Red Hannah," the last whipping post to be used in the United States.

In July 1776 the Declaration of Independence was read on the steps of the State House. A drummer boy led a procession of the Dover Light Infantry around the square. He carried a portrait of King George III. A bonfire was lit, and the president of the committee declared: "Compelled by strong necessity, thus we destroy even the shadow of a King who refused to reign over a free people."

While you're on the green, stop in at the **Hall of Records** (302-739-5314; www.state.de.us/shpo), 15 The Green, to see the original royal grant from King Charles II.

The **Biggs Museum of American Art** (302-674-2111; www.biggsmuseum .org), 4–6 Federal St. Open Wed.–Sun. There are 14 galleries to wander through, with colonial portraits and collections including Gilbert Stuart, Thomas Cole, Childe Hassam, and Asher Durand, to name a few. Delaware furniture and silver are also on display.

Delaware Agricultural Museum & Village (302-734-1618; www.agricul

The "log'd dwelling" at the John Dickinson Plantation.

turalmuseum.org), 866 N. DuPont Hwy. Open Tue.–Sun. year-round except closed Sun. in winter. There's a 1700 log house built by Swedes from white-oak logs. Enter the "Touch of History" section and you can play and interact with all sorts of exhibits.

Outside, Loockerman Landing Village offers restored historic buildings. An interpreter was sweeping the front porch of the farmhouse when we arrived. She escorted us through the house to see typical farm possessions. The blacksmith was pounding away, and his three-year-old son, Alex, wanted to climb up into the loft. Other buildings include the Silver Lake Mill, a school, chapel, a train station, Reeds General Store, and a barber shop. The exhibition hall houses horse-drawn equipment and farming implements dating from 1670 through the 1950s.

John Dickinson Plantation (302-739-3277; www.destatemuseums.org/jdp), six miles south of Dover at 340 Kitts Hummock Rd. Open Tue.–Sun. year-round. It contains a 1740 Georgian mansion, a reconstructed farm complex, a "log'd dwelling" that shows how slaves, free blacks, and poor whites lived, and a visitor center.

John Dickinson, sometimes called the "Penman of the Revolution," was a prolific writer for the colonists. It has been reported that he drafted the Articles of

Confederation in 1778. This colonial home, restored to the era of Dickinson's boyhood, contains furnishings of the period and has a formal English garden and also a household garden.

> ✻ The one-room "log'd dwelling" was typical of Kent County in the late 1700s. These log cabins were about 20 feet by 16 feet, with a brick chimney. They were sheathed with oak or pine clapboards and oak roof shingles, and the floors were either plank or dirt.

The visitor center has a display of 18th-century trash, including bottles, nails, buttons, and a thimble. A portrait of Samuel Dickinson hangs in the mansion, as well as one of his mother. His wife, Sally, wouldn't live here because of the mosquitoes. When we visited, curators were researching the colors used in paint at that time.

Dickinson inherited both the slaves and the land when his father died in 1760. By 1777 he had freed his slaves, though the manumission document required them to serve him for 21 years in exchange for food, clothing, shelter, and remuneration. But by 1785 he had freed all his slaves. The John Dickinson Plantation has interpreters to demonstrate various aspects of colonial life.

LODGING

COWGILLS CORNER B&B
7299 Bayside Drive, Dover, DE 19901
302-734-5743
The B&B is a working farm with a flock of sheep, beef cattle, and working border collies. Horses and dogs can be accommodated. The original structure was built in the 1760s. 2 guest rooms.

LITTLE CREEK INN
2623 N. Little Creek Rd., Dover, DE 19901
888-804-1300, 302-730-1300; www.littlecreekinn.com
The 1860 Italianate mansion is on the National Register of Historic Places. Cooking classes are given by the chef-owner. 4 guest rooms.

EVENTS

May: Old Dover Days; 302-739-4266

INFORMATION

KENT COUNTY CONVENTION AND VISITORS BUREAU
9 East Loockerman St., Dover, DE 19903
800-233-5368, 302-734-1736; www.visitdover.com

DELAWARE STATE VISITOR CENTER
406 Federal St., Dover, DE 19903
302-739-4266; www.destatemuseums.org/vc/

NORTHERN DELAWARE

This region of the state offers a variety of activities in historic towns and cities. There are mansions turned museums, the beautiful Brandywine River, gardens, and antiques shops.

ODESSA

Odessa is a town with three names in three centuries: At first it was Appoquin-imie, the original Indian name; by 1731 it became Cantwell's Bridge, after the man who operated the toll bridge across the Appoquinimink Creek; and in 1855 it was named Odessa, after the prominent Russian wheat and produce shipping port, perhaps with the hope that it would flourish as its Russian namesake did.

The Dutch first settled here in the 17th century. In 1664 the area was deeded to English Captain Edmund Cantwell. It was his son, Richard, who in 1731 built a toll bridge over the creek. A tannery was built in 1767 by William Corbit. Pro-duce was brought into town and then shipped down to the Delaware River and off to both foreign and domestic ports. Three homes built here in the 18th cen-tury are open to visitors, and you can wander a historic district of restored and pre-served 18th- and 19th-century homes. Many of the homes now in private hands are open for tours at various times of the year, usually in May, July, October, and December.

HISTORICAL SITES *and* MUSEUMS
Historic Houses of Odessa (302-378-4069; www.historicodessa.org), Main and Second Sts. Open Mar.–Dec., Thu.–Sat. Winterthur Museum owns and operates three houses from the colonial era and the Brick Hotel Gallery, a 19th-century tavern.

The 1774 **Corbit-Sharp House** was built by William Corbit, a Quaker tan-ner who had his business on Appoquinimink Creek. Some of the furnishings still in the house belonged to the Corbit family; others were made by local Delaware craftsmen. Upstairs, the drawing room is handsome, with blue decorating, a sparkling chandelier, and colonial revival furniture.

David Wilson owned the **Wilson-Warner House**; he was a local merchant and the brother-in-law of William Corbit. The house is furnished as it was when a bankruptcy inventory was prepared in the early 19th century.

The **Collins-Sharp House** is one of the oldest houses in Delaware, dating to the early 18th century. Educational programming takes place in this log and frame building. Cooking demonstrations using original recipes from the late 18th and early 19th centuries are available. Hands-on hearth cooking is a favorite with children.

NEW CASTLE

New Castle is a picturesque town filled with colonial and Federal houses and build-ings, many of them still lived in and used for offices. The streets are strollable and quiet. Tourists may be in evidence, but not huge throngs. William Penn first laid claim to two large land grants given him by King Charles II and the Duke of York in New Castle in 1682. Stroll around the streets near the water and you will come

The 1774 Corbit-Sharp House.

---

to a sign telling you about the historical significance of the site: "Landing Place of William Penn. Near here Oct. 27, 1682, William Penn first stepped on American soil."

Penn called on each of the three counties in Delaware to elect representatives to meet with delegates from Pennsylvania—the start of the Delaware tradition of representative government. Delegates adopted a constitution, which was the first such document in the colonies. Penn granted Delaware the right to its own separate assembly, and in 1704 the first Assembly of the Lower Counties met in New Castle.

HISTORICAL SITES *and* MUSEUMS

The green, laid out by Peter Stuyvesant in 1655 during the years when the settlement was called Fort Casimir, is still here; weekly markets and "great fairs" took place on it. A number of restored buildings line the sides of the green.

New Castle Court House Museum (302-323-4453; www.destatemuseums.org/ncch), 211 Delaware St. Open Tue.–Sun. The building dates from 1732; the colonial assembly met here until 1777, when the capital was moved to Dover.

Inside you'll see the original speaker's chair, portraits of some of Delaware's prominent men, and some excavated artifacts. Look through a cutout in the floor to see the dirt floor of the jail cells. We especially liked the painting of William Penn landing at New Castle.

The **Immanuel Episcopal Church**, on Harmony St., was built in 1703; inside, the high vaulted ceiling draws the eye upward. The graveyard has many early headstones to find and enjoy. The **Old Presbyterian Church,** on Second St., dates from 1707. Records indicate that it was the successor of the original Dutch Reformed Church of 1657.

The **Dutch House** (302-322-2794; www.newcastlehistory.org), 32 E. Third St., may be the oldest brick house in Delaware, dating from the late 17th century. Open Mar. 1–Dec. 31, Tue.–Sun. Sailors would stop here for a hot meal after leaving a ship, and they might even stay overnight. Now a museum, the house offers historical displays and artifacts. A spoon rack contains two spoons for a couple, with an additional one for each child. Several lighting pieces include rush lights and oil lamps. Look for the hutch table, a 16th-century Dutch Bible, and the courting bench. If you are here around the Christmas season, you'll see the house decorated as it would have been for the Dutch celebration of Twelfth Night.

Amstel House (302-322-2796; www.newcastlehistory.org), 2 E. Fourth St. Open Mar. 1–Dec. 31, Tue.–Sun. The house dates from the 1680s and the 1730s. Don't miss one of the earliest fanlight windows in the colony, and the colonial furnishings inside. Dr. John Finney built the house, and a number of signers of the Declaration of Independence visited here, as well as George Washington and Governor Nicholas Van Dyke.

George Read House (302-322-8411; www.hsd.org), 42 The Strand. Open Mar.–Dec., Tue.–Sun.; Jan.–Feb., Sat.–Sun. or by appointment. This house dates from 1801, when the owner decided to build the "grandest" house in the state. He was the son of a signer of the Declaration of Independence. Inside, the house has elaborately carved woodwork, relief plasterwork, gilded fanlights, and silvered door hardware.

We were taken with models of Kitty Read and her husband as he sat behind a screen and she worked on his silhouette. This technique was popular then, and we have enjoyed it with likenesses of our grandchildren.

The 2½-acre garden, the oldest surviving garden in the area, encircles the house. You will see parterre flower beds and a kitchen garden that was added later.

Take time to walk around town and look for **Packet Alley,** between the Strand

---

Another sign along the river marks the "Landing Place of William Penn" and describes the ceremony of taking possession: "Near here Oct. 27, 1682 William Penn first stepped on American soil. He proceeded to the fort, performed livery of seisen (the act of taking legal possession of property), he took the key thereof. We did deliver unto him one turf with a twig on it, a porringer with river water and soil in part of all."

The Read House is surrounded by two and a half acres of colonial gardens.

and the river, where you'll see a sign telling you what happened there: "Packet boats from Philadelphia met stagecoaches here for Maryland, the chief line of communication from the north to Baltimore and the south. Andrew Jackson, Daniel Webster, Henry Clay, David Crockett, Lord Ashburton, Louis Napoleon, Stonewall Jackson, Sam Houston, and Indians led by Osceola and Blackhawk en route to visit the Great Father in Washington all passed this way."

As you stroll around these streets, you will see window boxes filled with impatiens, heavy door knockers, brightly painted shutters and doors, and a variety of iron fences. New Castle's charm is undeniable but partly accidental, since much of the town's growth was stunted by a great fire in 1822 and the diversion of main railroad lines to Wilmington later in the 19th century. Thus the inevitable demolition of old buildings to make way for new ones stopped, leaving many colonial and Federal houses for you to enjoy.

LODGING

WILLIAM PENN GUEST HOUSE
206 Delaware St., New Castle, DE 19720
302-328-7736
This 1682 home has the original wide-plank floors. 4 guest rooms.

RESTAURANTS

ALEX'S SEAFOOD RESTAURANT
110 N. DuPont Hwy., New Castle, DE 19720
302-328-5666
A family-style restaurant; takeout is also available.

THE ARSENAL
30 Market St., New Castle, DE 19720
302-328-1290
The restaurant is in an 1809 former militia
barracks in the historic district.

**JESSOPS TAVERN & COLONIAL
RESTAURANT**
114 Delaware St., New Castle, DE
19720
302-322-6111; www.jessopstavern.com
English pub fare is served in this 1724 brick
house.

EVENTS

May: A Day in New Castle; 800-758-1550
December: Christmas in New Castle; 800-758-1550

INFORMATION

DELAWARE TOURISM OFFICE
99 Kings Hwy., Dover, DE 19901
866-284-7483, 302-739-4271; www
.visitdelaware.com

**VISITORS BUREAU OF HISTORIC
NEW CASTLE**
P.O. Box 465, New Castle, DE 19720-
0465
800-758-1550; www.ci.new-castle.de.us

WILMINGTON

The New Sweden Company founded Wilmington as Fort Christina in 1638; the name was changed by Quakers who developed the town a hundred years later. In 1638 Peter Minuit brought two ships, the *Kalmar Nyckel* and the *Fogle Grip,* up Delaware Bay and came ashore. Settlers on board had survived months of storms on the voyage, and they were relieved to land on a site now called The Rocks.

Lieutenant Colonel Johan Printz arrived in 1643 to lead the colony. The Lenni-Lenape called him "Big Tub" because of his massive size—he weighed four hundred pounds. He was supposed to defend the colony against aggression by the Dutch or English, keep good relations with the Indians, cultivate tobacco, raise livestock, make salt from ocean water, develop commercial fishing, and grow silkworms. The New Sweden Company wanted profit above all. Printz was considered a tyrant. From a settlement the town developed into a port and shipping center.

Today there is much to explore in Wilmington. The **Quaker Hill Historic District**, located downtown between Jefferson and Tatnall Streets, has homes dating from 1745. There are a number of museums, including the Delaware Art Museum, the Delaware History Museum, the Delaware Museum of Natural History, the Delaware Sports Museum, and the the Delaware Toy and Miniature Museum. The Delaware Center for the Arts, located on the Market Street Mall, offers a full schedule of events.

HISTORICAL SITES *and* MUSEUMS
The **Fort Christina Monument**, in Fort Christina Park (302-652-5629), stands where Peter Minuit landed after his voyage from Sweden. The sculptor was none

other than Carl Milles from Stockholm, whose work we admire every time we visit Sweden.

Maritime aficionados will want to visit the ***Kalmar Nyckel*** (302-429-7447; www.kalnyc.org), 1124 E. Seventh St. This vessel is a replica commissioned on May 9, 1998. (She may be out—we sailed alongside her in Newport harbor recently.)

The original vessel, commanded by Peter Minuit, left Gothenburg, Sweden, in November of 1637 along with the *Fogel Grip*. They lost each other in a violent storm in the North Sea, but both landed safely on Texel Island, in the Netherlands. After repairs they departed for the New World on December 31, 1637. They brought settlers from Sweden, Finland, Holland, and Germany, landing at The Rocks in 1638. The *Kalmar Nyckel* made four documented round-trip crossings of the Atlantic—more than any other ship carrying settlers at that time.

The original vessel was lost at sea in the 17th century. The three-masted replica built in the 1990s is used as a training vessel, and she also sails in tall-ship rallies and parades.

Holy Trinity (Old Swedes) Church (302-652-5629; www.oldswedes.org), 606 Church St., dates from 1698; it is the oldest active Protestant church in North America. Open Wed.–Sat. The iron numerals, 1698, are now on the belfry, although originally they were on the west wall over the main door. Inside, the pulpit is the oldest known in the country; Joseph Harrison carved it from black walnut donated by the congregation. The canopy was designed to project the voice of the speaker. Look carefully at one of the stained-glass windows, which has faint yellow sails and a red hull as a secondary scene in the glass.

The KALMAR NYCKEL

Take a tour of the vessel: The forecastle is in the bow and is the home of the foremast. The bowsprit extends forward, and under it is the longhead, with the ship's life-size figurehead lion.

The center section is the "waist" and is the home of the mainmast, cannon, and the capstan. Wood bars are inserted into the capstan so anything heavy can be raised or moved. The stern section is above the captain's cabin and is called the quarterdeck or the poop deck. It is the home of the mizzenmast and two swivel guns mounted on the rails on each side.

Each of the three masts, fore, main, and mizzen, is composed of two sections. The lowest is fixed permanently. At the head of each lower mast is a "mast top," and above it a "topmast," which can be "sent down" or lowered to increase stability in gales. Above the topmast is a flagstaff, where the vessel flies the flags of Finland, Sweden, and the Netherlands; the U.S. flag flies at the stern to indicate the registry of the ship.

Holy Trinity Church ("Old Swedes") in Wilimington dates from 1698.

During the 1700s men sat on the right and women on the left. A number of graves lie inside the church, including that of Peter Tranberg, a Swedish pastor. His portrait hangs with those of other early pastors on the balcony railing. Don't miss the model of the *Kalmar Nyckel,* the ship that brought the first Swedish settlers to Wilmington in 1638.

Walk out onto the South Porch to see the gravestone of Charles Christophersson Springer, who was born in Stockholm in 1658. He was kidnapped and put on board an English vessel bound for Virginia. There he "was sold like a farm animal" and held in "very slavery" for five years. After Springer's release he walked 400 miles to Delaware because he had heard that other Swedes lived there. He could read and write English and was called upon to draft wills, deeds, and additional legal documents for other Swedes. Here he became a church warden, vestryman, and trustee, as well as a justice on the New Castle court for 35 years.

The graveyard has a number of other interesting stones; the oldest marks the grave of William Vandever, who died in 1718.

The **Hendrickson House** was originally built by Andrew Hendrickson on Crum Creek, near Chester, Pennsylvania, in 1690. He built it for his bride, Brigitta, and they filled it with eight children. In 1958 the house was taken down and reassembled next to Holy Trinity Church. The curved staircase was reconstructed by following old marks on the wall. Now a museum, the house contains colonial furniture, a spinning wheel, pewter dishes, and cooking utensils commonly used in Sweden. For more information call the number for Holy Trinity Church.

Delaware History Center is a complex in the 500 block of Market Street Mall. It includes the Delaware History Museum, Old Town Hall, Willingtown Square, and a research library. The **Delaware History Museum** (302-656-0637; www.hsd.org), 504 Market St. Open Mon.–Sat. Delaware's history from the 1600s through the 20th century is offered through interactive exhibits.

Old Town Hall Museum (302-655-7161; www.hsd.org), 512 Market St. Closed at this writing. It dates from 1798 and was once the scene of both political and social events.

Willingtown Square (302-655-7161; www.hsd.org), 505 Market St. The square is composed of four historic buildings. The oldest dates from 1748. The square was named for Thomas Willing, who planned the village that became Wilmington. The buildings can be seen only from the outside: the Cook-Simms House, 1778; the Coxe Houses, 1801; the Jacobs House, 1748, and the Jacob and Obidiah Dingee Houses, 1771 and 1773.

Greenbank Mill (302-999-9001; www.greenbankmill.org), 500 Greenbank Rd. Open Mar.–Nov., Fri.–Sat. The mill dates from 1790, although historians think that there has been a mill here since 1677. It has an 18-foot waterwheel. You will see the mill, the clothing factory, and the farmhouse built by Robert Philips in 1794.

WINTERTHUR

HISTORICAL SITES *and* MUSEUMS

Winterthur Museum and Gardens (800-448-3883, 302-888-4600; www.win terthur.org), DE 52 (Kennett Pike), Winterthur. Open Tue.–Sun. year-round. Winterthur is one of the most remarkable museum complexes we have ever visited. It emphasizes decorative arts made or used in America between 1640 and 1860. No pains (or costs) were spared to make it one of the most complete and representative collections of Americana ever assembled. For example, one room was carefully removed from a 1680s house in Essex, Massachusetts, and meticulously put back together as a room in the museum.

E. I. du Pont, whose family had settled in the Brandywine valley in 1802, bought four tracts of land between 1810 and 1818 that eventually grew into a grand country estate. After his death Jacques Antoine Bidermann and his wife, Evelina, du Pont's daughter, acquired the land in 1837 and built a 12-room mansion. They named it for the Swiss city of Winterthur, ancestral home of the Bidermann family. After their deaths Evelina's brother, Henry du Pont, bought the property in 1867 for his son, Henry Algernon du Pont. His son, Henry Francis du Pont, became the moving force behind the further development of the mansion to house his growing collection of American art objects.

A period room with mural at the Winterthur Museum.

The wealth that originated in manufacturing explosives sometimes produced peaceful side effects—witness the Nobel Prize and the magnificent
collections and gardens of Winterthur. Henry Francis du Pont was well aware
that the industrial enterprises of his family had replaced and perhaps helped
destroy the agrarian nature of much of the middle Atlantic countryside. So he
entertained a pastoral vision for the role of the gardens: "My idea of Winterthur
is that it is a country estate Museum, to show the Americans of the future what
a country place and farm were like. I consider this investment in a way will give
quite as much pleasure to many as the Museum has."

H. F. du Pont started his collection with the purchase of a Pennsylvania-made
chest dated 1737, studied American crafts at a time when little research had been
done, and continued collecting. Du Pont also became interested in the decorative
art objects found in early American homes. His collection expanded to include
textiles, needlework, ceramics, glassware, metalwork, paintings, prints, books, and
newspapers.

Going further, he collected interior woodwork, paneling, fireplace walls, and
doors from houses built between 1640 and 1840. Interiors from houses all along
the eastern seaboard were purchased, dismantled, and reassembled in his mansion. A newspaper reporter once asked du Pont who his collection agent was and
received the reply, "You're looking at him."

MORE MUSEUMS IN THE AREA

It would be a pity for any visitor interested in American history to miss the other
magnificent museums and gardens northwest of Wilmington, even if their focus
is not primarily colonial. Most of them are associated with the du Pont family.

Hagley Museum, (302-658-2400; www.hagley.org), DE 141 (Powder Mill
Rd.). Open Mar.–Dec., daily; Sat.–Sun. the rest of the year. Hagley, on the original site of the du Pont mills along Brandywine Creek, is one of the best industrial
museums in the country, and it also includes workers' homes and a du Pont home
built in 1803. Wilmington has been associated with the du Pont family for much
of American history. E. I. du Pont arrived from France before the American Revolution and founded a black-powder plant at Hagley in 1802. He built his home,
named **Eleutherian Mills**, on the hill above the powder mill; with a speaking
trumpet he could direct the operation of the mill from his balcony. Du Pont also
gave buildings and money to Wilmington over the years.

Begin your tour in the museum to get an overview of the 230-acre site. Dioramas, film, and exhibits provide clear explanations of both the technological and
economic aspects of the industry. Once you could tell what a man did by looking
at his hands. The man who worked on stone wheels in the mill had little chips of
stone embedded in his hands. The man who tanned leather had brown hands from

the tannin in the leather. The man who worked in an office had smooth hands, and the farmer had hands full of calluses.

As the country expanded, the need for powder grew, and the du Pont company became the largest in America. Immigrants who had been starving in Ireland came to work in the mill. They worked 16 hours a day, seven days a week, with just two holidays a year—Christmas and the Fourth of July.

When there was an explosion at the mill, anyone in the area would likely lose his life. Sometimes the bodies were blown across the river, so the expression "across the creek" came to mean that someone had died. Du Pont and his family took a risk in building their home so close to the mill. There were explosions that damaged the house, and his son Alexis was killed in one of them. But du Pont's motto was "safety first," and he felt that there were fewer explosions because he lived on the site.

Eleutherian Mills contains furnishings that belonged to the family. Du Pont's great-granddaughter, Louise du Pont Crowninshield, was the last family member to live in the house, and the first floor remains much as she left it when she died in 1958.

Beyond Winterthur on Route 52 just over the Pennsylvania border lies **Longwood Gardens**, a vast and magnificent horticultural collection, both indoors and outdoors, with elaborate fountains (215-388-6741). See page 174.

Other notable manor and garden estates in the area include the **Nemours Mansion and Gardens** on Rockland Rd. (302-651-6912) and **Rockwood Museum**, 610 Shipley Rd. (302-761-4340).

LODGING

HOTEL DU PONT
11th and Market Sts., Wilmington, DE 19801
800-441-9019, 302-594-3100;
www.hoteldupont.com
This 1913 hotel has more than 800 works of art, hand-carved walnut doors, Italian marble, and medallions in the ballroom. Original paintings include those of three generations of Wyeths. 206 guest rooms.

THE INN AT MONTCHANIN VILLAGE
DE 100 and Kirk Rd., Montchanin, DE 19710
800-269-2473, 302-888-2133;
www.montchanin.com
The inn, a restored 19th-century hamlet, consists of a collection of historic buildings dating from 1799 to 1910. 28 guest rooms.

RESTAURANTS

COLUMBUS INN
2216 Pennsylvania Ave., Wilmington, DE 19806
302-571-1492; www.columbusinn.com
Dating from 1798, this building has colonial charm within its stone walls.

KRAZY KAT'S RESTAURANT
(at the Inn at Montchanin Village)
DE 100 and Kirk Rd., Wilmington, DE 19710
302-888-2133; www.montchanin.com
This restaurant is in the building that was once the village blacksmith shop. Creative cuisine is served along with feline decor.

DEEP BLUE BAR AND GRILL
111 W. 11th St., Wilmington, DE 19801
302-777-2040; www.deepbluebarand
grill.com
Seafood is the specialty in this downtown
restaurant.

THE GREEN ROOM AT HOTEL DU PONT
11th and Market Sts., Wilmington, DE
19801
302-594-3154; www.hoteldupont.com
This formal dining room has gold leaf ceilings, large chandeliers, and a piano balcony. The cuisine is Continental.

HARRY'S SAVOY GRILL
2020 Naamans Rd., Wilmington, DE
19810

302-475-3000; www.harrys-savoy.com
The restaurant sports a mural and fireplaces. Steak and seafood are specialties.

INFORMATION

DELAWARE TOURISM OFFICE
99 Kings Hwy., Dover, DE 19901
866-284-7483, 302-739-4271; www
.visitdelaware.com

**GREATER WILMINGTON CONVENTION
AND VISITORS BUREAU**
100 W. Tenth St., Suite 20, Wilmington,
DE 19801
800-489-6664, 800-422-1181, 302-652-
4088; www.visitwilmingtonde.com

Current Information

DELAWARE TOURISM OFFICE
99 Kings Hwy.
Dover, DE 19901-7395
866-284-7483, 302-739-4271
www.visitdelaware.com

Maryland

Historical Introduction
to the
Maryland Colony

C uriously, Chesapeake Bay, the great waterway that defines Maryland's eastern configuration, was little known to early European voyagers. John Cabot probably came no farther south than Maine or Nova Scotia in 1498, Giovanni da Verrazano was too far offshore to discern its mouth in 1524, and in the 1560s Pedro Menéndez de Avilés, Spanish governor of Florida, and French navigator Jean Ribault got no farther north than the Carolinas. Not until Captain John Smith set out in a shallop during the summer of 1608 did Chesapeake Bay and the Potomac River receive systematic exploration by Europeans.

With six gentlemen, seven soldiers, and a doctor, Smith undertook two voyages that summer, covering approximately 2,500 miles of the bay and the rivers and creeks that flow into it as he sought to reach the headwaters of each. The first voyage ended after Smith had been stung by a stingray at the mouth of the Rappahannock (now called Stingray Point) and returned to find Jamestown in chaos; but after restoring some order he set out again to complete his exploration.

A Refuge for Roman Catholics

Roman Catholics in England were being persecuted at the same time as the Puritans and wanted to find a place to live peacefully. They viewed the pope, not the monarch, as the leader of their church. Queen Elizabeth had been excommunicated in 1570, and by 1571 harsh penal laws against Catholics came into force. The Gunpowder Plot of November 1605, when Guy Fawkes and his co-conspirators tried to kill James I and blow up Parliament as it opened, further tarnished the image of Catholics.

Overleaf: Annapolis has the oldest state house in continuous legislative use in the United States.

THE *Remarkable* JOHN SMITH

Captain John Smith's shallop, about thirty feet long, had probably been brought to Virginia in sections in the hold of the *Susan Constant* and reassembled in Jamestown. It was open and could be sailed or rowed. In it the expedition experienced the usual vagaries of summer weather, including protracted calms and fierce squalls, one of which dismasted her. They also encountered Indian tribes repeatedly, sometimes in friendly exchanges of presents, but frequently in ambushes. To avoid what they regarded as savage treachery, they adopted a policy: "At our first meeting our Captaine ever observed this order to demand their bowes and arrowes, swordes, mantells and furs, with some childe or two for hostage, whereby we could quickly perceive, when they intended any villany."

About two weeks out on the first voyage, weary of rowing, eating bread spoiled by wet, and frightened by the onset of squalls, crew members began to urge Smith to turn back. He recorded his reply: "What a shame would it be for you (that have bin so suspitious of my tendernesse) to force me to returne, with so much provision as we have, and scarce able to say where we have beene, nor yet heard of that we were sent to seeke? . . . As for your feares that I will lose my selfe in these unknown large waters, or be swallowed up in some stormie gust; abandon these childish feares, for worse then is past is not likely to happen; and there is as much danger to returne as to procede. Regaine therefore your old spirits for return I will not (if God please) till I have seene the Massawomeks, found Patawomek, or the head of this water you conceit to be endlesse."

1,700-*mile Reenactment*

In 2006 congressional legislation established the Captain John Smith Chesapeake National Historic Water Trail, to be administered by the National Park Service. The John Smith Four Hundred Project, based in Chestertown, Maryland, planned a 1,700-mile reenactment of Smith's voyage from May to September 2007, using a replica shallop built in the *Sultana* shipyard and crewed by a dozen volunteers. Plans include visits to ports of call throughout the bay and its tributary rivers, as well as hourly postings of the voyage on the project Web site, www.johnsmith400.org.

The accession to the throne of Charles I in 1625 provided a better climate for Catholics because his queen, Henrietta Maria, was a Catholic. George Calvert, the first Lord Baltimore, had converted to Catholicism in 1625. He had been secretary to Robert Cecil, Earl of Shaftesbury, then clerk to the Privy Council, a secretary of state, and a member of the Council for New England that arranged for colonial grants from the Crown. As a loyal subject he had been awarded an Irish baronetcy and had invested in land in the New World, as a possible colony for

Catholics. When a prolonged visit to a settlement he had started in Newfoundland convinced him that winters there were too harsh, he sought land in Virginia but received land farther north in 1632. The charter from the king named the grant after Henrietta Maria, "Terra Mariae"—Mary Land. George Calvert died before he could begin to form his southern colony, leaving his land and his hopes to his twenty-six-year-old son, Cecil (Cecilius).

A Feudal Proprietary Charter

When we think of America as a "new" world we often forget how much was simply transposed from the old. Maryland began with a medieval land arrangement. George Calvert had persuaded Charles I to issue an all-encompassing proprietary charter, which was feudal in nature, giving Lord Baltimore title as "absolute Lord and Proprietor" not only of ten million acres of land but of its government as well. And Calvert need not pay duty to the Crown, other than a symbolic two arrows each year. He worked out his own subsidiary land grants, offering manorial rights, which meant that purchasers could collect rent and also a portion of yearly income. This system of manorial rights was an inducement for the aristocracy and gentry to buy land, thereby avoiding the need to finance the enterprise through selling shares.

After George Calvert's death, the second Lord Baltimore, Cecil Calvert, was determined to carry out his father's wishes. Cecil welcomed settlers of all Christian denominations, because he knew that not enough Catholics could be recruited to establish the new colony successfully. He provided generous incentives of land—one hundred acres for each settler, wife, and servant, fifty acres for each child under sixteen, and one thousand acres for settlers who brought five servants with them, as well as manorial status—yet the pressure for Catholics to emigrate had lessened, and many Protestants were uncomfortable with a Catholic proprietor.

It took Cecil eighteen months of planning to send his two ships, the *Ark* and the *Dove,* from England in November 1633. He himself did not sail to America but sent his younger brother Leonard instead as leader of the expedition and governor of the colony. After a stop in Virginia, the two ships, in March of 1634, sailed up into the St. Mary's River, near the mouth of the Potomac, with about 140 set-

MARYLAND *Time Line*

1632	1634	1635	1645
Maryland charter granted to Cecil Calvert, Second Lord Baltimore, by England's King Charles I	Settlers land at St. Clement's Island (now Blakistone Island); Leonard Calvert purchases Indian land and builds fort at St. Mary's City	First general assembly (law-making assembly of freemen) meets at St. Mary's City	Richard Ingle attacks St. Mary's; Maryland endures "the plundering time"

A building frame in preparation at Historic St. Mary's City.

tlers on board. Some were gentlemen who had acquired land and brought their families, but most were servants or indentured laborers who had to work to pay for their passage. The Yaocomaco and Piscataway Indians cooperated with the settlers as they built St. Mary's City, hoping to receive protection against the Susquehannocks.

Evolution of the Plantation System

The settlers established three main groups: St. Mary's, St. Clement's, and St. George's. They all went to work to become self-sufficient by raising crops and livestock. Tobacco was planted as the key cash crop and became very lucrative, but knowledge of the starving experience in Jamestown had led Lord Baltimore to

1646	**1649**	**1655**	**1667**	**1675**
Leonard Calvert returns and restores order	Virginia Puritans settle Anne Arundel, near Annapolis; Cecil Calvert creates an "Act Concerning Religion"	Puritans from Virginia defeat Governor William Stone's forces at Battle of the Severn	St. Mary's City incorporated	Cecil Calvert dies

> Lord Baltimore made a list of supplies for the settlers to bring on the voyage: "Victuals (like two bushells of oatmeale, one bushell of pease); Apparrell (three shirts, three paire of stockings, six paire of shoes); Bedding (canvas sheets); Armes (one musket, ten pounds of powder, one sword); Tooles (three shovells, five felling axes, nailes); Implements (one large frying-pan, one iron pot, platters, dishes and spoones)."

require that some land be cultivated for corn and vegetables. One aspect of the medieval land system—organizing groups of indentured servants and yeoman farmers in compact village and town settlements surrounded by outlying lands—was unsuitable to the development of the colony for two reasons: The original land grant incentives encouraged dispersion rather than centralization, and the economics of handling tobacco demanded waterfront property.

Within two years of his arrival, Leonard Calvert had begun organizing farming, the principal activity of the colony, on a manorial basis. From the outset, tobacco was the important crop for export, and plantations to grow it developed along the tidewater rivers of Chesapeake Bay; from there the crop could easily be shipped to England. By the turn of the century many large plantations were thriving and growing.

However, many of the indentured servants who had signed on for opportunity died, and the survivors were still living in poor conditions. Even after they had worked off their debts and become free, many did not have enough money to begin their own farms. But as more succeeded in buying and working small parcels of land, especially as tobacco prices rose after midcentury, they were replaced with African slaves.

Later generations of indentured servants had more opportunities, and some, like Daniel Dulaney, rose to professional eminence and political influence in the colony. Dulaney arrived in 1703 as a "redemptioner"—that is, he had to pay for his passage by serving a planter or other master. His planter was Colonel George Plater, who bought his indenture for four years. Dulaney was very useful as a clerk to Plater and also gained the experience of learning the law. By March 1707 he

MARYLAND *Time Line*

1688	**1694**	**1729**	**1755**
William III annuls Calvert charter; Maryland becomes royal colony	Capital moves from St. Mary's City to Anne Arundel Town (renamed Annapolis)	Baltimore Town established by charter	General Braddock leads expedition through Maryland to the west; French and Indians defeat Braddock's forces near Fort Duquesne

had fulfilled his indenture. Dulaney rose to prominence by his wits, riding circuits and winning cases to become a leading attorney, as well as acquiring land. By the end of his career he had been elected to the Annapolis Common Council and been appointed attorney general and judge by the governor.

Religious Turbulence and Civil Disputes

Throughout the first half of the 17th century, religion and politics were inextricably mixed in a home country headed for civil war, and even a remote colony originally tied to one religion could not escape sporadic turbulence. The Calverts, as well as most of the early settlers in Maryland, were Catholics tired of persecution in England. They had endured political and financial hardships throughout most of the Elizabethan era, fanned by the papal excommunication of the queen, the threat of the Spanish Armada, and the Gunpowder Plot. Yet, unlike the similarly persecuted Puritans of the Massachusetts Bay Colony, they established religious toleration in Maryland from the beginning. Perhaps it was in part a practical strategy to attract the needed settlers from a largely Protestant England, or an insurance against future intolerance aimed at Catholics. As it turned out, that insurance would be needed.

> When his indenture ended Dulaney received "a good suit of kersey or broadcloth, a shift of white linen, a new pair of stockings and shoes, and a new hat; also two hoes, one axe, and three barrels of corn."

Almost inevitably, religious alignments spilled over into civil disputes in the colony, and the rigid rules of the proprietorship helped create conflicts about land and trade. William Claiborne, secretary of state for Virginia, had received a commission from the Crown to develop Kent Island (near present-day Annapolis) as a trading station before Lord Baltimore's charter was in effect, and he resented becoming a tenant of a Catholic landlord. He thought he had the right to trade on his own, but Lord Baltimore insisted that trading had to be licensed by him. After a series of clashes in 1635, Claiborne returned to England on business, whereupon Leonard Calvert seized the island.

1769	1774	1775	1776
Maryland merchants adopt policy of nonimportation of British goods	Mob burns *Peggy Stewart* in Annapolis harbor	Association of Freemen formed by Maryland Convention	Maryland Convention declares independence from Great Britain; Ninth Provincial Convention adopts Declaration of Rights (Maryland's Bill of Rights)

Reproduction of an early dwelling at Historic St. Mary's City.

Claiborne, who would cause more trouble later, was a sign of worse to come. By 1642 civil war was raging in England, pitting supporters of Parliament, many of them Puritans, against the supporters of King Charles, many of them Catholic. In 1645 Richard Ingle, a London tobacco dealer and Protestant, appeared at St. Mary's in his ship *Reformation,* privateering in the name of Parliament. At his hands, Maryland was to suffer what became known as "the plundering time." Leonard Calvert sought refuge in Virginia. Many of the Catholic colonists were robbed and their homes burned, a chaos that lasted until Calvert was able to return in 1646. Ingle was eventually caught and executed.

Leonard Calvert died the following year. Back in England, Cecil Calvert, in

MARYLAND *Time Line*

1781	1783	1784	1814
Maryland ratifies, and thereby makes effective, the Articles of Confederation	George Washington resigns commission as commander in chief of Continental Army at State House in Annapolis	Treaty of Paris, ending Revolutionary War, ratified by Congress at Annapolis	British burn Washington; attack on Fort McHenry repelled

an effort to promote toleration and populate his colony, appointed a Protestant governor, William Stone, who had been forced to flee royalist Virginia. Stone encouraged Puritans driven out of Virginia in 1649 to settle to the north in Anne Arundel. That same year Lord Baltimore proposed the Act Concerning Religion, which was meant to protect the Catholics, by then a minority group. It assumed that since Christian unity was not possible, tolerance was the only way to achieve civil harmony. As a final result the two factions had to compromise, because the act made intolerance a crime among Christians.

Even wise colonial policies can fail, as this one did twice under the weight of turbulent events in the home country. When Charles I was executed in 1649 and rule passed to a Puritan Parliament, a split grew between Catholic authority in the southern counties of St. Mary's and St. George's and Puritan control of the northern ones, Anne Arundel and Kent. Parliament sent a commission to seize power in Maryland from the proprietor, creating instability that peaked in 1655, when Governor Stone, the Protestant whom Lord Baltimore had appointed to ease tensions, was defeated at the Battle of Severn River in Anne Arundel. Religious toleration returned in a compromise reached in London in 1657, whereby Lord Baltimore was reinstated as proprietor; and three years later that outcome was reinforced by the Stuart restoration, when Charles II assumed the throne.

But the pendulum was to swing again. By the time Protestants William and Mary ascended the throne of England in the "Glorious Revolution" of 1688, Maryland's Protestants had been chafing under Catholic authority and privileges for some time. When news of the new sovereigns reached the colony in 1689 and there was no sign that Lord Baltimore intended to recognize them (his messenger had died before leaving England), four men—John Coode, Nehemiah Blakiston, Kenelm Cheseldyne, and Henry Jowles—formed the Protestant Association, gathered 250 men, marched into St. Mary's, and took over the government without shedding blood. The legislature met, recognized William and Mary, and petitioned them for a royal governor. They did not get one until Sir Lionel Copley arrived in 1692, and in the interim the Protestant Association ruled the colony. At that point Lord Baltimore lost his authority to rule but not his title to lands or revenues. The new administration also managed to stop Catholics from voting—an ironic disenfranchisement that lasted until after the Revolutionary War.

French and Indian War

No battles of the French and Indian War were fought on Maryland soil, but an important meeting took place in nearby Alexandria, Virginia, at its outset. When British general Edward Braddock arrived in Virginia in 1755, he convened a conference with the governors of Massachusetts, New York, Pennsylvania, Maryland, and Virginia, to discuss war strategy. Maryland, having no western land interests, was less concerned than the other colonial participants.

Braddock was bitterly disappointed in the results of the conference when most of the colonial legislatures pledged only nominal funds and troops for the war to contain French expansion in their western lands. He led his troops through Maryland to the staging area at Cumberland, and from there into the wilds of Pennsylvania, where he built a military road over the mountains, suffered defeat near Fort Duquesne, and died of his wounds.

Moves toward Independence

Beyond the question of religion, the split between the lifestyles of southern and northern Maryland counties—plantation life and mercantile endeavors—widened during the 18th century. Annapolis, settled by Puritans from Virginia in 1649, had gained enough political clout from the "Glorious Revolution" in England to have the capital shifted from St. Mary's City by 1694 and thereafter prospered as the principal port, business, and social center of the colony.

Thus it is no surprise that the colony's reactions against the financial exactions of the mother country—largely to pay off the crushing debts from the French and Indian War—were parallel to those in other ports like Boston, Providence, New York, or Philadelphia. Simmering resentment to the Stamp Act of 1765 exploded around the return of Zachariah Hood from England. Hood, an unwary Annapolis merchant, had made the mistake of accepting a royal appointment as stamp tax collector for Maryland. When the news reached Annapolis, he was an immediate scapegoat, burned in effigy by a mob before he arrived, prevented from landing in the port, and finally forced to flee to New York.

Two years later the Townshend Acts of 1767 led to a boycott of British goods by merchants that lasted until the acts were repealed in 1770. After a brief lull, the Tea Act of 1773 again inflamed port cities throughout the colonies, and there were many replications of the Boston Tea Party. When the brig *Peggy Stewart* arrived in 1774 in her home port of Annapolis with a cargo of tea on which the tax had been

---

A curious set of circumstances during the two British campaigns produced our national anthem. Earlier, as the British troops were on their way to Washington, they took over the manor house of Dr. William Beanes. According to one version of the story, when some of the British soldiers came back after burning Washington—not until first having enjoyed the dinner that was prepared for President and Mrs. James Madison in the White House—they were tipsy with too much wine. Dr. Beanes arrested and jailed them for disturbing the peace. British officers then took him prisoner.

The rest of the story is more certain. Beanes's friends tried to arrange for his release and thought of Francis Scott Key. He was a well-respected and erudite lawyer who might be perfect for this mission. The British agreed to let him approach the British flagship and make his case. Key reminded the British officers on board that Dr. Beanes had treated wounded British soldiers, and they agreed to let him go. But they insisted he and Key must stay with the fleet until they had watched Baltimore go up in smoke. Key was able to see the flag on Fort McHenry through a spyglass and scratched his poem on the back of a letter.

---

paid, a mob refused all explanations and persecuted her owner, Anthony Stewart, until he set his own ship and cargo on fire to appease it.

As the Revolution began, the first constitution of Maryland as an independent state was ratified in 1776, finally replacing the Calvert proprietorship that had survived in remnants since initial colonization. But once again, as in the French and Indian War, Maryland soil was not destined to become a scene of battles, even though General Howe did pass through on his way to occupy Philadelphia in 1777. However, Maryland militias were active in all the major battles of the Revolution, from Long Island to Yorktown.

The War of 1812

By its location Maryland had escaped direct conflict on its own soil through the two major wars of the 18th century, but it was especially vulnerable in the War of 1812. Its land abutted Washington, the new capital of the nation, and Baltimore was known as a "nest of pirates," with 126 privateers in port. Baltimore clippers, two-masted topsail schooners built for speed, were very active when the government gave them a license to attack British shipping. They proved so troublesome to the British that a response was almost inevitable.

It came early in 1813 when Admiral Cockburn arrived with a dozen warships to blockade the Chesapeake, bottle up the port of Baltimore, and harass settlements on both sides of the bay. He established a base on Kent Island and burned Havre de Grace, among many other raids. When General Robert Ross arrived with more troops the following summer, the two forces combined for land and sea attacks on Washington and Baltimore, making 1814 the critical year of the war.

The attack on Washington came first. With the flexibility of amphibious warfare, the British used some ships to create diversions, while others landed the main invasion force at the Patuxent River. It met little opposition until it reached the Anacostia River at Bladensburg on August 24, where American troops had set up lines of defense and a pitched battle ensued. When the Americans were overwhelmed, British troops entered Washington that night, destroyed dockyards, arsenals, and barracks, and burned the Senate chamber and the Presidential Palace (White House), symbolic buildings at the core of government. The campaign had been successful, with deadly effect.

On September 12 the British fleet sailed to Baltimore, planning to burn the city as they had Washington. British troops landed at North Point, ready to march into the city and coordinate with the British fleet. But the American militia under Sam Smith had fortified Hampstead Hill to stop the invasion, and when General Ross was killed, his replacement found no way to overcome these obstacles and retreated. The British fleet had to get by Fort McHenry to reach Baltimore harbor. At 6:30 AM on September 13 the warships began bombarding the fort with a heavy barrage of mortars and rockets. They continued for twenty-five hours and finally gave up when the fort withstood this intense assault.

Regions *to* Explore

SOUTHERN MARYLAND
CENTRAL MARYLAND
EASTERN SHORE

SOUTHERN MARYLAND

Settlers arrived in southern Maryland in 1634, and their site at St. Mary's is a good place to begin a historical adventure. The 140 or so passengers who came ashore from the *Ark* and the *Dove* had to fend for themselves against mosquitoes that brought malaria, plant enough food crops to sustain them, and begin to grow cash crops such as tobacco. Fortunately, they had some help from friendly local Indians. This living-history town offers a window into the early life of the colony.

Today you will find pleasant countryside and the peace and quiet not found in cities. This tidewater wonderland attracts boaters who can poke up innumerable creeks and seek yet another perfect cove.

Calvert County, with its collection of charter boats, claims to be "Maryland's sportfishing capital." At Calvert Cliffs you can find fossils on the beach, and there are lighthouses to see, such as Cove Point Lighthouse, the oldest tower light on the Chesapeake.

Charles County offers Port Tobacco, with its Confederate historical past. The doctor who set the leg of assassin John Wilkes Booth lived here. Bird-watchers enjoy the parks and anglers the Potomac River.

St. Mary's County features the colonial capital of Maryland and the living-history museum of St. Mary's City. St. Mary's College of Maryland has been here since 1840. Sotterley Plantation is one of the few original plantations left.

Historical Introduction to St. Mary's County

In October 1633 the *Ark* and the *Dove* had been stopped at the mouth of the Thames because they had not taken an oath of allegiance to the king. After all who were visible on board had taken the oath, the ships were allowed to sail. They landed in Cowes on the Isle of Wight to await departure on their four-month voyage across the Atlantic. Although the gentlemen investors may have had cabins, the rest of the contingent lived in a space about 100 feet by 30 feet, night and day, for those four months.

They encountered a gale during their first days out, so they anchored in a harbor at Yarmouth. Another vessel came down upon the *Dove*, which forced her to cut her anchor and sail out to sea. The *Ark* followed, and for a time they had fair winds. Another storm struck and the ships were separated, each thinking the other had been lost, until they reached Barbados and were reunited. The *Ark* was said

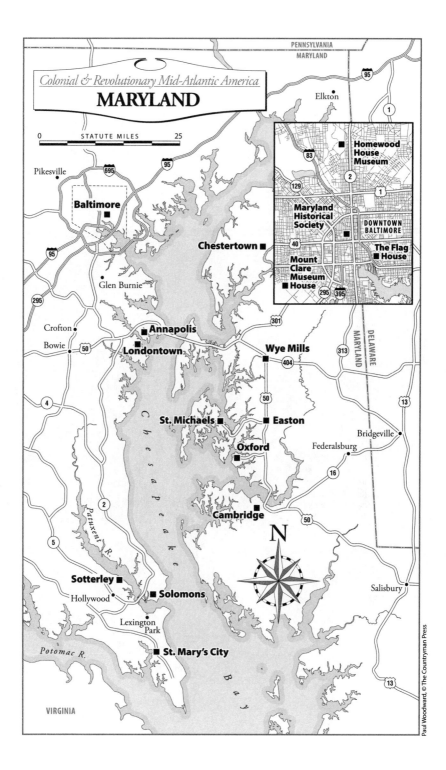

Colonial & Revolutionary Mid-Atlantic America
MARYLAND

STATUTE MILES
0   25

PENNSYLVANIA
MARYLAND

95

Elkton

1

Pikesville

695

95

Baltimore

Homewood
House
Museum

83

129

2

Maryland
Historical
Society

DOWNTOWN
BALTIMORE

Chestertown

40

The Flag
House

Glen Burnie

Mount
Clare
Museum
House

295

395

95

295

301

Crofton

Annapolis

Bowie

50

Londontown

Wye Mills

313

404

MARYLAND

DELAWARE

50

4

St. Michaels

Easton

Bridgeville

Oxford

Federalsburg

16

13

Cambridge

50

N

Salisbury

Sotterley

Hollywood

Solomons

Lexington
Park

Potomac R.

St. Mary's City

13

VIRGINIA

Patuxent R.

2

5

Chesapeake

Bay

Paul Woodward, © The Countryman Press

The Maryland Dove.

> The *Ark* was sorely tested on her voyage. Father Andrew White wrote, "At about 10 in the night a blacke cloud shed a pitiful shower upon us and presently a such furious winde as we were able to beare no cloth [sail] at all, and yet before we were able to take in our main[sail] a furious impression of wind suddenly came, and split it from top to toe and cast one part in the sea. This amazed the stoutest heart, even of the sailors, who confessed they had seen ships cast away with less violence of weather . . . the ship left without saile or government to the winds and waves floated like a dish til God were pleased to take pittie upon her."

to be "a shippe as strong as could be made of oake and iron, king built, making faire weather in great storms."

Both vessels survived the arduous voyage, landing on the shores of the St. Mary's River, a tributary of the lower Potomac. There in March 1634 they founded Lord Baltimore's colony at St. Mary's City, first capital of Maryland and now a major archaeological site for colonial history.

ST. MARY'S CITY

HISTORICAL SITES *and* MUSEUMS

Historic St. Mary's City (800-SMC-1634 or 240-895-4990; www.stmaryscity.org), 18751 Hogaboom Lane. Open mid-March–Nov., Tue.–Sun. The visitor center offers a helpful slide show and displays for orientation. Archaeological exploration has uncovered a number of ruins from the original city; more are waiting for future generations to excavate in open fields that were once filled with houses and other structures.

The museum adjoining the visitor center displays a wealth of military artifacts, including 1645 iron shot, cannon fragments, English flint, a 1650 sword, and parts of armor. House bits include a 1675 door hinge, iron keys, handmade nails, wall plaster made of oyster shells, pale green leaded glass, and a 1650 Dutch brick. The food display features a large 1661 pitcher by Morgan Jones, knives, pewter spoons, slipware cups from Staffordshire, England, and other ceramics. Medical instruments include a lancet for bleeding, forceps, and a bleeding porringer.

One of the most exciting discoveries took place in 1990 when three lead coffins were discovered. In 1992 Project Lead Coffin undertook the process of determining whether the coffins still contained original air from the 1600s, taking a preliminary look inside by means of a fiberscope, then lifting the coffins from the ground of Chapel Field, opening them, and analyzing the remains. NASA scientists were involved, and the procedure was carried out within a medical tent.

The small coffin contained the remains of a female child, along with traces of finely woven linen. The second coffin contained an older woman, who is considered perhaps the best preserved skeleton of a 17th-century colonist in North America. She was lying in a shroud with silk ribbons at her wrists, knees, and ankles. The third coffin revealed the skeleton of a man who wore a leather piece of clothing. The identity of the individuals has been established by Smithsonian Institution scientists as Philip Calvert, his wife Anne Wolsley, and an infant daughter, probably from the governor's second marriage. Philip Calvert was a half-brother to Cecil Calvert and served as a colonial official and governor of Maryland for a short time.

Two of the coffins are in storage, but the coffin of Philip Calvert is on display in the visitor center. All three coffins will eventually be reinterred in the brick chapel after it has been rebuilt. A walking trail will take you to the chapel, the first English Catholic chapel in the New World. The last of three chapels on the site was built of brick in 1667. Around the site are the unmarked graves of many colonists.

Take Chapel Road to the town center, where you can visit **Cordea's Hope**, a storehouse and office for Mark Cordea, a French Catholic immigrant who was a prominent member of the community; **Smith's Ordinary**, which offered food, drink, and lodging during colonial times; the **Calvert House**, home of Leonard Calvert, Maryland's first governor; the 1676 **State House**; and **Trinity Church**. Visitors to St. Mary's City are encouraged to "keep 17th-century time" to blend in with the interpreters, who want to speak with them in language of that era and follow its customs. You may meet Dan Clocker as he comes to town to drink, smoke, and tell stories, or Mrs. Nuthead, who loves to gossip as she runs the printing press. Chancellor Philip Calvert tries Captain Fendall for treason in the State House; Captain Miles Cook sells indentured servants from the transom of the *Dove;* and the Spray family continues cultivating its tobacco.

An interpreter keeps busy at Historic St. Mary's City.

Don't miss walking down to the river to go on board the *Maryland Dove* and talk with her crew, unless she is on a training cruise. As a faithful sailing replica of a small square-rigged ship from the 1630s, she gives visitors a chance to visualize a typical merchant vessel of the era. They carried lumber,

A house at Historic St. Mary's City.

tobacco, corn, furs, household items, and people. Now the *Dove*'s primary mission is educating people of all ages as she follows a busy schedule of port visits and cruises throughout maritime Maryland and adjoining states. In the process, she has served as a vehicle for experimental nautical archaeology, teaching maritime historians much about the capabilities of such vessels.

A model of the *Ark* is being built by Ray Miles. This 1:24 scale model will be placed next to Miles's model of the *Dove*. It will be almost seven feet long and six feet high. The model will be finished by the 2008–2009 season.

Also don't miss the **Godiah Spray Plantation**, located down the road on the other side of the visitor center. When

> As you stroll around the grounds you will see "ghost houses," which are wooden outlines marking the buildings that once stood there. Archaeologists have identified these sites, and eventually some of them will be reconstructed using 17th-century techniques.

we were there a group of schoolchildren were quizzing interpreters and getting good 17th-century answers. In between gardens, orchards, and barns stand the planter's house, a freedman's cottage, and tobacco houses; a path leads to slave quarters a hundred yards away.

LODGING

BARD'S FIELD B&B
15671 Pratt Rd., Ridge, MD 20680
301-872-5989
This historic home on Rawley Bay dates from 1798. 2 guest rooms.

THE BROME HOWARD INN
18281 Rosecroft Rd., St. Mary's City, MD 20686
301-866-0656; www.bromehowardinn.com
The inn dates from 1840 and is next to Historic St. Mary's City. The formal gardens are popular for weddings. 5 guest rooms.

RESTAURANTS

THE BROME HOWARD INN
18281 Rosecroft Rd., St. Mary's City, MD 20686
301-866-0656; www.bromehowardinn.com
Dinner is served Thursday through Sunday. Please call for reservations.

EVENTS

March: Maryland Day, St. Mary's City; 800-762-1634
October: Grand militia muster, St. Mary's City; 240-895-4990

INFORMATION

ST. MARY'S COUNTY TOURISM
23115 Leonard Hall Dr., Leonardtown, MD 20650
800-327-9023, 301-475-4200;
www.co.saint-marys.md.us/tourism

ST. MARY'S COUNTY HISTORICAL SOCIETY
P.O. Box 212, Leonardtown, MD 20650
301-475-2467; www.tqci.net/~smchs

SOTTERLEY

HISTORICAL SITES and MUSEUMS

Across the St. Mary's peninsula on the Patuxent River lies Sotterley (800-681-0850 or 301-373-2280; www.sotterley.org), 44300 Sotterley Lane, Hollywood, one of Maryland's many tidewater plantations during the colonial era. Open May 1–Oct. 31, Tue.–Sun. Lord Baltimore issued a manorial grant in 1650 to Thomas Cornwallis, who arrived on the *Ark* or the *Dove*. James Bowles built the first house here in 1717. After the latter's death, his widow married George Plater II, who named Sotterley after his ancestral home in Suffolk, England. George Plater III was a delegate to the Continental Congress and one of the first governors in the state of Maryland. Because Sotterley was a port of entry for the colony, the resident in the house was also the customs officer.

George Plater V was only five years old when he inherited the house, but he lost it later in a roll of the dice. He wanted to die in the house but didn't make it—his body was found in a nearby ditch. Some say that they can still hear the hoofbeats, see footprints, and even hear the fatal roll of the dice—George is apparently a friendly spirit when he comes to visit his plantation.

Richard Bolton created the Chinese Chippendale staircase and the ornate shell woodwork in the drawing room. The staircase has a break in the rail; its purpose may have been to signal a curve coming or to prevent a child from sliding down! The drawing room is considered by some to be one of the hundred most beautiful rooms in America, furnished with Adams and Hepplewhite pieces from London. In the front hall Chinese lattice-back mahogany chairs match the Chinese trellis stair. And like other great houses of the colonial era, it has an almost necessary feature—a secret staircase that leads from the bright red small parlor to an upstairs bedroom.

Sotterley is a working plantation, and you can visit the outbuildings, including tenant houses, smokehouse, and tobacco shed.

LODGING

THE VICTORIAN CANDLE
25065 Peregrine Way, Hollywood, MD 20636
301-373-8800; www.victorian-candle.com
This B&B is near Sotterley Plantation. 5 guest rooms.

Sotterly Plantation house.

SOLOMONS

The Solomons area is located where the Patuxent River meets Chesapeake Bay. The harbor is one of the deepest natural ports in the bay and a busy site for boat-building, sailing, and fishing. Many bugeyes were built here during the 19th century. The sky is equally busy with aircraft from the Patuxent River Naval Air Station.

HISTORICAL SITES *and* MUSEUMS

Calvert Marine Museum (410-326-2042; www.calvertmarinemuseum.com), 14200 Solomons Island Rd., offers a three-part emphasis on paleontology, estuarine biology, and maritime history. Open May–Oct., daily. The Calvert Cliffs are right next door, so to speak, providing a wealth of opportunity for exploration and collection of fossils. This museum explores maritime activity from long before the first settlers arrived. Fossilized remains and real live specimens make this a "don't miss" experience. There's even a real log canoe on display.

> Anna Weems Ewalt's grandfather used to tell the story of the time John Paul Jones's body was being transported back to Annapolis from France. He attributed the wild storm, which had all of the lighthouse windows leaking, to the fact that JPJ should not have been moved at all.

Outside, from a later era, stands the Drum Point Lighthouse, which was fully restored with the help of Anna Weems Ewalt, who was born in that very lighthouse. The doctor assisting her mother came by dory to the lighthouse, then located ⅛ mile offshore, the day before Anna's birth.

She described watching her grandfather clean the lenses on the lighthouse lamp daily at dawn; it was quite a job, because the kerosene flame smoked up the lenses. During a fog the bell had to be rung, which must have been earsplitting for the family to hear time after time after time.

LODGING

SOLOMONS VICTORIAN INN B&B
125 Charles St., Solomons, MD 20688
410-326-4811; www.solomons
victorianinn.com
This Queen Anne Victorian home dates from 1906. 8 guest rooms.

RESTAURANTS

THE CD CAFE
14350 Solomons Island Rd., Solomons, MD 20688
410-326-3877
Bistro fare; seafood is a specialty.

THE OLD FIELD INN
485 Main St., Prince Frederick, MD 20678
410-535-1054, 301-855-1054;
www.chesapeake.net/oldfieldinn
The place to go for a special dinner. The menu is innovative, specializing in seafood and beef.

CENTRAL MARYLAND

The state capital, in Annapolis, and the largest city, Baltimore, offer both history and entertainment for travelers. Besides that you can enjoy the shoreline of Chesapeake Bay in a number of different ways.

Baltimore County offers 175 miles of bay and creek shoreline for boaters and fishermen. You'll also find the third-largest concentration of thoroughbred horse farms in the country. And the city of Baltimore is where Francis Scott Key wrote "The Star-Spangled Banner." Its museums include the Baltimore & Ohio Railroad Museum, the National Aquarium, the Baltimore Maritime Museum, the Flag House & Star-Spangled Banner Museum, Homewood House, the Mount Clare Museum, and all the sites along the Inner Harbor, to name a few.

Anne Arundel County features Annapolis, with its wealth of colonial history, as well as the state capital and U.S. Naval Academy. Museums include the Hammond-Harwood House, the Paca House, the Maryland State House, and the Banneker-Douglass Museum. Annapolis is considered one of the prime sailing centers in the country.

ANNAPOLIS

Annapolis will always have a very special appeal for us because we spent most of our first year of marriage there. Robert was the assistant sailing officer at the U.S. Naval Academy, taking up his post in the fall of 1953. Life for us was wonderful and carefree—no house, car, or community obligations. We rented an apartment on Duke of Gloucester Street, just a few steps from St. Anne's Circle. On weekends we could sail on an academy yawl or knockabout, and often cruised for a couple of days with a group of midshipmen on *Royono,* a famous seventy-two-foot yawl donated to the academy.

Annapolis always has been and is now a thriving waterfront city, with salt water washing right up into the city dock at the center of its business district. This narrow slip of water juts in to meet the bottom of Main and Cornhill Streets. Almost everyone gravitates at one time or another to the dock area—always a busy place with fishing, charter, excursion, and pleasure boats coming in and going out. When we lived there, it was filled with bugeyes and skipjacks, among the last workboats to operate under sail; now it and the surrounding creeks are filled with pleasure sailboats that make Annapolis the premier sailing center of the Middle Atlantic states. And of course it has been home to another premier nautical institution, the U.S. Naval Academy, since 1845.

Such continued vitality, and the change that it inevitably brings, have not obscured the central colonial part of the city, either in ambience—it's still primarily a walking town—or in surviving buildings. Somehow the allure of an active boating port and capital city manage to coexist with a rich historical heritage stretch-

The Middleton Tavern overlooks the city dock.

ing back to the city's founding in the 17th century, enabling visitors to enjoy both worlds simultaneously.

Historical Introduction to Annapolis

Puritan settlers arrived in 1649 from Virginia after an invitation from Maryland's governor. They settled on the north side of the Severn River and called their home Providence. Within two years some of them moved across the river to the Annapolis peninsula to grow tobacco on its fertile land. Ships used the rivers and creeks to transport their crops back to England. Then a ship's captain was honored by the choice of his name, Proctor, for the town. Later it was called City by the Severn, the river on which it is located. Some records refer to it as Anne Arundel Town, Arrundell Towne, or Arundelton, all variant names of the county surrounding it.

In 1694 it became the capital of Maryland, when Governor Francis Nicholson moved the seat of government from St. Mary's City to this site nearer the center of the colony (a move that destroyed the prosperity of St. Mary's City but preserved its archaeological integrity). Nicholson directed his commissioners "to survey and lay out in the most comodius and convenient parte and place of said Towne six Acres of Land intire for the erecting a Court House and other buildings as shall be thought necessary and convenient." In 1694 Annapolis was chosen as the city's name to honor Queen Anne of England.

The city became an important and strategically located seaport, in addition to serving as the administrative center of Maryland during the Revolution. After the French entered the war in 1778, many British ships were diverted to European waters, and fast privateers sailed in and out of the harbor through a looser blockade. The Continental Congress met in the State House in 1783 and again in 1784 to ratify the Treaty of Paris ending the Revolution.

HISTORICAL SITES and MUSEUMS

You can begin to discover the sometimes hidden treats of Annapolis by heading for the **Annapolis and Anne Arundel County Conference and Visitors Bureau** (888-302-2852 or 410-280-0445; www.visitannapolis.org), 26 West St. Open daily. This center has racks of information on Annapolis, plus helpful staff to answer questions. One of the best ways to get a feel for Annapolis is through a walking tour—the ideal way to see a city full of narrow lanes and one-way streets. Your family may enjoy being directed by a guide in colonial costume who will pull relevant objects out of her basket as she reaches each new location. Our guide had a great deal of precise information, interspersed with anecdotes and stories, to make the history of Annapolis come alive.

In 1708 Ebenezer Cook wrote "The Sotweed Factor":

Up to Annapolis I went,
A City situate on a Plain,
Where scarce a house will keep out rain:
The Buildings fram'd with Cyprus rare
Resemble much our Southwark Fair.

By 1730 he had changed his tune in "Sotweed Redivivus":

Bound up to Port Annapolis,
The famous Beau Metropolis
Of Maryland, of small Renown
When Anna first wore England's Crown
Is now Grown rich and Opulent
The awful Seat of Government.

The earliest structures are plain, unadorned 17th-century houses like the one at 130 Prince George Street. This house was patterned after the utilitarian wood-frame houses common in English villages. The gambrel roof is topped by the very large central chimney typical of early colonial homes. Take a stroll down the smaller lanes like Pinkney, Fleet, Cornhill, and Francis Streets to see more of them, then walk the broader avenues like King George, Prince George, East, and Duke of

Annapolis will captivate architecture buffs, and it serves as a useful school for the evolution of architecture in America. As you walk around town, you will notice buildings marked with historic district plaques that are color-coded according to date and style. Colors signify time periods as follows: provincial green (17th century), terra cotta (18th-century colonial), blue (Federal), verdigris (Greek revival), aubergine (Victorian), and ocher (20th century).

A mannequin of George Washington presides in the State House.

Patriotic fervor for General Washington was expressed during a celebration the day before his resignation, presided over by Governor William Paca. Supplies for the evening were furnished by Mann's Hotel as follows: "ninety-eight bottles of wine, two and one-half gallons of spirits, nine pounds of sugar, a lot of limes, music and waiters, and a dozen packs of cards."

Gloucester Streets and around State Circle to spot some of the plaques on later and larger structures.

The **Maryland State House** (410-974-3400; www.mdwelcome.org), 91 State Circle. Open daily. The building dates from 1772 and has a distinguished history. It is the oldest state house in continuous legislative use in the United States and also served as the U.S. Capitol from November 1783 to August 1784.

George Washington resigned his commission as commander in chief of the Continental Army in the Old Senate Chamber. Look for the bronze plaque on the floor marking the spot where Washington stood on that day.

The official end of the Revolutionary War came with the signing of the Treaty of Paris in the State House in 1784. Charles Willson Peale painted a number of portraits for the State House, including one of Washington with Maryland's Tench Tilghman, his aide-de-camp, which hangs over the fireplace in the Old Senate Chamber. Call for more information on the State House, its exhibits, and opportunities for visiting its elegant chambers while the legislature is sitting.

From the State House, be sure to walk up the short block of School Street that links State Circle to Church Circle and visit **St. Anne's Episcopal Church.** King William III contributed the communion silver with his coat of arms on it in 1695. Nearly two centuries later, in 1893, the Sands Memorial Window won first prize for ecclesiastical art at the Chicago World's Fair. The oldest grave in the cemetery is that of Amos Garrett, the first mayor of Annapolis, who died in 1727.

From Church Circle continue east along College Avenue to **St. John's College** (443-716-4014; www.stjohnscollege.edu), 60 College Ave. It was founded in 1696 and became famous in the 20th century for its demanding liberal arts curriculum based on the classic texts of Western civilization. There is a legend that the treaty of peace with the Susquehannock Indians was signed under the large 400-year-old tulip poplar tree called the **Liberty Tree**, which was located on the front campus. The Sons of Liberty used to meet there to talk about separation from England. Because it was in the open, they could easily spot an outsider approaching in time to conclude their conversation. After the Revolution, when the Marquis de Lafayette returned to America in 1824, he reviewed the Maryland Militia under the tree. Francis Scott Key attended the school, and so did two nephews of George Washington, who graduated in 1796. However, the tree had to be cut down some years ago due to hurricane damage; a marker was to be placed at the site.

Reynolds Tavern on Church Circle dates from 1747. It is a fine place for a meal and overnight. You might want to try this recipe:

Reynolds Tavern Shepherd's Pie

1 lb. lean lamb, cubed
1 cup diced carrots
1 cup diced leeks
1 cup diced onions
  salt and pepper
3 lbs. mashed potato

Brown the lamb, remove, reserving the juices. Sauté the vegetables until soft. Return the meat and juices to the pan and mix well. Spoon into large buttered dish, spoon mashed potato over the top. Place in preheated oven (175–200°F) and cook until brown (30 minutes). Sprinkle top of pie with shredded cheese during the last 10 minutes of cooking.

From St. John's turn right onto King George Street to reach the **Chase-Lloyd House** (410-263-2723), 22 Maryland Ave. Open Mar. 1–Dec. 30, Tue.–Sat. It was partially built by Samuel Chase, a signer of the Declaration of Independence. In 1771 Chase sold his unfinished house to Edward Lloyd IV, who finished the building. Francis Scott Key married Mary Taylor Lloyd here in 1802.

The house is now a home for elderly ladies, "where they may find a retreat from the vicissitudes of life." You can visit the museum on the first floor. The Chase coat of arms decorates some of the family china on display. Look at the Italian marble mantel in the parlor, which depicts Shakespeare receiving keys from the Goddess of Wisdom.

The **Hammond-Harwood House** (410-263-4683; www.hammondharwood house.org), 19 Maryland Ave. Open Tue.–Sun. It was designed by William Buckland for Mathias Hammond in 1774.

While the house was in the process of construction, a change was made to reduce the height so that Hammond's neighbor, Edward Lloyd, would have a view of the harbor and the city dock.

 The Hammond-Harwood House holds a mystery. Hammond reportedly was having the house built for an unknown bride-to-be, who then eloped with someone else, so he resolved not to live in the house and left Annapolis. He died at the young age of 38, and the mystery of his forlorn love has never been solved. Ask about the tunnel under the house, which may have led down to the water. Two ancient keys were also found under the floor, one labeled "to the Secret Chamber" and the other "to the Secret Burying Place." Doesn't that stir your imagination?

The Chase-Lloyd House.

The "best bedchamber" was a showroom where the family displayed its decorative pieces. It is decorated with Chippendale pieces to reflect the high quality in the home. The chairs date from 1765; the tea table and bedstead are Chippendale. Two needlepoint pieces offer the 18th-century concept of classical mythology with the goddess Diana. The dining room has some Harwood family pieces, including the dining table, sideboard, chairs, and silver water urn and saltcellars. The northeast bedchamber has a 1789 portrait by Charles Willson Peale of Ann Proctor and her doll. Her doll is also in the collection.

Around the block on Prince George Street stands the **William Paca House** (410-990-4543; www.annapolis.org), 186 Prince George St. Open daily. Originally designed as a home and office for Paca in 1763, the house was later part of the elegant Carvel Hall, a vanished hotel that we remember from our stay in town during the 1950s. The restored house is open and furnished in period decor. The parlor has a Wedgwood appearance, with handsome white carving on Prussian blue paint above the fireplace. The original Paca gardens have also been replanted by the Historic Annapolis Foundation. Look for the unusual Chinese trellis bridge that matches the staircase in the house.

 In the dining room look for the "jib door," located below the window on the right; the window becomes a door leading into the garden.

On the other side of Main Street, the **Charles Carroll House** (410-269-1737; www.charlescarrollhoouse.com), 107 Duke of Gloucester St., was opened for visitors in May of 1993. Open Sat.–Sun., other times by appointment. Charles Carroll the settler (he is traditionally called this to distinguish him from the many other Charles Carrolls) owned the property of St. Mary's Parish, where the house and the church now stand. He built his home in the 1720s, perhaps using an older structure within the building. This two-and-a-half-story house was then among the largest in Annapolis.

His son, Charles Carroll of Carrollton, was born in the house in 1737; it is the only surviving birthplace of a signer of the Declaration of Independence in Maryland. He studied with Jesuits in Maryland, Belgium, France, and England, then returned in 1765 to work in his father's business. He was very active among the Patriots and served as a delegate to the Continental Congress for Maryland from 1776 to 1778, yet as a Catholic he was not allowed to vote. However, he was not only influential, but the wealthiest man in the colonies at that time.

The story of the Carroll House is not over yet. During archaeological exploration the foundation of the "Frame House," possibly a 17th-century building,

The Charles Carroll House.

was uncovered. Objects from the 1660s were unearthed in the adjacent "builder's trench," and broken dishes from the same era were also found on the property near the Eastport bridge.

Inside the house, the East Wing archaeological dig uncovered pieces from the late 1700s and may indicate that slaves lived and worked in that room. The collection of quartz crystals, polished stones, bone disks, and pierced coins may provide a link with African Americans, since both the pierced coins and bone disks relate to Kongo classical religion. Some tribes put transparent pieces such as glass near doorways to signify ancestral presence and protection.

John Adams wrote about John Paul Jones in 1779: "Jones has art, and secrecy, and aspires very high. . . . Eccentricities and irregularities are to be expected from him."

Jones claimed, "I wish to have no Connection with any Ship that does not sail fast for I intend to go in harm's way." He was known for his grit, daring, flamboyance, and determination.

The house also provides an unusual experience for history buffs because the walls, floors, and woodwork have not been restored; you can see the original forms of construction right in front of your eyes. The oldest wooden staircase in Maryland is here, and the original floors are put together with iron pegs, then a sign of wealth.

Outside, an 18th-century cistern on the west side of the house began a series of archaeological finds. Excavations continue in the gardens and along a 400-foot, 18th-century stone seawall. Core samples were taken to ascertain the makeup of the terraced gardens, which may eventually be restored to their original appearance.

U.S. Naval Academy (410-263-6933; www.usna.edu), Entrance Gate 1 at King George and Randall Sts. Open daily. Visitors 16 years and older need a photo ID. Although the academy was founded later than the eras covered by this book, its collections go back to the Revolution. There is a visitor center and museum covering American naval history, and tours are scheduled. The Naval Academy was opened at Fort Severn in Annapolis as the Naval School on October 10, 1845, by George Bancroft, secretary of the navy in President Polk's cabinet. The faculty consisted of four officers and three civilian professors. Initially, the course was five years—the first and last year at Annapolis and the intervening three years at sea.

The most remarkable building is the chapel, which dates from 1904 and is filled with stained-glass windows dedicated as memorials to naval heroes. Look for the Votive Ship, a model of a 15th-century Flemish carrack, which hangs from the ceiling in the rear of the nave. Walk downstairs to the crypt to see the sarcophagus of John Paul Jones, his commission as a captain signed by John Hancock, his membership certificate in the Society of the Cincinnati signed by George Washington, and the sword presented to him by King Louis XVI of France.

U.S. Naval Academy Museum (410-293-2108; www.usna.edu/museum), Gate 3, 118 Maryland Ave., Preble Hall. Open daily. The museum houses collections of ship models, paintings, uniforms, swords, and relics from the career of John Paul Jones. The Rogers Ship Model Collection contains 108 models dating from 1650 to 1850.

On your way between the chapel and museum, don't miss the Statue of Tecumseh, known by midshipmen as the "God of the C," the grade every cadet needs to pass courses. Pennies are tossed at him, and he also receives good-luck left-handed salutes. Before any athletic contest with the archrival, Army, Tecumseh undergoes a makeup session and puts on war paint. Tecumseh is a copy of the figurehead on the wooden battleship *Delaware*, built in 1819.

LODGING

THE ANNAPOLIS INN
144 Prince George St., Annapolis, MD 21401
410-295-5200; www.annapolisinn.com
Thomas Jefferson's physician lived in this home. 3 guest rooms.

CHEZ AMIS B&B
85 East St., Annapolis, MD 21401
888-224-6455, 410-263-6631;
www.chezamis.com
The building was a grocery store around the turn of the century. 4 guest rooms.

FLAG HOUSE INN B&B
26 Randall St., Annapolis, MD 21401
800-437-4825, 410-280-2721;
www.flaghouseinn.com
Two 1870 townhouses were combined to form this B&B in the historic downtown. 5 guest rooms.

GIBSON'S LODGINGS
110 Prince George St., Annapolis, MD 21401
877-330-0057, 410-268-5555;
www.gibsonslodgings.com
Restored and modern buildings in the historic district. 21 guest rooms.

HISTORIC INNS OF ANNAPOLIS
58 State Circle, Annapolis, MD 21404
800-847-8882, 410-263-2641;
www.annapolisinns.com
The three historic inns in this group, Governor Calvert House, Robert Johnson House, and Maryland Inn, are in the center of town. 124 guest rooms.

REYNOLDS TAVERN
7 Church Circle, Annapolis, MD 21401
410-295-9555; www.reynoldstavern
.org
This building dates from 1747, and the guest rooms are decorated with period pieces, with the addition of modern amenities. 3 guest rooms.

THE 1908 WILLIAM PAGE INN
8 Martin St., Annapolis, MD 21401
800-364-4160, 410-626-1506;
www.williampageinn.com
The home dates from 1908 and is in the historic district. 5 guest rooms.

RESTAURANTS

GALWAY BAY
61-63 Maryland Ave., Annapolis, MD 21401
410-263-8333, 410-263-8989;
www.galway2006.com
An Irish restaurant and pub in the historic district.

MIDDLETON TAVERN

2 Market Space, Annapolis, MD 21401
410-263-3323;
www.middletontavern.com
This 18th-century building overlooks the
city dock and serves Maryland dishes.

REYNOLDS TAVERN

7 Church Circle, Annapolis, MD 21401
410-295-9555; www.reynoldstavern
.org
An 18th-century dining room for lunch,
dinner, and English afternoon tea; the pub
is in the original tavern kitchen.

TREATY OF PARIS AT THE
MARYLAND INN

58 State Circle, Annapolis, MD 21401
800-847-8882, 410-216-6340;
www.annapolisinns.com/dining.php
The Treaty of Paris was ratified here in
1783. Continental cuisine is served with a
French flair.

EVENTS

May: William Paca Garden plant sale of
18th-century plants; 410-267-7619
November: Hammond-Harwood House
colonial dog show (parade of dogs featured in English painting from the 18th
and 19th centuries); 410-263-4683
November: Tavern traipse, St. Clair
Wright History Center; 410-267-6656

INFORMATION
ANNAPOLIS & ANNE ARUNDEL
COUNTY CONFERENCE AND
VISITORS BUREAU

26 West St., Annapolis, MD 21401
888-302-2852, 410-280-0445; www
.visitannapolis.org

ANNAPOLIS WALKABOUT

223 S. Cherry Grove Ave.; Annapolis,
MD 21401
410-263-8253

CAPITAL CITY COLONIALS

101 Severn Ave., Annapolis, MD 21403
410-295-9715; www.capitalcity
colonials.com

DISCOVER ANNAPOLIS TOURS

Annapolis, MD 21403
410-626-6000; www.discover
-annapolis.com
Tours leave from Annapolis & Anne Arundel County Visitor Center, 26 West St.

HISTORIC ANNAPOLIS FOUNDATION

Shiplap House, 18 Pinkney St., Annapolis, MD 21404
800-603-4020, 410-267-7619;
www.annapolis.org

HISTORY QUEST

99 Main St., Annapolis, MD 21401
410-267-8146; www.annapolis.org

U.S. NAVAL ACADEMY/ARMEL-
LEFTWICH VISITOR CENTER

52 King George St., Annapolis, MD
21402
410-263-6933; www.navyonline.com

WATERMARK

P.O. Box 3350, Annapolis, MD 21403
800-569-9622, 410-268-7601, x104;
www.watermarkcruises.com
Tours, cruises, and charters

LONDON TOWN

This site is a reconstructed "lost town" of London. It is a pleasant place to visit, with landscaping and flowers in season. Take a walk down to the river and relax.

HISTORICAL SITES *and* MUSEUMS

Historic London Town and Gardens (410-222-1919; www.historiclondontown .org), 839 Londontown Rd., Edgewater. Open Tue.–Sun. Brown House closed for tours Jan.–Mar. Archaeologists are currently excavating part of late 17th- and 18th-century London Town. It was a busy ferry crossing on the route through the colonies. From the 1680s travelers going north or south crossed the South River here. The town received ships to take tobacco to Britain for sale. Slaves and white indentured and convict servants also arrived in the port.

William Brown built his home in the early 1760s on the banks of the South River. He was a carpenter, ferry master, tavern keeper, and builder. His home features header bond brickwork of the Georgian period. Enter and you will be in the hall where guests were greeted. Hogarth prints on the walls illustrate the activities of an evening. Tea, which was valuable, was kept locked up. The floor cloth has the "tumbling block" pattern. Look for an original Murphy bed, which was filled with corn husks. In the Great Hall the innkeeper rented out clay pipes. He served cider, ale, punch (made of rum, brandy, and citrus.) Our guide, a wench wearing a mobcap, shift, petticoat, and bodice, had a "tussy mussy" filled with herbs in her "Lucy pocket."

The Lost Towns Project has identified several building sites at London Town that date from the late 1700s. Wooden posts were sunk three to four feet into the ground. They are identified by discolorations in the clay subsoil. Archaeologists map the post holes to determine building patterns.

Dr. Richard Hill was born in 1698. Trained as a physician, he had an interest in plants for medicinal properties and was a regular correspondent with a member of the Royal Society in London. America's foremost naturalist at the time, John Bartram, visited Hill at his home in London Town. Hill sent four plant specimens to England, and these plants are the core of the Richard Hill Garden at London Town. They are tall goldenrod, Jerusalem oak, Quinzy root (rattlesnake master), and wild senna. Some of them were known to housewives of the day, and some of them were thought to cure bronchitis and dog bites. The Woodland Trail offers many other plants.

EVENTS

September: Colonial market days, featuring a plant sale and the annual London Town Autumn Tea; 410-222-1919

BALTIMORE

Baltimore evolved from Jones Falls, a town established by Governor Calvert at the site of what is now the downtown. In the 1720s there was a gristmill there, and in 1750 flour was shipped to Ireland and a wharf was built for expanding business. During the same period Fells Point, founded in 1732, was becoming an important 18th-century shipbuilding center. These two settlements grew together into the city of Baltimore. By the end of the century the settlement had become a major economic center, with a population of 20,000.

Baltimore was an important port that produced many ships for the Continental Navy during the Revolution. Privateers (privately owned warships) also used Baltimore for a base as they sailed out to capture British ships. Fells Point once had twenty shipyards, including some that built the famous Baltimore clippers in the last quarter of the 18th century and the first quarter of the 19th. These fast schooners had the distinctive clipper bow and were the forerunners of the larger, square-rigged clipper ships developed for the California trade in the middle of the 19th century.

We remember Fells Point in the 1950s as a run-down district with many abandoned buildings. There was no access to the harbor front. Two decades of harbor renewal have changed all that. Fells Point is now bustling with renovated and reconstructed buildings housing shops, pubs, and restaurants along the waterfront and surrounding blocks.

The Inner Harbor is filled with all kinds of attractions for visitors and residents alike. Years ago the area was unattractive, with decrepit warehouses, but a transformation took place. Now you can spend a day or more enjoying one museum and attraction after another, including the Maryland Science Center, the IMAX Theater and Davis Planetarium, the National Aquarium, and the Top of the World

---

How can the USS *Constellation* be both the first and the last sailing ship in the U.S. Navy? The easy answer is that three ships have carried the name. The first was a frigate launched in 1797 with a string of "firsts" to her credit—first to be built, put to sea, engage and defeat an enemy, under the command of Thomas Truxton. The second was a sloop of war launched in 1854 that sought out Confederate ships during the Civil War. She was not the last U.S. Navy ship with sails, but the last one to depend on them alone, with no auxiliary power. And the confusion is more than a matter of two ships with the same name, since the original frigate was in the same yard being broken up as the sloop of war was being built, and some of the old timbers were used in building the new ship. Further, when Baltimore rebuilt the sloop of war in the 1990s, some sections were built to look like the original frigate. The confusion and the controversy it created stopped there, though, because the third ship of that name, built in 1961, is an aircraft carrier.

observational floor in the World Trade Center. In the middle of it all is the USS *Constellation,* the last sailing vessel built by the U.S. Navy.

HISTORICAL SITES *and* MUSEUMS

The Flag House & Star Spangled Banner Museum (410-837-1793; www.flag house.org), 844 E. Pratt St. Open Tue.–Sat. year-round. Rebecca Flower Young was a flag maker in Philadelphia during the Revolutionary War. Her daughter, Mary Pickersgill, learned to sew flags and lived in this house from 1807 to 1857. She made the "star-spangled banner" that flew over Fort McHenry when the British bombarded the fort in 1814. We now associate huge flags with car dealers and shopping centers, but this one beats them all: It was 30 feet by 42 feet. It has 15 stars and 15 stripes, the official design of the American flag from 1794 to 1818.

A portrait by Charles Willson Peale depicts Colonel Benjamin Flower, commissary general of military stores, carrying a sword given to him by General Washington for saving the military stores and magazines of the army "and successfully removing also blankets, shoes and clothing so much needed by the army at that time." He also saved the Liberty Bell by moving it to the Zion Lutheran Church in Allentown, Pennsylvania, in 1777. Flower was an uncle of Mary Pickersgill. Mary's flag-making shop has a chest with bolts of fabric, a desk, and a flag spread out on the floor. Mary's bedroom was large and contained a trundle bed for her daughter. Afternoon tea was also served there.

The modern museum adjacent to the house has a Great Flag Window—a glass wall the same size, color, and design of the original Star-Spangled Banner. Visitors can see a video in the theater and also peruse the exhibits.

The Maryland Historical Society (410-685-3750; www.mdhs.org), 201 Monument St. Open Wed.–Sun. year-round. This fine museum offers extensive collections and displays on Maryland's history. Furniture on display dates from as early as 1634 and includes pieces made by John Shaw, a pre-Revolutionary cabinetmaker in Annapolis. English silver dates from the 1700s. Trade goods include a 1675 kettle and an English copper kettle used to trade with the Indians. You can see a life mask of Charles Carroll of Carrollton.

The Carroll family began with Charles Carroll the settler, who left Ireland in 1688 to find freedom as a Catholic. His son Charles Carroll of Annapolis became wealthy. The third Charles Carroll, of Carrollton, was the only Catholic signer of the Declaration of Independence (as well as the last surviving signer) and the richest man in America before and after the Revolution. The fourth was Charles Carroll Jr., who built Homewood in Baltimore. To add to the confusion, there was another prominent Charles Carroll, known as "the barrister," who was a distant cousin.

This is one of Mrs. Carroll's favorite recipes:

Macaroons

1   pound (3 cups) almonds, blanched
1   teaspoon rose water
4   egg whites
2   cups sugar

Place almonds and rose water in blender, cover and blend until nuts are very fine. Beat egg whites until frothy. Gradually add sugar and beat until stiff. Fold in finely blended almonds. Drop by teaspoonsful onto baking sheets covered with brown paper. Bake at 300°F for 25 minutes. Makes approximately eight dozen cookies.

A new wing, the Carey Center for Maryland Life, offers three stories of space. "Looking at Liberty: An Overview of Maryland History" is the centerpiece. Images and objects are combined with oral histories.

Homewood House (410-516-5589; www.jhu.edu/historichouses), 3400 N. Charles St. Open Tue.–Sat. year-round. The money to build the house was a wedding present from Charles Carroll of Carrollton to his son Charles Carroll Jr. and his wife, Harriet Chew, in 1800. Charles Carroll Jr. began building the Palladian-style villa the following year and was intent on making it a statement of his wealth and social position. He was an alcoholic, and eventually Harriet left him.

The house has high ceilings and a view of the harbor. The reception hall has green walls and diamond-shaped patterned floor cloths. The drawing room is in blue, with a tea set on the table and a harp in the corner. Every room in the house is decorated with period pieces.

Mount Clare (410-837-3262; www.mountclare.org), 1500 Washington Blvd. Open Tue.–Sat. year-round. It was built in 1760 as a summer home for Charles Carroll the barrister (a Protestant and distant cousin of Charles Carroll of Carrollton). Charles and his wife, Margaret Tilghman, entertained Martha Washington and the Marquis de Lafayette. The parlor contains Mrs. Carroll's French furniture of Louis XV style. Mirrors are in gilt frames, and the draperies are gold colored. The dining room contains all Carroll furniture. A cupboard displays Chinese export porcelain. Upstairs, the master bedchamber has a canopy bed, brass bed warmer, commode chair, and a cradle.

Fort McHenry National Monument and Historic Shrine (410-962-4290; www.nps.gov/fomc), E. Fort Ave. Open daily, year-round. The fort was built from 1798 to 1803. It was designed in the French star shape, with five bastions to produce crossfire against attackers. The Fort McHenry Guard, composed of volunteers and Park Service employees, presents programs on weekends during the summer. A drumroll calls the men to assembly, and as they take their places visitors have the distinct feeling that they are watching men preparing to defend the fort again.

A 15-star, 15-stripe flag is raised, and the men report to their posts. The fun begins when a member of the garrison attempts to slip past a guard or someone from the outside tries to enter the fort. Guards need to be on their toes to spot an unauthorized attempt.

Those representing the Third Artillery Regiment wear dark blue wool coats with gold trim and round felt hats topped with red plumes and carry smoothbore muskets. The Maryland Militia wear blue coats with red facings and half-moon-shaped hats. The Sea Fencibles unit wears seaman's attire of 1814.

Visitors can choose to interact with any of the divisions. Some of them will be in the barracks cleaning their weapons, playing games, or reading an 1814 news-

The PRIDE of BALTIMORE

Shipyards in Fells Point were a main source of Baltimore's prosperity throughout the 18th and early 19th centuries, and their most famous vessel type was the Baltimore clipper. These extremely fast and versatile schooners became privateers during both the Revolution and the War of 1812, preying on British shipping in both cases. The *Pride of Baltimore,* an authentic replica of the *Chasseur,* a schooner built at Fells Point in 1812, was launched in 1977. (The name of her model proved prophetic, for on a cruise to British and Mediterranean waters in 1813–14 the *Chasseur* captured or sank 17 ships.)

Representing the city, the *Pride of Baltimore* logged over 150,000 sea miles visiting many ports along both coasts of North America, on the Great Lakes, and in Atlantic and Mediterranean Europe. We saw her in several of them and had a chance to go on board and chat with her volunteers. Then disaster struck during a voyage home from Europe on May 14, 1986, when a white squall, a microburst with hur-ricane-force winds, hit without warning. The ship capsized and sank quickly, with the loss of the captain and three crew members. Because there was no time to radio for help, the eight survivors drifted in a raft for more than four days before being picked up by a tanker.

Naval architect Thomas Gillmer of Annapolis designed her replacement, *Pride of Baltimore II,* to have the same appearance but more space below and modern safety features, including watertight compartments, external as well as internal ballast, and two auxiliary engines. Like her predecessor, she sails the world to represent Baltimore. She too suffered one serious problem at sea while racing from England to Spain in a tall ships event. On September 5, 2005, a 45-knot squall combined with heavy swells cracked the bowsprit and brought down the rig, but no one was hurt. She returned to Baltimore in early 2006 to be remasted and then resumed her regular schedule.

paper. You will think you are living in a different age as you question the members of the guard. (For more on the fort and on Francis Scott Key, see pages 286–87.)

Although not in our time frame, the **Inner Harbor** has been transformed into a real showplace. From an area of urban decay and decline, the now-attractive waterfront is lined with new or reconstructed buildings. You can start at one end of the Inner Harbor and spend all day learning about science or history and enjoying the sights, with plenty left over to see on another visit. You can't miss the sloop USS *Constellation*, the lightship *Chesapeake*, the submarine USS *Torsk*, the Coast Guard cutter *Roger B. Taney*, and, in nearby Fells Point, the Baltimore clipper reproduction *Pride of Baltimore II*, if she is not cruising.

LODGING

ABACROMBIE FINE FOOD AND ACCOMMODATIONS
58 W. Biddle St., Baltimore, MD 21201
888-9BADGER, 410-244-7227;
www.badger-inn.com
This row house in the Mount Vernon Cultural District dates from the 1880s and is across the street from Meyerhoff Symphony Hall. 12 guest rooms.

ADMIRAL FELL INN
888 S. Broadway, Baltimore, MD 21231
866-583-4162, 410-522-7380;
www.admiralfell.com
Eight connected buildings dating from the late 1770s were renovated to form this inn in Fells Point. 80 guest rooms.

CELIE'S WATERFRONT INN
1714 Thames St., Baltimore, MD 21231
800-432-0184, 410-522-2323;
www.celieswaterfront.com
This 1880s row house has been renovated and offers a brick courtyard garden in back. 9 guest rooms.

INN AT HENDERSON'S POINT
1000 Fell St., Baltimore, MD 21231
800-522-2088, 410-522-7777;
www.hendersonswharf.com
This 1893 building overlooking the water was once a tobacco warehouse. 38 guest rooms.

SCARBOROUGH FAIR B&B
1 E. Montgomery St., Baltimore, MD 21230
410-837-0010; www scarborough -fair.com
This 1801 home is in the historic Federal Hill neighborhood. 6 guest rooms.

RESTAURANTS

ALDO'S RISTORANTE ITALIANO
306 S. High St., Baltimore, MD 21202
410-727-0700; www.aldositaly.com
Regional Italian dishes with seasonal ingredients.

DA MIMMO RISTORANTE
217 S. High St., Baltimore, MD 21202
410-727-6876
Italian cuisine served in a 200-year-old building.

GERTRUDE'S IN THE BALTIMORE MUSEUM OF ART
10 Art Museum Dr., Baltimore, MD 21218
410-889-3399; artbma.org/shop
Innovative menu featuring regional foods inspired by chef John Shields's PBS show.

JORDAN'S STEAKHOUSE
8085 Main St., Ellicott City, MD 21043
410-461-9776; www.jordanssteak house.com
Live music adds to the ambience of this upscale restaurant, rebuilt after a fire.

PHILLIPS SEAFOOD
301 Light St. Pavilion, Harborplace,
Baltimore, MD 21202
410-685-6600;
www.phillipsseafood.com
Fresh seafood on the harbor front.

TRUE AT ADMIRAL FELL INN
888 S. Broadway, Baltimore, MD 21231
410-522-2195; www.admiralfell.com
The cuisine is creative, with fresh local
foods.

EVENTS

July: An old-fashioned Fourth of July
weekend, Fort McHenry; 410-962-4290
September: Defender's Day—Follow the
Flag, the Flag House & Star-Spangled Banner Museum; 410-837-1793. The celebration begins there and continues to the
Star-Spangled Weekend, Fort McHenry;
410-962-4290.

INFORMATION

BALTIMORE VISITOR CENTER
401 Light St., Baltimore, MD 21202
877-225-8466, 410-837-4636; www
.baltimore.org

EASTERN SHORE

This shore, remote from urban expansion in the Baltimore-Washington corridor on the other side of the bay, escaped most intrusions of the modern world. It retained a more relaxed rural lifestyle throughout the 19th century and the first half of the 20th. Then in 1952 the completion of the Bay Bridge began changing all that, but not quickly or irreparably. The pace is still slower on the other side of the bridge, and the people who have lived there for generations value their traditions.

The Eastern Shore is peppered with colonial homes, still lived in, wonderful harbors and creeks to explore by boat, and a number of old inns and museums to preserve its agricultural and maritime heritage. Like the South Shore in Massachusetts or Bucks County in Pennsylvania, it's an area that invites you to wander around and savor the colonial atmosphere of old towns, as well as the virtually unchanged land-and-seascape of winding tidewater rivers.

WYE MILLS

Today's visitors will see old equipment and new in Wye Mills.

HISTORICAL SITES *and* MUSEUMS

Wye Oak State Park was famous for its 460-year-old Wye Oak, which overlooked the colonists even when they first arrived. It was 95 feet high, had a trunk 21 feet in circumference, and stretched to a horizontal spread of 165 feet. But it toppled on June 6, 2002, during a thunderstorm. The white oak is Maryland's state tree.

Wye Mill (410-827-6909; www.historicqac), MD 662 off US 50, was built in 1671, reconstructed in 1720, and then again in 1840. It is the earliest industrial-commercial building in continuous use in Maryland. Robert Morris, a major financier of the American Revolution, bought flour for the American troops in Valley Forge from it and paid 10,000 pounds sterling, which was about $50,000 then.

Old Wye Episcopal Church (410-827-8484; www.toad.net/wyeparish), 14114 Old Wye Mills Rd. Open daily. This church was built in 1721. It has high-box pews, a raised central pulpit, and a Palladian window.

EASTON

Today Easton is a pleasant town with well-maintained colonial, Federal, and Victorian architecture. In 1954 a renovation plan was created by the Committee for the Colonial Restoration of Easton to preserve or re-create the architecture in town. The historic district is right next to the four-block-long shopping district. Boutiques, antiques shops, art galleries, and restaurants offer whatever you are looking for.

HISTORICAL SITES and MUSEUMS

Easton was settled in the late 17th century. The oldest Quaker frame meeting-house still standing in America is the 1683 **Third Haven Friends Meeting House** (410-822-0293; www.pym.org/southern-gm/third_haven/index.html), 405 S. Washington St. Open daily year-round. It was built at the headwaters of the Tred Avon, and people arrived by boat for the meeting; monthly meetings lasted all day. William Penn preached here, and Lord Baltimore attended services.

The **Historical Society of Talbot County Complex** (410-822-0773; www.hstc.org), 25 S. Washington St., includes a Quaker cabinetmaker's cottage from the 1700s, a period garden, and a museum. The museum is open Mon.–Sat. year-round. The Joseph Neall Cottage (1795) and the James Neall House (1805) are open to the public for tours daily at 11:30. The museum gardens are maintained by the Talbot County Garden Club, and the perennial beds are very colorful.

LODGING

THE INN AT EASTON
28 S. Harrison St., Easton, MD 21601
888-800-8091, 410-822-4910;
www.theinnateaston.com
The mansion dates from 1790 and is in the historic district. Rooms have original artwork, and some have claw-foot tubs. 7 guest rooms.

TIDEWATER INN
101 E. Dover St., Easton, MD 21601
800-237-8775 or 410-822-1300;
www.tidewaterinn.com
This Georgian-style inn built in 1949 is decorated with 18th-century reproduction furnishings and features a handsome spiral staircase. 114 guest rooms.

ST. MICHAELS

St. Michaels, on the Miles River, is remembered for its legendary naval trick during the War of 1812, when its residents foiled a British naval attack by snuffing out all lights at ground level and hanging lanterns in the tops of trees. This caused the British ships to aim their guns high and shoot over the town.

The town was very much alive as a colonial shipbuilding center during the late 17th and early 18th centuries. Today St. Michaels is appealing to those with a nautical bent. You can wander around the anchorage to gaze at gorgeous boats. Anyone will enjoy the shops and restaurants in this attractive town.

HISTORICAL SITES *and* MUSEUMS

Chesapeake Bay Maritime Museum (410-745-2916; www.cbmm.org), Mill St. Open daily year-round. This 18th-century complex focuses on the maritime history of the area and Chesapeake Bay.

As you enter the museum you'll see an overview of the Miles River—a "drowned river" in geological terms—and its many uses and vessels. The Indians made their canoes by burning and then scraping out the inside of a log with oyster shells; the

Replica of Captain John Smith's shallop at the Chesapeake Bay Maritime Museum in St. Michaels.

sample on display is partly finished to show the process. Colonists arrived and planted tobacco, with sassafras as a secondary crop during poor tobacco years, and they used the river to bring in supplies and ship out the crop. To harvest the wealth of the bay, fishermen, oystermen, and crabbers developed distinctive watercraft that are exhibited throughout the museum—sailing log canoes, bugeyes, and skipjacks—maintaining one of the few continuous traditions of sailing workboats in America. The museum traces the culture of Chesapeake watermen who have worked the Bay long and hard for generations; some have family roots going back to the 17th century.

> Among maritime superstitions are beliefs that bad luck will come to a boat containing anything blue, a hatch cover upside down, a red brick used as ballast, or a leaf, nut, or twig from a walnut tree on board. Worse yet is a woman on board, or changing the name of a boat, or watching three crows fly across the bow.

A model of the *Peggy Stewart* is in the museum collection. She was a merchant ship owned by Anthony Stewart and named for his wife. There was a great deal of resentment in colonial Maryland after England imposed a tax on tea. Stewart had 17 chests of tea on the ship, and the tax was paid. But a mob insisted that he set fire to his own ship, which he did, and it sank off Windmill Point in Annapolis on October 19, 1774. A windmill once stood on the site, but now the surrounding area is reclaimed land and lies in between Bancroft Hall of the Naval Academy and Annapolis Harbor.

LODGING

THE INN AT PERRY CABIN
308 Watkins Lane, St. Michaels, MD 21663
800-722-2949 or 410-745-2200;
www.perrycabin.com
After the War of 1812, an aide-de-camp to Commodore Oliver Hazard Perry built part of his house here to resemble Perry's cabin on his flagship. Ask about the secret door in the library. The property is now owned by Orient-Express. 80 guest rooms.

THE PARSONAGE INN
210 N. Talbot St., St. Michaels, MD 21663
800-394-5519, 410-745-5519;
www.parsonage-inn.com
This inn was built in 1883 of bricks from the original owner's brickyard. 8 guest rooms.

ST. MICHAELS HARBOUR INN, MARINA, & SPA
101 N. Harbor Rd., St. Michaels, MD 21663
800-955-9001, 410-745-9001;
www.harbourinn.com
A resort on the waterfront, convenient to boaters. 46 guest rooms.

WADES POINT INN
Wades Point Rd., St. Michaels, MD 21663
888-923-3466, 410-745-2500;
www.wadespoint.com
Set on the water 5 miles from St. Michaels, this 19th-century home was built by a shipwright. 26 guest rooms.

RESTAURANTS

THE CRAB CLAW
304 Mill St. at Navy Point, St. Michaels, MD 21663
410-745-2900; www.thecrabclaw.com
Fresh crab and other seafood; no credit cards.

ST. MICHAELS CRAB HOUSE
305 Mulberry St., St. Michaels, MD 21663
410-745-3737; www.stmichaelscrab house.com
On the water in a 1830s oyster-shucking house and serving all kinds of seafood.

THE INN AT PERRY CABIN
308 Watkins Lane, St. Michaels, MD 21663
410-745-2200; www.perrycabin.com
The cuisine is innovative, delicious, and beautifully presented.

OXFORD

Oxford, on the Tred Avon River, was once a stomping ground for pirates, including Stede Bonner and Blackbeard Teach, when they needed repairs on their ships. Because of its location and sheltered anchorage, it was popular as a port of entry for the colony. London and Liverpool stores started branches in town, where they exchanged goods for tobacco.

One of the town fathers, Robert Morris, for whom the main street is named, was killed unexpectedly by the wadding from a ceremonial cannonball; his son was a signer of the Declaration of Independence.

Tench Tilghman, another Oxford resident, rode from Yorktown to Philadelphia on October 17, 1781, to tell the Continental Congress that Cornwallis had surrendered. As Washington's aide-de-camp he was well known for his bravery. He was buried in the Oxford Cemetery, and a monument stands by his grave as a memorial. Look across the cove to see **Plimhimmon**, which was the home of his widow, Anna Maria Tilghman.

Today Oxford remains quiet, an oasis untouched by the clutter and traffic of many small towns. And when you get to the other end of Morris Street you are back in farmland. If you have arrived on the ferry, you are right on the main street. It's a wonderful town to stroll.

Anna Maria Tilghman lived as a widow for 56 years surrounded by mementos of her husband's wartime service. Each year on her wedding anniversary she would retire to a private room and unwrap the relics of her deceased husband—his uniform and ceremonial sword awarded by Congress.

HISTORICAL SITES *and* MUSEUMS

Oxford-Bellevue Ferry (410-745-9023; www.oxfordferry.com), N. Morris St. and The Strand, has been operating since 1683—continuously—the only one in the country with such a record. Even if you have no pressing reason to get to the other side (most visitors don't), it's worth the ride just for the fine views down stretches of the Tred Avon.

Oxford Museum (410-226-0191; www.portofoxford.com), 101 S. Morris St. Open Mon, Wed., Fri., Sat., Sun. year-round. Displays include information on Scottish settlers in the area in 1747, a cabin door piece from the ship of Captain Jeremiah Banning from the 18th century, a trunk from the same family, and cut-glass pieces from the Tilghman family. Also silver knee buckles from the 18th century.

LODGING

ROBERT MORRIS INN
314 N. Morris St., Oxford, MD 21654
888-823-4012, 410-226-5111;
www.robertmorrisinn.com
The original house was built before 1710 by ships' carpenters and has wooden-pegged paneling and hand-hewn beams. 35 rooms.

CAMBRIDGE

Cambridge, on the Choptank River, was founded in 1684, mostly for the purpose of collecting customs fees. Tobacco was the cash crop during colonial times; now the region has changed to truck farming. A farmers market takes place on Tuesday and Friday, 8 to noon. High Street is lined with houses from the 18th and 19th centuries.

If you would like a view of **Cambridge Creek**, where skipjacks moored, head down to the harbor. Skipjacks are unfortunately vanishing as the last sailing fishing fleet in the country.

HISTORICAL SITES *and* MUSEUMS

Dorchester County Historical Society (410-228-7953; www.intercom.net/npo/ dchs), 902 La Grange Ave., offers the Meredith House, the Nield Museum, and the Goldsborough Stable and Herb Gardens. Open Wed.–Fri. year-round.

The Meredith House has three floors of collections, including clothing, portraits, and dolls. A schoolmaster's desk dates from 1730 or earlier. Needlepoint portraits of George and Martha Washington are hung in the hall. The Governors' Room pays tribute to the six elected governors from Dorchester County. The furnishings in the room include a Victorian sofa, Victorian chairs, and an Empire desk. A star of Bethlehem pattern quilt dates from 1762.

The Nield Museum is chock-full of more collections, including arrowheads

The Meredith House and Nield Museum.

from 5,000 years ago collected on Taylors Island, stone axes, trade pots from the late 17th century, and a dugout canoe. The stable dates from 1790 and now houses a collection of horse-drawn vehicles that were used in Dorchester County. The gardens are sectioned as follows: fragrance, health, beauty, and cooking.

LODGING

CAMBRIDGE HOUSE
112 High St., Cambridge, MD 21613
877-221-7799 or 410-221-7700;
www.cambridgehousebandb.com
This Victorian house is in the historic district. 6 guest rooms.

INFORMATION

DORCHESTER COUNTY OFFICE OF TOURISM
2 Rose Hill Place, Cambridge, MD 21613
410-228-1000; www.tourdorchester.org

TALBOT COUNTY VISITOR CENTER
11 S. Harrison St., Easton, MD 21601
410-770-8000; www.tourtalbot.org

CHESTERTOWN

Chestertown, on the banks of the Chester River, was founded in 1706, although it had been designated as a town as early as 1668. Many waterfront homes were built during the 1700s, and a number of them are identified on a walking tour.

HISTORICAL SITES *and* MUSEUMS

Washington College was founded in Chestertown in 1782 and is now the 10th-oldest institution of higher learning in America. George Washington was instrumental in the founding of the college and in 1789 received a doctor of laws degree there. The **Hynson-Ringgold House**, 106 S. Water St., dates from 1743 and is now the home of the Washington College president.

At the end of the block and across the street is the **Customs House,** High and Water Sts., which has Flemish bond brick construction. Nearby, furious citizens organized Chestertown's own version of the Boston Tea Party. On May 23, 1774, they boarded the brig *William Geddes,* moored in front of the Customs House, and threw the cargo of tea into the river. The chamber of commerce sponsors a reenactment of the 1774 tea party in May.

The Georgian house across the street, at 101 N. Water St., is called **Widehall**. It was the scene of much action during the Revolutionary era because the owner, Thomas Smythe, was the head of Maryland's provincial government from 1774 until the state's first constitution emerged in 1776. The house, which has an unusual freestanding staircase, got its name because of the large hall and staircase on the street side.

The house at 107 Water St., called **River House**, was also owned by Thomas Smythe and dates from the 1780s. Woodwork from one of the second-floor rooms now resides in the Chestertown Room of Delaware's Winterthur Museum.

The oldest house in town is the **Watkins-Bryan House**, 109 N. Water St. This merchant's home dates from 1740. Esau Watkins received the land as a wedding gift.

The **Nicholson House**, 111 N. Queen St., was built by Captain John Nicholson in 1788. He was the youngest of three brothers, all active during the Revolu-

Legislation in 1732 contained the following complaint: "That diverse Persons . . . do raise and keep large Quantities of Swine, Sheep, and Geese . . . whereby not only the Grass necessary for the Support of the Cows and Horses of the Inhabitants is consumed, but that also, the Ground is so rooted up, and the Streets so broke, that in Winter or wet Weather, they are almost impassable; also, that the Swine there are so numerous and ravenous, that they break into Warehouses where grain is stored, and that several young Children have been in Danger of being devoured by them; and that the Inhabitants cannot preserve their Gardens and Inclusures from being broke down and destroyed by them."

tion. John was commander of the Continental sloop *Hornet,* James was head of the Maryland navy, and Samuel later commanded and supervised the construction of the navy's USS *Constitution.*

The **Geddes-Piper House**, 101 Church Alley, is the home of the Kent County Historical Society (410-778-3499; www.hskcmd.com). Open May–Oct., Sat.–Sun. or by appointment. This 1780 house was saved by neglect and therefore has original rooms. The front parlor received gifts of furnishings from a number of families. Don't miss the teapot collection in an 18th-century Irish breakfront. Upstairs, the Victorian sitting room has a fainting couch, smelling salts, period garments, and crazy quilts.

The **Schooner *Sultana* 1768 and the Sultana Center** (410-778-5954; www.schoonersultana.com), Cross St. Open Tue.–Sat. year-round. The original schooner *Sultana* dates from 1767 when her keel was laid at Benjamin Hallowell's shipyard in Boston. The Royal Navy purchased her to monitor colonial shipping, specifically to enforce the Townshend Acts, which imposed duties on tea,

The Geddes-Piper House.

paint, paper, lead, and other items. She patrolled Chesapeake Bay from October 1769 through August 1770, searching inbound ships. In July of 1770 she sailed up the Potomac River and moored near Mount Vernon. Lieutenant Inglis and Master David Bruce dined with George Washington. In 1771 and 1772 American sailors increasingly objected to being searched. In Newport, Rhode Island, citizens gathered, and Master David Bruce wrote in his log: "The people of Newport threatened to board us, cut us off [the anchor], and burn the Schooner." After several similar encounters she was recalled to England.

The *Sultana* is a reproduction of the 1768 schooner. She was constructed from original plans and launched in 2001. Now she is a school ship on the Chesapeake, teaching bay ecology and colonial maritime history to students. Public sails are available from Chestertown, Annapolis, Baltimore, and Alexandria, Virginia. Dockside vessel tours are given during special days, and on special weekends she gathers with other historic vessels.

The Sultana Project also initiated the John Smith Four Hundred Project, to reenact the first European exploration of Chesapeake Bay in 1608. Their shipyard on the Chester River built a replica of John Smith's shallop. We saw her on display at the Chesapeake Bay Maritime Museum in the summer of 2006 during a 15-month museum tour that was completed in April 2007. Then she set out to retrace Smith's voyage in May with a group of 14 explorers, historians, naturalists, and educators on board through the 1,700-mile route. You can check out their progress on www.johnsmith400.org. Afterward the shallop will be rowing and sailing around the Chesapeake with a crew of 12 volunteers.

> Preserving the Chesapeake by understanding the cultural and economic value of the bay is a goal of the Sultana Project. As children and adults sail, they develop a sense of value in preserving the tidewater region, which is threatened by development. Teaching colonial and Revolutionary history is a part of this plan, so that future generations will understand the life and livelihood of our maritime ancestors.

LODGING

BRAMPTON INN
25227 Chestertown Rd., Chestertown, MD 21620
866-305-1860, 410-778-1860;
www.bramptoninn.com
This 1860 plantation house is situated on 20 acres. 10 guest rooms.

GREAT OAK MANOR B&B
10568 Cliff Rd., Chestertown, MD 21620
800-504-3098, 410-778-5943;
www.greatoak.com
This brick Georgian-style house overlooks the bay and has 12 acres of gardens and lawns. 11 guest rooms.

WHITE SWAN TAVERN
231 High St., Chestertown, MD 21620
410-778-2300; www.whiteswan
tavern.com

This site has been in use since before 1733; a tavern was established here in 1793. An archaeological dig here in 1978 uncovered coins dating to 1694, marble pieces from fireplaces, a glass tumbler, a wineglass, medicine bottle pieces, blue and gray stoneware, brass drawer pulls, chamber pots, chargers, and cups, all currently on display. 6 guest rooms.

RESTAURANTS

BLUE HERON CAFÉ
236 Cannon St., Chestertown, MD 21620
410-778-0188; www.blueheroncafe.com
Regional ingredients and seafood specialties.

KETTLEDRUM TEA HOUSE
117 S. Cross St., Chestertown, MD 21620
410-810-1497
Afternoon tea on antique dishes; dinner is also served.

WHITE SWAN INN
231 High St., Chestertown, MD 21620
410-778-2300; www.whiteswantavern.com
Afternoon tea offers tea and hot cider in winter, and iced tea and lemonade in the summer.

EVENTS

May: Chestertown Tea Party festival; 410-778-0416, 410-810-2968; www.chestertownteaparty.com
October: Chestertown tea time house tour of 15 houses; 410-778-3499
November: Downrigging weekend, the *Sultana* Project, with other tall ships sailing to Chestertown; 410-778-5954.

INFORMATION

KENT COUNTY OFFICE OF TOURISM
400 High St., Chestertown, MD 21620
410-778-0416; www.kentcounty.com

NEW YARMOUTH TOURS
Stephen Mumford, 410-778-3221, www.chestertowntours.com.
We met Stephen, dressed in period clothing, in Fountain Park for a tour of historic sites with commentary, ending at the Geddes-Piper House.

Current Information

MARYLAND OFFICE OF TOURISM
217 E. Redwood St.
Baltimore, MD 21202
866-639-3526, 410-767-6329
www.choosemaryland.org

Resources

Colonial Period

Bearor, Bob. *Leading by Example: Partisan Fighters & Leaders of New France, 1660–1760*. Westminster, MD: Heritage Books, 2003.

Boorstin, Daniel J. *The Americans: The Colonial Experience*. New York: Random House, 1958.

Calloway, Colin G. *The Scratch of a Pen: 1763 and the Transformation of North America*. Oxford and New York: Oxford University Press, 2006.

Cuneo, John R. *Robert Rogers of the Rangers*. New York: Oxford University Press, 1959.

Fischer, David Hackett. *Albion's Seed: Four British Folkways in America*. Oxford and New York: Oxford University Press, 1989.

Greene, Jack P. *Pursuits of Happiness: The Social Development of Early Modern British Colonies and the Formation of American Culture*, Chapel Hill: University of North Carolina Press, 1988.

Hawke, David. *The Colonial Experience*. New York, Kansas City: Bobbs-Merrill, 1966.

Kennedy, Roger G. *Rediscovering America: Journeys through Our Forgotten Past*. Boston: Houghton Mifflin, 1990.

Illick, Joseph E. *Colonial Pennsylvania: A History*. New York: Charles Scribner's Sons, 1976.

Kammen, Michael. *Colonial New York: A History*. New York: Charles Scribner's Sons, 1975.

Leder, Lawrence H. *America 1603–1789: Prelude to a Nation*. Minneapolis: Burgess Publishing, 1972.

Lewis, Tom. *The Hudson: A History*. New Haven, CT: Yale University Press, 2005.

Middleton, Richard. *Colonial America: A History, 1607–1760*. Cambridge, MA, and Oxford: Blackwell, 1992.

Reich, Jerome R. *Colonial America*. Englewood Cliffs, NJ: Prentice Hall, 1989.

Starbuck, David R. *The Great Warpath: British Military Sites from Albany to Crown Point*. Hanover, NH: University Press of New England, 1999.

———. *Massacre at Fort William Henry*. Hanover, NH: University Press of New England, 2002.

Vrooman, John J. *Forts and Firesides of the Mohawk Country*. Johnstown, NY: Baronet Litho Co., 1951.

Revolutionary War

Amar, Akhil Reed. *America's Constitution: A Biography*. New York: Random House, 2005.

Bellico, Russell P. *Chronicles of Lake George: Journeys in War and Peace*. Fleischmanns, NY: Purple Mountain Press, 1995.

———. *Sails and Steam in the Mountains: A Maritime and Military History of Lake George and Lake Champlain*. Fleischmanns, NY: Purple Mountain Press, 1992.

Bohrer, Melissa Lukeman. *Glory, Passion, and Principle: The Story of Eight Remarkable Women at the Core of the American Revolution*. New York: Atria Press, 2003.

Commager, Henry Steele, and Richard B. Morris. *The Spirit of Seventy-Six: The Story of the American Revolution as Told by Participants*. 2 vols. New York, Indianapolis: Bobbs-Merrill, 1958.

Ellis, Joseph J. *Founding Brothers: The Revolutionary Generation*. New York: Alfred A. Knopf, 2004.

Ferling, John. *A Leap in the Dark: The Struggle to Create the American Republic*. New York: Oxford University Press, 2003.

Fischer, David Hackett. *Washington's Crossing*. Oxford and New York: Oxford University Press, 2004.

Kelly, C. Brian. *Best Little Stories from the American Revolution*. Nashville, TN: Cumberland House, 1999.

McCullough, David. *1776*. New York: Simon & Schuster, 2005.

Raphael, Ray. *A People's History of the American Revolution: How Common People Shaped the Fight for Independence*: New York: New Press, 2001.

Stember, Sol. *The Bicentennial Guide to the American Revolution. Volume II: The Middle Colonies*. New York: Saturday Review Press, E.P. Dutton, 1974.

Wood, Gordon S. *The Radicalism of the American Revolution*. New York: Penguin Press, 2004.

———. *Revolutionary Characters: What Made the Founders Different*. New York: Penguin Press, 2006.

Also, each state has a *Bicentennial History* in the States and Nation Series, published by W.W. Norton, New York. Also, each state has *A History of the American Colonies*, KTO Press (A U.S. division of Kraus-Thomson Organization Ltd.), Millwood, NY.

Biographies

Brady, Patricia. *Martha Washington: An American Life*. New York: Viking, 2005.

Chernow, Ron. *Alexander Hamilton*. New York: Penguin, 2004.

Ellis, Joseph J. *His Excellency George Washington*. New York, Alfred A. Knopf, 2004.

———. *American Sphinx: The Character of Thomas Jefferson*. New York: Alfred A. Knopf, 1997.

Grant, James. *John Adams: Party of One*. New York: Farrar, Straus and Giroux, 2005.

Isaacson, Walter. *Benjamin Franklin: An American Life*. New York: Simon & Schuster, 2003

Randall, William Sterne. *Benedict Arnold: Patriot and Traitor*. New York: William Morrow, 1990.

Index

Maps are indicated by font in bold.

H

Haddonfield, NJ, 228, 229

Haddonfield Information Center, Haddonfield, NJ, 229

Haddonfield Inn, Haddonfield, NJ, 229

Hagley Museum, Winterthur, DE, 274

Hague, NY, 114

Hall Of Records, Dover, DE, 262

Hammond-Harwood House, Annapolis, MD, 302

Hammond-Harwood House Colonial Dog Show, Annapolis, MD, 307

Hammonton, NJ, 241

Hancock House, Hancocks Bridge, NJ, 225

Hancocks Bridge, NJ, 225

Hank's Place, Chadds Ford, PA, 182

Hans Herr House, Lancaster, PA, 196

Harrisburg, PA, 203, 204, 213

Harry's Savoy Grill, Wilmington, DE, 276

Hattie's, Saratoga Springs, NY, 93

Havens House Museum, Shelter Island, NY, 44

Haydn Zug's, East Petersburg, PA, 200

Head House Square, Philadelphia, PA, 166

Heidelberg, Lower Manhattan, NY, 36

Hendrickson House, Wilmington, DE, 272

Henry Hudson's Half Moon, Albany, NY, 89

Henry Knox's Birthday Celebration, New Windsor, NY, 66

Herkimer, NY, 130, 131, 133

Herkimer County Chamber Of Commerce, Herkimer, NY, 131

Herkimer Home State Historic Site, Little Falls, NY, 130

Hermitage, Ho-ho-kus, NJ, 246

Hessian Powder Magazine Museum, Carlisle, PA, 203

Hideaway Suites, Rhinebeck, NY, 71

High Falls, NY, 77

Hill-Physick-Keith House, Philadelphia, PA, 166

Hiram-Burton House, Lewes/Cape Henlopen, DE, 259

Historic Annapolis Foundation, Annapolis, MD, 307

Historic Fallsington Day, Fallsington, PA, 184

Historic Fallsington, Fallsington, PA, 183

Historic Hotel Bethlehem, Bethlehem, PA, 190

Historic Houses Of Odessa, Odessa, DE, 265

Historic Inns Of Annapolis, Annapolis, MD, 306

Historic Lancaster Walking Tour, Lancaster, PA, 194

Historic London Town and Gardens, London Town, MD, 308

Historic Morven, Princeton, NJ, 236

Historic Richmond Town, Staten Island, NY, 39

Historic Rock Ford Plantation, Lancaster, PA, 194

Historic Smithton Inn, Ephrata, PA, 199

Historic St.Mary's City, St. Mary's City, MD, 291

Historic Waynesborough, Paoli, PA, 176

Historic Yellow Springs, Chester Springs, PA, 177

Historical Society Museum, York, PA, 199

Historical Society Of Talbot County Complex, Easton, MD, 315

History Quest, Annapolis, MD, 307

Hobbit Hollowfarm, Skaneateles Lake, NY, 141

Ho-Ho-Kus, NJ, 246

Holiday House Tour, East Hampton, NY, 48

Hollywood, MD, 295

Holy Trinity (Old Swedes) Church, Wilmington, DE, 270

Home Sweet Home Museum, East Hampton, NY, 47

Homewood House, Baltimore, MD, 311

Hope, NJ, 245

Hopewell Furnace, Birdsboro, PA, 179

Hopewell Junction, NY, 71, 72

Hotel Du Pont, Wilmington, DE, 275

Hotel Du Village, New Hope, PA, 188

Hotel Roger Williams, Lower Manhattan, NY, 34

Hotel Utica, Utica, NY, 133

Hotel Wales, Lower Manhattan, NY, 34

Howe Caverns, Howes Cave, NY, 135

Howell Living History Farm, Titusville, NJ, 232

Howes Cave, NY, 134, 135

Hudson, NY, 80, 82

Hudson House Restaurant, Cold Spring, NY, 69

Hudson River Cruise, NY, 71

Hudson River Cruises, Poughkeepsie, NY, 76

Hudson River Maritime Museum, Kingston, NY, 76

Hudson River Valley, NY, 50–82

Lower Hudson River Valley, NY, 52–69

Mid-Hudson River Valley, NY, 69–82

Hudson Valley Tourism, NY, 52